Republic of Intellect

NEW STUDIES
IN AMERICAN INTELLECTUAL
AND CULTURAL HISTORY

Howard Brick, Series Editor

REPUBLIC *of* INTELLECT

The Friendly Club of New York City
and the Making of American Literature

Bryan Waterman

THE JOHNS HOPKINS UNIVERSITY PRESS
Baltimore ·

Publication for this book has been aided by a grant from the Abraham and Rebecca Stein Faculty Publication Fund of New York University, Department of English.

The Johns Hopkins University Press
2715 North Charles Street
Baltimore, Maryland 21218-4363
www.press.jhu.edu

Library of Congress Cataloging-in-Publication Data
Waterman, Bryan, 1970–
    Republic of intellect : the Friendly Club of New York City and the making of American literature / Bryan Waterman.
        p.   cm.
    Includes bibliographical references and index
    ISBN-13: 978-0-8018-8566-2 (hardcover : alk. paper)
    ISBN-10: 0-8018-8566-3 (hardcover : alk. paper)
    1. New York (N.Y.)—Intellectual life—18th century.
2. Intellectuals—New York (State)—New York—Biography.
3. Friendly Club (New York, N.Y.) 4. Fraternal organizations—
New York (State)—New York—History—18th century. 5. New
York (N.Y.)—History—1775–1865—Biography. 6. United States—
Intellectual life—1783–1865. 7. American literature—Societies, etc.—
History—18th century. 8. American literature—1783–1850—History
and criticism. I. Title.
F128.44.W37 2007
974.7′03—dc22   2006019853

A catalog record for this book is available from the British Library.

For Stephanie

{ CONTENTS }

Acknowledgments ix

Introduction. "There exists in this city, a small association of men" 1

PART ONE. ASSOCIATIONS
Prelude. Pictures at an Exhibition 17
One. "The Town is the only place for rational beings": Sociability, Science, and the Literature of Intimate Inquiry 24
Two. Dangerous Associations: The Illuminati Conspiracy Scare as a Crisis of Public Intellectual Authority 50
Three. Unrestrained Conversation and the "Understanding of Woman": Radicalism, Feminism, and the Challenge of Polite Society 92

PART TWO. INDUSTRIES OF KNOWLEDGE
Prelude. James Kent, Legal Knowledge, and the Politics of Print 145
Four. The Public Is in the House: William Dunlap's Park Theatre and the Making of American Audiences 154
Five. "Here was fresh matter for discourse": Yellow Fever, the *Medical Repository,* and *Arthur Mervyn* 189

Coda. The End of the American Enlightenment: Samuel Miller's *A Brief Retrospect of the Eighteenth Century* 231

Appendix. Friendly Club Membership and Nineteenth-Century New York City Historiography 243
Abbreviations 249
Notes 251
Index 311

Illustrations appear following page 142.

{ ACKNOWLEDGMENTS }

Though it may seem like an academic cliché to begin a list of acknowledgments by invoking your book's topic, I can't imagine a way through these paragraphs without suggesting that several friendships and friendship circles have been instrumental to this book's production. While I was still conducting research for the dissertation that preceded this book, friends in New York gave me a place to sleep, sometimes for several weeks at a time over consecutive summers. Lane Twitchell, Adriana Velez, John Rothermich, and Shelley Turley fall into that first category. This circle extends to Brian Aitken, Andrea Evers, Shar Taylor, and Lisa Dickey, who provided hospitality (often for my family as well) during research or conference trips to Washington, D.C. Along with Dave Barber, who has since become a New Yorker himself, they have been collectively known as "the DC crew." In Boston, where I was completing my degree, the friendship of Mark and Pandora Brewer sustained us through times when Stephanie and I weren't sure whether the investments we were making in graduate school would ever pan out. I could not have been happier, after we had moved to New York, when Farrell Lines and Rebecca Maury moved to Philadelphia and became more fully integrated into this widening cohort. As the manuscript neared completion they put me up for the good part of a summer and gave me a room in the attic for writing and for the two hundred pounds of books and files I had sent there. Rachel Poulsen and Missy Bradshaw, whom we had known as long as anyone, gave our family a place to stay in the weeks following September 11, 2001, when we could not yet return to our apartment downtown; earlier they had provided lodging and fellowship in Chicago during an early run at the academic job market. At least since the enormous Thanksgiving party Karen Slade threw in New York in 1999, the bulk of this group, with additions and removals here and there, has referred to itself as the Northeast Corridor Social Club, at least a partial reference to the research I had undertaken.

Another, more widely scattered group, partly overlapping with the first, has enjoyed near-annual reunions since the mid-1990s. Known to members as the Friendly Order of the Olympic Flask, again partly in homage to the club I was writing about, this friendship circle also provided intellectual and emotional fellowship: Elbert Peck presides, and additional members include Brian Kagel, Eric Jones, and Jeremy Zitter along with several people named in the previous paragraph. These overlapping circles—doctors, lawyers, artists, writers, editors, economists, academics, and more—have given me repeated occasions to think about what happens when friendship turns into intellectual and cultural collaboration (and vice versa), how conversation works as an institution of culture, and how the emotional bases of friendship—and its limits—can force you into productive moments of self-examination. These friends have put up with several years of walking tours of lower Manhattan, gory recitals of New York's yellow fever epidemics, and convoluted plot summaries of Charles Brockden Brown's fiction. They have also enriched a significant portion of my life through their exchanges, which I anticipate will continue long into the future. We could not have asked for better friends.

Living in downtown New York for the last five years, I have claimed membership in two other circles with strong eighteenth-century antecedents, and whose fellowship has been key to maintaining my sanity through this project. Thanks to Dan, Julia, Meg, Wolf, Tim, Sarah, and especially Derick Melander and Sacha Jones for letting me into Record Club (a modern Anacreontic Society of sorts) after an extended stint as visitor. I wrapped up the final draft of the manuscript in 2004–2005 at Fresh Salt (146 Beekman Street, between Front and South). Thanks to Fresh Salt's regulars, staff, and proprietors—especially Jason Connolly and Sara Williams—who all made the end of the work day something to look forward to. Oyster outings with Jason, Nicole, Dave, and Steph were especially rewarding. It seemed especially appropriate to finish writing this book in a tavern of sorts in lower Manhattan during the last days of the Fulton Fish Market.

Academic friendships, many of which have long since transcended pedagogical or professional affiliation, have assisted materially and emotionally at every stage as this book took shape. My greatest intellectual debt is to Susan Mizruchi, who oversaw not only the dissertation but the process of turning it into a book. Jill Lepore served as an early reader and mentor. They, along with Richard Wightman Fox, set the high standard of historical scholarship and writing to which

I continue to aspire. Several mentors and friends have supported this project by writing recommendations on my behalf for fellowships or teaching positions: Nancy Bentley, Richard Fox, Chris Grasso, Virginia Jackson (who also generously provided a place to stay one summer in Princeton), Jill Lepore, Chris Looby, Susan Mizruchi, Saundra Morris, Cyrus Patell, and Mary Poovey. Thanks to John Brooke and Seth Cotlar for sharing unpublished work.

A number of people deserve my thanks for reading individual chapters or sections of chapters, sometimes in multiple drafts, or for offering advice on book or fellowship proposals: Jennifer Baker, Dave Barber, Mark Brewer, John Brooke, Caleb Crain, Cynthia Davis, Robert Dimit, Niki Eustace, Elaine Freedgood, Marilyn Gaull, Jenni Green, Robb Haberman, Phil Harper, Catherine Kaplan, Jon Klancher, Chris Looby, Sam Otter, Mary Poovey, Jeff Richards, Laura Rigal, Nancy Ruttenburg, David Shield, Eric Slauter, Gabi Starr, and John Waters. One of my longest-standing intellectual co-conspirators, Joanna Brooks, braved the entire manuscript, after having provided valuable advice on many smaller details over several years. She has been a model, mentor, and close friend for fifteen years, since we were undergraduates publishing an independent college newspaper, and I count myself very fortunate that we both wound up as early Americanists.

The English Department at New York University has offered me the opportunity to live in the city—and neighborhood—I have spent so long researching; it has also provided me with a terrific cohort of colleagues and wonderful students on whom I could test ideas. Special thanks to Elisabeth Shane for research assistance at a crucial juncture and Jessie Morgan Owens for help with illustrations and permissions. I have benefited from audience feedback at the University of South Carolina, University of California at Santa Barbara, University of Memphis, Penn State–Harrisburg, the New York Academy of Medicine, and the Library Company of Philadelphia, as well as at meetings of the Society of Early Americanists, Modern Language Association, the Atlantic History Workshop at NYU, the Omohundro Institute of Early American History and Culture, the North American Society for the Study of Romanticism, BU's Americanist Forum, and NYU's Americanist Group.

I offer special thanks to my colleagues at the Charles Brockden Brown Society and participants in its biannual meetings, especially to Phil Barnard, Elizabeth Dillon, Michael Drexler, Fritz Fleishmann,

Jared Gardner, Sean Goudie, Janie Hinds, Mark Kamrath, Bob Levine, Sam Otter, Jeff Richards, Nancy Ruttenburg, Stephen Shapiro, Ezra Tawil, Evert van Leeuwen, Wil Verhoeven, and Ed White, many of whom have offered years of intellectual fellowship on multiple continents. Thanks to John Holmes for sharing electronic files of Brown's correspondence.

Several institutions and their donors made research for this book possible: the New-York Historical Society, the Gilder Lehrman Institute of American History, the Boston University Humanities Foundation, Princeton University Libraries, the Historical Society of Pennsylvania, the Library Company of Philadelphia, and the New York Academy of Medicine. I thank librarians at all of these institutions, especially Jim Green at the Library Company, Arlene Shaner at the New York Academy of Medicine, and Al Bush at Princeton's Firestone Library, the last of whom has been nudging me in the right direction for a very long time indeed. I appreciate permission to publish materials from these libraries' collections. I also appreciate the fellowship and assistance of Marvin Taylor and Mike Kelly of the Fales Library and Special Collections at New York University. Toby Appel at Yale's Cushing/Whitney Medical Library answered questions about Elihu Smith's manuscript diaries over several years. Karie Diethorn, the Museum Curator at Independence National Historical Park, provided helpful information about James and Ellen Sharples's portraits of club members and helped me track down "my" William Johnson.

A Goddard leave for junior faculty at NYU gave me time for final revisions to the manuscript. Thanks to deans Richard Foley, Mary Carruthers, and Catherine Stimpson for that support. Additional thanks to deans Carruthers and Stimpson and to the Humanities Council at NYU for partially funding the 2004 Charles Brockden Brown Society meetings, "Circles and Circulations in the Revolutionary Atlantic World," and an accompanying library exhibit and catalog.

Early versions of chapter 2 and chapter 5 appeared in the *William and Mary Quarterly* and *American Literary History*, respectively. I thank the editors of those journals, Chris Grasso and Gordon Hutner, as well as their anonymous reviewers for suggestions that helped me refine my arguments. I thank the publishers of these journals, the Omohundro Institute of Early American History and Culture and Oxford University Press, respectively, for permission to incorporate previously published material.

At the Johns Hopkins University Press I have been very fortunate to work with Bob Brugger and Howard Brick and appreciate the suggestions—stylistic and substantive—I have received from each and from the Press's anonymous reviewer. Thanks to Michael Baker for eagle-eyed copyediting and to Carol Zimmerman for efficiently moving the book through production.

I have reserved my final paragraph for my friendliest circles. My parents, Dennis and Lois Waterman, gave me a love of reading and writing that has served me well. They and my parents-in-law, Jack and Marlene Smith, have been extraordinarily supportive of my academic endeavors. My daughters, Anna and Molly, are older than my interest in the Friendly Club, but just barely. They have been patient as I took much time away from them to write. I rejoice with them that I'm finally finished. Stephanie has been patient, too, through more than I care to admit. She has been my best friend, virtually from the moment I met her in 1991. I couldn't think of dedicating this book to anyone else.

Republic of Intellect

"There exists in this city, a small association of men"

T HIS book tells the story of an intimate circle of young men who lived in New York City in the politically and socially turbulent 1790s—an age of revolutions and counterrevolutions in politics, manners, and writing—when governmental structures, religious experience, scientific knowledge, gender norms, and principles of association all served as subjects of fierce debates in person, in correspondence, and in print. Meeting on Saturday nights in each other's homes to pursue scientific and moral truth through "unshackled" conversation, these friends also assisted one another as they published in a broad range of literary forms.[1] Made up of doctors, lawyers, scientists, merchants, playwrights, poets, editors, a novelist, and a minister, the Friendly Club produced much of what we now consider the cornerstones of early American literature. Its members also inaugurated American legal and medical publishing, and some of them held local and national political office. They founded a theater and multiple journals, and they ushered into being the fiction of Charles Brockden Brown, America's first novelist of international distinction.

By the end of the nineteenth century, the Friendly Club would be legendary in the multivolume, gilt-edged memorial histories of New York City, held up as examples of the city's and the nation's early intellectual vitality. If at times these popular histories exaggerated the club's list of members and visitors—even George Washington was supposed to have been a regular attendee—they recognized the basic fact that no group in the new United States boasted such a concentration of persons who would figure so prominently in so many fields, a recognition that has persisted to the present. The historian Henry May's estimation of the club as "perhaps the most brilliant of all the [early republic's] organizations of earnest and enlightened young men" owes its effulgence to the stature most club members had attained by the time they died, but it accurately assesses as well the extraordinary amount and variety of writing produced even in their early years.[2]

None of this mattered to Friendly Club members in the fall of 1798. That season, local concerns trumped literary ambitions as an epidemic of yellow fever emptied New York shops and homes and monopolized what conversation remained in town. Instead, club members feared for their lives, and with good reason. New York had lost hundreds to yellow fever in 1795; a much more severe epidemic had nearly decimated Philadelphia two years before that. Those with means fled into the countryside; those who remained died by the dozen, especially in crowded waterfront neighborhoods, where streets that reeked of garbage and spoiled goods served as the seat of commerce and as home to thousands of immigrants and other urban poor. A month into the epidemic, on the afternoon of 19 September, the sun bearing down out of doors, a 27-year-old poet and physician named Elihu Hubbard Smith, the Friendly Club's central force, vomited something the texture and color of coffee grounds, delivered a single-word self-diagnosis—"Decomposition!"—and died, a victim of what would be the worst outbreak of the disease in the city's history.

For just over a week, as his own fever progressed, Smith had nursed a young Italian physician named Joseph Scandella, who had come to the United States in order to research the epidemic disorder that had plagued port cities up and down the eastern seaboard each of the past five summers. The previous winter, when Smith had agreed to compile for Scandella a "Catalogue of publications, in the United States, on Yellow Fever," the two had formed a fast friendship. When Smith learned that Scandella had recently returned from fever-stricken Philadelphia and languished unattended in a coffeehouse, he took Scandella into his own rooms and added him to his regular medical rounds, which included boat trips to see patients in Brooklyn and visits to the New-York

Hospital, where he was a staff physician. Smith's nights were plagued by "incongruous dreams," humidity, and the relentless buzzing and biting of mosquitoes. The mosquitoes had appeared that season in unusually large numbers, some observers noted, though no one knew that the insects were transmitting a disease that would leave more than two thousand dead in a matter of months.[3]

Smith died surrounded by his medical colleagues Samuel Latham Mitchill and Edward Miller, rising figures among New York physicians. With Smith they had founded and coedited the *Medical Repository*, the new nation's first medical journal, then in its second volume. Smith's housemates, a young lawyer named William Johnson and an aspiring novelist, Charles Brockden Brown, oversaw his burial in the cemetery of the Wall Street Presbyterian Church, where Edward Miller's brother, Samuel, was a collegiate pastor. Then Johnson and Brown boarded a ferry and fled the "pestilential, desolate, and sultry city" for "the odors and sprightly atmosphere" of Perth Amboy, New Jersey, thirty miles away, where another friend, the playwright William Dunlap, kept a country home.[4] "It was when the ravages of pestilence had become so tremendous," Samuel Miller later wrote, "when scarcely any passengers were to be seen on the streets but the bearers of the dead to the tomb . . . that [Smith's] friends, bedewed with their tears, and followed to the grave, the remains of a young man, in some respects one of the most enlightened and promising that ever adorned the annals of American science."[5] Brown sent his brother the news: "The die is cast. E.H.S. is dead. O the folly of prediction and the vanity of systems." A few days later, he added that Smith's death had "endeared the survivors of the sacred fellowship . . . to each other in a very high degree; and I confess my wounded spirit and shattered frame will be most likely to be healed and benefited by their society."[6]

The death of Elihu Hubbard Smith likely led to the Friendly Club's premature climax; its formal activities—other than organizing Charles Brockden Brown's first magazine effort, the *Monthly Magazine, and American Review*—are difficult to trace once Smith's diary comes to its abrupt conclusion. In the turbulent fall of 1798, the club included Smith, Brown, Dunlap, Johnson, Mitchill, and the Miller brothers, as well as a recently appointed state supreme court justice, James Kent, and Dunlap's brothers-in-law, the merchants William and George Woolsey. Diverse in politics, religion, and profession, their circle came together on the principle that such association facilitated self-improve-

lent in the City of New-York (1799); in the satirical poem *A Political Green-House, for the Year 1798,* written by Smith's Connecticut friends; as the template for an episode in Brown's fever novel *Arthur Mervyn* (1799–1800); in another American medical magazine in 1814 and James Thatcher's 1828 *American Medical Biography;* in Dunlap's 1815 biography of Brown and his 1832 *History of the American Theatre;* and in the entry on Brown in Evert Duyckinck's canon-making *Cyclopaedia of American Literature* (1855), to cover only the first half-century of its circulation.[12] In spite of his early age of death, the tale helped ensure Smith's inclusion over a century later in that who's who of American cultural aristocracy, the *Dictionary of American Biography.*[13]

Such circulation, which also provided Smith's friends with their own opportunities for public recognition, reveals the group's confidence that reputation served as a counterweight to republican injunctions toward anonymous participation in public discourse.[14] For young men of this educated, ambitious, and upwardly mobile demographic, the public performance of being informed and informing others—of being a man of information—was as important as the specific knowledge one had to convey. With this point in mind, recall Smith's final diary entries, which emphasized the relationship between a knowledge culture and being *known* in his account of the ailing Scandella: "The history of this most accomplished, & unfortunate man is calculated to awaken the deepest interest & foster the profoundest regrets." Even in his final days, Smith cannot help but worry about how audiences might receive a new publishing project. His imagined Scandella biography would not depend simply on medical information for its utility, although Smith would likely use it, as he had his professional friendship with Scandella, to further his particular medical views. Its "moral incidents," to recall Brown's initial telling of the story, would make the Italian traveler a martyr for knowledge, a model for other seekers after truth and purveyors of useful information. Smith's friends followed this same pattern in telling the story of his death.

This self-conscious attempt not only to shape American culture but moreover to write themselves into positions of influence and reputation, illustrates the Friendly Club's usefulness as a case study for understanding the relationships between literary and intellectual cultures in the late-eighteenth-century United States. The primary social form this book examines—the intimate conversation circle—helped bring into existence and serves as a template for reuniting the diaries, medical journals, newspaper essays, novels, reports of traveling physicians and jurists, memorial biographies, and literary histories that provide this book's subject matter, genres in which Elihu Smith was memorialized and in which he had worked himself (with the exception of the novel, which he eagerly consumed but did not produce). The gentlemen's conversation club, a principal Enlightenment form, allowed its members to enact on a miniature scale their ideal principles for public debate, what one critic has described, reading Charles Brockden Brown's fiction, as a "juridical public sphere" in which readers would converse about and judge morals and knowledge in relation to the material they voraciously read.[15] This conception underlay most of their publications and public activities just as it defined their imagined republic of intellect.

In post-Revolutionary New York City, this larger public sphere could be found or facilitated in a variety of spaces outside the club. Though recent histories of this era have rightly emphasized the complementary significance of voluntary association and print culture in producing the new nation's public sphere, most of this work has emphasized the ways in which politics dominated public discourse.[16] Friendly Club members did not so much compete with their many acquaintances who were politicians (as, at times, were members like Kent and Mitchill themselves) as they hoped to influence moral and intellectual structures of a broader sphere that subsumed political discussion. In this effort, they believed, their chief competition was the clergy. For Friendly Club members, whose partisan views were not uniform, the divide between "modern philosophers" and "religionists" was more significant than the division between Federalists and Jeffersonians. They saw the decade's partisan turmoil as inimical to the progress of knowledge and hoped to supplement or supplant the seemingly relentless focus on domestic and international politics with what Smith called "communications . . . of a more permanently useful nature."[17]

To do so they took advantage of a range of publishing opportunities. Smith, who had published newspaper verse and edited a volume of American poems before moving to the city in 1793, started his writing career in earnest following New York's 1795 yellow fever epidemic, when his medical history of that season appeared in a collection edited by Noah Webster. William Dunlap saw several of his own plays staged before he became manager of the Old American Company and, eventually, founded the new Park Theatre in 1798. Charles Brockden Brown began his career as a newspaper essayist, then novelist, and finally a magazine editor, all with the assistance of his fellow club members. In perhaps the most literal incarnation of a "juridical public sphere," James Kent established a program of legal education at Columbia that emphasized reading broadly in the century's most important philosophical works; with William Johnson as a court reporter, he saw his decisions printed in order to establish a body of new American precedents, while at the same time securing an Americanization of British common law tradition. In addition to taking advantage of or establishing such print outlets, Friendly Club members belonged individually and collectively to a range of additional associations, from the Manumission to the Mineralogical, most of which gave rise to additional oratorical or publishing ventures.

Such disparate literary endeavors united in the premium they placed on "information."[18] Contemporary documents rarely define "information" with any more specificity; broad lines distinguished "men of information" from the uninformed. The distinction implied that such men knew not only about current events at home and abroad but also were familiar with the latest publications in science, philosophy, and belles lettres.[19] Becoming informed—by newsprint, correspondence, domestic and imported journals, or through participation in voluntary associations—qualified one to govern what observers then and now understood as an "information revolution."[20] As participation in public discourse broadened and forums for such participation multiplied, information of all sorts—from news of global importance like the events of the French Revolution to studies of South Carolina soils—became more pressing and plentiful than it had been in earlier generations. Face-to-face communication and letters gave way to a new profusion of print media distributed among personal acquaintances and via a constantly improving postal system.[21]

As Friendly Club members repeatedly witnessed and sometimes experienced themselves, this overabundance of political, scientific, and social information generated anxiety among many elite authorities. Though this situation eventually gave rise to the creation of disciplinary knowledge and to the consolidation of the liberal professions, such consolidation forms only part of the Friendly Club's story. Clashes between epistemological frameworks (played out, for example, in conflicts between "religionists" and "modern philosophers") and intramural professional competition (such as the fierce medical rivalry over the subject of yellow fever) often had more immediate public visibility than the structural shifts that would eventually result in the emergence of disciplinary thinking and a culture of elite professional expertise.[22]

Scholars most often treat the literature of this period, including the writing of Friendly Club members, as contributing to new forms of nationalism; those treating "the American Enlightenment" more generally have similarly emphasized ways in which the political writing of the founding generation both led to and interpreted the American Revolution.[23] This book both challenges and complements such approaches by examining ways in which the Friendly Club's literary offerings were perhaps less oriented toward a new nationalism than to the authority-making rituals of civic fraternity that constituted a transnational intellectual culture.

Shifting how we approach these authors and texts requires a serious consideration of club members' reading as well as their writing, and so this study begins from a late-eighteenth-century definition of the term *literature* that was expansive enough to accommodate the extraordinary range of writing such figures produced and consumed. Arguing that *literature* in this period "meant all the forms of written discourse and the uses of literacy," Michael Warner quotes New York newspaper editor and Friendly Club acquaintance Noah Webster to support his point: "*Literature* comprehends a knowledge of the ancient languages, denominated classical, history, grammar, rhetoric, logic, geography, &c., as well as of the sciences."[24] When Friendly Club members planned to establish a "Literary Journal," their design "reaches to every division of literature & while it comprehends, at once . . . letters & arts, customs & manners, the history of nations & the peculiarity of individuals,—it becomes alike the *Manual* of Science & of Conversation."[25] The final phrase sums up the connections between "literature" (broadly conceived), a professionally diverse circle like the Friendly Club, and the information networks that made up the republic of intellect.

Taking the period's definitions of literature seriously has two effects crucial to the story I tell here. First, such an approach looks beyond post-Revolutionary politics to recognize ways in which the European Enlightenment had broader influence in the American 1790s than has previously been recognized. Robert Ferguson's argument that the "American Enlightenment does not quarrel with religious orthodoxies as its French counterpart does" is only partly correct. Elihu Smith's reading of Condorcet's *Sketch for a Historical Picture of the Progress of the Human Mind,* for example, reinforced his belief in the human capacity for perfectibility, which drove a serious wedge between him and his orthodox Congregationalist friends and former teachers. More than simply representing a "moderate Enlightenment," Smith and his friends aimed to create a new intellectual order in which "undeceived and reforming man" would expose the "nakedness & insufficiency of Religion" and replace "her with the lovely & unsophisticated form of Truth."[26] Smith and his friends may not have succeeded in this effort, but we must recognize it nonetheless in order to see the ways in which they conceived of a range of authorial practices as directly competing with clerics and others for government of the public sphere.

Recognizing the catholicity of the period's category of "literature" also means that some familiar ways of describing the writing produced in this period—as promoting a "collaborative" form of authorship, or as displaying a "devotion to factuality"—gain added significance.[27] The Friendly Club's literary output reveals the effects of collaboration across professional lines and demonstrates that a broad cultural predilection toward "facts" may have had less to do with Protestant didacticism than with attempts to "validate Enlightenment canons of knowledge," as John Bender has described the literary situation in England in the same period.[28] This means that even the group's more recognizably "literary" offerings—poems, novels, plays—often read by modern critics in terms of early national politics or nationalism, may have had meanings more closely related to broad philosophical debates than to emerging nationalist ideologies.

The comparison to late-eighteenth-century English literature is instructive, not least because Friendly Club members understood the republic of intellect to be transatlantic in scope and aimed for correspondents and audiences overseas as well as at home. In early 1798, Elihu Smith wrote to John Aiken, the editor of the *Monthly Magazine, and British Register,* to complain that the "conductors of the ablest literary works in Gt. Britain" routinely offered "imperfect, partial, & erroneous" accounts of American "affairs, manners, opinions, & institutions." Smith set out to rectify the problem by offering the Friendly Club's services to the journal as American correspondents. He writes:

> There exists in this city, a small association of men, who are connected by mutual esteem, & habits of unrestricted communication. They are of different professions & occupations; of various religious & moral opinions; & tho' they coincide in the great outlines of political faith, they

estimate very variously many of the political transactions of the men who have, from time to time directed the councils of the nation. This diversity of sentiment, however, as it has never affected their friend-ship, has made them more active in investigation; & tho' they may have formed different judgments concerning facts, has led them to a general concurrence in the facts themselves. Natives of America, & of remote parts of the Union, they are in habits of constant communication with several of the States, & are well informed of the state of letters, science, & opinions in these States, with some few exceptions.[29]

Smith's letter is one of the few descriptions of the club written dur-ing its activity. Its implications, though, are as structural as they are bound to a specific set of individuals. They indicate broad networks of communication that would both facilitate better information and also expand a European audience for the club's medical, literary, and nationalistic endeavors. As a sample, Smith enclosed brief biographical sketches of America's leading poets, the elder Connecticut Wits, which both the club's own *Monthly Magazine* and Joseph Dennie's *Farmer's Museum* also eventually serialized.[30] But Smith's letter emphasizes above all else the importance of the circle of friends whose services he offers: "It is for you to judge how far the correspondence of such a knot of men may be of consequence to your Work," Smith told the editor, "or of value to your curiosity . . . a means of readily furnishing you with the publications made in the United States; with such occasional re-marks as may enable you to estimate them properly." They will offer, presumably because more current and regularly updated, "a species of information which no books can furnish."[31]

Smith's efforts to establish this correspondence help to clarify the Friendly Club's nature and social functions. Smith emphasizes that the club's diversity of occupation and sentiment helps to produce a "concurrence in the facts themselves," pointing to the Enlightenment ideal of "departmentalizing" the processes of knowledge collection as a means of increasing efficiency and comprehensiveness. He intended such efforts to consolidate both knowledge and the social authority to convey it, and to position him and his friends as men of observation and information. At the same time such language signals what I label a protodisciplinary knowledge culture—one that recognizes the need to subdivide knowledge production and has begun to do so by attaching specialized knowledge to different professional enterprises. The club, as Smith describes it, plays a very specific function in this nostalgic effort to bring together various "investigations" and "communications" in an Edenic state of universal knowledge. That specific function had to do with friendship. Ideally, any tensions that may have arisen from the diversity of religious, moral, and political opinion would be counteracted by the friendly bonds that provided the rationale for gathering in the first place.

The cultural politics of association were not always so irenic. Collective distinction had its shadowy sides. "Animated by the example, assistance, & social exertion of others, there are no heights of science too arduous for me to attempt to surmount," Smith wrote in the preface to one volume of his diary, only to follow that sentiment with a "survey" of the "busy multitude" surrounding him: people "little thoughtful of knowledge & reputation but as instruments to acquire [wealth]," "too lazy to inquire," and, perhaps most damning of all, "busy in oppressing others, from whose humiliation they expect distinction."[32] If circles of influence were bound by friendship's energies, many Americans in the late eighteenth century sometimes worried they were being left outside the associations that really mattered or that others had united in conspiracies against them. Other dangers followed closely on the age's encomia to friendship. Unbridled conversation, even between friends, could breed licentiousness or encourage infidelity. It could, furthermore, disclose differences that posed significant challenges to friends of varying politics or opinions. If Smith and most club members aligned their literary energies with unrestraint and free inquiry, they were less unified in their opinions regarding propriety in mixed-sex conversation. If the Friendly Club came into existence as part of a broad cultural celebration of civic association, by century's end there were many who eyed assembly suspiciously and wished to police its limits.

My account of the Friendly Club and the forgotten literary and intellectual structures it represents falls into two parts. Part 1 considers the varieties and meanings of friendship and voluntary association in the late-eighteenth-century city: highly gendered social forms that were commonplace if, at times, controversial. These chapters seek to situate the Friendly Club within its contemporary discourses of friendship and association (chapter 1), including anxiety about secret or exclusive associations (chapter 2), and questions about proper modes of conversation in mixed-sex society (chapter 3). Part 2 identifies and examines specific examples of what I call the "knowledge industries" in which club members participated. As an example of such institutional fields of knowledge production I examine James Kent's performances in the lecture hall, courtroom, and most importantly in print (treated here in a brief prelude to part 2), followed by discussions of Dunlap's ambitions for and management of the theater (chapter 4) and Brown's fever novel *Arthur Mervyn*, which emerged alongside his clubmates' *Medical Repository* in the midst of fierce debates over the sources and treatment of the disease (chapter 5). As institutions of the public sphere, these knowledge industries depended in various ways on the style of intellectual fellowship the club afforded its members, and they all contributed to the group's ultimate goal of generating social authority and effecting social change by collecting and disseminating moral and scientific knowledge. Together these chapters represent the first effort to make collective sense of this group's diverse output, and in doing so to account for the full vitality and variety of early U.S. writing.

In some ways, *Republic of Intellect* treats subjects that did not yet exist. It is about New York City before it was the preeminent American metropolis; about American literature before any such tradition had fully cohered; about the disciplining of knowledge and the formation of professional identities before knowledge was disciplinary and modern professional identities fully formed. It examines a group of young men, most of whom would go on, in their adult lives, to dominate the fields in which they practiced, yet I write about a period of their lives that preceded their eventual fame and, in some cases, their most significant contributions to American culture. In part, *Republic of Intellect* tells how New York became the city it is; how American literature came to distinguish itself; how knowledge came to be controlled by expert professionals; how a handful of prominent Americans moved toward their eventual fame. But it tells a larger cultural history as well, for more than any similar group in the new United States, the Friendly Club was situated at the generic, geographical, and professional crossroads of American society and at the primary point of entry and exit for transmissions within a transatlantic intellectual culture. Before his early death, Elihu Smith, in his careful record of social and intellectual life in New York, anticipated correctly that his diary would be useful to a future readership, precisely because it would open up a world of association in its preservation of "the characters of my friends—of their friends—finally, of all those distinguished personages, with whom, accident, or design have made me acquainted."[33] *Republic of Intellect* aims to deliver on that promise.

I. ASSOCIATIONS

Pictures at an Exhibition

O N a rainy afternoon in the fall of 1797, the three editors of the newly established *Medical Repository* traveled by carriage to the rural farm of Horatio Gates, a famed general in the American Revolution, to view an international celebrity on display: Thaddeus Kosciusko, "the Washington of Poland." Kosciusko, who had fought alongside Gates during decisive battles in the Revolution, had recently been released from a Russian prison, where he had been locked away for leading a Polish nationalist uprising in the mid-1780s. Elihu Smith's record of the event in his diary offers instructions for understanding the relationships he and his contemporaries imagined between friendship, reputation, and scientific observation, issues that called the Friendly Club into existence and occupied much of its collective activity. "Kosciusko came in, leaning on a crutch, & with one assistant," Smith wrote:

> He is tall, muscular, & his face somewhat thinner than would be expected from his limbs. His complexion is light & delicate, with a slight intermixture of red; his eye blue; his hair short, dark, & unpowdered. The countenance is more indicative of reflection than fancy, of fortitude than of force. He appears to have been laden with care, & anxiety. The ready flexions of his brow bespeak him to have suffered great & long-

continued pain. He recd. numerous wounds & was confined in a solitary dungeon many months before they were in any way cured. Nothing but a most vigorous constitution could have supported him. He has nearly lost the use of one thigh; & a sabre-wound on his head is not yet healed. He speaks english, but not correctly, & with a foreign accent & pronunciation. His demeanor is interesting & proper. We talked of the Comet; & he appeared well versed in Astronomy. A reply made by him to a remark addrest to him by me, marks the simplicity & sincerity of his character. Speaking of his residing again in the United States I said to him—"You will find a great many old friends, & a great many new friends." He returned "that he had made some new friends, whose acquaintance gave him pleasure, but that his principal delight was in the society of his former friends."[1]

The account, something of a set piece among Smith's briefer summaries of daily affairs, deserves quoting at length for three reasons. First, the density of telling detail Smith lavishes on his subject illustrates well the intensity with which he and his fellows conceived of themselves as scientific observers of moral character as well as environments. Second, the account demonstrates the importance of social settings and networks of association—often highly exclusive ones—to such quests for knowledge. Third, it emphasizes that for Smith and others like him, friendships old and new were fundamental not only to the production of public knowledge and reputation but also to a rigorous and systematic effort at self-understanding.

In keeping with his role as scientific writer and editor, Smith begins with an almost ethnographic overview of Kosciusko's permanent features, fashion choices, and manners. The catalog of facial features and complexion gives way quickly to an interpretive mode derived from the science of physiognomy, popularized in the late eighteenth century by the work of the Swedish theologian Johann Casper Lavater. Smith scrutinizes the soldier's countenance to discern his character ("reflection" is stronger than "fancy," "fortitude" outweighs "force"), although as was often true of physiognomical readings of celebrity subjects, Smith's serves mostly to justify the subject's preexisting reputation. Artificial indicators of the general's republican values ("short, dark, & unpowdered" hair) confirm information Smith gleans by careful scrutiny of the soldier's facial structure itself (the creased and careworn brow). Governing the entire account is a sympathetic tone, in the late-eighteenth-century sense of the term *sympathy*: a resonance between two similarly attuned bodies. Smith's recognition of Kosciusko's virtues confirms like qualities in himself, qualities cultivated through the social rituals of urban association.[2] That is, the observer's painstaking scrutiny of his surroundings ultimately yielded self-knowledge as Smith turned Kosciusko and himself into joint subjects of natural history. "I believe that I comprehend the character of my own mind," Smith wrote in the preface to the final volume of his diary, an assertion he followed quickly by affirming the importance of "the example, assistance, & social exertions of others" to his intellectual endeavors.[3]

The concerns for social standing and self-knowledge implicit in Smith's entry resurface, and are perhaps even more fully expressed, in another set of events Friendly Club members took part in that season. Beginning with a series of three-mile walks out of town, a number of club members sat for portraits by the British artist James Sharples, an occasional visitor to their Saturday evening meetings.[4] The following summer, "Mr. Sharples's COLLECTION OF PORTRAITS of distinguished Characters," as the *Daily Advertiser* billed it, went on public display "at no. 104 Broadway, opposite Trinity Church."[5] Visiting the show, club members saw themselves exhibited as exemplars of civic virtue, just as Kosciusko had been. Readers who noted the newspaper advertisement and could afford the price of admission would have viewed a curious collection of characters indeed: nearly two hundred small chalk pastels, life-sized heads and shoulders, almost all preternaturally rigid profiles. Among the collection were several people viewers may have encountered outside on the city streets or among the other attendees in the makeshift gallery: Alexander Hamilton, the New Yorker who until 1795 had been Washington's treasury secretary; Samuel Bard, a founder of the New-York Hospital; local patriot-heroes and politicians like General Gates, Colonel Aaron Burr, and George Washington, who had relocated from New York to Philadelphia along with the federal government only eight years earlier.[6]

What did it mean, at the end of the eighteenth century, for someone to produce, collect, and display such a series of characters? Or to seek membership in such a collection? To modern viewers, Sharples's portraits are remarkable for their uniformity, for the way their subjects seem almost interchangeable—hardly an indication that such portraits seek to scrutinize and preserve idiosyncrasy or individual character. One answer, then, to the question of these portraits' meaning lies in the rec-

lap's real passions, though, were painting and playwriting. In the late 1780s his father had sent him to London to study painting with the American artist Benjamin West, though Dunlap abandoned his lessons and spent his three years there in theaters, taverns, and the New York Coffee House, a favorite with American expatriates. When his father finally called him home to New York, Dunlap returned to find the theaters reopened (they had been closed temporarily when the triumphant American colonists had turned British occupants and loyalists out of the city) and a "native" play, Royall Tyler's *The Contrast,* in the midst of a successful run. Within two years, New York's Old American Company, which Dunlap would eventually manage, was staging Dunlap's work.[7] Sometime between the fall of 1793 and the fall of 1794, Smith, William Woolsey, and Dunlap, along with a handful of additional friends—most, like Smith, Connecticut natives and Yale graduates—founded the Friendly Club, which they conceived as a weekly literary conversation in a member's home for the purpose of promoting general knowledge and refining their literary sensibilities.

New York City in the 1790s was not the United States' leading intellectual center, if such a determination depends on the size and activity of public learned societies like Philadelphia's American Philosophical Society or Boston's American Academy of Arts and Sciences. Philadelphia remained the medical stronghold of the new nation, though Columbia faculty like Samuel Latham Mitchill, a Long Island native educated in Edinburgh, worked tirelessly to promote New York as an alternative training ground for physicians.[8] Some historians have dealt harshly with New York's performance: in a city where "population, commerce, industry, wealth, and geographic location might have led one to expect the development of an array of institutions for promoting knowledge rivaling or surpassing the achievements of Philadelphia, nothing of the kind occurred."[9] The presumed reasons include the devastation visited on the city during the Revolution, the shift of the national capital to Philadelphia and the state capital to Albany, and one reason club members themselves repeated frequently: "the eager cultivation & rapid increase of the arts of gain, & . . . the neglect of elegant & useful science, of the arts of genius, taste, & society."[10] Business boomed, the 33-year-old lawyer James Kent wrote to his brother in May of 1796. "But the Business Life of this City is very unfavorable to literary Pursuits which are the Source of all that is precious & happy." Still, even Kent, who seems to have enjoyed urban life least of all the club members, recognized some literary advantages of a vibrant port city: "My Library . . . swells very fast," he added, noting that he had just purchased a new edition of Voltaire in 92 volumes.[11] Other members were unabashedly enthusiastic about what New York offered. Even at the onset of the epidemic that would claim Smith's life, William Johnson heckled Dunlap, confined to the countryside: "I commiserate your situation: so destitute of intellectual food: You had better leave a dull uninteresting country scene & join us. The Town is the only place for rational beings." Writing on the same sheet, the bedridden Smith added news about their latest project: a newly formed Mineralogical Society that met in Mitchill's offices at the college.[12]

If New York's intellectual environment did not have the prestige of Philadelphia and Boston institutions, this situation may, in fact, help to explain some of the city's appeal to this group, as well as its members' various successes. New York, rapidly growing, was a wide-open arena in which they could distinguish themselves in medicine, law, business, belles lettres, and publishing forms attached to the professions. Living outside the shadow of watchful parents and teachers, this circle of literary friends—many of whom eschewed their parents' religious orthodoxy—enjoyed an exhilarating measure of independence. Their accomplishments belie the lamentations of historians for New York's intellectual inactivity. Neither Boston nor Philadelphia could boast, in the 1790s, a publishing record as diverse or significant as the one Friendly Club members established in New York. Understanding that varied output requires a step back to consider the written and social forms that facilitated and supplemented these diverse publications: forms that emphasized the importance of intellectual association to the emergence of the first U.S. literature.

Varieties of Urban Association

In New York City in the 1790s, the public face of civic life was visible in clusters of male bodies that crisscrossed the city in one another's company, attending meetings of groups with names like the Horanian Society, the Calliopean Society, the Tammany Society, the Marine Society, and the Manumission Society. This "associational world"—the networks of relations that gave rise to a "deliberative public sphere"—was the world into which Friendly Club members were born.[13] The century and especially the decade before their births witnessed exponential growth in the number and variety of such civic associations. Friendly

Club members belonged to a variety of organizations prior to and during the club's years of activity.[14] As a teenager in Philadelphia, Charles Brockden Brown had helped to form a "Belles Lettres Club," whose members hoped to trace "the relations, dependencies, and connections of the several parts of knowledge" as they jointly pursued "literary improvement."[15] Smith knew at least some of Brown's group while he studied medicine in Philadelphia; on returning to Connecticut in 1791 he participated in a similar literary circle with other young "Hartford Wits."[16] Most Friendly Club members found their earliest models of intellectual association in student clubs at Yale; several of them had participated together in the Brothers in Unity, established for "the improvement of science and friendship." Only James Kent had belonged to the rival Linonia Society, organized "for the promotion of Friendship and social Intercourse and for the Advancement of Literature." Such clubs prepared elite young men to assume positions of leadership in communities, states, and the new nation's government.[17]

New Yorkers formed or joined a range of similar associations in the 1790s for several distinct reasons: intellectual development, especially literary and scientific (Calliopean, Horanian Literary, Belles Lettres, Uranian, Agricultural, Mineralogical); moral reform (Manumission, Emigrants); leisure, music, dining, or other gentlemanly amusement (Anacreontic, Sub Rosa, Belvedere); professional development and fellowship (Medical); financial insurance or commercial networking (Mechanics, Marine); evangelical (Missionary); the ostensible transmission of secret or mystical knowledge (Freemason, Black Friar); and patriotic, nationalistic, or partisan networking (Democratic-Republican, Tammany). The following decade would witness continued diversification, including the New York African Society for Mutual Relief. Some but not all of these associations represented themselves in public—in newspaper notices, public society orations, parades, or entries in the new annual city directories.[18]

Although voluntary societies served a variety of intellectual, civic, political, commercial, humanitarian, and leisure interests, and sometimes overlapped in their topical pursuits, their common claim to foster fraternal feeling often had pragmatic benefits that transcended specific concerns. Membership in one club often led fellows to seek membership together in another; groups in one city or country extended honorary memberships to individuals in distant places as a way to advertise the reach of their information networks and promote reputations beyond local settings. Smith, for example, was voted an honorary member of the Massachusetts Historical Society shortly before his death, a sign of his advancing national reputation as a medical writer and editor.[19] Middling and elite groups depended on the networks of privilege that resulted; a short leap could carry those with sufficient privilege from membership in voluntary associations to the governing boards of hospitals, colleges, or churches, or to political office or appointment.

Publicly visible collectivity—what one historian, writing about a later period, calls "the performance of people in association"—facilitated the production of personal reputation in an urban civic culture. Spectacular parades of thousands of citizens marked a diverse range of occasions, from the imminent ratification of the Constitution in 1788 (a parade in which William Dunlap and Samuel Mitchill may have marched as members of Noah Webster's short-lived Philological Society), to major events in the French Revolution, to annual Independence Day celebrations, to visits by or funerals of political or other civic leaders, including an extraordinary memorial march for George Washington in 1799.[20] Often underwritten by city government and recounted in newspapers and broadsides, such spectacles of public association were not tableaux of the city's actual demographics so much as they were highly scripted, semiofficial, and often partisan corporate self-representations.[21]

Membership in the bar, the Congress, the Order of the Cincinnati, the militia, or any of the groups that collectively made up such parades helped define one's public character. Over the course of the 1790s, the opportunities for such public association proliferated at an amazing rate. In 1788, the Philological Society was the only intellectual society to stake a public presence in a parade more specifically organized to celebrate "the various branches of mechanicks" and their contributions to ratification. In the New Year's Eve 1799 procession to memorialize George Washington, affinity for workers was displayed by voluntary association rather than craft; elites were organized into merchant societies or the liberal professions. The groups to which one could belong formed a sort of continuum from governmental bodies and political parties to professional, vocational, or ethnic ones.

Through events like these, Friendly Club members and their contemporaries demonstrated that their places in civic society were structured not simply by individual station or reputation but by their positions in the multiple groups and networks of civic life. The expansiveness of one's choices and the number of memberships one held signaled the privileges of social status.[22] In the case of Washington's parade, groups and individuals with varying degrees of autonomy also struggled to define themselves publicly and politically by association with the deceased.[23] At the same time, such events upheld cultural hierarchies in details like "Twenty-four Girls, in White Robes, with White Surplusses and Turbans, Strewing Laurels during the Procession," or, later in the parade, "The General's Wife, in Mourning, Led by two black servants in complete mourning with white Turbans." Elites used such symbolic choreography—bodies put into the service of more abstract social values—to throw into relief the more implicit symbolism of the group formations that made up the remainder of these parades, which served to reinforce networks and identities based on vocation, profession, and political standing.[24]

The increasing numbers and diversity of associations, particularly but not limited to those with political emphases, made rights of assembly a topic of continual debate throughout the decade. Controversy stemmed from tensions between publicity and secrecy, between federation and faction, perhaps because contemporaries recognized in acts of spectacular association the ways in which such groups worked so powerfully to mediate public identities or provide the basis for collective determination. The exclusive nature of most fraternal organizations had long made clubs the subject of popular curiosity.[25] Because secret societies like the Freemasons made some outsiders nervous, such groups made their existence known and advertised their civic utility in order to alleviate public anxieties about the secret knowledge they were said to transmit.[26] Secret societies would come to generate an enormous amount of discussion during the Bavarian Illuminati scare at the turn of the century, but throughout the entire post-Revolutionary period debate raged over the question of who could assemble, for what purposes, and whether or not such groups needed state sanction.[27]

Histories of intellectual and literary culture in late-eighteenth-century New York—most of which highlight the Friendly Club because of its roster of prominent members—rarely differentiate between this group's style of association and the range of other associations in the city. Representative of other private conversation circles, the Friendly Club stands apart from most forms of civic association in its privacy. Unlike Webster's Philological Society of the late 1780s or the Calliopean Society of the 1790s—two groups with which the Friendly Club has often been confused—Smith and his fellows did not cultivate a public reputation for their club during the years of its existence. It could not be found in city directories, and its members did not march under a banner in public parades. Although they joined more visible organizations together, Smith and his friends designed the Friendly Club as a haven from public life that would offer them a space for the unrestrained conversation they believed was required to discover moral and scientific truths about one another and the world they lived in. This freedom would ideally foster, protect, and even depend upon a diversity of sentiment—even on sensitive topics like religion and politics, which were taboo topics in many public societies.

As a group, Friendly Club members imagined themselves as inheritors of the Enlightenment republic of letters, which had ideally transcended politics and nationalism.[28] Club members would not have considered their group to have much in common either with the city's young Federalist groups or with the Democratic-Republican societies, which club member William Woolsey derided in a letter to a friend as attracting "the lowest order of mechanics, laborers, and draymen."[29] Nevertheless, the group believed that the truths discovered in their insular conversations would have social effects. Smith even argued to the Federalist editor Joseph Dennie, a fierce partisan and Anglophile, that natural science could supply an antidote to partisan strife, a belief he held even as some Federalists had begun to hold up Jefferson's scientific interests as evidence of religious infidelity.[30]

Smith's confidence that the republic of intellect could remain above politics shines through in his decision to bring the Millers and Mitchill into Friendly Club activity in 1798, at the highpoint of national partisan tensions and despite the fact that William Woolsey privately "condemn'd" the Millers as democrats.[31] When several Friendly Club members helped to found the Mineralogical Society in the summer of 1798, it was similarly characterized by its cosmopolitanism and bipartisanship (it included Solomon Simpson, a Jewish watchmaker and past president of the city's Democratic-Republican society). The following year, Samuel Miller promoted the club's literary-scientific *Monthly Magazine, and American Review* to the Massachusetts minister, geographer, and Federalist propagandist Jedidiah Morse as the project of a politically mixed group.[32] In spite of its attempts to withdraw from public view and to eschew political controversy, the Friendly Club would be affected by partisan disputes. An account of the club written

years later by William Dunlap even suggests the club came to an end
when partisan conflict at the turn of the century became insurmount-
able.[33] Even so, Friendly Club alumni and others sought to preserve
a learned culture in the city that was more patrician than partisan, as
political opponents joined forces to found the New-York Historical
Society and other intellectual institutions.[34]

If these differences separated the Friendly Club from other associations in the era, its greatest commonality with the world of civic sociability lay in its overt emphasis on friendship. Like association more
generally, friendship held specific meanings in relation to commercial
society, politics, and Enlightenment intellectual culture.[35] Commenta-
tors then and now have recognized ways in which friendship facilitated
economic relations, provided a democratic model for political relations,
and opened up networks for the dissemination of knowledge. Toward
the turn of the century, new notions of "romantic friendship"—disinterested emotional relationships based on elective affinity—took the
Enlightenment's idealization of friendship and added a crucial dimension: an emotional economy in which true friendship was nearly as
scarce as discussion of it was abundant.[36] The difficulty of finding a true
friend sent young people on searches for those sympathetic individuals
who would fill that role. An emphasis on sympathy, affinity, and likeness made this form of romantic friendship predominantly (though not
exclusively) a same-sex affair. To one male correspondent early in the
decade, Charles Brockden Brown wrote: "Friendship is, perhaps, more
pure but certainly not less violent than love. Between friends there must
exist a perfect and entire similarity of disposition. . . . Soul must be
knit unto Soul."[37] The relationship between the intense emotion of
romantic friendship and Enlightenment modes of intellectual inquiry
justified rituals of conversation, familiar correspondence, and club life
itself. Such notions of friendship, club members believed, led not only
to the production of self- and general understanding but also to several
forms of writing used to record or display this new knowledge.

Conversation, Correspondence, Club: Accounting for Association in Smith's Diary

This hybrid of Enlightenment scientific sensibility and romantic friendship emerges most clearly from Elihu Smith's diary, the single most
important source on the Friendly Club. Made up of six hard-backed
notebooks of various sizes, comprising nearly four hundred thousand

words, the extant diary—whose title Smith constantly adjusted—begins with "Vol. III" on Smith's 24th birthday, 4 September 1795. (Smith destroyed the first two volumes, embarrassed by their preoccupation with a failed romantic interest.) Smith's notebooks are generically miscellaneous. They include diurnal entries; drafts of letters, essays, and poetry; notes on reading, including occasional transcriptions or translations; case histories from his medical practice; an unfinished utopia; genealogical narratives of himself and biographies of childhood friends; and a meticulous record of his "industry": the number and size of pages he read and wrote each month (fig. 6). Much more than a record of individual consciousness, Smith's diary serves as an account of public associations, private conversations, collective reading patterns and textual circulation; class privilege, political tensions, and literary ambition; public health, private opinion, literary and cultural institutions, and, not least, the importance of friendship itself to such undertakings.[38] In a letter encouraging his sister Fanny to imitate his regular diary practice, Smith argued that "Journalizing" allows us to "obtain correct notions" as we attempt to "arrange our ideas on paper." By so "recur[ring] to the pen," he advises, "when we attempt to methodize, [we] shall discover what indeed we do know."[39] Conversation, correspondence, and club life all worked in similar ways. Like the club, Smith's "diurnal duty" would provide a tool for self-understanding and a repository for tentative ideas, warm-up drills for public performances.[40]

The diary offered Smith a place to account for the club's industry as well as his own. On a Sunday morning in September 1795, Smith penned in the first pages of "Vol. III" a detailed, if frustrated, narrative of the Friendly Club's development. Searching for the cause of the club's recent and repeated failure to meet on the designated Saturday evenings, Smith begins the history by listing the club's original ten members, a network based largely on marital relations and Connecticut origins: William Dunlap, William and George Woolsey, Prosper Wetmore, Horace, Seth, and William Johnson, Thomas Mumford, Smith himself, and Lynde Catlin. Beginning at the end of this list, Smith attempts as he writes to sort out the reasons so many of these friends had not lived up to his expectations of club life: Catlin married, and the "'cat-ish fondness' of his wife, & perhaps, his own indifference" separated him from his friends; Seth Johnson suffered poor health and traveled for business; Mumford moved; others were too unpunctual to be dependable. New members James Kent and Charles Adams, like

George Woolsey, were more regular, but the core membership consisted of "W.W. Woolsey, W. Dunlap, W. Johnson, & Smith, [who] have been punctual, with scarcely any exception, when in Town," and whose "absence must, materially, affect the meetings of the Club."[41]

A catalog of inactivity and indolence, Smith's diary entry imagines specific forces—commerce, illness, and especially marriage—as inimical to the club's industry.[42] The previous evening, with four members absent on business and the rest undependable, neither Smith nor others knew where to assemble. Even if they had met, the entry makes plain the double-edged effects of limited membership; while Smith, with characteristic secretarial skill, can account for every member, present or absent, on a given night, he is also aware that the failure of even a few members to attend can prevent a necessary quorum not because of bylaws but required by the demands of conversation itself.

Conversation was the club's raison d'être, its organizing principle, and Smith used his diary in part to record and evaluate the broad-ranging discussions he conducted with these and other friends. In club members' understanding, "conversation" meant something more than mere talking; it was what made the cardinal virtue "industry" possible. Throughout his diary Smith scrutinizes strangers' speech—just as physiognomists did faces—as a means of discerning character.[43] He also classifies even the most casual of conversations using a pseudo-Linnaean vocabulary. In order for conversation to deserve its name, it had to be frank, spirited, and directed toward detecting and eliminating error or conveying useful information. It could be sharply focused or "general" and still be "efficacious" or to one's "advantage." It could be "pleasant," even "ingenious," and still be "desultory." It had to be "sufficiently consistent," however, "to admit of character, or denomination."[44]

The Friendly Club defined itself by conversational style rather than formulating a constitution or set of rules. Friendly Club conversations aimed for three goals. In one of the earliest retrospectives on the club, William Dunlap recalled the first of these, what he called "unshackled intellectual intercourse": "All form was rejected by the 'friendly club,' and but one rule adopted, which was that the member who had the pleasure of receiving his friends at his house, should read a passage from some author, by way of leading conversation into such a channel as might turn the thoughts of the company to literary discussion or critical investigation."[45] This single rule makes plain the second defining characteristic of the club's conversational aims: its subordination of conversational pleasure to scientific or critical ends.

An article titled "On Conversation," from the group's *Monthly Magazine, and American Review* for July 1800, sets forth the third conversation goal these members shared: principles of politeness could not be allowed to frustrate conversation's best effects. "If my companion be wrong in thinking me in error, and in thinking me *self-confutable*," the author of this essay argues, "let the truth show itself upon experiment. Let him take his own way, and, by putting questions, as many as his wishes, finally detect his own folly." The article contrasts such conversational "philosophers" with "polite men"; if a person asks friends to question erroneous beliefs, or insists, even, that fundamental terms (like "conversation" itself) be defined clearly, that person would risk violating the rules of polite society, which constitute, in the writer's view, "merely the art of pleasing, directly, by soothing the vanity or banqueting the passions of others, or, indirectly, by avoiding accusation, and helping others to conceal their incapacity or ignorance."[46] Whereas "politeness," earlier in the century, had characterized the "free conversation" of gentlemen's clubs, here the term connotes all that is false and constraining, something to set aside among true friends.[47] Conversation that was frank rather than polite facilitated and even embodied the club's ideals of friendship and collectivity; it provided the ritual through which individuals were bound in corrective mutual improvement and the production of knowledge.

The Friendly Club's preferred mode of conversation depended on virtuous participants. When the early member Prosper Wetmore became entangled in shady business transactions in the winter of 1795, the club voted to revoke his membership. His continued presence, they determined, was itself inimical to the openness and sincerity they desired. When, "much to our regret," he attended the meeting on 19 December of that year, "[c]onversation was heavy—& the evening on the whole, unpleasant."[48] To be morally useful, Smith and his fellows believed, conversation required extraordinary discipline and seriousness. In one diary entry, Smith found "fault" with himself and his friends for allowing "gaiety & frolic" to "give a looseness to [their] conversation" and resolved "to put an end to this, in myself; & to attempt to check it, in others." This was not to take the pleasure out of conversation; Smith found one female friend's highly refined conversation "an Entertainment still superior" to a good evening at the theater.[49]

Ideal conversation depended not only on discipline but also on superior information, the sort garnered from wide-ranging reading, various professional activities, and correspondence that allowed members to interact with other trusted observers. Smith used these standards to evaluate club meetings in general as well as individual interactions. At one particularly profitable meeting, for example, Kent read aloud, "with great marks of satisfaction," a set of letters William Dunlap had received that day from the British writers William Godwin and Thomas Holcroft. The same night's discussion included William Johnson's reading of "Gibbon's character of Mahomet" and an extract from "St. Pierre's Theory of Tides," and Smith was called on to read an original poem he had just completed by request for a mixed-sex meeting of the Anacreontic Society.[50] At another meeting, Johnson's reading of a selection by Hume "excited comments on various modes, & on the best mode, of Reading. Each read, in turn—we criticized—& with some improvement, & much diversion." Following this they compared "the excellence, evidence, & spirit of different Religions—& on the proper conclusions to be drawn from a decided preference to either."[51] Information, comparison, evaluation, improvement: these were conversation's—and the club's—ideal ends.

In contrast to such lively discussions, Smith laments club nights when discourse does not move beyond the "politics of the day," when "trivial talk [is] not worthy the name of conversation." As harsh in his judgment as he was idealistic in his standards, he lamented on another occasion, when political discussion made for "pitifully rambling & uninstructive" conversation, that he and his fellow club members "do not give a higher and efficient character to this little association, which certainly is not wanting in capacity & information, & ought to be devoted to something better than mere amusements." Sated with the day's news, "one yawned, another stretched himself, a third dozed, & all were stupid."[52]

Taken together, such entries offer a coherent theory of friendship's relationship to reputation and to scientific observation. Smith's desire to make himself "the subject of inquiry" provided another primary motivation for keeping his diary and participating in club life. "What is of more importance, to man, that the knowlege [sic] of man?" Smith asks in the introduction to the diary's earliest volume—one he eventually destroyed, preserving only the preface: "What [is] so useful to an individual, as an acquaintance with himself?" Such an undertaking required empirical investigation, he believed, a "science" by which "our own hearts" might be "discover[ed]" and "our actual character" brought "before the penetrating eyes of our own understandings." Such precision could only come by "composing an actual history of himself."[53] The forms by which the poet-physician mediates his self-performance are both literary and scientific as he places himself on the dissecting table of his own mind and wields a historian's pen like a scalpel.

This scientific process of self-inquiry becomes collaborative performance not only in conversation—or even in Smith's decision to include friends' biographies in his diary—but also in the social uses to which he put the diary even as he produced it. Contrary to modern assumptions about the privacy of the diary form, Smith and friends often read aloud from their journals to one another, especially after long separations.[54] In such ways, their diaries did not simply trace individual intellectual progress but also aimed to "stimulate abler men to investigation."[55] For Smith the relationship between individual and collective identities was the key to "investigation" itself—the search for founding principles of self and society, morality and science. Such principles are clear in the title he eventually assigned to the diary: "Memoirs: or Notices concerning the Life, Studies, Opinions, and Friends, of E.H. Smith." The term "Friends" may stand out to twenty-first-century readers who have been taught to think of the diary, like the novel, as a form of writing closely aligned with the emergence of modern liberal individualism.[56] But Smith clearly indicated that his diary was to be less an individual record than a group portrait. "To those into whose hands my papers may come, when I cease to exist, they will be valuable," he wrote in the preface to one volume, "for my connections in many instances, have been with those, who either have been, or promise to be, in some good measure, distinguished actors in the scene around me."[57]

In entries like these, conversation and correspondence provide the social practices fundamental to ascertaining "undiscovered truth." If the diary records ways in which Smith used conversation both to evaluate character and to further friendship and inquiry, it places equal emphasis on correspondence. Smith "design[ed]" in late 1795 to "preserve copies" of his correspondence in the diary in part to index "my own mind," making it possible to aid "the treasures of memory, the riches of reflection," but also to "exhibit . . . a view of my business, feelings, sentiments, the condition of my friends, &, occasionally, perhaps, the history of former periods."[58] The diary owes much of its bulk to the

letters Smith drafted in its pages, and the same reasons that led Smith
and others like him to valorize conversation and diary keeping underlay
Smith's sense that scientific and moral inquiry depended on familiar
correspondence. "Letters are designed as substitutes for conversation,"
he wrote to Idea Strong, a female friend from his childhood, and "may
be considered as analogous to the intercourse of neighbors" or to "partnerships & marriages" and as such "ought to be engaged in with some
caution, & much meditation." From mutual improvement of the immediate authors ("the acquisition of knowledge & virtue") they would
extend their benefits to "advance human happiness" in general. Letters
between friends, Smith suggests, could even reveal to their authors the
laws by which the world and its inhabitants operated. Public utility
and personal pleasure are, for him, interdependent, as Smith engages
his correspondent in an activity that will cultivate the ability to "discern
our failings, & correct them."[59]

Smith's scientific ambitions for his familiar correspondence are evident in such passages. "Shall we not, mutually," Smith wrote to another
friend,

> by becoming reciprocally admitted into the very inmost soul, each of
> the other, be better & more enabled, to draw forth the latest [latent?]
> qualities which lurk there unimproved & perhaps unknown, & bring
> them out to day, & cultivate them into useful importance? Can cold, ir-
> relevant, & generalized communications, do this? Have they the genial
> warmth necessary to stimulate the slumbering germ of benevolence, foster
> it's slowly unfolding bust, support it's feeble stalk, & expand it's fragrant
> blossoms to bless and beautify the world? . . . This can only be hoped
> from unfolding the interior of the heart. And this letters should do.[60]

Delineating generic conventions for correspondence, Smith seeks here
to win his reader, a friend who had complained about Smith's demands
for self-disclosure, using language that draws both on the sentimental
excess of the culture of sensibility and the language of scientific husbandry. Two aspects of the theory Smith sets forth in passages like
these deserve careful notice. First, though the process of self-examination as Smith describes it may seem simply to secularize Puritan forms
of self-scrutiny (which also gave rise to diary forms like the one he
used), a crucial difference exists: religious forms of self-examination begin with a fixed understanding of ideal selfhood—the individual's place

in divine order as revealed by Scripture—whereas Smith's is a process of discovery, of inquiries into unknown aspects of one's own character as well as into other regions of the natural world. Second, Smith attempts a model of friendly and collaborative inquiry—both into knowledge of the self and into the surrounding natural world—that privileges difference over likeness. Differences in individual temper, Smith argued, allow for greater profit in collaborative inquiry.

This model puts friendship not simply in the service of science but also promotes the intimacy on which publicly useful collaborations must be founded. Friends discover knowledge in the external and in one another's "very inmost soul[s]." The vocabulary of scientific husbandry ("slumbering germ," "feeble stalk," "fragrant blossoms") reminds us that with many of his correspondents Smith exchanged literal information about the natural world, comparing and classifying plants and birds and soils found in various parts of the United States; but here hearts unfold like flowers, and the "undiscovered truths" he inquires after are deeply personal. With this friend, Smith takes the position of the teacher, as he often does with reluctant correspondents—proselytes to his method of understanding self and world—but he also makes a plea for his friend to help him "draw forth" parts of himself to which he might not have access on his own. Correspondence, like conversation, constitutes a collaborative method for self-knowledge as well as for the utilitarian production and distribution of knowledge.

Club members worked in several literary forms that depended on and facilitated friendly collaboration. Smith's diary-bound letters stand as one of the most obvious examples. He apparently planned to publish them at some point, along with the rest of his memoirs; he kept them in his diary, he explained to his friend Theodore Dwight, because they contained a "history" of "the state of my mind, & progress of my studies."[61] Letters circulated among small networks of friends, though they sometimes aimed to prompt correspondents to public action and publication. Such friendly forms of communication had long been idealized in Enlightenment science and mercantile contexts as essential to the dissemination of news and useful information and to the progress of scientific knowledge.[62]

The correspondence preserved in Smith's diary bore an intimate relation not only to "the progress of knowledge" but also to Smith's belief in human perfectibility, the doctrine that most set him apart

as a "philosopher" from his religiously orthodox friends. Self-knowledge, a prerequisite to general knowledge, was collaborative in nature,
and bit by bit, virtuous human beings could push one another toward
moral perfection through such inquiry. "Have I a fault?" Smith asked
another correspondent. "Does my friend know it? & will he not strive
[to] correct it? Have I penetrated, in a new direction, into the region of
undiscovered truth? & shall I not impart, of the fruit of my discoveries,
to my friend?"[63] Smith's confidence in such "penetrat[ions]" saturates
his diurnal entries and correspondence alike. In some passages he even
converses with himself, as in this instance of his tendency to berate
himself for indolence: "Shall I ever do better? Poh! What a question is
that for one who believes in the perfectibility of man! . . . There is such
a thing as Volition, you know. Yes, & I know how feebly it is exerted,
where it ought to be rapid & penetrating as the lightnings."[64]

The Friendly Club's communal reading practices were designed
to foster such "rapid & penetrating" conversation, as is evident from
Smith's account of "[a] very well-spent evening" with the club in late
1797, with Johnson, Smith, and William Woolsey present, and Edward
Miller a visitor:

> I read Gilbert Wakefield's criticism on the Style of Hume—from the
> [London] Monthly Magazine. Conversation on the style of Hume,
> Robertson, Gibbon, Gillies, &c.—on the historical fidelity of Hume—
> Mrs. McCauley & Mr. Whitaker—Dr. Henry's History, & Andrew's
> continuation—character & conduct of Charles 1st of England—of the
> Stuart's—Whitaker's defense of Mary of Scotland—his theory of Gov-
> ernment—the present David Hume & others—doctrine of necessity of
> liberty to profession of science—France—Russia—effects of Peter 1st,
> of Catherine II.—particular estimation of what she has done—compar-
> ative view of other countries—effect of climate—China—its improve-
> ments, morality & population—De Pauw read on this last point—An-
> derson, & Sir Geo: Stanton—Royal Society—compared with other
> Societies—state of Spanish literature—state of Spain—probability of
> a revolution—effects—on Italy—France—agriculture of those coun-
> tries—of America—comparisons—commerce—President [Adams]'s
> speech—opinions concerning it—comparative literary merit of Adams
> & Washington—information of American merchants—physicians—
> lawyers—bar of Connecticut—Phila., N. York—Georgia claims—me-
> morial to Congress—state of society there—&c. &c.[65]

Whether Smith composed such an entry after the fact or, acting in a secretarial role, jotted notes as the meeting was in progress, the entry highlights the interplay between communal reading and conversation, as well as the multiple meanings of "association" at play in the gathering: both the association of individuals requisite to conduct such a wide-ranging exchange of opinions and information, and the "association of ideas," itself a concept fundamental to the philosophical and psychological models club members valued most.[66] Association psychology held that ideas were perceptions that emerged in response to nervous vibrations in the brain, and that "whatever renews the vibration, renews also the perception." Hence ideas left corporal markers on the body, material thought-maps that could be retraced and patterns that could be replicated. Smith's account of the club's conversation seeks to chart such routes. Club members took such principles from earlier thinkers like David Hartley as well as from contemporaries like Joseph Priestley, William Godwin, and Erasmus Darwin. If association psychology underlay the entire eighteenth-century culture of sensibility, it also explains the enduring celebration of friendly association.[67] One of self-examination's chief ends rested in recognizing the impressions left by associations—friendships and early associations in particular—that helped to make up one's character.

From Association to Publication: Friendship and Literary Collaboration

In the fall of 1795, both Smith and the Friendly Club had come to crisis moments in their respective histories. Low on funds, Smith contemplated the unhappy prospect of returning to Connecticut. If he were to stay in the city, he needed some means of support in addition to the meager funds provided by his private medical practice. To forestall such an occurrence, the club's "capacity & information" would have to be directed more effectively than it had been toward print media.[68] Recently he and Johnson had discussed with Noah Webster the possibility of taking editorial control of Webster's newspaper, the *Minerva*. Smith also considered opening a bookstore. The most ambitious publishing project he and his friends had so far plotted, though, was "a Periodical Paper; somewhat on the plan of the Spectator," the famous London daily edited early in the century by Addison and Steele.[69] (The *Spectator* had famously represented itself as being in part the product of a gentlemen's conversation club.)[70] Such a paper, he felt, would allow club members to serve as special observers of metropolitan manners and current events, but their view would extend as well to the whole natural world.

With the introduction of new members between 1795 and 1798, the club not only maintained a successful conversation circle but also secured its place in two centuries of the city's historiography. It would do so in large part because the new members who replaced the lackluster founders were all writers of one sort or another, as opposed to the group of merchants they displaced. In the fall of 1795 neither the group's collective output nor its members' individual reputations were particularly substantive: Smith had collaborated with Connecticut friends on satirical political poetry, published other occasional newspaper verse, and edited *American Poems,* though none of the projects had his name attached; Dunlap had seen a small handful of his plays staged; Charles Adams was the vice president's son, but his law practice was not particularly distinguished. Nor was William Johnson's. James Kent perhaps had the most prominent reputation of any Friendly Club member, as Columbia's first professor of law, but his initial series of lectures had not been particularly successful. The others—the Woolseys, Wetmore, and the remaining Johnson brothers—were merchants.[71] More than any of their projected intellectual endeavors, what made this group of friends most visible at this point in its history was its members' participation as officers—Smith himself was the secretary—of the city's Manumission Society and African Free School.[72]

In stepping up collaborative publishing endeavors after 1795, the group had multiple options open to them. Several eighteenth-century literary genres depended on sociable forms similar to theirs. Familiar and public correspondence carried news, scientific reports, queries, and answers between individuals and scientific societies, as the "epistolary genre became the dominant medium for creating an active and interactive reading public" in this period.[73] Magazines, often advertised as published "by a society of gentlemen," frequently carried items in epistolary form, creating for readers a sense of privileged information. Correspondence between learned societies laid the groundwork for more formal published "transactions" and established networks of intellectual authority.

Society orations, a genre in which several club members participated and published, also emerged from the world of civic association. In their oral form, typically delivered at regular meetings or anniversary celebrations, such addresses offered the opportunity for individual men to appear in public, to declare association with others who were also socially powerful, and to demonstrate a degree of learning and oratorical ability. Following the address, society officers would appoint an official committee to visit the speaker and request that the oration be published (fig. 7). These rituals served both to protect the speaker from accusations of self-promotion and to publicize one's membership in a larger society by printing the names of the Committee on Publication. Reciprocally, a prominent speaker could confirm the group's collective sense of self-importance.[74]

More than most contemporary private circles, the Friendly Club learned the value of coming together to promote publishing endeavors. Unlike some other groups, the club did not translate its club practice into literary sketches, as did some Calliopeans in their serial for the *New-York Magazine*, "The Club" and "The Drone." Nothing in the voluminous archive left behind by Friendly Club members resembles the most famous representation of club life from eighteenth-century America, the mock epic *History of the Tuesday Club*, written in Baltimore at midcentury. No Friendly Club counterpart exists for Dunlap's satirical portrait of the earlier Philological Society in his unpublished play *Cuttgrisingwolds*, which poked fun both at individuals and at the formalities that dominated society meetings. Rather, Friendly Club members' individual and collective literary aims were both more civically oriented and more ambitious than those of most earlier or contemporary conversation circles.[75]

Prior to the Friendly Club's existence, its future members had published more poetry than any other genre. In the years immediately following the American Revolution, an international demand for American cultural productions had enabled some Americans to craft celebrity identities as public poets. The Connecticut native Joel Barlow, for instance, seventeen years older than Smith and a member of the original circle of Hartford Wits with Smith's former teacher Timothy Dwight, secured subscription lists for an epic poem of America that included the king of France.[76] Though they never attempted a poem on the scale of Barlow's *Vision of Columbus*, several future Friendly Club members, including Smith, Brown, Dunlap, Mitchill, and sometime member Richard Alsop, all found an outlet for their early writing in newspaper poetry, a genre and print form particularly suited to facilitating literary friendships. Poems in newsprint were easy to clip or transcribe in order to send them to friends or to keep in commonplace books.[77] The bulk of the poems Smith anthologized in *American Poems, Selected and Original* had originally been published in newspapers in Philadelphia, New York, Hartford, and Boston. Poetry could be easily reproduced and provided useful fodder for social conversation and debate.[78] Poetic exchanges in particular seemed an ideal form for cultivating friendly sentiment, useful information, and moral action.

Such a poetic correspondence may actually have been responsible for introducing Elihu Smith to Charles Brockden Brown in Philadelphia in 1791. The poetic exchange that scholars have long called the "Ella-Birtha-Henry" correspondence, though it predates the formation of the Friendly Club itself, stands as the earliest literary collaboration between people who would become core club members. It also illustrates a mode of collaborative publication that both prefigures and contrasts the types of projects the club would take up later in the decade. A detailed consideration of the exchange, then, reveals one model of friendship's relation to collaborative literary production in the period. Made up of thirty-two poems in two Philadelphia newspapers between February and August 1791, the correspondence consisted of poems addressed back and forth between Elihu Smith (Ella), Charles Brockden Brown (Henry), and one of Brown's Quaker friends, Joseph Bringhurst (Birtha).[79] The *Gazette of the United States* for 20 April 1791, two months into the exchange, and just before Henry began to contribute, carried a note in which its editor, John Fenno, "acknowledges with gratitude the favors he ha[d] received from his poetical correspondents ELLA and BIRTHA," who "would do honor to any miscellany whatever. The readers of the *Gazette* have doubtless been pleased, and their pleasure will be heightened to surprise, when they are informed that ELLA is but a youth of 17" and that "[t]he authors are unknown to each other."[80] (The claim about Ella's age is off slightly; Smith was 19, though he had composed some of the poems years earlier.) Fenno assumes that part of the appeal of these poems will be the mystery of the poets' identities as their anonymous exchange unfolds.

The series began on 23 February 1791 with a poem in which Ella characterized his poetic persona: "The Volunteer Laureat, An Ode; for the Birth-Day of the President of the United States."[81] Framing his poetry from the outset as filling a civic duty, Ella subordinates his genius to the voice of the nation. With the next few poems he publishes, however, Ella's mode shifts abruptly, from the political to the parlor romance. The *Gazette*'s readers learn that these sonnets, published ten days apart, are "Sent to Miss —— ——, with a Braid of Hair" and to "Mrs. —— ——, with a Song," signaling the poems' place in polite society as well as political landscapes. In the second of these poems addressed to anonymous women, Ella calls on "[s]ome kindred genius" to "awake the trembling lyre, / And give to far posterity his [Ella's, presumably] praise."[82] The call for a kindred poet to sing his praises drew a response almost immediately; "Birtha" offered the *Gazette* a poem titled, simply, "To Ella." It begins by soliciting Ella to produce more poetry: "Strike, Strike again thy silver-sounding lyre / Ella, thou darling of the God of verse."[83] Two poems later, Ella takes the bait and writes an ode in which he calls Birtha's voice the "voice of *Truth*" and expresses gratification at being asked to produce more poetry ("Deep from my soul the grateful sighs arise").[84]

The slippage between an occasional masculine pronoun and feminine pseudonyms suggests, perhaps, a similar tendency in friendly literary correspondence to slip back and forth between romantic friendship and homoerotic attachments. In the exchange now fully underway, "Friendship, trembling o'er the strings, / Breathes on the lyre unutterable things," and the poets' effusions become increasingly interdependent. "See my soul, in fancy rise," Ella finishes the ode, "BIRTHA, seraph, opes the skies." Birtha returns the compliment in his next offering, using the same image: "Borne on the undulating breeze, / Thy heaven-taught Notes *my* Spirit seize, / And waft it to the sky."[85] This poem is dated in Delaware on 10 April, apparently following Bringhurst's move there from Philadelphia; for the authors (and the readers who imagine them), the poetic exchange now closes geographical gaps, building on Fenno's image of two young poets who do not share physical proximity.

Brown's contributions as Henry first appeared not in Fenno's paper but in Benjamin Franklin Bache's *General Advertiser, and Political, Commercial and Literary Journal,* a daily paper made up primarily of shipping announcements and advertising, political news (from a partisan perspective opposite to Fenno's), correspondence on the theater, and original and selected poetry and anecdotes. Most of the poetry featured in Bache's paper was occasional verse and doggerel copied from London, New York, or Boston papers, some with pseudonyms or initials. In early April Bache reprinted, from the *Gazette,* Ella's poem titled "ODE. To Birtha." This poem generated a response from Brown (as Henry), who had published poetry in the *General Advertiser* beginning the previous fall. On 25 April, Bache printed Henry's "Sonnet Written after hearing a Song sung by three Sisters,"[86] in which Henry makes reference to "Ella's lays" and implies that the sisters' song was, in fact, Smith's newspaper poetry set to music. Quickly reprinted by Fenno in the *Gazette,* the poem inaugurated the three-way correspondence.[87]

Henry's poem, like Ella's and Birtha's exchange-in-progress, illustrates one of the chief points to be made about this style of poetry, known in the 1790s as Della Cruscan verse: the way in which its self-referentiality focuses primarily on authorizing the production of more verse.[88] Ella's original poems provoked Birtha's response, which called forth a return from Ella. Similarly, in Henry's "Sonnet," Ella's poetry has provoked the sisters' song, which provokes Henry's poem. Before long Henry's attention has been turned to the praise of the other two poets themselves.[89] When Ella, Birtha, and Henry called on one another to strike again the lyre, they emphasized the importance of this early Romantic poetry to the cultivation not only of their mutual identities as public poets but also of a form of sensibility they and others saw as fundamental to moral order and intellectual commerce.[90]

The Ella-Birtha-Henry correspondence served as a training ground for later projects with the Friendly Club that would channel the fraternal feeling generated by such writing into more ambitious and socially useful directions, the search for scientific truth in particular. For example, the connection underlies the club's 1798 American edition of Erasmus Darwin's long scientific poem *The Botanic Garden,* which Smith prefaced with a Della Cruscan poetic epistle to the author (who has inspired this "kindred spirit to strike the sacred lyre"). Smith's dedicatory poem recounts a history of print technology's effects on scientific improvement, culminating in a "proud column" raised to "bear inscribed, immortal, DARWIN'S name."[91] The performance of poetic sympathy— like the American reprinting of Darwin's scientific poem itself—aims not only to disseminate Darwin's art and thought but also to secure transatlantic reputation as poet-scientists for the American editors as well.

By the middle of the 1790s, Smith and friends had turned from poetry to magazine writing and editing to secure their fame and harness their utilitarian energies. Although the *Medical Repository* would be the most successful publishing venture launched by club members, as early as 1795 Smith projected a literary magazine called *Proteus,* an idea that would eventually be realized by his friends in 1799 as the *Monthly Mag-*

azine, and American Review. Smith's early prospectus for the magazine
suggests the club's belief that a magazine entirely "devoted to the entertaining & useful performances, relative to the Arts & Sciences" would
usefully contrast American newspapers, which had become dominated
by politics.[92]

Smith framed the need for such a magazine within a history of
American "News-Papers" and "Journals." The traditional dearth of "Literary Journals" in America, he writes, had been long compensated for by
"the peculiar excellence of our News-Papers," which appealed, in their "superior cheapness" and "frequent impression" to the ideal American reader:
"the enlightened, inquisitive, & frugal yeomanry of the United States."
However, the debates over the Constitution, followed by ongoing news
of the French Revolution, had transformed newspapers from economi-
cally affordable transmitters of "elegant & useful communications" into
political scandal sheets concerned with nothing but "public contests &
private intrigues." Even the most trivial contemporary events and political debates had "usurped" newsprint, banishing "communications of
a less interesting, but more permanently useful nature."[93]

The club's projected publication would call the bluff, Smith suggested, on what is really interesting and to whom. Smith acknowledged
that newspapers "contain everything to gratify the eager curiosity of
the politician" but complained they have "nothing to satisfy the more
temperate appetite of the scholar, the philosopher, or the man of literary leisure." Worse, they offered nothing to reading women, who had
been completely excluded from national politics. Smith called on men
who understood the connection between "knowledge" and the "liberty,"
"virtue," "tranquility & happiness of a nation," to join their efforts to
take control of American publishing outlets.[94]

Part of the problem for American publications, as Smith described
it, rested with the audience. American citizens cared less about reading than about money and baser forms of amusement, in spite of the
fact that they enjoyed the most democratic educational opportunities
in human history. The type of publication such an audience needed,
then, was precisely the opposite of what American newspapers offered.
Smith envisioned a publication devoted entirely to "literary & scientific
entertainment," something that would free educated professionals of
the burden of having to conduct extensive research outside their profession in order to gain further knowledge. But his ideal magazine would
be important to writers as well as to potential readers: "As literature is

not a profession in this country, it is true, that few can devote themselves to the composition of considerable works; yet, among those who
have cultivated the sciences, with any success, there are scarcely any,
who do not, at times, divert themselves by lighter compositions, or by
writing on detached parts of those sciences to the study of which they
have especially attended."[95]

In other words, Americans did not lack authors—for "considerable"
or "lighter" works—so much as they needed a "repository" to collect
and arrange what had already been written. Providing such a forum for
useful information would be a public service, even as it would create
a reading public. Smith imagines these future readers, even those not
inclined to serious study, gleaning information and rational amusement
from articles designed to be brief: "To these the man of business can
recur, while he waits for an expected guest, lingers at an ill-attended
appointment, or patiently submits to the operations of his hair-dresser.
From these, even the self-complacent beau, & the fashionable fair-one,
may catch an unexpected ray of knowledge, while they sip their morning coffee, or their evening tea." In editing this "*Manual* of Science &
of Conversation," the editors expected "assistance from their friends"
and from gentlemen observers from different parts of the United States
to convey local information, an aspiration Smith would renew in the
Medical Repository a few years later.[96]

Like his diary and like the Friendly Club itself, the magazine Smith
described would above all emphasize collaborative processes of intimacy,
inquiry, and authorship. When the club's *Monthly Magazine* emerged
at the end of the decade, with Brown at the helm, members consistently
represented it as an effort undertaken by friends. "There is a *Society* or
club of about 10 gentlemen," Samuel Miller wrote to Jedidiah Morse,
soliciting his support, "who meet once a week, to consult about the
Magazine, & concert plans to make up its contents & to promote its
interests."[97] Brown highlighted friendship's energies even more directly
in a letter to one of his brothers. "Eight of my friends here, men in the
highest degree respectable for literature and influence," he wrote, "have
urged me so vehemently to undertake the project of a magazine, and
promised their contributions and assistance to its success, that I have
written and published proposals." He added that the club's energetic
support was key: "The influence of my friends, and their unexpected
and uncommon zeal, inspire me with a courage which I should be unable to derive from any other quarter."[98]

By the point at which Brown wrote these descriptions of the club's role in producing the *Monthly Magazine,* he had established himself as a novelist, and club members had worked together to promote other endeavors, including Dunlap's new theater, James Kent's Columbia law lectures, and the *Medical Repository.* Members hoped that their individual successes would translate into collective visibility. Considering the effects of Brown's potentially controversial novels on his friends' reputations, Smith exclaimed on one occasion, "What different sentiments will [his writing] excite! And how much rancour, & misrepresentation must he encounter! And not he alone, but all those who are united to him, by the ties of friendship, & bonds of resembling opinions." Although he seems to express some ambivalence here—the tide of public opinion could turn against them, after all—Smith ultimately trusts "that we shall put forth the conductors of virtue, & turn aside, or disarm the lightnings of superstitious fury" as they improved, rather than compromised, their reputations and established themselves as their generation's intellectual leaders.[99]

This is the history the club members worked together to realize and created for themselves in retrospect. Three decades after the club ended, in his *History of the American Theatre* (1832), Dunlap forged a literary history that featured his early friends' contributions to American literature and to his own early career. Brown, Johnson, and Smith, he writes, were his closest friends among the "band of pioneers" of New York's literary culture. "To such men" were his own "dramas . . . read and submitted."[100] Dunlap's account, which echoes his discussion of the group in his 1815 biography of Brown, furthers a practice of tracing literary history through particular friendships, an act that also served to secure his place—and the places of his friends—in a canon of American letters.

|||||||||||||||||||||||||||||||||||||||||||||||||||||||||||||||||||||||||||||||||||||||||||||||||||||||||||||||||||||||||||||||||||||||||||||||||||||||||||||||||||||||||||||

TWO

Dangerous Associations

The Illuminati Conspiracy Scare
as a Crisis of Public Intellectual Authority

Iɴ late January 1797, Elihu Smith returned to his hometown, Litchfield, Connecticut, for a visit to family and friends, in part to confront his rapidly developing notoriety as an "infidel." The principal showdown on this point took place one evening in the parlor of U.S. Senator Uriah Tracy. With him were the senator's wife, Susan Bull Tracy—Smith's childhood teacher, now one of his most intimate friends and correspondents—and her three oldest children. The controversy stemmed most immediately from a forty-page letter Smith had written to another Connecticut friend, Theodore Dwight, in which he had candidly defended his loss of faith in Christianity—a courageous move, he believed, given Dwight's stringent orthodoxy and the already audible rumblings of a holy war waged by Connecticut's Standing Order ministers against "philosophy." Led by Theodore's brother, the new Yale College president Timothy Dwight, the campaign responded to the violence and godlessness of the French Revolution. The force of this counterrevolutionary response, Smith believed, had "deformed" his friends' thinking; for their part, they worried for the state of Smith's soul. Theodore had discussed Smith's letter with mutual friends, including Mrs. Tracy, and had put it—or at least its contents—into circulation. Anticipating such an event, Smith carried with him that evening his original drafts of the letter, as composed and revised in his diary.[1]

Not quite a week earlier, Smith had taken the mail stage from New York to New Haven and a one-horse sleigh from there to Litchfield, leaving him plenty of time to anticipate this performance. Five long days had passed before a chance arose to present his case to Mrs. Tracy. On the last night of his visit, after "various" conversation, he struck an orator's pose, his diary open, the audience seated, as if he were reading to them from a new novel by Elizabeth Inchbald or Thomas Holcroft. He read for over an hour, first from Dwight's confrontational letter, then from his response: a tortured history of faith lost and found and lost again, from his childhood education, through his early teenage years at Yale, and beyond, when he had studied at Timothy Dwight's Greenfield Hill Academy. His best defense, he believed, would be to lay before Mrs. Tracy the entire correspondence, which he did, despite the children present and the entrance, during the reading, of two more adults. Smith believed himself motivated only by sincere disclosure: "I did not wish any to suppose I was driven to shew, what I would otherwise have concealed," he wrote of the event in his diary, "but on the contrary, that I had a willingness & even a desire, to acquaint them with its contents."[2]

But the scene as Smith recounts it still feels forced, anxious, and the risks incurred were high. Susan Tracy and Theodore Dwight were among his oldest friends; he had long worried what effects his disclosure of disbelief would have on Dwight in particular. (Tracy already knew his views, though by making them public he perhaps placed her character in question if she defended him.) He was even more concerned about his parents' reactions.[3] And despite protestations that he did not fear prosecution under Connecticut's antiblasphemy laws, the prospect did haunt him. He discussed his predicament extensively with sympathetic club members and fellow doubters Dunlap and Brown. The former had his own religious tensions with his brothers-in-law the Dwights; the latter had spent several years caught up in religious arguments with his childhood Quaker friends.[4] But Smith still "could not get it out of my head, till I had run over, in imagination, the manner in which such a prosecution would, probably be conducted; the part I should act; the conduct of my friends, & others; & the result of the whole. I think I do not fear it."[5] He cast himself as hero in a courtroom drama; in such an event he would emerge a martyr for the cause of truth. But the mention of "my friends, & others" suggests that such martyrdom could not escape more intimate contexts.

This realization was magnified for Smith by the threat religious tension posed to the collegiality of the Friendly Club itself. While Smith had yet to describe the club, in his letter to the London *Monthly Magazine*, as containing a "diversity of sentiment," which rather than "affect[ing] their friendship, has made them more active in investigation,"[6] the diary belies such idealism, as he worries that corroding relationships with early friends might spread to the minority of Friendly Club members who maintained conservative religious beliefs, William Walton Woolsey in particular. Woolsey, like his Dwight brothers-in-law, was a devout Christian and arch-Federalist who would help to bankroll early waves of New York evangelicalism in the nineteenth century. As Smith's friendship with Theodore Dwight showed early trouble signs, Smith fretted that Woolsey, "less cordial towards me, than [he] has been wont to be," might withdraw his intimacy as well: "I fear that his religious opinions will, eventually, estrange his heart intirely from me."[7]

As the diary bears out, religious differences did prove a hard test of many of Smith's early friendships. The Dwights, Woolsey, Uriah Tracy, and Smith's parents all manifest suspicions of the books and ideas that had proved so attractive to him and so many of his New York friends. A few weeks after Smith ended his Connecticut visit, Mrs. Tracy wrote to say that her husband, troubled by Smith's intellectual direction, had forbidden her from reading a collection of Dissenting British sermons Smith had given her, a follow-up to the copy of William Godwin's *Enquiry Concerning Political Justice* he had given her two years earlier. Though the senator continued to write Smith letters on political topics, Smith's disavowal of his childhood faith precluded the former intimacy of their friendship, as Tracy feared that profligate reading or city life had imperiled his young friend's eternal salvation. In the spring and summer of 1798, these concerns only intensified for Smith's Connecticut friends, when word began to circulate—and to be taken quite seriously by many—that a conspiracy of Bavarian atheists had established Jacobin networks throughout Europe, masterminded the French Revolution, and now sought to seduce young Americans by infiltrating literary societies and Masonic lodges, thereby gaining control of government, voluntary associations, and the print public sphere.[8] Elihu Smith died only a few months into the Bavarian Illuminati scare, but the test of his early friendships survived him; on his death the most pressing question in the minds of orthodox friends and family was, Did he die a deist?[9]

The scene in Uriah and Susan Tracy's parlor indicates a host of forces that characterized literary, intellectual, and political cultures at the end of the eighteenth century. Recent political historians have shown convincingly that through the 1790s Federalists and Jeffersonian Republicans cultivated increasingly different views on the nature and regulation of public expression, but Smith's predicament also reveals ways in which such conflicts also reveal late-Enlightenment crises of epistemology and public intellectual authority as they raised questions about who had avenues to knowledge adequate to warrant the public's trust.[10]

During the cultural conflicts of the late 1790s, the club's Enlightenment ideals of unregulated conversation and scientific progress came under attack by Anglo-American cultural conservatives. In England, Edmund Burke, an early proponent of Illuminati conspiracy theories, asserted more generally that unrestrained conversation in radical societies had fomented sedition. In a move that resonated with some Federalist opinion on the issue of "self-created societies" and, later, the need for a Sedition Act, Britain's government required debating societies to be licensed and outlawed discussion of religion and politics in such settings. Arguing against the Dissenting minister Joseph Priestley, who had championed free discussion as essential to scientific progress, Burke attacked Enlightenment science as authorizing new forms of licentiousness.[11] During the Alien and Sedition and Bavarian Illuminati crises, similar debates took place in the United States, with "reading and debating societies" falling suspect for social conservatives. Some opponents of the Federalist antisedition measures complained that even "the taste for reading" had "declined" because of governmental pressure.[12]

Smith's case suggests that the overwhelming emphasis some historians have placed on partisan divisions may obscure the relationship between the early republic's public sphere and its knowledge cultures, whose boundaries were not national and whose most fiercely fought battles in the era cannot be simply reduced to partisan perspectives. These knowledge cultures included a range of emerging disciplinary and professional forms of knowledge production and dissemination— the traditional liberal professions of medicine, law, and the clergy—and also slowly gave rise, beginning in this period, to new categories of professional authors, magazine editors, and critical reviewers. In this moment of professional consolidation, which one scholar memorably termed "the organization of American culture," new forms of accreditation and professional association, which would ultimately result in the concentration of professional and social authority, initially generated significant tensions among professionals whose training and theory remained extraordinarily disparate. These new knowledge-producing professions competed internally and with one another for credibility with American audiences.

As Smith's and his friends' experiences bear out, debates about religious toleration, skepticism, and establishment all played roles in these conflicts that did not always align with partisan divisions and should not be underestimated in their own right. In the late eighteenth century, plebeian religious leaders posed one set of challenges to the ministerial elite.[13] But religion was not simply at stake on the margins. The increasing professionalization of medicine and law in particular resulted in competition with ministers, who had long held a high place in colonial social hierarchies, particularly in New England.[14] Certainly such contests were framed in partisan terms at the time, but many Jeffersonian ministers, like the eventual Friendly Club member Samuel Miller, were loath to let the Federalists claim the religious high ground, and some Federalist intellectuals, like Smith, were unwilling to let ministers monopolize morality. Taking seriously the peculiarly religious cast of the political and cultural conflicts of the late 1790s opens up an understanding of the ways in which faith and doubt facilitated not only competing epistemologies but also competition among the professions for intellectual authority in the new nation.

Friendly Club members framed these contests not in partisan terms but as a battle between "philosophers" and "religionists." For them, as for their ministerial opponents, the stakes could not have been higher as these new intellectuals privileged rationalism over Christianity or called for religious toleration and an end to the traditional privileges of religious establishment.[15] Friendly Club members' engagements with these debates ranged from the most intimate contexts, as fault lines ran through friendships and families, to the most public, as they set about careers publishing in various intellectual and literary contexts. As in the German political philosopher Jürgen Habermas's seminal account, the public sphere as club members understood it emerged first within the familial and friendly context of the bourgeois parlor before moving outward to include literary and political spheres.

If Smith's crisis of faith and his religious friends' reactions offer a fruitful context for understanding Anglo-American countersubversive discourse more broadly, these situations also relate to the issues at stake in Charles Brockden Brown's novelistic debut, *Wieland; or the Transformation*, which he completed while living with club members in the summer of 1798 and saw to press as yellow fever began to break out that fall. To the extent that literary critics of the early republic have followed or paralleled the important work of new political historians, they have explored ways in which political partisanship affected literary publication in the period. In this context, Brown's novels have themselves come to occupy a significant place in literary critical narratives of the emergence of an American public.[16] But as with other Friendly Club productions, Brown's novels have meanings that are lost when partisan contexts overshadow religious ones. Their prioritization of epistemology over politics indicates a cultural politics of knowledge in which debates over the place of religious authority in the public sphere circulated at times against the currents of partisan propagandizing.

For members of the Friendly Club cohort, more than control of the federal government was at stake in these struggles. They saw themselves as engaged in a competitive if sometimes covert struggle with their clerical associates for control of the circulation of moral and scientific knowledge in the republic of intellect. In their minds, partisan politics, as Smith had declared in the draft prospectus for *Proteus*, had "usurped that place" in American publications previously reserved for "communications" of a "permanently useful nature."[17] Smith's generic history highlights his desire to keep inquiries into science, morals, and literature apart from the pressing concerns of popular politics and even European revolutions, events he saw as fleeting—and prone to promote faction—rather than revealing universal truths.

If Smith's Connecticut friends feared for his soul in the year that preceded his death, the religious skeptics among the Friendly Club feared the ability of the clerical elite to claim secret and superior knowledge as they equated all dissent with seditious conspiracy and generated images of an American public in peril. Even more dangerous, from the rationalists' view, these countersubversives claimed divine authorization for their actions; their associate Jedidiah Morse, for example, felt compelled beginning in 1798 to publish his warning cries against the Illuminati because of the "public station" he held "under GOD" as a Massachusetts minister.[18] Smith, Brown, Dunlap, and other club members rejected such claims to divine sanction as dangerous. Smith's rejection resulted in a protracted struggle to salvage his early friendships. In *Wieland,* Brown offered memorable illustrations of just how dangerous religious voices could be.

Infidel Philosophers and Their Audiences:
Elihu Smith's Apostasy

The simmering anxieties over the place of religion in public life, which would eventually boil over in the Illuminati scare, had literary dimensions that registered even in as intimate a context as Smith's parlor reading and the account he made of it in his diary. The tension between Smith and his early friends over his departure from Christian orthodoxy threatened not only to end important friendships but also to topple entire literary structures as he understood them to function. His correspondence with Susan Tracy and Theodore Dwight, embedded in the diary alongside the account of Smith's public reading of the long letter to Dwight, reveals fundamental characteristics of the literary culture that fostered the club's other writing projects, including Brown's novels, Dunlap's plays, and Smith's own miscellaneous compositions.

Smith's parlor performance, correspondence, diary, and even his limited writing for the theater all reveal a fundamental concern with the audience's response. The month prior to the events at the Tracy home, when Smith attended the first and only production of his opera, *Edwin and Angelina,* he obsessed about audience reactions. Scanning his fellow audience members as much as watching the performance of his play, Smith noted that "a fellow in the Gallery, was comfortably asleep; while Mrs. Brett [the lead actress] shed tears—the only ones, I suspect, which fell from any eyes, during that Scene."[19] A few months after the parlor reading at the Tracy home, in March 1797, he fretted as well over audience response to his letter to Dwight. Dunlap, recently returned from Connecticut, bore news that Theodore Dwight had continued to circulate his letter "to several friends: some condemn, some defend: [they] asked about my Opera," Smith complained in his diary, "but not about me."[20] The audiences for the letter were both more and less concrete than those for *Edwin and Angelina.* He had himself, by March 1797, read both his and Dwight's letters to several New York friends, and he could anticipate individual responses to it perhaps better than he could predict a theater audience's. He had sensed that this "important paper" would eventually become public in some form, and even placed it at the head of a new volume of his memoirs, with the implication it would remain there as an introduction to his intellectual history once the memoirs were published.[21] He could not, however, control how widely Dwight would circulate the letter without his permission.

Smith's comment on the scene at the Tracy home, that he "did not wish any to suppose I was driven to shew, what I would otherwise have concealed," points to a particular audience problem in the period. Smith's decision to proclaim his disbelief—and to do so at the hearth of a Christian home—suggests a measure of confidence in his sincerely spoken but carefully prepared text. The reading was intimate but calculated against the odds of convincing listeners, if not of his unorthodox positions, then of the purity of his motives for adopting them. His actions, though, betrayed an uncharacteristic failure of confidence in mutual inquiry. "I was especially desirous," he writes of the encounter in his diary, "of acquainting Mrs. T with my sentiments, in a more methodic way than I could well do, in conversation."[22] The emphasis on a different method than the conversational model suggests different results: the aim of eighteenth-century oratory more broadly to make "the will of the auditor the instrument of [his or her] own surrender." Smith's parlor reading bridges the chasm between private self-examination and public performance of that examined self, a divide that characterized what one scholar calls the period's "elocutionary revolution."[23] Writing to Mrs. Tracy a month after the event, Smith "can not . . . think otherwise than that [she] preponderates on my side of the question." Could his words have done other than "carry conviction to [her] mind"?[24] Like his favorite author, William Godwin, Smith believed that "a sincere rational language would of itself be persuasive."[25] Yet as months passed and his correspondences grew increasingly strained, his confidence in sincere, artless, rational language waned a bit. His trips to Connecticut in January 1797 and the summer of 1798 can be understood as an acknowledgment of the limits of familiar letters, as he attempted through an intense social regimen to substitute his physical presence for the textual self-representation whose circulation and reception seemed increasingly out of his control.

Smith's literary friendship with Theodore Dwight, in particular, seemed destined to suffer. As members of the younger wave of Hartford Wits, the two had collaborated earlier in the decade with Richard Alsop, Lemuel Hopkins, and Mason Fitch Cogswell on the anti-Jeffersonian, anti–French Revolution *Echo* poems, published in Connecticut newspapers. But by the middle of the decade, Smith's declining faith in Christianity and his growing confidence in rationalism and human perfectibility began to outweigh his political affinities with such friends. Escalating partisan vitriol—especially when allied with claims to religious certainty—made Smith uncomfortable, just as his own movement away from Christianity greatly concerned his friends. Religious conservatives like the Dwights, in one historian's apt phrase, feared "a new breed of learned men was infiltrating Connecticut's [and America's] natural aristocracy."[26] Questions of faith aside, the prospect of losing someone like Smith, who had clear publishing ambitions in several fields, would have been regarded as a serious blow to the conservative Congregationalist cause.

Smith, in turn, also understood the failing friendships to be an enormous loss. He had likely made Theodore Dwight's acquaintance in 1787 when, at age 15, just having graduated from Yale, Smith studied for two years with Theodore's older brother until he was deemed old enough to enter on professional education. (Smith suspected, though, as he told Dwight in his long autobiographical letter, that his father had sent him to Timothy Dwight in hopes of winning him back to Christianity, after his undergraduate years at Yale had brought on his first crisis of faith.)[27] In 1791, after Smith had returned to Connecticut from a year of medical study in Philadelphia, he and Dwight renewed their friendship. In Smith's letter to Dwight, his correspondent comes off by implication as a rather stodgy, aristocratic arch-Federalist, worried about Smith's creeping democratic tendencies down to minor details of style and generic convention, such as his failure to use formal titles when addressing letters. But Smith deeply valued Dwight's lighter side, his "love of everything, which promotes conviviality and merriment," including his facility for punning.[28] He initially hoped that Dwight's willingness to confront him on his changing opinions signaled the persistence of his friendship: "He would not, he could not, have written thus, did he not love me."[29]

Susan Bull Tracy's friendship was even older—and perhaps dearer—than Dwight's. In a 1797 sketch of his childhood Smith composed in his diary, he recalled her (then "Miss Bull," twelve years his senior) with an eroticized longing: he had been her "particular favorite, often admitted to sit on her lap, receive her caresses; & she uncommonly beautiful & engaging," with "a voice wonderful in its sweetness & delicacy, of that particular frame that it reaches irresistably [*sic*] to the inmost recesses of sensibility, & moves it in uniform."[30] His first mention of her in the extant diary hints at intrigue surrounding their relationship. During a fall 1795 visit to Litchfield, he made a long morning visit to Mrs. Tracy during which "she accounted to me for her long epistolary silence, & in [a] way which was equally unexpected & astonishing." He learned that "unfounded malice" on the part of "one who is under the greatest obligations to us both" was to blame for her failure to write. The details he included in the diary were deliberately few. "This note is sufficient to preserve the facts in my memory," he writes, "& I will spare myself the odious task of detailing them," but he implies that someone has accused them of inappropriate intimacy in their friendship.[31]

Smith had, during that visit, left Mrs. Tracy with a copy of Godwin's *Political Justice*, which he hoped would serve as the grounds for epistolary exchanges and perhaps even convert Mrs. Tracy to his brand of freethinking. Smith exulted, for similar reasons, in her warm reception of Mary Wollstonecraft's *Vindication of the Rights of Woman*, another work he admired as a cornerstone of what was just beginning to be called "the New Philosophy."[32] Smith had an unaffected regard for Susan Tracy's mind. "An equal education would have placed Mrs. T. far before Miss Wollstonecraft," he wrote in his diary during the 1795 visit.[33] Whatever the reason their relationship inspired "malice" in some, the friendship—and the correspondence—seemed at this juncture poised to survive, and Smith felt he could "speak freely" with her about his views on "the foolishness of superstition," his epithet for all religion.[34]

While Smith's theories of friendship and sincerity influenced nearly every social and publishing project he undertook in the 1790s, his most careful statements on the subject emerge from his correspondence with Dwight and Tracy from 1796 to 1798. In early 1796, not quite three years after Smith had moved to New York, when he began to fear that Theodore Dwight's friendship was waning, the potential damage to Smith's theory of friendship loomed large. Confronting Dwight by letter, Smith asked how their correspondence had "fallen into this tardy, interrupted, & starved, kind of intercourse."[35] Making a similar inquiry of Susan Tracy later that year, he outlined his expectations of their exchanges. "[Y]our letters were my great encouragers," he wrote, "by [their] ceaseless inquiries after more certain science & more blameless morals."[36] Her letters encouraged friendship; friendship was the foundation of moral inquiry, the method for philosophical and scientific certainty, the antidote to intellectual or spiritual submission.

In another letter to Mrs. Tracy, written a year before his public airing in her parlor of the Dwight correspondence, he had framed his views on collaborative inquiry as a response to the increasing professionalization and disciplinarity of knowledge:

> What! shall I implicitly receive an opinion for truth, & blindly practice what it directs because you [a lawyer, physician, priest] tell me it is truth? Shall I bow my reason to your authority, & tamely yield my faith to whatever you require? By what right do you assume the direction of my conscience? Shew me the patent by which you are commissioned, point me out it's author, and give me proof, unequivocal proof, that he is indeed it's author. You falter! You cannot do it? I know it. Your power is usurpation, & you are either deceivers, or deceived—or both.[37]

The cultural authorities who require blind obedience, he tells Mrs. Tracy, are "legions surround[ing] the temple of Truth; & often, while they seem to invite our approach, are preparing to circumvent, or entangle us in the labyrinths which their unhallowed hands have wrought in the majestic groves which environ it." The image betrays his anxiety about religious authority in particular; professionalized clergy resemble pagan priests who transformed sacred groves into dense mazes to prevent sincere inquirers from getting at the truth. "I can see that what mankind have mistaken for the clear sky of truth, is no more than the mist of error; but tho' I perceive & am convinced of the deception, it forms a cloud too thick for me to penetrate. It is thro' the loopholes only, which the brisk breeze of discussion sometimes forms, that I can discern the celestial azure." Smith apologizes a few lines later for this purple prose, but his point remains: truth cannot be trusted to arbitrary authority. It must be approached instead through "the brisk breeze of discussion."[38]

A few weeks after initially confronting Dwight about the state of their correspondence, Smith received a letter from his friend, confirming that a gap *had* developed in their sentiments. Smith's omission of polite titles and failure to address his letters at the bottom rather than the top (as convention dictated) were taken by Dwight as signs of Smith's growing democratic tendencies; unchecked, these small infidelities could lead to larger moral subversion. Smith did his best to convince his friend he meant no disrespect and "struggle[d] in vain to give language to [his] sentiments of sorrow for your regrets, of love for your love, & of constancy for your constancy," an apt description of his idealization of reciprocal friendship, even as it suggests a creeping failure of confidence in the ideal.[39] A few weeks later, Dwight unexpectedly turned up in New York, allowing Smith over nearly a week to pass "several hours most pleasantly" in the "rare society of a long—& well-beloved friend."[40] Following Dwight's return to Connecticut, Smith expressed relief that his friend had "lost none of his attachment to me," but retained some anxiety that "his heart is, or will be, estranged from me—in consequence of the difference in our metaphysics," since his friend "must regard with pain one who he apprehends is doomed to perdition."[41]

Smith sought through his letters over the next several months to cement the friendship, perhaps anticipating the more forceful confrontation that would follow. While he had felt "sorrow[ful]" that Dwight had treated him, in earlier letters, as a "suspected person," he still

> discovered, or thought that I discovered [during Dwight's visit], in your eye, your voice, your manner, that tenderness which I felt in my own bosom, & which mutually constituted so large a portion of our happiness, & my spirits were calmed. Am I then deceived? Will you, can you, tell me I am not? I do not know whether I ought to estimate your friendship so lightly, but whether it be from the sense I entertain of your merits, or from the powerful effect of early associations, there is something in the idea of forfeiting your affection like the pain supposed to accompany the forcible separation of soul & body.[42]

Here Smith takes, in relation to Dwight, the same position of scrutiny with which he attempts, in the diary, to regard himself. Though their letters have occasioned misunderstanding, during Dwight's stay in New York Smith had the opportunity to read body language rather than written words for signs of sympathy, a corporeal resonance with the "tenderness which I felt in my own bosom." But uncertainty remained, and a tone of sincere desperation governs the letter, a note Smith would sound repeatedly for the duration of these correspondences.

Here, as elsewhere in his writing, Smith imposes medical metaphor and interpretation onto his theory of friendship. "[T]he powerful effect of early associations" is, for Smith, scientific principle, drawn from the association psychology of David Hartley, Erasmus Darwin, and others. The word "effect," like the Lockean term "impression" he uses so frequently elsewhere, conveys his sense that an individual is never formed apart from the forces exerted by "associations." To undermine this reality of human experience would inflict an amputation, "the forcible separation of soul & body." In contrast to friendships entered into as adults, he argues, with "a spirit too temperate to have their dissolution inflict any deadly wound," that those "associations [formed] in youth [which] grow & become consolidated with the increase of our mental powers & attainments, are, as it were, intertwined with our very existence: to rend them asunder is to annihilate our greatest joys."[43] Within this discourse of friendship, Smith articulates a natural history of self, a way to anatomize the series of associations that make up a human being.

The letter to Dwight, carefully revised and transcribed before Smith sent it, forms the heart of Smith's diary as we receive it. In it Smith illustrates in detail his medical-literary theory of friendship, which comprises a mixture of rational self-justification and sentimental expression. Smith begins the letter by holding his ground, using the same plain salutation—"To Theodore Dwight"—that his friend had earlier found so offensive; but he also seeks to seduce his reader in the body of the letter by way of address ("my dear friend") and flattery ("How much soever we may vary in opinion, I can never be insensible to the proofs of [your] uncommon friendship"). The language of friendship, even as it presents Smith as a particularly sensible friend, also scripts Dwight's reader response into the letter itself. Smith further prepares Dwight for the difficult declarations that follow by affirming his standard of "sincerity & freedom": "You will at least be convinced that I am honest; that I mean to think & act right, whatever you may believe concerning the real nature of my sentiments & conduct." Motive makes up the crux of the matter; if epistemology divides them, Smith aims to preserve fraternity on the ground of sincerity. At the same time, Smith still seems to hope that the projection of sincerity, coupled with the language of rational authority, might compel his friend to recognize the reasonableness of the positions he has taken.

With these strategies in mind, Smith grounds his defense in what might be called scientific autobiography, a hybrid of the clinical histories he routinely drew from his patients and the long-standing tradition of Puritan spiritual autobiography. He attempts, through this doubting pilgrim's progress, to provide experiential justifications for his philosophy, to portray his disbelief as sincere, rational, and, moreover, a natural outgrowth of Christian ideals and his own initial efforts to defend

Christianity against its detractors. He expresses gratitude, for instance, for parents who taught him morality and virtue, but he resents their insistence that "the religion of Christ was the only foundation of morals." This "misfortune" led him to abandon morality at Yale when older classmates convinced him that Christianity was false. In his limited "understanding," he acquired "many foolish habits . . . and was preserved from others, probably, by my immature age alone." Thus, when he was sent after graduation to Dwight's Greenfield Hill Academy, he was a perfect candidate for regeneration at the hands of a sentimental father figure: "Was it strange, then, that the eloquence, the judgement, the understanding, the uncommon virtue, of Dr. Dwight—the address which he peculiarly possesses of attaching youth to him, the more than paternal kindness which he shewed me . . . should gain an easy conquest over opinions, hastily taken up, without reflection"?[44] As a storyteller, Smith is an anatomist; he seeks to dissect and explain as he cuts through the tissue of anecdotes that have produced him.

In this self-analysis, Smith provides for Theodore Dwight not only a narrative of his childhood faith, doubt, and reconversion—the first half of the basic story he would tell and retell as he attempted to justify his disbelief to friends—but also a cause-and-effect account of this period of his life that differed from the one his friends and parents probably held. His "restor[ation] to christianity," he argues, had less to do with spiritual regeneration than with "[t]he cares of Dr. Dwight." Because this restoration also brought him back to "morality . . . founded on reason, as well as habit," he sincerely owes Theodore's brother thanks: "It is to [Dr. Dwight], more perhaps than to any other man, that I owe that love of virtue, which I now feel."[45] Such a flattering expression of gratitude (disclosing, perhaps, the guilt that must have come with turning his back on Dwight's indoctrination) may have been less than heartening to Smith's readers, however. Should not his conviction have been due more to Christ than to Dwight?

Attributing to Timothy Dwight his sense of reasonable virtue, and characterizing his first doubts as childish and immoral, Smith sets the stage for a defense of his current disbelief. In the letter's second draft Smith inserts the crucial formulation: "In reasoning with me, Dr. Dwight taught me, also, to reason; & while he inspired virtuous resolutions & religious faith, he excited a spirit of inquiry, & a disposition to examine the foundations of that faith & the reasonableness of those resolutions." This examination of Christianity's foundations—inspired by Timothy Dwight, not William Godwin—ultimately led him to see his religion as unreasonable and inconsistent with its own moral ideals. Could God be such an inefficient organizer, he wondered, to offer a plan of salvation that would save so little of his creation? "'Strait is the way, and narrow is the road, which leadeth unto life eternal—and *few* there be that find it,'" he quotes. "*Few* there be, who find it! What must I think of a being who having infinite fore-knowledge, must have foreseen the fate of man; who had infinite power to prevent it, if he would—and yet would not?" God, possessing all knowledge—the wildest Enlightenment fantasy—has failed to use it for the greatest good. A being who hordes knowledge for its own sake can claim neither moral authority nor Smith's affection.[46] Smith placed his faith instead in humanity's capacity to direct its own progress.

In Smith's autobiographical account, religion was to blame for its own undoing. In other words, he writes to his friend, "I had overrun belief, in striving to support it." Reason, as taught by Dr. Dwight, was the method. This idea, the core of his defense to Dwight, bears similarities to a passage from Smith's "Ode Written on Leaving the Place of My Nativity," a poem published before he left Connecticut for Philadelphia and reprinted in the *Gazette of the United States* as part of the Ella-Birtha-Henry correspondence. In the poem he bids farewell to familiar Litchfield landmarks, then pauses at the local church building,

> Where the mild Sabbath called my constant feet,
> Still let me think how frequent on thy seat,
> Deep-musing thought had found a heavenly home;
> For there the Soul, when bigot rage was raised,
> And fiery zeal threw crimson o'er the face;
> Or when the vengeance of the Lord was praised,
> And torture shook the tenements of grace,
> Or priestly warmth upraised the rod,
> Or Dulness nodded o'er the word of God;
> Could look with mild complacency around;
> And age where inborn worth was found,
> Or goodness glowed upon the face of youth,
> Or native innocency shone,
> Or beauty softened on the lip of truth,
> Or dove-like Pureness fixed her throne;
> Could gaze content with fond delight,

Grow better at the sight,
Grateful would swell for what was given,
And rise, in glowing rapture up to heaven.[47]

As in his defensive letter to Dwight, here Christianity's inconsistencies pointed him toward more correct principles. The passage stands out in his sentimental tribute to Litchfield for its tension between his "constant feet" (which bring him to meeting each Sabbath) and what turns out to be the ultimate source of the "Deep-musing thought [that] had found a heavenly home."

Through the first three lines of the passage the speaker's thought appears to be elicited by what he hears in church. The fourth line, however, changes the meaning of those that immediately precede it; the sermon, rather than enticing the poet to religious awakening, provokes disaffection through its "bigot rage." Suddenly the "Still" that begins the second line means "contrary to" rather than "continuing to": it undermines the "constant feet" (the habit of religious performance) rather than continuing the sentimental recollections that had so far formed the content of the poem. Or perhaps it shows his constancy to be rewarded by higher understanding. What he gains from attending church meetings is not spiritual insight or nourishment but "Deep-musing thought" provoked by the preacher's ineptness, bigotry, and dullness. In contrast to a message of "torture" and fear of the "upraised . . . rod," the poet sees innate beauty and perfectibility—"native innocency" and "inborn worth"—in the parishioners around him. From this passage emerges a sense that his dissatisfaction with religion grew, initially at least, out of religious conviction. Importantly, the final sentiment here is religious; when the "Soul" swells, it "rise[s] in glowing rapture up to heaven"—despite the sermon rather than as its result.

Later in his life, Smith's disdain for unjust ministers would transform into disillusionment with the Christian God. But even after he came to repudiate the Bible and Christianity, he preserved the idea of a sacred textual canon, replacing the Bible with other sacred texts of sorts—Richardson's oeuvre, for example: sacredness founded in a truth Smith could rationally comprehend. The move to replace the Bible with truer works was probably something Smith had discussed with Brown, who had used similar arguments when attacking Scripture in his letters to his and Smith's Quaker friend, Joseph Bringhurst, the "Birtha" of their earlier poetic exchange: "I esteem [Richardson] inferior to none

that ever lived, as a teacher of virtue and the friend of mankind, but
the founder of the Christian Religion," Brown wrote in one letter, but
when it came to the literal truth of biblical accounts, "Does not my
reason compel me to give the preference to the performance of Richardson?"[48] In Smith's poetic tribute to Litchfield, God can still claim
the poet's heart as he leaves home (he says so in the poem's final line),
but he has already introduced a host of voices that compete for his allegiance: Science, Ambition, Fame, Knowledge and Learning, and others. These forces would ultimately push Smith from moderate to radical deism, from a person who "bow[s] with soul resigned" to a "Father
of Heaven" (despite a faltering faith in the institutional church) into
someone who rejects that Heavenly Father on several moral grounds.

The argument that he "had overrun belief, in striving to support
it" consolidates Smith's narrative in a nutshell. His disbelief has less to
do with attacking Christianity, he argues, than with his sincere initial
attempts to defend it rationally. At this point he must address one of
Dwight's gravest concerns, that his "belief in the *perfectibility of man*"
was based on an unwise allegiance to William Godwin. Smith must
demonstrate that his belief in human perfectibility—which is linked
closely, he admits, to his disbelief in Christianity—results from his
own careful reasoning rather than from British radicalism. "[T]hese
few lines," he assures Dwight, contain "the mental progress of seven or
eight years." He had not quit praying in Jesus' name, he writes, until he
was "intirely satisfied that this name had no superior efficacy over any
other." His "morning & evening devotions" gave way only gradually to
a belief in perfectibility, an "obnoxious doctrine," he facetiously tells
Dwight, which is quite easily explained:

> Man is an animal formed with certain capacities. These are not unlim-
> ited—for then he would cease to be Man. But they are improvable; &
> that in two ways—first by culture or exercise; & secondly, by an heredi-
> tary propagation, to a certain degree, of that culture: there can be no
> doubt that the child of a native of Connecticut is born with a greater
> aptitude to receive minute impressions, than a child of one of the stupid
> inhabitants of Labrador. When we read the history of man, we must
> be sensible that he has undergone a gradual refinement of manners,
> & acquired, gradually an amazing fund of ideas & consequent powers,
> which he had not at first. We have every reason, therefore, which our
> knowledge of his capacities, & of his history, can offer, for believing

that he will continue to improve: or, in other words, that he is likely to approach still more towards perfection. This capacity for progressive advancement towards excellence, is denominated *perfectibility*—which, you will observe neither implies that man will ever become *perfect,* nor that he is not vicious & weak, & imperfect, *now.* . . . Those who admit that man is a perfectible animal, mean that he is an animal susceptible of all the improvement consistent with human nature.[49]

This portion of the letter's first draft captures a number of points on which he and Dwight would agree, as well as a major blind spot on Smith's part. The ethnocentricity of his Connecticut chauvinism, first of all, forms the heart of their shared notion of natural aristocracy. Smith's belief in perfectibility does not suggest that all men are created equal, a point he does not bother to reconcile with his typical Lockean psychology. Some souls—those born in Connecticut (apparently, to Smith, the apex of white humanity)—are a few steps ahead in the game. This view made men like Theodore and Timothy Dwight (and Smith, too) uneasy about democracy, but Smith reassures his friend that his endorsement of perfectibility was not a vote for social leveling. What Smith seems consistently to miss, however, is the gulf that separates him from his friend on questions of epistemology and human nature. For Dwight, human nature was far from perfectible; it required redemption, by Christ, from its depraved state. Smith claims to know what he does about human nature by reading "the history of man." Only one Book, by contrast, is necessary for Dwight to arrive at his certainty about human nature, a book Smith rejects as inconsistent and immoral.

Smith counters Dwight's accusation that he has ridiculed Christianity with a lesson in comparative religion. His approach here anticipates but also differs sharply from the nineteenth-century comparativists who would follow; his ethnocentrism is more unabashed, and his failure of faith in Christianity does not lead to the liberal "natural theology" of later generations of doubters. Rather, Smith turns the tables on his friend and charges Dwight with having spoken lightly of other faiths. Theodore does not "hesitate to express [his] contempt," for example, for "all the idle stories of Mahomet" or other religious traditions:

Thousands, millions of people, fall down before a stock, a stone, a leek, an onion; place the most implicit confidence in the wondrous transmigrations of Vishnou, the rainbows that surrounded the infant nose of Tohi, and the earthly immortality of Teshor Lama; & thousands, & millions of men, perhaps, repose all their hopes of happiness, present & to come, on these incredible fictions, & would consent to martyrdom in their support. Yet you do not hesitate to load these tales with every epithet of scorn, & to regard the wretches who believe them, with compassion, or horror, or disgust.

Though Smith insists that he does not place Christianity on the same level as onion worship, the implication remains; but rather than chastising his friend for insensitivity, he unexpectedly uses the implication to argue that Dwight's ridicule reveals a mindset he and Smith share: "We both refuse to assent to what appears absurd in our eyes; tho' millions receive it as sacred and divine." Bringing it even closer to home ("[H]ave [you] never made Deism the subject of your ridicule?"), Smith claims a right to his friend's polite respect, no matter how much Dwight may think Smith to be mistaken. It cannot be "proper," he concludes, to assert a surety of one's own belief "with scorn, with ridicule . . . & when a native of Egypt should be with us, I do not think we should act either justly or politely, to speak contemptuously of his humble adoration of the *leek*."[50]

Smith's final tactic in the letter returns to what has remained, for the most part, implicit in his defense: that moral inquiry ought to be open ended, that whatever knowledge emerges from sincere investigation requires adoption into one's system of thinking, regardless of the consequences. His growing belief in perfectibility, he wrote earlier in the letter, eventually proved "hostile to the dogmas" of Christianity: "The Atonement, Regeneration, Election, the Fall, Original Sin, &c. &c. all fell before it in orderly succession." The logical extension of this idea, he realizes, will test his friendships: "If I discover what is Truth—is it not a rational act of mine, which has for it's [sic] object the illumination of mankind? Nay, is it not incumbent on me to remove, as far as in me lies, every obstacle in the way of men towards happiness? And if Religion be an obstacle—to remove religion?" Smith revised this passage to make it even more forceful: he will "expose the nakedness & insufficiency of Religion, to strip her of all her delusive ornaments, point out her hitherto concealed deformities, compare her with the lovely & unsophisticated form of Truth, & hold her up to the temperate regard, & for the rational dereliction; of undeceived and reforming man."[51]

Over the course of the letter, Smith sets aside his method of correspondence as friendly inquiry and uses his discourse of friendship both
to demand his friend's tolerance and to gain the moral upper ground.
By professing his friendship, he sets an expectation for his friend to
do the same, regardless of their divergence of opinion. Smith brings
this strategy to its fullest use in the letter's conclusion, where he usurps
Dwight's position as a mourner for lost sheep: "To you, my friend, I am
bound by a thousand ties: your very errors strengthen my attachment
. . . [but] I can not but lament that you have not attained to clearer
views of the foundation of morality, & to a more consistent notion of
it's injunctions." The rhetorical move also allows him to offer Dwight a
model for toleration, valuing friendship over religious difference. Only
if Dwight follows his example will friendship remain a method for collaborative inquiry; otherwise their differences will not provoke further
knowledge, even if Smith hopes they will continue to facilitate "attachment."[52]

The results of Smith's letter and its public performance were not at
all what he hoped they would be. In response to Uriah Tracy's objection
to Joseph Fawcett's Godwinian sermons, which Smith had left to circulate among his Litchfield friends, Smith wrote Susan Tracy a careful
response, drafting it over five days in February. "I can not but compas-
sionate your situation," he wrote, "but, in sincerity I must regard that of
another, as still more pitiable. He must, indeed, be wretched, who fears
inquiry; who so doubts the soundness of his faith as to tremble at every
opposition."[53]

Senator Tracy's function as a rival in the narrative Smith creates
here becomes explicit—and borders on impropriety, since Smith criticizes a husband to his wife, comparing Tracy to the Dey of Algiers, a
popular figure for sexual and political tyranny in the name of religion.
Smith's unrestraint on this point, he claims, derives from his philosophical creed: "[N]o censor can restrain the operations of intellect.
He who possesses the undisturbed faculty of thought, may well deride
the pigmy violence of a thousand Omars. Yet, I say not this from any
indignation I bear against Mr. T. on this occasion. My only emotion is
regret: and more on his account, than on yours." The move to expose
his true feelings becomes a dominant trope of the letter. "I have, no longer, any *personal* reason for concealing any letter which I have written
to you," he writes. "You once requested my leave to impart the contents
of certain of my communications to Mr. T.: I was foolish enough, at

that time, to have objections. They have long since vanished. Hereafter, I would willingly have the world my confidant." Showing Mr. Tracy their correspondence might actually "remov[e] any unpleasant doubt that may sometimes overcast his mind" about Smith's friendship with his wife, if sincerity and truth-telling had the moral force he believed them to possess. "Why will you not so far imitate my example . . . as to make me the depositary of your sentiments?" he writes. "Indeed, have I not a right to claim this act of confidence from you?"[54] The plea for intimacy is blunt, drawing on the language of legal rights more than intimate disclosure. He stakes a similar claim by making himself and Mrs. Tracy a "we"—uniting them regardless of the course she plans the friendship to take.

Six months pass in the diary, and his claim is still unfilled. In August he wrote her again, the "interrupt[ion] of our correspondence" having called her friendship into question. Rather than discussing the dynamics of intimate exposure, as in his last letter, he dwelled now on silence. He had earlier written to her "with a freedom & sincerity calculated to display, at once, the depth & disinterestedness of my friendship," but his letter had met only "that afflicting silence, so destructive of all the advantages of friendship, so threatening to its very existence." What other than silence could be more threatening to someone whose very sense of self depended on friendly communication? He throws out possible motives for her failure to write: an offense taken by his interfering in her family affairs, or a "fear of improper inferences; inferences unjust to me and cruel to you; to be drawn from the continuance of our correspondence," or perhaps she has even been "induced to change [her] opinion of my character & principles."[55]

The letter suggests Smith's desperate attempt to salvage a friendship he knows has been damaged; his ideal of free and open communication as a sign of sincerity and intimacy has backfired, and as the friendship fails, so have the forms of communication on which it depended. He comes close to blaming his disbelief as the source of the fracture but reminds her that rationalism does not numb sensibility: "The armor of that philosophy I cherish is not such 'thick-ribbed steel' as to repel the attacks of a fortune so malignant. I have not cherished a firmness so adamantine that I can behold all the tendered & long-cherished sympathies of life perish around me unmoved, or undismayed. . . . The meanest worm writhes under the foot that tramples on it."[56] When, a few months later, Uriah Tracy passed through New York to

Philadelphia, he stopped to deliver letters from Smith's parents. "Our conversation . . . but glanced on [Tracy's] family," Smith writes. "Never have I heard a syllable, directly or indirectly, from Mrs. Tracy, since my last letter. My correspondence there is, I fear, at an end. Our friendship, too, I fear. . . . If this winter pass without a line from her . . . I must relinquish my hopes of a renewal of our correspondence—& strive to forget our friendship."[57] He would also have to reconsider his views on friendship's moral force as escalating cultural struggles over truth, public expression, and literary culture would put him at even greater odds with these friends.

The Illuminati Crisis and Public Intellectual Authority

To Uriah Tracy, and to Timothy and Theodore Dwight, Smith must have seemed living proof of the dangers "infidel Philosophers" posed to young American intellectuals, a reminder, perhaps, of their former friend Joel Barlow, who now, living in Europe, was reputed to have renounced Christianity and joined in with French revolutionaries. Timothy Dwight, from the moment he took control of Yale in 1795, saw himself as engaged in a battle for the souls of his pupils and had already spent years resisting first the spread of Unitarianism and then what he considered the leveling effects of the French Revolution and the philosophical writing that provided its underpinnings. Federalist opposition to "self-created" Democratic-Republican societies also helped to predispose cultural and political conservatives to believe claims, beginning in 1797 and 1798, that the French Revolution had been the result of plots laid by the Bavarian Illuminati. From 1798 through the early 1800s, Federalist newspaper publishers and clergymen spent an extraordinary amount of print space and time at the pulpit warning their listeners and readers against the conspiracy.

Scholars have long viewed the Illuminati scare as an important episode in early American history, primarily as it illustrates the extremes of the partisan divisions that preceded and followed Jefferson's election in 1800.[58] But the incident went beyond American politics. A transatlantic affair, it was made possible, in fact, by intellectual networks through which books, bodies, correspondence, and criticism crisscrossed the Atlantic Ocean. The actual Illuminati emerged from struggles between clergy and university professors during the European Enlightenment. Founded in 1776 by Adam Weishaupt, a law professor at the Jesuit-controlled University of Ingolstadt, the Illuminati sought to infiltrate and assert control over the government, thereby wresting the school and other public institutions free from clerical control. In the early 1780s the secret society expanded to around 3,000 members, mostly by converting Masonic lodges to its purposes. In the late 1780s, the Bavarian government published a stash of papers it had seized in an effort to stamp out secret societies in general and the Illuminati in particular. The governmental crackdown and exposé put a quick end to the order, but the threat of the group's secret survival has fueled conservative conspiracy theories from the 1780s to the present.

The late 1790s witnessed the major thrust of an international anti-Illuminati crusade, which came in response to the bloody excesses of the French Revolution. An exiled French Jesuit, the Abbé Augustin Barruel, who had already written a book about the persecution of the priesthood during the Revolution, published in 1797 and 1798 a four-volume exposé of the Illuminati that assigned the group direct responsibility for France's political turmoil. Barruel was preceded, for American readers, by John Robison, a professor of natural history at Edinburgh—with whom Samuel Mitchill had been personally acquainted during his education there[59]—who in 1797 published his *Proofs of a Conspiracy against All the Religions and Governments of Europe, Carried on in the Secret Meetings of Free Masons, Illuminati, and Reading Societies.* Both authors took up Edmund Burke's claim that midcentury philosophes had conspired to bring about the popular uprising; according to Barruel and Robison, these thinkers, ultimately through the agency of Masons and the Illuminati, were not only responsible for the overthrow of religion and government in France but also for conspiring to infiltrate and seize control of all the governments in the world, including the fledgling one in the United States.[60]

The American campaign against the Bavarian Illuminati was driven by close associates of the Friendly Club. The campaign's most forceful voice belonged to Jedidiah Morse, a 37-year-old clergyman from Massachusetts on whose behalf Smith and Johnson had testified in a copyright case involving his *American Geography.*[61] Morse in turn served as an informal New England agent for the *Medical Repository* and would also be called on, in 1799, to help promote the *Monthly Magazine, and American Review.* Second only to Morse among anti-Illuminati crusaders were Timothy and Theodore Dwight. Other Congregationalist clergymen and Federalist politicians and propagandists throughout New England spent the spring and summer of 1798 delivering alarmist orations and sermons, many of which were immediately sent to print and distributed throughout the country.

Historians typically date the campaign's beginning to a Fast Day sermon Morse preached on 9 May 1798, in his hometown of Charlestown, Massachusetts; his jeremiads built on Timothy Dwight's two forceful sermons at Yale the previous fall, published as *The Nature, and Danger, of Infidel Philosophy*. On 4 July 1798, Theodore Dwight thundered against the Illuminati at a Federalist Independence Day oration in Hartford while his brother did the same in New Haven. All three described in graphic terms various dangers the Illuminati posed. Timothy Dwight focused on the role played by his old imagined nemesis, Voltaire. Morse targeted the Freemasons. As the nation approached the presidential elections that would result in Jefferson's "Revolution of 1800," Theodore Dwight in particular attempted to attach the rhetoric and claims of the anti-Illuminati crusade to a political assault not only on Jefferson's party but on the vice president himself. He did so by imagining himself an Illuminatus. "If I were about to make proselytes to illuminism in the United States," Dwight told his Hartford audience, "I should in the first place apply to Thomas Jefferson, Albert Gallatin, and their political associates."[62] While Smith shared his friends' Federalist politics to the last, to the point of calling Jefferson, in a letter to a Federalist friend, "jacobinical almost to lunacy,"[63] the Dwights' growing tendency at the end of the decade to conflate Jeffersonians, Jacobins, deists, and atheists must have unsettled him.

During the summer of 1798, the climax of Smith's two-year standoff with Dwight coincided not only with the onset of the Illuminati conspiracy scare but also with Brown's return to New York, where he completed and published *Wieland* and began drafting its sequel, *Memoirs of Carwin the Biloquist*, works that have often been read by critics in relation to the political turmoil of 1798. The Friendly Club's encounter with the conspiracy theories began prior to Jedidiah Morse's Fast Day sermon in May; months earlier, on New Year's Day, Smith took notes in his diary on the appendix to a recent volume of the British *Monthly Review*, which had included excerpts from Barruel's multivolume exposé of the Illuminati. Smith responded skeptically and at length. He questioned Barruel's knowledge "concerning the highest order of Freemasons." How could he have such knowledge without being one? If he had been one, Smith believed "he could not have exposed their secrets." Other questions abounded: why would Masons participate in an atheistic campaign, when Smith had always assumed that they were "friendly to Xtianity"?[64]

William Dunlap also encountered anti-Illuminati propaganda prior to the publication of Morse's Fast Day sermon. On a visit to Dobson's booksellers in Philadelphia in April 1798, Dunlap looked through Robison's volume and pronounced it "at least a curious book" before meeting Brown for tea, where they may have had occasion to discuss what Dunlap had read.[65] From the start, then, club members engaged with these theories in a transatlantic context of countersubversive discourse, anti-Jacobinism in particular; religion, not national partisan politics, was key to their reading, as several of their favorite British Jacobin writers had been—or would soon be—dragged into the fray.

Through the summer of 1798, as Smith traveled through Connecticut to shore up the damage caused by his disclosures to Dwight, the Illuminati dominated conversations as well as Federalist oratory. Smith first picked up a copy of Robison's *Proofs of a Conspiracy* at his father's house. Upon returning to New York, where he found that Brown had arrived in his absence, Smith read through parts of Timothy Dwight's *The Nature, and Danger, of Infidel Philosophy*, to which he refers in his diary as "Two Sermons." A few days later, Morse delivered to Smith in person a printed copy of his anti-Illuminati Fast Day sermon. By late July, after Brown, Smith, and Johnson carried on "a long conversation, chiefly on a suitable catastrophe" for *Wieland* (for which they were already correcting page proofs of early chapters), Smith had finished reading Robison's book along with Theodore Dwight's Independence Day oration.[66] The proximity to Brown's scene of composition was fortuitous; Dunlap noted in an early August diary entry that Brown was already working on *Wieland*'s sequel, in which he had "taken up the schemes of the Illuminati."[67]

The friends' responses to their countersubversive associates reveal much about key conflicts for intellectual authority in the new nation's public sphere. Some opponents—even staunch Federalists like the New Hampshire editor Joseph Dennie, one of Smith's many correspondents—criticized the clergy for bringing politics to the pulpit.[68] From the perspective of people like the Dwights and Morse, however, religion was the central issue in public life, and politics was simply one arena they saw as especially vulnerable to the influence of infidelity. Although Smith left less in his diary than he had about Barruel to indicate how he read the Morse and Dwight pamphlets or responded to their authors in person, Dunlap was more forthcoming and suggests that for him religion was the central issue. In early August, Dunlap received gift copies of Timothy Dwight's two "Sermons against Infidels" (*Nature, and Danger*), along with Theodore Dwight's Independence Day oration.[69] Dunlap had long expressed concern privately over an emotional distance from his brothers-in-law over religion and politics. In May 1798, when Dunlap first read *Nature, and Danger,* he regarded the sermons as "an intemperate farrago of falshood and abuse." When he finished reading Robison's book in early August, he judged it "a strange mixture of knowledge & prejudice, truth & error, and another proof of the avidity with which we make every circumstance bend to the favorite System." His response to Robison included his exasperation at the "perseverance" with which "these religionists believe or pretend to believe the necessary connection between Religion & morality: with what impudence [they] inculcate that without Religion a man cannot be virtuous."[70] Though he maintained a polite face to the Dwights in person, Dunlap set to work on responses to the orations and on a satirical novel he called *The Anti-Jacobin,* whose title character was a Francophobic minister modeled on his brother-in-law.[71]

It was one thing to harbor such sentiments in private. It was another thing altogether to take them public, though Brown, Smith, and Dunlap had all long contemplated, as Smith put it in his letter to Theodore, how best to "expose the nakedness & insufficiency of Religion."[72] To promote their philosophical positions they chose the novel and the stage as vehicles, already favorite targets of their ministerial friends.[73] For Timothy Dwight, not only were these literary forms morally dangerous, they were the very opposite of masculine intellectual labor: "When the utmost labor of boys is bounded by history, biography and the pamphlets of the day, girls sink down to songs, novels and plays."[74] In Smith's position, in spite of his sincere respect for his former teacher, the clergy had for too long exercised its own stranglehold on the public sphere by pretending to speak with the voice of God, a voice he did not believe interfered in human affairs. Brown, Smith, Dunlap, and Johnson, who ironically appropriated from Dwight the moniker "infidel philosophers" and appreciated the humorous deflation of religion in Thomas Paine's infamous *Age of Reason,* conceived of literary professionalism as the province of moral observers like themselves, which placed them in direct competition with religious authorities. As Smith had put it to Mrs. Tracy, clerical exhalations produced a "mist of error" that could only be dispersed by spirited and unrestrained conversation.[75]

The conflict boiled down to epistemological difference. Smith's premium on discussion helps explain his attitudes toward claims of divine authority. In an article titled "Prayer," composed in his diary on his 25th birthday—only a few months before he would write his manifesto to Dwight—Smith explains that, convinced of the "falsity of Christianity," he had along the way "ceased to employ the name of Christ" in his prayers. Later, satisfied with the deist doctrine that "the Supreme Being" did not intervene in human affairs, he stopped "petitioning" God for favors and simply offered "praise & thanksgiving." Tempted to quit praying altogether, he continued to praise God for some months "because I would be satisfied of the reasonableness of discontinuing it, before I should actually" do so. The passage ends with a birthday resolution: "[P]eriodical exercise of this kind is inconsistent with the notions I entertain of the structure & constitution of the Universe, & henceforth I am resolved to discontinue it." Prayer ultimately becomes unacceptable for Smith; not only does God apparently not hear prayer, but more importantly he does not speak in return. To someone for whom inquiry depends on the "brisk breeze of discussion," such a being was of no use.

Talking Dogs and the Public Sphere: Publicity, Conspiracy, and Religious Voices in Brown's First Fictions

Smith's portrait of a silent and possibly nonexistent God anticipates the premise for *Wieland,* Brown's first published novel, in which a stranger named Carwin enters the Wieland family's rural Pennsylvania family circle and supplants its conversation, unbeknownst to them, with an impersonation of God's voice. And to disastrous effect: the group hears a series of mysterious voices that culminates in young Theodore Wieland's conviction that God has commanded him to murder his wife, children, and sister in Abrahamic acts of sacrifice. (He succeeds in all but the last before he becomes convinced of his deception and kills himself.) When modern critics consider Brown's hints in *Wieland* and in its unfinished sequel that Carwin, the villainous ventriloquist, is a proselyte to a secret society that resembles the Bavarian Illuminati, the typical response has been to read the novel as aligned with countersubversives like the Dwights.[76]

The connection, on closer examination, is not so easy to make. Brown never used the term "Illuminati" in his novels; readers who posit him as a countersubversive often rely on a more explicit connection between Carwin and the group drawn in Dunlap's diary. In the year of the Alien and Sedition acts, these critics suggest, Brown offered his debut novel as a Federalist brief on the dangers of alien influence; what Carwin has done to the young Wieland family, infidels and aliens may do to the new nation.[77] Another common critical approach exploits the personal link between Brown and the Federalist clergy. One of the most frequent claims critics have made about the Friendly Club, in fact, is that its members were responsible for perceived reactionary elements of Brown's fiction and for what biographers describe as his turn from intellectual radicalism to cultural and political conservatism.[78] Even critics careful to distinguish between political pamphleteering and novel writing draw biographical conclusions regarding Brown's apparent anxieties "about Enlightenment rationalism, foreign infiltration, 'artistic' and marketplace duplicities, and American vulnerability."[79]

But if Friendly Club sources reveal a deeply entrenched skepticism among most of this group toward the Illuminati conspiracy theories, and suggest furthermore that religion, not politics, was the group's chief concern, how should we understand Brown's engagement with the conspiracy scare? Smith's and Dunlap's diaries and correspondence reveal an abundance of evidence to confute claims that the Friendly Club was "largely a Federalist group with ties to New Haven orthodoxy, united in nothing so strongly as their hatred for the French Revolution and Jacobin rationalism."[80] Once we recognize that what most united the club's inner circle—Smith, Brown, Dunlap, and Johnson in particular—was not an antipathy toward Jacobins or Jeffersonians but a shared derision of established Christianity, we can begin to recognize ways in which this skepticism fuels Brown's *Wieland* and haunts his entire novelistic career in significant ways. From this vantage point, *Wieland,* a cornerstone of the early American literary canon, stands not as a warning cry against the breakdown of civic authority but as a dramatic illustration of the reasons that religious voices should be suspect sources of knowledge.[81]

Wieland stands as a warning against the desire for "sensible intercourse" with God;[82] its incomplete sequel, which describes Carwin's earlier proselytization by an Illuminati-like secret society, makes a broader warning still; it sets forth a theory of publicity that reveals how both works engage contemporary debates over public intellectual authority. In *Memoirs of Carwin*, which tells the ventriloquist's life story leading up to the events recounted in *Wieland*, Brown suggests how publics are conceived and, like those who long to hear God's voice, are often deceived. Although critics tend to treat the two works separately, the terms of the sequel's discussion of publicity are useful for recognizing the religious content and context of Brown's fictional debut.

From the first of his *Memoirs*, Carwin stands as a rather compelling emblem of publicity. Three episodes illustrate different ways in which Carwin allegorizes the public sphere. The first comes prior to his original discovery of his talent for ventriloquism. While hiking in a canyon one day, singing a "rude ditty," Carwin elicits an unexpected response:

> After finishing the strain, I paused. In a few seconds a voice as I then imagined, uttered the same cry from the point of a rock some hundred feet behind me; the same words, with equal distinctness and deliberation, and in the same tone, appeared to be spoken. I was startled by this incident, and cast a fearful glance behind, to discover by whom it was uttered. . . . The speaker, however, was concealed from my view. . . . A few seconds, in like manner, elapsed, when my ditty was again rehearsed, with a no less perfect imitation, in a different quarter. . . . To this quarter I eagerly turned my eyes, but no one was visible. . . . Five times was this ditty successively repeated, at intervals nearly equal, always from a new quarter, and with little abatement of its original distinctness and force.[83]

The episode can be read as a publication fantasy; Carwin's voice, behaving like a printed text, enters circulation, leaves his body behind, and reconstitutes him as an audience member as it moves without him, constantly returning from various quarters. This characterization of the experience of disembodied publicity draws on the same trope Smith and his Hartford Wit associates used when they circulated their anonymous neo-Augustan political satires under the title *The Echo*.[84] In both cases, the figure suggests an audience that has sent its own voice into circulation, a circle of audience-author relations typical not only of republican print generally but of the type of magazine publishing the friends would conduct through the first decade of the nineteenth century.[85]

In Carwin's case, as seen in a second episode he narrates, the circle of author-audience relations quickly became one in which he delighted in possessing a "superior power" over his audience. Leaving Western

Pennsylvania for Philadelphia in search of education, young Carwin successfully tricks a group of his friends into thinking that his "favourite Spaniel," Damon, can utter "clearly distinguished English words."[86] He prefaces the talking dog trick—which has nothing to do, of course, with the dog's training or skill—with a more aboveboard routine, as he has taught his pet to respond to "simple monosyllables" and to "comprehend my gestures." "If I crossed my hands on my breast," Carwin explains, "he understood the signal and laid down behind me." This part of the performance, in which Damon played a legitimate part, still aimed to deceive, because the means by which Carwin manipulated the dog's behavior were not apparent to the audience. "[T]o a stranger [his actions] would appear indifferent or casual," Carwin explains, "[and] it was easy to produce a belief that the animal's knowledge was much greater than in truth, it was." If Carwin exposes himself to his implied auditor (unidentified, but intimately familiar, we are given to believe, with the events of *Wieland*), the scene itself illustrates the creation of credulity; Damon's audience "separated lost in wonder, but perfectly convinced by the evidence that had been produced."[87]

Here, too, Carwin can be seen as an allegory of the republican print sphere; there he sits, a member of the audience, responsible for yet also disconnected from the disembodied voice that successfully claims the audience's belief.[88] Building on a long tradition of reading Carwin as reflecting various attitudes toward American authorship, one recent critic writes that "authorship itself is ventriloquism writ large." Like Carwin, "the author extricates his voice from the physical limitations of the body and the psychosocial contours of his personality and usurps the voices of others in the interests of fabricating a plot."[89] In this scenario, however, unlike some others Carwin orchestrates, his voice does not come out of thin air; it has simply taken possession of an unwitting spaniel. The voice does not, strictly speaking, pretend as it did repeatedly in *Wieland* to be disembodied; it just pretends to come from someone else's body. Significantly, Damon's first utterance is an argument for "the dignity of his species and capacity of intellectual improvement," a shrewd implication that those who speak in the voice of "the people" actually stage an elaborate form of political theater. Playing on his audience's superstitions or gullibility for his own amusement or benefit, Carwin serves less as an emblem of republican publicity than as a warning about insider manipulations of "the public."[90]

A third instance from the *Memoirs* more clearly relates to the events in *Wieland*. At one point Carwin considers feigning a voice from heaven and manipulating his aunt into altering her will in his favor. Although he does not follow through on the plot, at this crucial juncture a character named Ludloe enters the story. Carwin's pursuer and accuser at the end of *Wieland*, Ludloe figures in the prequel as both a paternal benefactor and as a member of a secret association that conspires to establish a one-world government. As a literary narrative Carwin's *Memoirs* really gains momentum not in these early rehearsals of Carwin's ventriloquial mischief—not even when his dog tricks threaten, as in this third instance, to roll over into *God* tricks. Rather, as Ludloe presses him to confess the origins of his secret skill, Carwin comes to the realization that he is close to giving away his deepest secret. The vocal and verbal talents that confirm Carwin's sense of superiority and his deepest sense of identity become instead a source of vulnerability and paranoia. The secret of his "biloquism," the one secret he keeps from Ludloe, the one that had "modelled" his "character" and that reads easily as an emblem of the public sphere, leads only to insecurity at having peeked behind publicity's screen. Carwin's knowledge of how publics work leaves him always looking over his shoulder. The tricks he has pulled on others, he worries, are bound to return and do him in.[91]

Carwin's refusal to tell Ludloe about his secret skill (about which his implied auditor and the reading audience are already aware) keeps the story interesting. The reader, for whom Carwin's confidant is a surrogate, should identify vicariously with Carwin's anxiety. Rhetorically, Brown implies, a half-disclosed secret generates interest and authority.[92] This fact suggests a relationship between reading audiences and the disclosure of secret knowledge, crucial to understanding Carwin and early American literary culture alike. In the proliferating information economy of the eighteenth century, an advertisement that one possesses secret knowledge grants the bearer superiority, as young Carwin realized, and the transmission of the secret facilitates an imagined author-audience transaction that establishes an imagined intimacy between author and audience. The trick is to gain the reader's confidence by making it seem as if one possesses exclusive information.

If in Carwin's *Memoirs* Brown delineates the manipulation of audience paranoia, if in *Wieland* he had already outlined the disastrous effects of linking claims to divine sanction and confidence in the supernatural with such aspirations for social authority. Brown structures *Wieland* on a series of religious pretensions, mishaps, and misunderstandings, beginning with the elder Wieland's discovery of a pamphlet, "written by one of the . . . Albigenses, or French Protestants," which lays out "the doctrine of the sect of Camissards." This book sets him on the path of religious fanaticism that results first in his emigration to North America and ultimately to his death, when he apparently bursts into flames while praying. These early moments in the Wieland family history offer two important insights into the novel's ultimate attitude toward religion. First, Brown's choice of religious orientation for the patriarch of this ill-fated family—a line running from the Camisards to the Albigenses, representing centuries of religious extremism—sets the stage for the novel's later extended attention to the intervention of good and evil spirits.[93] Second, Brown suggests that the elder Wieland's predisposition to religious delusion—and his spontaneous combustion—may both have medical explanations. When he stumbled onto the fateful pamphlet, his "mind was in a state peculiarly fitted for the reception of devotional sentiments" (that is, he was young, poor, and depressed).

Reflecting on her father's devotion and his death, Clara poses two means of explaining these events: "Was this the penalty of disobedience? [T]his the stroke of an invisible hand? Is it a fresh proof that the Divine Ruler interferes in human affairs[?]" Or were there natural explanations: "the irregular expansion of the fluid that imparts warmth to our blood, caused by the fatigue of the preceding day, or flowing, by established laws, from the condition of his thoughts?" Here Brown tips his hand toward the latter, citing Italian medical journals with accounts of similar cases; later he cites Erasmus Darwin's discussion of "mania" in his medical compendium *Zoonomia,* the first volume of which Samuel Mitchill had prepared in 1796 for American publication. Darwin's volume includes a discussion of *Mania Spes Religiosa* (or "superstitious hope"), including accounts of people who hear disembodied voices calling them to repentance. Darwin classifies mania in general as "increased actions of the organs of sense." Both generations of Wielands appear to have been so diseased.[94]

If *Memoirs of Carwin* warns about the mechanics of public delusion, *Wieland* argues that a "superstitious hope" in supernatural beings and divine intervention may predispose some to grave error, if not mental disorder. The most concentrated evidence for this reading comes in the novel's climax, when Theodore Wieland, who has already butchered his young family at what he understood to be a divine command, attempts next to murder his sister, Clara, before he finally commits suicide by plunging a penknife into his neck. Just prior to this sensational scene, Carwin spends nearly two chapters defending himself against the implication that he has unleashed this violence. He does so by carefully retelling everything Clara, the novel's principal narrator, has already recounted. When Carwin comes to the part of his story where Clara herself, while sleepwalking, nearly falls over the edge of a cliff, he reveals to Clara that he was in fact her savior; he prevented her plunge by "break[ing] [her] slumbers" with a "powerful monosyllable" repeated twice: "hold! hold!" He chose this word, he explains, in part for literary effect, as it is the "mode in which heaven is said by the poet to interfere for the prevention of crimes." An asterisked footnote quotes the relevant lines from Shakespeare ("—Peeps through the blanket of the dark, and cries / Hold! Hold!"), and Carwin moves forward with his self-defense.[95]

Whether we are to read the footnote as placed there by Clara (a sign of the rigor with which she has tried to make sense of the story she is simultaneously narrating and recovering from) or by Brown (a sign of his own literary acumen) the quotation from Shakespeare reveals a set of concentric circles, layers of quotation, that when peeled back reveal the novel's preoccupation with religious experience and ecclesiastical authority in the production of the early American public sphere. At the outermost ring of these circles, Brown narrates Clara's voice, and one of them provides the authoritative footnote. Clara in turn narrates Carwin's voice. Carwin quotes Shakespeare. Shakespeare gives voice to Lady Macbeth, nervous about Duncan's pending murder and afraid that God will intervene to prevent it. The layers of quotation within quotation most obviously emphasize the similarities between ventriloquism and authorship, resemblances many critics have recognized as significant. And yet more is at stake here, for at the core of these concentric rings of quotations, occupying the innermost circle, there is no original or originating authorial voice at all, certainly no heavenly interference, as Lady Macbeth had feared, but rather the paranoia of a fictional character who imagines how an intervening God *might* stage "the prevention of crimes." In Shakespeare's play, of course, God fails to intervene, and the murder goes off as planned. Similarly, in Brown's novel the heavens remain silent and readers are left with an open question regarding Carwin's complicity. Whether or not Carwin cast the voice that Theodore Wieland took to be God's, a family has been sacrificed. There was no ram caught in the Wieland family's thickets.

The concentric set of voices in this passage crystallizes *Wieland*'s religious dilemma: will God intervene in human affairs, either to inspire such Abrahamic human sacrifice or to prevent horrific murder in his name? A majority of the novel's characters desire either to be subjected to or to wield the authoritative force of an interventionist God. Theodore wants to see and hear one; Clara believes herself protected by one; Carwin impersonates one; and, in the passage just discussed, Lady Macbeth fears one, as did the senior Wieland. The editorial footnote—which by generic definition exists to provide authoritative commentary—offers an appropriate rejoinder to such a quest. If God won't intervene, the note seems to suggest, then Shakespeare will, or perhaps Erasmus Darwin will, as the novel pits literary-historical parallels and medical explanations for Wieland's behavior against his own religious understandings. The authoritative footnotes replace—displace, perhaps—the voice of God. In *Wieland*, a deist conception prevails of a God a lot like Carwin, who admits to having "rashly set in motion a machine, over whose progress [he] ha[s] no controul." Clara speculates, as she begins to narrate the novel, that the "Deity . . . has chosen his path [and] admits no recal." Her desire for intervention, like Theodore's, has been disappointed, but the violent nature of their joint disappointments suggests that the novel offers a warning as much as it stakes out a theological position. In providing what Brown called, in the preface, "some important branches of the moral constitution of man," *Wieland* argues against the utility—and for the dangers—of faith in divine intervention, and offers pointed parodies of Calvinist Christianity and Quakerism alike in its illustrations.[96]

Carwin, as one historian has convincingly shown, belongs to a tradition of ventriloquists who, unmasked, expose the pretensions of religious authority. They act, that is, as Enlightenment figures of demystification.[97] But Carwin does even more. He stands for what one recent public sphere theorist calls "publicity's secret,"[98] and does so by commenting not so much on the actual Illuminati conspiracy but on the means by which shrewd narrators like John Robison, Jedidiah Morse, or the Dwight brothers sought to capitalize on fears of conspiracy by claiming secret knowledge. Other satires of the countersubversives worked in similar ways. John Cosens Ogden, an Episcopalian rector in New Hampshire, authored a widely reprinted pamphlet in which he turned the tables and accused Dwight and Morse themselves of being the true secret combination of conspirators. The "New England Illuminati," his pamphlet proclaimed with mock seriousness, was a secret cabal "designed to increase the power and influence of the clergy." Like Brown, Ogden opposed the countersubversive clergy primarily on religious, not political, grounds. Like Dwight, Ogden decried infidelity, but he also argued that Connecticut's establishment laws had authorized an "ecclesiastical state, ruled by the *President* of the *College,* as a *Monarch.*"[99] In "tak[ing] up the schemes of the Illuminati," as Dunlap wrote, Brown similarly critiqued the countersubversives and outlined a competition among different kinds of intellectuals over newly significant knowledge industries, the management of public information, and representations of public opinion.

Countersubversives may have been particularly disposed to paranoia about the Illuminati's alleged invasion of America precisely because, as long-standing power and information brokers, they understood the ways in which "the public" was often a representation conceived in secret and put into circulation.[100] In this light, the Illuminati scare has a literary context within the transnational republic of intellect, particularly as the circulation of printed sermons and orations, correspondence, and journalistic criticism all reveals struggles to define a public sphere that encompassed but was not limited to the partisan press of the American 1790s. Conservative intellectuals described the Illuminati, for this reason, as attempting to gain control of the engines of intellectual and literary culture.

This strand of the anti-Illuminati fears was stressed most by Timothy Dwight, though Robison had laid the groundwork. In *Proofs of a Conspiracy* he had printed a letter purportedly written by one of the order's leaders, which included a declaration that the Illuminati aimed to "acquire the direction of education—of church management—of the professorial chair, and of the pulpit. We must bring our opinions into fashion by every art—spread them among the people by the help of young writers. . . . We must take care that our writers be well puffed, and that the Reviewers do not depreciate them; therefore we must endeavor by every mean[s] to gain over the Reviewers and Journalists . . . [and] the booksellers, who in time will see that it is their interest to side with us."[101] The letter demonstrates an acute awareness of the ability of interested parties to manipulate the institutional bases of the public sphere. Another purported Illuminati document in Robison's book similarly posited "[a] Literary Society [as] the most proper form for the introduction of our Order into any state where we are yet strangers."[102]

Seated as Yale's president, Dwight was extremely anxious to influence literary culture, especially as it affected the Christian indoctrination of young people in the new nation. In *The Duty of Americans, at the Present Crisis*, his 1798 Independence Day sermon, he declared his belief that infidels had already penetrated "every place of power and trust, and [insinuated themselves] into every literary, political, and Friendly society."[103] Following Barruel and Robison, he framed the battle with Jacobin and Illuminati conspirators as a battle for literary eminence in which Voltaire—who had long been Dwight's imagined foe and was also Barruel's special target—plotted to make himself a literary celebrity by controlling the international flow of printed information.[104]

In an 1801 sermon (a late statement in the debates, though Dwight apparently never lost his conviction of the conspiracy's existence) Dwight again emphasized the Illuminati's monopolization of the public sphere: infidel writings "have assumed every form, and treated every subject of thought. From the lofty philosophical discourse it has descended through all the intervening gradations to the news-paper paragraph; from the sermon to the catechism; from regular history to the anecdote; from the epic poem to the song; and from formal satire to the jest of the buffoon."[105] The hierarchical catalog includes high and low genres intended for audiences of elite, middling, and lower classes. And yet, the problem goes beyond the circulation of dangerous printed matter, in spite of his conviction that the Illuminati had successfully infiltrated all media and placed a stranglehold on all genres. Dwight worried even more about the effects of face-to-face "action and influence,"[106] a sign of the distrust bred by the ways in which the conception of a monolithic "public" could conceal secret movements and behind-the-scenes machinations, an explicit vote of no confidence in an anonymous republican print sphere. Brown's analysis of the public sphere, though it stemmed from a different set of concerns, suggested the sources for Dwight's particularly suspicious subjectivity, the fate of those who know that publics are imaginary relationships generated through representations and that they can be manipulated by powerful interests behind the screen.

The Ghost of Elihu Hubbard Smith in Brown's *Edgar Huntly*

If Brown's first novel, with its religious voices poised to destroy domestic tranquility, shares Smith's confidence in rational over religious explanations, it also shares a shaken confidence in the ability of all audiences to think rationally. The failures of Smith's correspondences with Dwight and Tracy altered Smith's philosophy of friendship and his belief in the necessary force of sincerity. In contrast to what he had written Theodore Dwight earlier about the importance of early associations, Smith wrote in the summer of 1797 to another Connecticut friend, Sally Pierce, that "we are not to expect a great deal from early-formed friendships, as such; & that, therefore, we ought not, greatly, to regret them." Those who abandon us "are ordinary minds" and must be replaced by "superior" ones. If early friendships could not endure, he had earlier written to Mrs. Tracy, they must be considered part of the "sacrifice" required by earnest inquiry, however painful such separations may be.[107]

The realities of Smith's personal and professional life—the absorption of his intellectual energies in promoting his own medical journal, Brown's fictional career, and Dunlap's theatrical enterprise (which occasionally offered him a venue for his own literary productions)—increasingly made it plain that he enjoyed greater sympathy with Brown, Dunlap, and his roommate William Johnson than he did with his old Connecticut friends. In August 1796, as the tension with Dwight was increasing, Smith scraped together enough money to visit Dunlap at his summer home in Perth Amboy, where Brown would arrive from Philadelphia. One morning, after reading an edition of the London *Monthly Review*, Smith joined his two friends for a country walk. They searched out a "three-partile Tree, emblem of our friendship, which we discovered, & made our own, last year." Here their impulse to transpose natural history onto their friendships comes through vividly. "We had some doubt which stock belonged to each," he writes. "For each of us had fixed upon his own. We readily agreed that the slenderest one, & which grew in the middle, must be Charles's; & after many examinations, the reason of size determined me that the westernmost must be mine. This proves to be the fact."[108]

Smith renders friendship as natural and as factual as a tree, but as uncommon as one with three trunks. As an emblem it serves to remind them that their lives are intertwined, their friendships symbiotic. By discovering it they make it their own. As it grows, it will continue to signify the friendships that grow as well, as well as the support each trunk offers the others. (Brown, apparently, needed the most support.) The language of "examination" lends scientific self-importance to their sentimental musing and self-examination. Dunlap, Brown, and Smith, along with William Johnson, formed a group within the Friendly Club whose opinions most resembled one another's. They nicknamed themselves "infidel philosophers," poking fun at the Dwights. They chided one another when literary allusions in their letters borrowed too heavily on "the Vulgar cant of the religionists."[109]

These were the friends with whom the adult Smith chose to cast his creative lot; to a large degree they replaced his earlier creative dependence on Hartford's Wits, though Smith continued to obsess about losing Dwight's and Tracy's friendships. Then, just before Smith was to visit Connecticut in June 1798, Mrs. Tracy broke her long silence in response to a brief letter he had ventured. "I am reinstated in all her friendship," Smith writes in the diary. Though he is "sorry to find her converted, by the French Revolution, to Christianity," he resolves not to "unsettle her faith," to leave her this "intellectual opium. . . . She will still be one of the most excellent of women."[110] Smith's summer visit to Connecticut included calls on upwards of 150 people in less than three weeks. Smith could not have known that his death was only weeks away; he more likely feared that the erosion of his friendships might spread.

On his first morning in Litchfield he spent "nearly the whole forenoon" at "Mrs. Tracy's. This was the renovation of ancient pleasures, augmented by the presence, & intelligent conversation of her daughters, who are now old enough to contribute to the delights of confidential intercourse."[111] Did the "confidential intercourse" center on their friendship, his lack of faith, his opinions of Senator Tracy's decision to control his wife's reading habits? He does not say. During his few days in Litchfield before and after a quick trip to Hartford, where he spent time with Theodore Dwight, he had tea with Mrs. Tracy several times and read to her one afternoon from the moderately feminist newspaper essays of Brown's friend Frances Paxton, as well as some of Brown's own Philadelphia newspaper sketches, "much to her gratification." This performance was a scaling back from the evening over a year earlier, when he had read for more than an hour from his correspondence with Dwight; it was less personal, more appropriate, the sort of thing he might have done in any mixed-sex setting with less intimate friends. Three days before Smith returned to New York, he and a friend drank tea again with Mrs. Tracy, and then she silently slips from his story. He makes no mention of letters written to or received from her during the two and a half months before his diary ends.

emy, then lost it again in a mature and considered way that brooked, in Smith's own view, no return. In Brown's revision, the angst that fills Smith's diary on this subject, especially in his correspondence with Dwight and Tracy, has vanished like the apparition in Huntly's bedroom.

In Waldegrave's ghost, Brown offers a figure of anxieties over publication and reminds us of the ways in which Smith's correspondence with Dwight and Tracy reveals crucial aspects of the literary culture of the early republic. Smith's letters, part of his diary, intended for eventual publication as his memoirs, defy easy generic categorization (they are, after all, simultaneously letters, diary entries, and drafts of potentially public memoirs) and thus complicate usual divisions between public and private in relation to these forms. Even as letters addressed to individual readers, they encompass larger audiences. He communicated them in a variety of other settings (in Mrs. Tracy's parlor as well as to intimates in New York; or circulated by Dwight among Connecticut friends). These semipublic disseminations of Smith's autobiographical statements were risky given the generally negative response to his religious transformations and the broader cultural tensions at play over issues of religion, rationalism, and religious authority. The results illustrate the difficulty, at the end of the century, of separating the literary from the political public spheres, the experimental, examined, and sincere self from the performed.

Moreover, the consequences of Smith's attempt to articulate his deism have even larger literary and political ramifications. While most accounts of the eighteenth-century public sphere have followed Habermas's description of the "audience-oriented subjectivity" produced by letters, diaries, and parlor conversation—modes of representation shaped to maximize audience approval—Smith's experience illustrates the costs incurred when the audience simply would not embrace the performance. So considered it reminds us of the very human struggles elided by ideal-typical accounts of the subjectivity produced by the emergence of a modern public sphere.[117]

Edgar Huntly's dilemma over Waldegrave's letters differs from the one confronting Brown and his friends with Smith's memoirs. Edgar plans only to transcribe them for Mary Waldegrave's use; they would, in other words, be "privately published." Brown and company initially intended a broader publication, in print, of Smith's papers. Although Brown is notorious for undertaking projects he never completed, it is tempting to read his portrait of Waldegrave as a fictional case against publishing Smith's memoirs.[118] *Edgar Huntly*'s composition coincided with a visit to Connecticut made by Brown and Johnson in the summer of 1799, where they visited several of Smith's former friends and possibly his family. Did the family ask them not to publish? Did the friends make the decision on their own, as Huntly does in Brown's novel? Or, in the context of increasing public resentment toward infidel philosophers like themselves, intensified by the escalating anti-Illuminati campaign, did they hesitate to mar their friend's memory by associating him with ideas even less politically tenable among his peers than they had been before? After 1800, Federalist-Congregationalist partisans like Timothy Dwight largely succeeded in cementing the association between deism and the threat of Jacobin subversion. Deists among founding-era Federalists kept their disbelief private, for the most part, or eventually experienced reconversion along with others during the heightened religiosity of the 1820s and 1830s.[119] The utopian fires that fueled rationalist philosophers early in the 1790s had largely gone out; in spite of the Federalists' feeling of defeat in 1800, the crisis of intellectual authority they had encouraged did not end in the secularists' favor.

||||||||||||||||||||||||||||||||||||||||||||||||||||||||||||||||||||||||||||||||||||||||||||||||||||||||||||||||||||||||||||||||

THREE

Unrestrained Conversation and the "Understanding of Woman"

Radicalism, Feminism, and the Challenge of Polite Society

I N early November 1796, just as he was beginning to contemplate his self-defensive letter to Theodore Dwight, Elihu Smith was interrupted in composing his regular Saturday afternoon correspondence by William Johnson, who returned to their new rooms at 13 Cedar Street, having just purchased "a new Novel—by the author of 'Man as he is'—intituled 'Hermsprong, or Man as he is not.' He began to read it to [William] Dunlap, who was here, & I threw aside more serious employments, to become one of his hearers. [Charles Brockden] Brown came in. We were pleased; & I propose to read this new book—whose author seems to be treading in the *profane* steps of [William Godwin's 1794 novel] 'Caleb Williams.'"[1] Of course Robert Bage's *Hermsprong* (1796) would delight these friends. The titular protagonist, having been nurtured in North American forests by an Indian tribe, arrives in England, where he uses his uncivilized outsider's vantage point and his skill at witty and frank conversation—what he calls "plain and simple truth"—to slaughter one by one the landed gentry's sacred cows: the importance of rank, title, and property; male superiority and women's ornamental refinement; patriarchal authority and filial duty; and the corrupt patronage by which an aristocratic class controls sycophantic clergy and magistrates.

Over the next week Smith recorded further details of *Hermsprong*'s reception by club members and their larger social circle; these details allow us to outline important aspects of the club's reading habits. Smith finished the novel's first volume in a day, started straightaway on the second, then, deciding his friends should hear it, hurried around town to rally them. That evening he read aloud to an audience of Johnson, Brown, Dunlap, and Mrs. Dunlap. He "began the volume anew," he writes, "& did not quit it, till it was finished. The reading has given us uncommon pleasure; we pronounced the book an excellent one; & I have half resolved to undertake the mechanical task of compiling, out of it, a Comedy." At the end of the month Smith noted with pleasure that the British *Monthly Review* for September 1796 had given *Hermsprong* a "liberal" review, "& the spirit of a Godwinite breaks forth in the selection of extracts," confirming their evaluation of the novel's worth and their assessment of its cultural politics.[2]

This particularly enthusiastic example of a common scene of late-eighteenth-century reading offers just one instance of many on record in which literary association—in this case, the sheer pleasure of sharing a new novel with a group of friends—structured the daily experiences of informal reading audiences just as it did formal meetings of groups like the Friendly Club. We can learn much from such descriptions. The consumption of the new novel, for example, took place in a mixed-sex setting and was absorbing enough to cause Smith to set aside other work and contemplate new literary projects. The audience valued the novel for more than pleasure; Smith's aim to undertake a dramatization would be a public service, "mechanical," duty driven. Judging by Smith's description of the novel as printed in two volumes, Johnson appears to have purchased the pirated Dublin edition instead of the original London edition's three, suggesting the efficiency of colonial printing and transatlantic circulation, including the circulation of British magazines and critical reviews, which contributed to the impression that they shared with European authors a common intellectual sphere.

Most of all, these entries outline the process by which Smith and his friends assimilated a new work into their understanding of modern fiction, including the place of fiction in the republic of intellect. Though the author's identity remained unknown to the friends, Smith framed his account by reference to their favorite recent novel, William Godwin's *Things as They Are, or the Adventures of Caleb Williams*, published just two years earlier. The comparison between these particular books might seem odd at first. Stylistically Bage's novel is more Goldsmith than Godwin, lighthearted where the latter is urgent, even anxious. But if profanity sold the book to Smith, on this score the novel had much to offer; as the *Monthly Review*'s treatment made plain, a "Godwinite" would be pleased by *Hermsprong*'s attempt to give the established church and other aristocratic power bases a sincere and solid thrashing.[3]

Another series of events recounted in Smith's diary over the same period of time speaks to the philosophical uses of fiction that drew the group to Bage's novel and led its members to cultivate "Godwinite" identities. A week after William Johnson introduced *Hermsprong* to his friends, William Dunlap read to the same audience his new play, *Tell Truth and Shame the Devil*, adapted from a French one-act "dramatic proverb," *Jerome Pointu*. Smith worried that the play might be "too moral to succeed" in America. "Our audiences must have a plentiful dose of fun," he writes, "to make even a drop of morality palatable," a sentiment that recalls his interest in producing a comedy based on *Hermsprong*. If Smith was not accurate in his prophecy regarding Dunlap's play, he at least thought he was. When the play was staged in January 1797 Smith recorded his frustration with the audience's response: "The night was extremely cold—the audience thin—the piece moral—is it wonderful that it did not produce bursts of applause? Yet there was some, in several parts. But not enough to satisfy the wishes of one, who longs to see a deserving piece well received."[4]

Dunlap's *Tell Truth* relates to Bage's *Hermsprong* not only chronologically and thematically—they both feature spirited young protagonists who aim to expose the vice and folly of unrighteous elders—but also through an explicit reference to Godwin in Dunlap's adaptation. As the play's second act opens, Semblance, a vicious patriarch and a corrupt lawyer, laments the current state of society, epitomized by his ward, Tom, who has set out to unmask Semblance as a hypocrite:

> My ward, Tom . . . undertaking to be a critic, politician, reformer. Lord! Lord! how times have changed since I was young! . . . Formerly a clerk would sit all the week at his desk, and scarcely allow himself time for a walk on Sunday: but, *now,* they are men of spirit, wits, judges of authors, and critics at the Theatre; and we shall have a stripling of four-and-twenty tell you that the basis of all English law is violence and injustice, and advise you to read *Godwin.* I have no patience![5]

Like Lord Grondale, the aristocratic patriarch in *Hermsprong*, Semblance—whose name obviously indicates deceptive surface and appearance—covers up his own licentiousness by expressing indignation that a young person of no rank should dare to call him on his errors. Semblance expands the list of Tom's sins to include upstart literary criticism, an apparent analog of judging one's elders, and a clear indication of the connections Dunlap drew between literary culture, politics, and reform. But Dunlap gives what could be read simply as the manifestation of a generation gap a measure of philosophical significance through the reference to Godwin. Suddenly, Tom's designation elsewhere in the play as a "preacher of sincerity"—a characterization akin to Hermsprong's self-proclaimed "vice" of "frankness"—takes on more meaning. Both *Hermsprong* and *Tell Truth* frame sincerity in opposition not only to falsehood but also to customary systems of deference and politeness that curtailed conversation based on the class, sex, or age of speakers and listeners.

As Dunlap's reference to Godwin suggests, the notion of sincerity celebrated by Dunlap and Bage shared philosophical foundations with the book that, even more than any work of fiction, kept club members occupied for a significant portion of the 1790s: Godwin's *Enquiry Concerning Political Justice, and Its Influence on Morals and Happiness* (1793), which had been published a year before *Caleb Williams*, with a revised London edition reprinted in Philadelphia in 1796. Brown hailed the book in 1795 as "my Oracle" and Smith viewed its morals as "more pure" than the New Testament.[6] Dunlap, thrown into raptures by *Political Justice*, launched a correspondence with the author.[7] Within months of the group's enthusiastic reading of *Hermsprong*, Godwin's treatise would be at the center of Smith's controversy with the Dwights and the Tracys.[8] In addition to considering the work politically dangerous, Smith's friends blamed it, in large part, for destroying his Christian faith.[9] Moreover, Uriah Tracy had agreed with the Dwights that it was particularly harmful to female readers, a point the senator fixed by forbidding his wife to read it and possibly curtailing her year-long discussion of it with Smith.[10]

The emphasis these conservative Friendly Club associates placed on the potential effects of radical thought on female readers helps to deepen our understanding of the gulf that separated Smith from his former friends and mentors and Dunlap from his brothers-in-law: rifts between friends and family that stand for divisions in the larger cultures

of the new nation. The Friendly Club's self-consciously gendered reading and conversation speaks both to Godwin's notion of sincerity and
to the controversial feminism of his eventual wife, Mary Wollstonecraft. For Friendly Club members, Godwin and Wollstonecraft—even
before news of their marriage was public knowledge in America—pre-
sided over what promised to be a new age of reason and intellectual
improvement. With a host of other writers bent on propagating similar
ideas, they aimed to launch a revolution of manners among men and
women in the republic of intellect.

Of course these issues cannot be separated from the politics of
Godwin's and Wollstonecraft's reputations at the end of the century,
when they went from being among the most celebrated authors in Europe and America to being spurned by former friends and becoming
the special targets of the anti-Jacobin, countersubversive right. Conservatives allied Godwin's political philosophy with the extreme disorder
of the French Revolution, fearing that one would follow in England.
Godwin and Wollstonecraft's marriage in 1797, an international news
item, drew derisive commentary in the rapidly growing anti-Jacobin
press. More scandalous than their marriage, though, were Godwin's
actions following the birth of their daughter in August 1797 and Wollstonecraft's death only weeks later.[11] Within months, along with his
wife's *Posthumous Works*, Godwin published *Memoirs of the Author of a
Vindication of the Rights of Woman*, in which—acting on his own confidence in truth-telling and the moral force of sincerity—he frankly
outlined Wollstonecraft's intellectual and sexual histories, including
accounts not only of her romance with Gilbert Imlay, an American adventurer who had abandoned her and their illegitimate daughter soon
after their return to London from Revolutionary France, but also her
romantic obsession for a married man, the painter Henry Fuseli, and
finally Godwin's own premarital sexual relationship with her, which
resulted in her second out-of-wedlock pregnancy, the child who would
grow up to become Mary Shelley. Perhaps even more shocking than
Godwin's detailing of her sexual history, he also recounted her repeated
suicide attempts on being abandoned by Imlay. The *Memoirs* scandal-
ized even the couple's friends and admirers. The poet Robert Southey,
who like some Friendly Club members had once "all but worshipped"
Godwin, thought the philosopher had "strip[ped] his dead wife naked"
and left her corpse exposed to public view.[12]

Smith had associated Wollstonecraft with Godwin long before

the two writers actually became romantically involved; he discussed them together in a conversation with Susan Tracy as early as November 1795.[13] This intuitive connection, like Smith's association of *Hermsprong* with *Caleb Williams,* exemplifies a larger process central to club members' reading: the habit of establishing links among newly published texts in order to create a canon from which they drew inspiration and with whose authors they sought to establish intellectual commerce. In drawing such connections, Smith anticipated later critics who would organize Godwin, Wollstonecraft, Bage, and other oppositional authors into a cohesive group (the "British Jacobins").[14] This process also offered grounds for self-praise and a celebration of their readerly acumen. In 1795, for example, when Dunlap first attempted to establish a correspondence with Godwin, the reply, which arrived in early 1796, included Godwin's congratulations on the accurate "conjecture of there being considerable intimacy" between him and Thomas Holcroft.[15]

The process of assembling information about their favorite authors was more gradual than scholars usually recognize; in retrospect, we have much more information about such thinkers and their texts than could possibly have been available to late-eighteenth-century American readers. This should caution against quick conclusions about readers' opinions, based solely on their appreciation of texts whose social implications were just being discerned. The news of Wollstonecraft's marriage and death, for example, arrived in so fast a succession that they hardly made individual impact on American readers, yet American readers seem not to have encountered Godwin's memoirs of his wife for months after their London publication. Records of the club's reading, attended to closely, can lead to better conclusions about the appeal of specific topics and arguments, and in turn facilitate the emergence of a more careful portrait of early American intellectual landscapes than the one allowed by simplistic assertions about their endorsements or disavowals of a general "radicalism."

Club members clustered a series of authors under the general heading "Godwinian," including Bage (whom they did not know by name), Holcroft, and the young poets Robert Southey and Samuel Taylor Coleridge;[16] scientific writers like Erasmus Darwin (whose scientific poetry set a model for Mitchill and Smith), Thomas Beddoes, and Joseph Priestley; and feminist writers like Mary Hays, Helen Maria Williams, Elizabeth Inchbald, and especially Mary Wollstonecraft. Some, but not all, of these writers published under the imprint of Joseph Johnson, for whose *Analytic Review* Mary Wollstonecraft and others wrote and reviewed, though often anonymously. Club members were also in awe of French and German authors they considered philosophically and aesthetically progressive, such as Condorcet, Volney, Dumarsais, Christoph Martin Wieland, Schiller, and, closer to the turn of the century, the playwright August von Kotzebue. Friendly Club members had their favorite imported magazines, too, which were also left-leaning: the *Monthly Review,* the *New Annual Register,* and the *Monthly Magazine.* As they did with Godwin and Holcroft, club members sought out what information they could about anonymous publications and the biographical details about "the private history of the Author[s]" they most enjoyed.[17]

Godwin's and Wollstonecraft's transatlantic reputations and notoriety have often been traced through their influence on Brown, who repeatedly discussed women's rights in Wollstonecraftian terms and tested Godwin's philosophical principles as he measured his own fiction against *Caleb Williams.* Beyond questions of individual influence, however, British Jacobin writing structured the Friendly Club's participation in debates about the philosophy of mind and about women's capability for intellectual improvement. These issues arose in Dunlap's plays and playhouses, in Smith's correspondence with female friends, and in Brown's fiction. They also formed a significant part of the appeal of radical British and European writers to club members.

A major discrepancy seems to exist, however, between club members' embrace of Wollstonecraftian feminism and their unwritten and perhaps unconscious homosocial constitution. Probing that inconsistency yields fruitful interpretations of key texts club members produced, including Brown's *Alcuin* (1798) and *Ormond* (1799). This investigation also yields new understanding of the place of mixed-sex friendship and conversation in the history of gender in Federal-era America by revealing the limitations and complex configurations of American feminism and intellectual "radicalism" in the decade. Specifically it allows us to see ways in which a hoped-for revolution in understandings of gender and society remained partial even for progressive thinkers, limited in part because the Godwinian ideal of a clash of minds—a template compatible with the club's guiding principles—came into conflict with cultural pressures to maintain politeness of speech in mixed-sex society.

"Godwin came and all was light!"

From the early nineteenth century on, critics have referred to Brown as "the Godwin of America,"[18] and ever since his first twentieth-century biographer brought Elihu Smith's unpublished diaries to bear on Brown's life and fiction, scholars have made much of a passage in an unsent letter to Brown in which Smith outlined his friend's transition from a Rousseauistic wanderer in a world of his own imagination to a searcher, above all, after truth. "Now & then a ray of truth broke in, but with an influence too feeble to dissipate the phantoms, which error had conjured up around you," Smith wrote of Brown's romantic past. But *"Godwin came and all was light!"*[19] To read this history as a rebuke would be a grave misinterpretation, given that Smith elsewhere in the letter refers to Godwin, without irony, as "the Sun himself." But even critics who recognize Smith's own adoration of Godwin have failed to consider carefully the specific appeal of Godwin and his circle to the Friendly Club, when so many of their contemporaries and associates could see him only, in Theodore Dwight's vitriolic phrase, as "a philosophical madman . . . from whom our cosmopolites have drawn the most important articles of their creed."[20]

These highly varied responses demand some explanation of the work the Friendly Club's "cosmopolites" considered so pure and their "religionist" friends so dangerous. A sprawling treatise of over eight hundred pages, *Political Justice* inquires into the nature of government and the nature of mind, a dense combination of political philosophy, psychological theory, and morals. Its author, on its publication in 1793, was a 37-year-old former Dissenting minister who since the late 1780s had participated in radical publishing circles in London as a magazine writer and critic, though such biographical details would become apparent to his American readers only over the course of several years. (All the while they enjoyed his anonymous contributions to the *New Annual Register.*) They encountered in his imposing text, which some of them read only after encountering the subsequently published *Caleb Williams,*[21] a bold work that announced itself in opposition to monarchical government (and government in general) and in favor of universal benevolence and the progress of knowledge. Providing a utilitarian critique of Lockean individualism, it argued that all action should be undertaken by a standard of justice for the greatest portion of society possible: "The first object of virtue is to contribute to the welfare of

mankind." The criteria for determining what was "just" depended to
some degree on the ability of careful observers to project the effects of
given actions or ideas. This notion, in turn, depended on an associa-
tionist and materialist conception of mind in which all thought, like
all physical motion and force, is bound together in unending chains of
cause and effect. In this way, the scientific mindset that revealed the
laws of the physical world could be trained to illuminate as well a science of morality.

This set of core principles made up the crux of Godwin's "doctrine
of necessity," a foundational tenet for the work as a whole. "In the life
of every human being there is a chain of causes," he wrote, "generated
in the lapse of ages which preceded his birth, and going on in regular
procession through the whole period of his existence, in consequence of
which it was impossible for him to act in any instance otherwise than
he has acted."[22] Derived at least in part from the Calvinism of Godwin's
early years, Political Justice's deterministic system nonetheless allowed
for "voluntary action," interventions in these "chain[s] of causes" based
on alterations in one's beliefs. If voluntary actions are based on one's
opinions and one's opinions are subject to change, then benevolent men
can undertake the work of leading the mass of humanity into higher
understanding of moral laws—inserting their influence, that is, into the
chains of cause and effect that determine individuals' behavior.

This belief necessitated Godwin's emphasis on sincerity, which he
laid out clearly in five propositions: "Sound reasoning and truth, when
adequately communicated, must always be virtuous over error: Sound
reasoning and truth are capable of being communicated: Truth is om-
nipotent: The vices and moral weakness of man are not invincible:
Man is perfectible, or in other words susceptible of perpetual improvement."[23] If one discerns the motives by which another person acts, one
can to some degree predict that person's behavior. Antithetical to the
state's government by threat of force, Godwin's program was, instead,
the architecture for a progressive and optimistic intellectual republic
whose citizens were men and women of benevolence, a republic that
depended on free inquiry and free expression, and on the ability to
shape public opinion.

Political Justice bestowed on Godwin a celebrity both immediate
and meteoric. In William Hazlitt's famous retrospective account of the
era, Godwin "blazed as a sun in the firmament of reputation," especially
among young bourgeois writers with radical leanings. Samuel Taylor

Coleridge, the same age as Smith and Brown, wrote poetry in Godwin's honor; William Wordsworth, another contemporary in age, reportedly encouraged a student friend to throw aside his chemistry books "and read Godwin on necessity" instead. Based on the Friendly Club's experience and interactions with contemporaries, Godwin's writings appear to have enjoyed a broad audience of earnest young intellectuals in America, as well. *Political Justice* was available from American booksellers as early as May 1793; excerpts appeared in magazines in New York and other cities beginning that summer. Godwin's fame only escalated with *Caleb Williams,* one of the most popular novels in America in the 1790s.[24] An American edition of the novel was published in 1795 by the same Philadelphia bookseller who would publish the first volume of Brown's *Arthur Mervyn* (1799). Another Philadelphia printer put out American editions of the revised version of *Political Justice* (1796) and Godwin's later collection of essays on education, *The Enquirer* (1797), which club members also read, debated, and recommended to friends.[25]

The Friendly Club's enthusiasm for British Jacobins unsettles easy understandings of the partisan divisions in Federal-era American culture, but it also belies the group's reputation with historians as political conservatives who engineered Brown's supposed movement from radicalism to conservatism.[26] When Dunlap eventually received replies from Godwin and Holcroft, Smith sent the news to Brown in Philadelphia along with the injunction that "[w]e must do something to convince these men that we are worthy to receive some moments of their consideration."[27] The friends' eagerness for anecdotes about these writers was gratified beginning in early 1798 when the group encountered a young actor and recent émigré, Thomas A. Cooper, who had been mentored by Godwin and Holcroft in London. (Not until Cooper's arrival did the group realize Godwin had once been a clergyman.)[28] Cooper, who eventually joined Dunlap's Old American Company, provided club members with copious information about their favorite writers' physical appearances, fashion sensibilities, and personal relationships—Godwin's acquaintance, for example, with Mary Hays, another novelist they enjoyed and had already inferentially categorized as "Godwinian."[29]

Godwin's appeal to this circle had multiple dimensions.[30] They shared with him a belief in the doctrine of human perfectibility; a resistance to established authority, especially of the clergy; a desire to harness the "engines" of literature for purposes of moral reform and the dissemination of philosophical and scientific principle; and especially a celebration of inquiry, what Godwin called the "intercourse of mind with mind." Godwin's idealization of "unreserved communication . . . among persons who are already awakened to the pursuit of truth," which "accustoms us to hear a variety of sentiments,"[31] perfectly suited the friends' rationale for the club itself.

Friendly Club members above all shared Godwin's faith in progressive education—central to *Political Justice* and *The Enquirer,* but also to the writing of his future wife, Mary Wollstonecraft, who blamed unequal systems of male and female education for the deficiencies of mind that prevented most women from making useful contributions to society. Though Godwin rarely articulated feminist positions himself, his conception of mind and education—as well as his emphasis on marriage's complicity with a corrupt system of private property—made Godwinian thought eminently compatible with Wollstonecraft's argument that, given equal education, women would be capable of the same intellectual and professional achievements as men. Wollstonecraft's *Vindication of the Rights of Woman* (1792), which included her most influential statements on this theme, had enjoyed success on both sides of the Atlantic since its publication even as the events flowing from the French Revolution made the subject of women's participation in politics a major topic of debate in Europe and America.

Though she was always a controversial writer, Wollstonecraft had broad support in America among the same sectors that embraced Godwin's writings, including most Friendly Club members.[32] Smith was a professed fan from the *Vindication* forward; one of the few letters from another person he transcribed in his diary is a 1794 letter Susan Tracy had written to a male relative in defense of Wollstonecraft. Brown, too, was strongly influenced by Wollstonecraft, as were his parents, who owned copies of her texts as well as Godwin's. The Friendly Club circle read together Wollstonecraft's translation of C. G. Saltzman's *Elements of Morality,* a progressive primer for schoolchildren, and her *A Short Residence in Sweden, Norway, and Denmark* (1796), an account of travels undertaken with her infant daughter and without male escort, which William Johnson had purchased a few months before he brought home *Hermsprong.*

If Friendly Club members already admired Wollstonecraft, her *Short Residence* fixed their affection. Wollstonecraft wrote the book as a series of letters to her American lover, Gilbert Imlay, following his abandonment of her and their daughter, Fanny. Godwin, who had met Wollstonecraft years earlier and had not been favorably impressed either by her or her feminist treatise, later wrote of *Short Residence* that "if ever there was a book calculated to make a man in love with its author, this appears to me the book." On the other side of the Atlantic, not much later than Godwin encountered it, Elihu Smith recorded that he read the book's first few pages "with melancholy satisfaction" and that he stayed up long past midnight to finish it. "This is more a view of the author, than of the country she travelled thro'," he wrote of it in his diary, "there being but little information which is to be treasured up; yet the work is pleasing, & abounds with remarks, not the product of a common mind."[33] Writing about it to Susan Tracy a few days later, he said the book had

> given me some information, some pleasure, but more pain. I could wish you to read it, as it opens a new vista into the soul of this admirable woman, but that I fear it would be the occasion of a melancholly too afflicting, & which you have every reason in the world to shun. In this work, Miss W. appears wounded, afflicted, desolate. She is a mother, & is deserted. There is an air of mystery thrown over the whole book, perhaps only so because I am ignorant, of circumstances well known in Europe, but which at this distance I cannot penetrate. It has, of consequence, interested me the more, & excited new eagerness to discover what is the cause of her evident unhappiness. At present I will not hazard a conjecture, as, in all probability, I shall soon be able to obtain a true statement of facts.[34]

Against this backdrop of romantic melancholy and mystery, the group received news of Wollstonecraft's marriage to Godwin a year later with total enthusiasm. "Miss Wollstonecraft is now the wife of Mr. Godwin," Smith announced in a letter to his friend Idea Strong in October 1797, convinced that the news would give her "a lively gratification," particularly as Wollstonecraft "is probably rendered as eligible, by this match, as she can desire" and would have both the intellectual support and the financial means to support her in "the cultivation of those sciences in which she so much delights" and in her "successive & interesting publications."[35] (The couple's financial situation was never so rosy.) When word of Wollstonecraft's death arrived only a few weeks later, Smith lamented that "[t]he loss of 50,000 french & as many Austrians, on the Rhine or in Italy, would have affected me less."[36]

Such investment in biographical circumstance reveals the degree to which club members had idealized these writers not simply for their ideas but as key exemplars for participation in the republic of intellect.[37] On this assumption—the most significant point on which this group sided with British Jacobins—literature was an "engine," something capable of pushing society toward reform by promoting correct moral views. Recognizing this philosophical and sometimes reform-oriented program for fiction is crucial to understanding much of the writing Friendly Club members produced in the 1790s. Although Thomas Holcroft pioneered this approach in *Anna St. Ives* (1792), Godwin fixed the template in *Caleb Williams,* which he intended, as he wrote in the preface, to communicate truth to "persons whom books of philosophy and science are never likely to reach."[38] Even the progressive early poetry of Coleridge and Southey confirmed Smith's, Brown's, and Dunlap's shared sentiment that generic diffusion itself should be subordinated toward reformist ends; poems, plays, and novels would reach audiences that philosophical treatises may not, and by different means: by capturing readers' imaginations.

The program for reform-minded fiction laid out by the British Jacobin writer Mary Hays in the September 1797 *Monthly Magazine* bears striking similarity to Brown's stated fictional principles, suggesting, if not his direct indebtedness to Hays's essay, at least their mutual indebtedness to Godwin. In Hays's view,

> [t]he business of familiar narrative should be to describe life and manners in real or probable situations, to delineate the human mind in its endless varieties, to develope the heart, to paint the passions, to trace the springs of action, to interest the imagination, exercise the affections, and awaken the powers of the mind. A good novel ought to be subservient to the purposes of truth and philosophy[.] . . . The language of the novelist should be simple, unaffected, perspicuous, yet energetic, touching, and impressive. It is not necessary that we should be able to deduce from a novel, a formal and didactic moral; it is sufficient if it has a tendency to raise the mind by elevated sentiments, to warm the heart with generous affections, to enlarge our views, or to increase our stock of useful knowledge. A more effectual lesson might perhaps be deduced from tracing the pernicious consequences of an erroneous judgment, a wrong step, an imprudent action, an indulged and intemperate affection, than in painting chimerical perfection and visionary excellence, which rarely, if ever, existed.

Hays's chief example of this form of authorship was, predictably, the "author of Caleb Williams."[39] Brown and Smith had corresponded about Hays's 1796 novel *Memoirs of Emma Courtney*, and they likely encountered this essay as well, as they were careful readers of the *Monthly Magazine*.[40] Hays's description fits both the agitated style and the utilitarian rationale Brown hoped to copy in his own career as a novelist, which began within months of this essay's publication.

This understanding of literature's ability to carry philosophical conviction helps to explain club members' enthusiastic dissemination of Jacobin texts among family and friends. Such choices had more at stake than mere literary taste. What people chose to read carried philosophical and political implications of the highest order. Members who styled themselves "philosophers" and embraced Godwinianism as an alternative to Christianity set about to convert male and female relatives and friends alike, though with various degrees of transparency about their motives. Though Smith defended *Political Justice* to Theodore Dwight in part as compatible with the metaphysics of Dwight's grandfather, Jonathan Edwards (whom Godwin indeed cites on certain points), he appears to have been more enthusiastic about the possibility that Godwin could win over "the votaries of Jesus" to "our Philosophy."[41] Smith gave copies of *Political Justice* and *Caleb Williams* to Mrs. Tracy, to his sisters, and to his friend Idea Strong, along with books by Bage and Inchbald. He was even willing to enlist believers in his cause; he had given the sermons of Joseph Fawcett, a minister with Godwinian leanings, to his parents and to Susan Tracy. "I would sustain [you] by my principles, & protect [you] by my counsels," Smith wrote to his sister Abigail to accompany copies of *Caleb Williams* and his own *Edwin and Angelina*.[42] Along with Godwin, Smith wanted to believe that the reception of truth was necessary, inevitable, and that the appropriately conditioned mind would receive the forcible impressions of truth without resistance.

British Jacobins and the Politics of American Reading

Unlike most British writing of the late 1790s, in which Jacobin and anti-Jacobin positions were starkly demarcated, the writings of Friendly Club members (Brown and Dunlap in particular) have been characterized as both Jacobin and anti-Jacobin, Jeffersonian and Federalist, radical and conservative.[43] Part of the problem critics face in arguing for or against the "radical" character of Brown's writing lies in the different areas—politics, religion, class, sexuality—to which scholars look for evidence of "radicalism." If the term refers above all to democratic efforts to broaden the public sphere and to resist political aristocracy, the Friendly Club's record is mixed. The broadening they desired had less to do with extending rights to common people than with an ide-ology of natural aristocracy that rewarded intellectual merit and chal-lenged power bases like hereditary wealth and the clergy. "It is in the Political part of his work, that this writer is most exposed to the charge of fancifullness," Smith wrote of *Political Justice* in his long letter to Theodore Dwight; in letters to other friends he took specific exception to Godwin's criticisms of the American "executive" or presidency. "We are not yet, even in America," he wrote to Idea Strong, "sufficiently instructed to bear a purely democratical government."[44] The union Smith embodied of moderate Federalism and religious skepticism has precipitated mixed readings of the club's politics; in their own time it allowed members on one hand to shore up the social privileges of class and gender and on the other to challenge some entrenched forms of cultural authority.[45]

One challenge in seeking to answer questions about the group's radicalism, especially in relation to a chronology of their reception of British Jacobin writing, stems from a lack of documentary evidence. Smith's diary, which contains such a careful account of his reading and the group's discussions, ends with his death in September 1798; William Dunlap's volumes from 1799 to 1806 are lost. In the absence of a firm date for the group's reception of Godwin's *Memoirs* of Mary Wollstone-craft, and given the fact that Brown's works like *Alcuin* and *Ormond* have both been read in contradictory terms—as among the most radi-cal expressions of feminist argument in the early republic or as evidence of Brown's supposed turn toward anti-Jacobinism and Federalism—the task of placing these writings in a history of the group's reading is more difficult than critics have credited.[46]

The available sources indicate that religion and gender, rather than local or national politics, were key points in the group's attraction to the New Philosophy. Reading the memoir of a man interred by the French Jacobins, for example, Smith seized on and translated a description of "a New Religion" the prisoners had invented on rational principles, as well as the memoir's account of the Girondist martyr Madame Ro-land, whose "energy & virtue," Smith thought, placed her "character, in my eyes, far above that of any woman who I now recollect to have become celebrated in the history of nations."[47] Smith recommended the memoir to Brown along with Dumarsais's *Analyse de la Religion chrestienne; Essay sue le Prejuges contenante l'apologie de la philosophe,* "the fount whence the Philosophers of the New School have drawn their delightful, vivifying, & invigorating, waters; the work which most deserves to be the Manual of the *little children of Truth.*"[48]

Members like Smith, who believed fiercely in "the right to think"[49] and in the possibilities of collaborative inquiry into self-knowledge, assented to Wollstonecraft's proposition that men and women shared equally such capacity for rational development. Smith hoped the "children of Truth" would include his family members, especially his sisters. "Women," he wrote to his youngest sister, Fanny, "are formed for something nobler than merely to be wives & mothers." In the same letter he exhorted her to cultivate "the attributes of a moral being, of which to think yourself is one of the first." His exhortations to "think [of] yourself" as a "moral being" constituted Smith's way of discouraging dependence on Christian foundations for morality.

If resistance to religious authority and traditional gender roles (especially regarding education) were the two points on which the group most identified with British Jacobin writers, these were also two areas on which cultural and political conservatives focused much of their reactionary rhetoric. Just as they featured in British anti-Jacobin writing as stereotypes of romantic radicals, especially after 1798, Godwin and Wollstonecraft suffered the wrath of American conservatives. Following suggestions from Robison and Barruel that women were chief targets of the Illuminati conspiracy, both for their capacity to exert female influence and to reproduce the order,[50] Timothy Dwight argued in his orations that the infidel philosophers who led the Illuminati aimed to make American women into "bawd[s]" and "strumpet[s]," and to induct them into a "promiscuous and universal concubinage."[51] By the end of the century Godwin and Wollstonecraft—jointly the embodiment of religious and sexual radicalism for conservatives—were even accused by American conservatives of being actual members of the Illuminati.[52]

"Seducting Suppositions":
Gender and the Scene of Conversation in Alcuin

The provocative views on religion and gender that drew club members to European radicals also drove Brown's first wave of fictional output in the late 1790s. These issues find an especially strong place in the composition and publication of *Alcuin* in 1797–98; in several other pieces published in the Philadelphia *Weekly Magazine;* in *Wieland,* which took up most of Brown's summer and early fall in 1798; and in *Ormond,* which was composed in New York in December 1798 and published in January 1799. They even characterize his two "late" and much-maligned domestic novels, *Clara Howard* and *Jane Talbot* (both 1801), which also take up religion, gender, and Jacobinism in important ways.[53] Only yellow fever (in the serialized opening to *Arthur Mervyn* and other sketches published in Watters's magazine in 1798) and somnambulism (in the lost manuscript for his first completed novel, *Sky-Walk* and in 1799's *Edgar Huntly*) can compete with controversial debates on religion and gender for space in Brown's early productions. Of these works from his first year of intense literary production, *Wieland* is most preoccupied with religion, and though it betrays Brown's interest in gender debates, as in the Wieland siblings' equal access to education and Clara's determination to manage her own property, gender in *Wieland* does not enjoy the prominent attention given to it either in the earlier *Alcuin* or in the later *Ormond,* where explicit discussions of women's education and social status take center stage. Although they do so in ways that aim to vindicate women in general and Wollstonecraft in particular, these books also offer insight, perhaps unexpectedly, both into the homosocial constitution of the club's conversational space and into gender politics in the new American republic.

One of the most debated topics in Europe and America in the 1790s, women's rights had been the subject of popular discussion in the United States even before the publication of Wollstonecraft's *Vindication of the Rights of Woman.* Still, if Wollstonecraft's book merely "expressed what a larger public was already experiencing or was willing to hear," in its wake Americans could hardly bring up the topic without reference to her thinking and, eventually, to her biography.[54] *Vindication's* circulation—as an import, in four separate American editions, and in excerpts in several American magazines—helped to increase discussion of women's education and participation in public life. Together with increasing literacy rates and growing urban populations, Wollstonecraft's book helped create a new "woman-centered" print public, in which "Americans discussed and debated women's familial, social, economic, and political roles."[55]

Susan Tracy's comments on Wollstonecraft, written in January 1794

and transcribed by Smith in his diary almost two years later, anticipate several of the topics that Brown would emphasize in *Alcuin* and
Ormond; Wollstonecraft's "proposed amendments in the Education of
Women" constitute her chief concern. Tracy agrees that women should
study science and also values Wollstonecraft's arguments for women's
entrance into the professions. Women would make good merchants, she
wrote, and are even capable of the "courage & fortitude" necessary to be
surgeons. They are not often given a chance to manage property or to
learn law, she acknowledges, but there is no reason they could not. Like
men, women differ individually in temperament. Tracy also falls back,
like Wollstonecraft herself, on religious justifications for her feminism
and may have been comforted by the work's pious tone. "Is there danger in enlightening the understanding of Woman," Tracy asks her correspondent, but raises this question particularly "as it respects practical
religion, & the great duties we all owe to God's Family on earth?" Even
if the limitations she places on the "practical" applications of an enlightened woman's "understanding" seem at first to narrow the possibilities for
women's public utility, the final phrase of her question suggests a confidence that female improvement is a matter of universal importance.

   If questions about women's rights and intellectual capacity were
never far from the club's reading and conversation, they were carried
on, among some members at least, without Susan Tracy's or even Wollstonecraft's piety. As readers, club members encountered feminist issues in *Hermsprong*'s reform agenda; in Holcroft's *Anna St. Ives;* in the
works of Elizabeth Inchbald, Helen Maria Williams, Erasmus Darwin,
and Mary Hays, as well as in French writing by Condorcet and Madame Roland, all writers whose publications were eagerly read by these
and other Americans. In the months surrounding *Alcuin*'s composition, the topic seems to have heated up significantly in Anglo-American culture. In August 1796 and a year later, in the fall of 1797, Smith
worked on his own utopian scheme, perhaps spurred on by Brown's
work-in-progress. Smith's plan included women's equal inclusion in a
state-sponsored educational system (at least up to the university level),
even though it clearly excluded them from political office.[56] Brown
had already completed a significant portion of *Alcuin* when the group
began its enthusiastic reading, in the spring and summer of 1797, of
Mary Hays's novel *Memoirs of Emma Courtney* (1796), but there can be
little doubt that its subject matter, including a critique of women's education, resonated with Brown. Hays had also published several essays

on women's intellectual capacity in the *Monthly Magazine*, which club members read and discussed regularly within months of each issue's publication in London.[57]

Brown's engagement with the cultural conversation on women's rights in the spring of 1798 with *Alcuin* meant something quite different than it would have even a few years earlier, even if most Americans were not yet aware of the scandalous contents of Godwin's posthumous *Memoirs* of his wife.[58] By the time Brown's dialogue was published, the anti-Jacobin publishing establishment in Britain had begun its crusades against the New Philosophy, which either unsexed women, critics claimed, or made them sexually licentious. By the summer of 1798, anti-Illuminati orators and pamphleteers were paying special attention to questions of gender in their assault on the alleged conspiracy (though they were not yet invoking in print Wollstonecraft's sexual history). Their arguments were bolstered by fiction like Hays's, which in spite of her claim that her heroine was being held up as a "warning" nevertheless portrayed a woman driven by both passion and principle to propose an extramarital affair with the man she loves. Even more damning were early word-of-mouth reports of Wollstonecraft's own illicit behavior. In the face of such rumors, support for her among Friendly Club members still ran high: "Many ridiculous stories have been propagated" about Wollstonecraft, Smith wrote to Idea Strong as early as the summer of 1796, "but there are so many fools & so many knaves interested in decrying her, that I choose not hastily to credit what they say." In any case, he reassured her, "the truth of any sentiment does not depend, in the least, on the character of him who utters it."[59]

Understanding *Alcuin, a Dialogue*, however, may require one to set aside Smith's position on this matter, inasmuch as Brown used "character"—in the sense of fictional personae—to set forth philosophical arguments. The book consists of an exchange between a young schoolteacher named Alcuin and an urban *salonierre*, the wealthy widow Mrs. Carter. The two take up topics ranging from women's participation in politics (Alcuin's opening question is "Pray, Madam, are you a federalist?") to education, marriage, and property. Mrs. Carter voices Wollstonecraft's arguments, in the dialogue's first phase, against the exclusion of "one half of mankind" from the "usefulness and honour" attendant to the "liberal professions" and maintains that the "tendency of rational improvement is to equalize conditions" between men and women. Though she believes the United States affords women more opportunity for mental progress than any other country in human history, it is still "manifest that we are hardly and unjustly treated." She sees herself as "exempt from the grosser defects of women, but by no means free from the influence of a mistaken education." As "rational beings," she believes, their options should be the same as men's.[60]

Alcuin's responses to these arguments are not antifeminist so much as they question the liberal foundations of Mrs. Carter's (and Wollstonecraft's) thought. Rather than assume that education and the professions should be accessible to both sexes, he asks whether the current state of education and professional life yields the greatest good to society. In this way, *Alcuin* stages a dialogue between Wollstonecraft and Godwin on reform, pitting against one another ideas Brown and his friends found attractive in both writers, and using the dialogue form to force reconciliation or to seek common ground where he has found discrepancy. (Brown was extraordinarily prescient in this regard, given that Godwin's *Enquirer* and his revisions to *Political Justice* were influenced, most scholars agree, by Godwin's conversations with Wollstonecraft.) If Mrs. Carter's arguments are consistent with Wollstonecraft's feminism, Alcuin's jealousy of Mrs. Carter's leisure echoes Godwin's critique, especially in *The Enquirer,* of the liberal professions. "[I]ndeed," Alcuin says, he has "but little [respect] for any profession whatever" that prioritizes "gain" over "usefulness." Instead, it would be "prudent" to determine "those advantages" that would flow from opening the professions to women before actually doing so; perhaps, he suggests, reform needs to go deeper than simply admitting women into a system that is fundamentally flawed.[61]

At this early point in the discussion, educational issues move to the fore, and Mrs. Carter scores points not only by revealing the problems of traditional gender training ("What think you of female education? Mine has been frivolous. I can make a pie, and cut out a gown") but also by forwarding Wollstonecraft's argument in favor of coeducation. Gender-segregated schooling, she declares, has created separate cultures for men and women, complete with separate languages and systems of manners, separate "ideas, maxims, and pursuits," to the effect that meaningful mixed-sex communication is stifled: "All intercourse between [the sexes] is fettered and embarrassed. On one side, all is reserve and artifice; on the other, adulation and affected humility. . . . The man must affect a disproportionate ardour; while the woman must counterfeit indifference or aversion. Her tongue has no office, but to belie the sentiments of her heart, and the dictates of her understanding."[62] Mrs. Carter's line is particularly damning, for false education has not merely prevented women from developing intellectual faculties, it actively works to undermine what feelings ("heart") and reflective capacity ("understanding") have already been cultivated. At the same time, the problem is Godwinian as well, since the situation forecloses on the possibility of sincerity. With this in mind, we can see that Mrs. Carter's concluding sentiments, which some critics have read as lackluster or "unoriginal,"[63] make perfect sense. When she concludes that friendship is essential to a true marriage, she offers more than a clichéd description of the companionate ideal, for the very possibility of mixed-sex friendship—within marriage as well as without—has been threatened, she believes, by educational programs that prevent sincere conversation between men and women.

This threat bears on *Alcuin* itself, a literary performance that both takes mixed-sex conversation as its central topic and attempts to represent such an exchange in its own form. In representing a conversational situation described by its participants as fundamentally problematic, Brown would seem to benefit from the possibilities afforded for fictional characters to model an ideal type of conversation between the sexes. As one critic has pointed out, as much as *Alcuin* is about women's rights, it also models "a specific kind of conversation in mixed company," an alternate "salon society" that complements the all-male Friendly Club.[64] In *Alcuin*'s third part, which remained unpublished in Brown's lifetime, Alcuin resumes the conversation by reporting on a visit he claims to have made to a utopian society that did not acknowledge sexual distinction. More utopian even than this "paradise of women," though, the dialogue forwards the notion that educational reform may make professional life and marriage compatible with men's and women's mutual participation in the republic of intellect, where a widow and an impoverished schoolteacher could actually rise to prominence by putting their abilities to the service of the larger society.

"Conversation" itself takes center stage in the dialogue. In the several pages of exposition that preface the actual exchange between Alcuin and Mrs. Carter, Alcuin provides extended commentary on the social setting, including his initial fears that the degree and style of performance required by genteel parlor society will preclude his participation. Mrs. Carter's apartment, which she keeps for her brother, a physician, serves as "a sort of rendezvous of persons of different ages and condi-

tions, but respectable for their talents and virtues." The "instructive society" sought out by these young intellectuals, however, remains bound
by social conventions of politeness, gentility, and the period's oratorical culture. "[C]onversation," as Alcuin puts it, "is a *scene.*" His anxiety
about social artifice suggests that the blend of instruction and rational
entertainment offered by Mrs. Carter's coterie exists in tension with
the demands of appropriate fashion and poise; its conversation may not
be as "unfettered" as he imagines. These requirements almost discour-
age him from attending her lyceum: "I looked at my unpowdered locks,
my worsted stockings, and my pewter buckles. I bethought me of my
embarrassed air, and my uncouth gait. I pondered the superciliousness
of wealth and talents, the awfulness of flowing muslin, the mighty task
of hitting on a right movement at entrance, and a right posture in sitting, and on the perplexing mysteries of tea-table decorum."[65]

Importantly, Alcuin's anxieties are explicitly gendered; if at first his
hesitancy stems from "the pride of poverty" and "the bashfulness of
inexperience," his catalog of reservations also suggests a simultaneous
discomfort with looking at women's suggestively covered bodies (the
muslin gowns seem "awful," perhaps, for what they both disclose and
suggest to the imagination) and with being onstage himself (his performance anxiety regarding oratorical posture). Unaccustomed, it seems,
to a social and intellectual sphere under female government—an educational situation that is the inverse of his schoolroom, where he spends
"[e]ight hours of the twenty-four" enforcing rote learning—Alcuin
finds Mrs. Carter's mixed-sex tea-table, with its "careless and unfettered," "abrupt and sententious," "fugitive and brilliant, and sometimes
copious and declamatory" conversation to be a mystery, albeit one that
eventually overcomes his hesitations and claims his attention on repeated occasions.[66]

At this point, instead of simply modeling ideal intellectual interactions between men and women, the dialogue begins to suggest that
mixed-sex conversation may prove difficult to dissociate from what
Mrs. Carter eventually calls "the sexual distinction"—that is, from
physiological differences between the sexes. From Alcuin's point of
view, the bodily mysteries thinly veiled by muslin line up with the mysteries of tea-table ritual and, ultimately, present a topic that the promiscuous constitution of the conversation requires, under principles of
politeness, to remain uncommented upon. One critic makes a similar
point by identifying in *Alcuin* "a slippage between two adjacent literary

genres: the philosophic dialogue and the seduction narrative."[67] This generic ambivalence comes into focus, tellingly, when the conversation between Alcuin and Mrs. Carter turns to the difference between mind and body. The possibilities for mental development, according to Alcuin, are "the same" regardless of sex, because "the sexes are equal" in terms of "the principle of thought"; however, he argues, the body has been universally recognized to be the seat of "the sexual distinction," and "[w]e all know," Alcuin puts it suggestively, "what is the final cause of this distinction."

Here Alcuin asserts universal knowledge as a way to maintain a euphemism. Although the word "cause" remains ambiguous—it is not clear whether he means that sexual reproduction is the reason for this distinction, or merely the consequence of it—everyone knows, he seems to say, that sexual intercourse propagates the species, and so no need exists to talk about the subject aloud. Nevertheless, the question does resurface, in the dialogue's third part, which circulated privately among club members and their larger social circle but remained unpublished until it appeared in William Dunlap's 1815 biography of Brown. Part III establishes, among other things, that Alcuin has an easier time broaching such tough subjects with other men rather than with women; in order to imagine a utopian society without sexual distinction, Alcuin fantasizes about a conversation with another man in which he has the freedom to explore such ideas. Even though Alcuin's interlocutor during his visit to the imaginary society is male, when their discussion arrives at the subject of sexual knowledge, Alcuin stops short of relaying this portion of their conversation to Mrs. Carter. "It may not be proper" to continue, he suggests. "This is a topic on which, strange to tell, we cannot discourse in the same terms before every audience." Perhaps he should write it down for her, since "decorum would not perhaps forbid you to read, but it prohibits you from hearing." Mrs. Carter, however, will have nothing of this double standard. What she reads she may as well hear: "There are many things improper to be uttered, or written, or to be read, or listened to, but the impropriety methinks must adhere to the sentiments themselves, and not result of the condition of the author or his audience." Nevertheless, she allows him to refrain from relating the details on sex among the utopians, and Alcuin's failure to push his account to its conclusion seems an uncanny parallel to Brown's failure to see the sequel through to the press, presumably because he and Smith considered the treatment too risqué.

If the issue of sexual content in polite conversation goes unremarked for the remainder of the dialogue, one explanation for Alcuin's reluctance to breach conversational decorum may be found back in the earlier, published portion. Toward the end of part II, when sex becomes the topic of conversation, Alcuin abruptly concludes his first conversation with Mrs. Carter by both acknowledging his sexual arousal and leaving its details concealed. "When I reflect on the equality of mind" between the sexes, he confesses,

> and attend to the feelings which are roused in my bosom by the presence
> of accomplished and lovely women; by the mere graces of their exterior,
> even when the magic of their voice sleeps, and the eloquence of eyes is
> mute, and, for the reality of these feelings, if politeness did not forbid,
> I might quote the experience of the present moment—I am irresistibly
> induced to believe that of the two sexes, yours is, on the whole, the su-
> perior.[68]

Three things seem particularly worthy of comment here. The first is Alcuin's tendency to reveal as much as he conceals (he discloses his arousal by their exchange only to disavow its appropriateness as a topic of conversation), which is in part, I think, what allows one to identify in *Alcuin* elements of the seduction tale. Second, Alcuin makes this disavowal in the name of "politeness," which prevents him from spelling out the details of his arousal beyond the suggestion, a few lines later, that it prevents him from "reason[ing] dispassionately on this subject." And third, Alcuin's ability to slide so effortlessly from encomia to "the equality of mind" that distinguishes "accomplished and lovely women"—terms whose parallel placement within the sentence in which they appear would seem to suggest they should be taken as synonymous—into a list of "the mere graces of their exterior."

Alcuin has, in other words, elided the question of Mrs. Carter's intellectual capacity by focusing on his own sexual attraction to her in terms that conflate intellectual interest with sexual preoccupation. (We do not learn whether the attraction is mutual, but Brown suggests elsewhere—in Clara's initial encounter with Carwin in *Wieland*, for example—that women's sexual arousal by male interlocutors poses similar challenges to conversation.) Alcuin follows his semiconfession of his sexual feelings for Mrs. Carter with a declaration that the arousal he experiences in her presence is "impossible to feel for one of our own sex." The failure of mixed-sex conversation in *Alcuin* can be seen then to have roots simultaneously in idealized fraternity and in a form of homosexual panic. And while the idea that men in the late eighteenth century could not be sexually aroused by same-sex conversation is belied at every turn in familiar letters that testify to the erotic bonds of friendship, this seems a curious but important argument to have emerged, in the late 1790s, in a dialogue on "the rights of women" written by a member of a group that welcomed Wollstonecraft's ideas but that apparently never considered admitting women as members. As one critic has argued, "*Alcuin* gains coherence if one understands that Alcuin and Mrs. Carter are pursuing different ideological agendas." Hers is aligned with "the plight of women" and his with "impoverished intellectuals." It may be correct to assert that this division results from Brown's "divided loyalties," but the dialogue also accurately represents a style of mixed-sex conversation that was still difficult in the mid-1790s.[69]

Alcuin's keen interest in education and its formal and thematic emphasis on debate and conversation suggest its proximity to Godwin's *Enquirer,* which Brown read during the same months he was composing the dialogue. Taking education as an overarching focus, Godwin presented the collection of essays "not as *dicta,* but as the materials of thinking."[70] This notion—that writers could offer, rather than specific solutions to social problems, a set of materials to encourage debate among readers, and that dialogue itself would promote social progress—anticipates social formations like the club or even like the larger mixed-sex circles in which members participated as the likely setting of literary reception. When Smith was testing the waters for Brown's new work, he read it aloud both to the club and to mixed-sex audiences of friends to gauge the potential response. Even if these settings constituted an ideal audience formation to receive Brown's dialogue, they also seem to have raised or at least acknowledged specific problems of mixed-sex society. Based, perhaps, on such test readings, Smith and Brown decided not to publish the dialogue's continuation, with its portrait of a sexless society.[71]

Ormond *and the Fate of Wollstonecraftian Feminism in America*

When Brown returned to these topics in *Ormond,* less than a year after *Alcuin* was published, he produced a dystopian counternarrative to *Alcuin*'s unpublished "paradise of women." The novel opens in New York, where Stephen Dudley, a merchant who lives in comfort with his unnamed wife and his daughter, Constantia, loses his fortune to a con-

fidence man, leaving him helpless before merciless creditors. Humili-
ated, Dudley takes his family to Philadelphia, where they change their
family name and start a new life. A new set of disasters arises: Mrs.
Dudley's death, Dudley's sudden blindness, and Philadelphia's 1793 yellow fever epidemic come in quick succession. Constantia, pushed to the
novel's fore by these events, faces an even more severe trial when she
encounters the megalomaniacal Ormond, who like Ludloe in *Memoirs of Carwin* turns out to be an international revolutionary radical
with purported connections to "an adventurous and visionary sect" of
schemers. Ormond, sexually aroused by Constantia's intellectual abilities, abandons his superficial mistress and attempts to turn Constantia's
rationalism against her, to seduce her by force of mind. When this fails
he resorts to more traditional gothic fare: he arranges her father's murder, imprisons her in a country mansion, and threatens her with rape,
murder, and necrophilia. Somewhat miraculously, through a "desperate" and "random" blow with a penknife, Constantia kills her attacker
and eventually relocates to Europe with her lifelong friend—and the
novel's narrator—Sophia Courtland.[72]

Publicity for *Ormond* promised that it would engage recent events of
global consequence, and indeed the novel invokes the French Revolution at several key moments, though obliquely.[73] Many critics have read
the novel as reactionary to such events, and (similar to readings that
posit *Wieland* and *Memoirs of Carwin* as politically conservative) often
take for a starting point the implication that Ormond is a Godwinian
and an Illuminatus. From this view, Constantia's rationalist education
renders her vulnerable to a nearly successful seduction and makes her
story a cautionary tale against the dangers of adopting Wollstonecraftian ideals. Other critics read Constantia as a feminist heroine and
discern a more progressive political agenda on Brown's part. Yet another set of influential readings suggests a more conflicted combination
in the novel of reactionary anxieties and radical principles.[74] Another
critic has recently argued that *Ormond* maintains a "commitment to
some form of feminism," perhaps even "a homosocial, feminist utopia-
nism," even as it seeks to correct "Wollstonecraft's overinvestment in
reason and abstract principle, and even in manliness and heterosexual-
ity."[75] On this view, the novel's sensational climax, in which Constantia
murders Ormond in self-defense, "refuses the chivalric, heterosocial
fantasies of antijacobin literature," though this critic also designates
Ormond as Godwinian and the novel as anti-Jacobin.

Such a reading assumes that *Ormond* responds to the controversy generated by the 1798 publication of Godwin's *Memoirs* of Wollstonecraft. But even if this chronology of reception and production is accurate, the novel certainly was not recognized in such terms by the anti-Jacobin establishment in England. The *Antijacobin Review* saw *Ormond* as filled with "disgusting and pernicious nonsense," including an implied defense of suicide in Mr. Dudley's temporary temptation to take his own life when he loses his fortune. The review denounced Brown's second published novel as a product of "the brain of phrenzy ... the effusions of a pragmatic enthusiast!" and its author as "a madheaded metaphysician!"[76] If *Ormond* cannot be so easily classified as anti-Jacobin, other meanings available at the time of its initial publication and transatlantic reception need to be more fully discerned.

Ormond emerged directly from a nexus of Friendly Club discussions of education, gender, religion, and politeness. It tests—and ultimately vindicates—many of the club's foundational tenets, in particular its members' confidence in the efficacy of women's education and improvement. First and foremost a novel about female education, *Ormond* takes up the same issues and arguments Brown dealt with in *Alcuin*. At the same time, the novel develops *Alcuin*'s response to other ideas associated with British Jacobins and in doing so helps to illuminate some of the contradictions that plague the Friendly Club's commitment to Wollstonecraftian feminism, especially the group's failure to create a gender-inclusive club culture. Though *Ormond* invokes Godwinian keywords at crucial moments—most significantly in Ormond's attempt to seduce Constantia in part by invoking Godwin's arguments against marriage—the novel is populated more obviously by a series of female characters who illustrate different models of experience and education, with specific reference to arguments on education put forward in Wollstonecraft's *Vindication of the Rights of Woman*. Structured on a series of seduction stories in which Constantia's virtue and her enlightened education are put to the test, the novel contrasts Alcuin's acknowledgment that both decorum and sexual arousal inhibit his ability to converse with Mrs. Carter. In *Ormond,* the titular villain actually uses conversation's rational and sexual appeal as his primary avenues toward seduction.

Brown's dystopian portrait of perverted rationalism should not be misunderstood as either a simplistic repudiation of positions he entertained in *Alcuin* or as a sign that in the fall of 1798 he suddenly found his cultural politics dramatically transformed. As were Alcuin's and Mrs. Carter's, Constantia's views in many regards—with important exceptions, such as her opinions about marriage—are alternately Wollstonecraftian and Godwinian, most often a combination of the two. She has been educated by her father in a manner consistent with Wollstonecraft's recommendations; her "ardent thirst of knowledge," which follows on her father's similar desires, is gratified by "meditation and converse" with him, as well as by "books and the pen."[77] Compare this description to *Alcuin*'s paradise of women, where "the same method of education is pursued with regard to both sexes," based on multiple "avenues [to] knowledge": "Conversations, books, instruments, specimens of the productions of art and nature, haunts of meditation, and public halls, liberal propensities and leisure . . . within the reach of all."[78] Poverty and gender prevent Constantia from full use of these resources, but her education clearly surpasses many women's, including *Alcuin*'s Mrs. Carter. Aiming to prevent Constantia from merely becoming "alluring and voluptuous," Stephen Dudley attempts to help her become "eloquent and wise" by teaching her Tacitus and Milton instead of Petrarch and Racine, and physical science and philosophy of mind—Newton and Hartley—instead of music or drawing. "These accomplishments," we are told, "tended to render her superior to the rest of women."[79]

Central to Constantia's education, and among its most pleasurable fruits, are the same social habits that were central to the Friendly Club: conversation, correspondence, reading, and friendship itself. Conversation, as Constantia's "chief employment," offered her "benefits of the highest value" as her father taught her about "the moral history of mankind" based on his youthful observations of Italian landscapes and revolutions. Constantia also takes "intellectual amusement" in her "uninterrupted correspondence" with her friend Sophia, which is apparently how the latter has the intimate knowledge necessary to narrate the novel. So, too, is Constantia the subject of correspondence among friends, as the narrative structure also bears out: *Ormond* is framed as one enormous letter from Sophia Courtland to the mysterious I. E. Rosenberg, who lives in Germany but is for some reason "deeply interested" in Constantia's fate as well as in "[s]ociety and manners" in the United States more generally.[80]

The parallel between Constantia's intellectual habits and the Friendly Club's preoccupations implies that the novel asks not only what will come of equal access to education but also, as in *Alcuin*,

whether mixed-sex society can function on the same principles as seg-
regated company. Idealized habits of unrestrained conversation apparently have their dangers in mixed company, as Constantia's mind is
precisely what makes her attractive to Ormond. The sexual excitement
generated by his conversation apparently renders her, in turn, vulnerable to his attempts at seduction. Brown contrasts Constantia with
Ormond's original victim of seduction, his mistress Helena Clewes, a
textbook example of Wollstonecraft's arguments against typical female
education. The narrative takes pains to point out that Helena is not
merely "silly or ignorant"—not the sort of fallen woman who has been
corrupted by reading novels, in other words. Rather, her "understanding bore no disadvantageous comparison with the majority of her sex."
Her problems are systemic. Whereas Constantia has been educated
to be "eloquent and wise," all of Helena's training has been focused
on singing: "Her voice was thrilling and melodious, and her utterance
clear and distinct," but her talents have been "calculated to excite emotions more voluptuous than dignified." Helena has none of Constantia's
ability to discern men's character by "exercis[ing] her judgment," and
so she is an easy target not only for Ormond but also for Constantia's
reformist impulses; Helena's "defects" make Constantia eager to "assist
her in repairing [the] deplorable error" of her education. Unfortunately
for Helena, Ormond has become infatuated with Constantia. Rejecting Constantia's advice that he marry Helena, Ormond abandons his
mistress instead, precipitating her suicide.[81]

Helena stands and falls both as a representative of traditional femi-
ninity and as a figure of friendship's failure, suggesting that the ill effects
of a faulty female education include obstacles to same-sex friendship as
well as to mixed-sex conversation. Though Constantia has received an
ideal education, she constantly fails to find the friendship she so desires.
In spite of Sophia's prior indication that Constantia's letters to her were
unremitting, she later locates Constantia's loneliness in the "distance"
that separates Constantia and Sophia, which "forbade communication"
and so increased Constantia's eagerness to meet someone "congenial
with her principles, sex, and age." If Helena offers one example of the
potential to fill this void—albeit a friendship that ultimately fails—the
second possibility arrives in the form of a mysterious woman "whose
person and face instantly arrested [her] attention." Like Constantia's,
we are told, the stranger's "aspect was heroic and contemplative" rather
than "seduc[tive]," and that she appeared to be someone in whom "the

female was absorbed . . . in the rational creature." Her appearance seems to confirm Constantia's intuition, on first hearing stories about the newcomer, that this might finally be someone who will "prove worthy of her love."[82]

In this newcomer, Martinette de Beauvais, the novel offers another model of female experience and education, as well as another possibility for friendship to flourish. In a synopsis of her life story that takes up two chapters of the novel—relayed in a conversational style that "denoted large experience, vigorous faculties, and masculine attainments"—she describes her own education as "conducted on the justest principles," one that resembles Constantia's, with the exception that her understanding of events in Europe appears to flow from "a better means of information than books." A child of mixed nationalities and parents who perpetually traveled, Martinette describes herself as "a girl, prompt, diligent, inquisitive," possessed of "versatile curiosity and flexible organs." When her parents died she was placed in an Italian seminary under a lascivious priest. Martinette works the priest's perverse interest to her advantage by letting him teach her in "metaphysics and geometry," including "the newest doctrines respecting matter and mind." Her greater education comes not only through book learning but also experience, when she escapes from Father Bartoli and becomes the traveling companion of a wealthy woman, a situation that allows "[n]ew avenues to knowledge, by converse with mankind and with books, and by the survey of new scenes." Her experience expands significantly when she falls in love with a young adventurer and "political enthusiast" who "proposed no other end of his existence than the acquisition of virtue and knowledge." Together they emigrate to America to fight in the Revolutionary War against the British; her husband dies in a British prison, and Martinette carries her revolutionary fervor with her to France, where she numbers herself among the Girondists in the Revolution there. Like Constantia, Martinette has "panted after . . . friendship," though unlike Constantia she pined even more for "liberty"; ultimately, friendship, like marriage—following the death of her husband the revolutionary—is something Martinette feels compelled to "sacrifice" in order to keep her "liberty inviolate."[83]

Martinette, like Helena, presents not only a potential object for Constantia's affection (though like Helena she removes herself suddenly from the scene, ending the possibility that she will become intimate with Constantia) but also the occasion to reflect on the effects of a particular model of female education. Where Helena had only been allowed to cultivate ornamental qualities, Martinette, like Constantia, had received a solid scientific and philosophical education. Unlike Constantia's, her education is augmented by travel, observation, and participation in major world events, a proximity to revolution that Constantia envies. Early on we learn that Constantia's father has taught her that the "most precious materials of the moral history of mankind are derived from the revolutions of Italy"; later, after her initial sight of Martinette but before they are intimately acquainted, she fantasizes that this woman somehow maintained personal access "to the actors in the great theatre of Europe." The scope of Martinette's experience makes Constantia self-conscious of "her own slender acquirements," a "humiliation" that is compounded when Martinette reveals her personal intimacy with Volney and other philosophes and Enlightenment literary celebrities.[84]

Martinette's military history raises the issue of gender ideology. During Martinette's elaboration on her revolutionary activities, Constantia recoils in revulsion when her new friend confesses to have volunteered for a potential suicide mission, reminiscent of Charlotte Corday's notorious assassination of Marat only a few years earlier. With no visible "symptoms of disgust or horror" Martinette details other bloody scenes in which she participated, including the murder of thirteen officers, two of whom were former lovers who had renounced their allegiance to the Revolution. When Constantia interjects, "But a woman—how can the heart of women be inured to the shedding of blood?" Martinette reminds her that women have the "capacity to reason and infer," that they, like men, are subject to "the influence of habit." Caught up in the torrent of revolution, she tells Constantia, she "felt as if imbued by a soul that was a stranger to the sexual distinction."[85] Whereas Constantia had initially been attracted to Martinette for her proximity to events of the French Revolution, here she confronts a tendency to romanticize revolution (one apparently shared by her father) without a clear understanding of the toll its violence can take.

Though on one hand Martinette resembles the Amazonian figures who were staples of anti-Jacobin fiction,[86] she also prefigures Constantia's own capacity for violence in the novel's conclusion. Constantia's self-defense markedly contrasts an earlier experience, when she was attacked by would-be rapists in Philadelphia and was incapable of protecting herself. If anti-Jacobins pointed to violent women as a sign of

the corruption bred by the French Revolution and by Wollstonecraftian feminism alike, Brown vindicates Constantia's "masculine attainments" and uses her capacity for violent self-defense as an argument
against gender essentialism.[87]

Such a vindication of Wollstonecraft may still be perfectly consistent, of course, with the idea that the novel stages an anti-Godwinian
critique. Taking this approach, at least one critic reads the novel as a
rewriting of Godwin's *Memoirs,* with Constantia a surrogate for Wollstonecraft herself, and Ormond a combination of Imlay and Godwin,
seducers who appealed to Wollstonecraft's radicalism and rationalism
to get what they wanted sexually.[88] Yet even if evidence existed that
Brown had read the *Memoirs* by the time he wrote *Ormond,* such an
interpretation is difficult to support. Contrary to the almost universal
assumption of the novel's critics, Brown insists that Ormond is neither an Illuminatus nor a Godwinian. Brown does invoke the Illuminati conspiracy scare (again, without naming it), but primarily to set
Ormond apart from the sect. While in Berlin, we are told, Ormond
encountered a group that closely resembles the Illuminati: "schemers
and reasoners who aimed at the new-modelling of the world, and the
subversion of all that has hitherto been conceived elementary and fundamental in the constitution of man and of government . . . reformers
[who] had secretly united to break down the military and monarchical
fabric of German policy." But he also met others, who "more wisely,
had devoted their secret efforts, not to overturn, but to build; that, for
this end, they embraced an exploring and colonizing project." *These* are
the visionaries Ormond joins, which seems a clear indication that readers were to understand him as something other than an Illuminatus.[89]
Though Sophia initially identifies Ormond's cabal as "wiser" than the
Illuminati, she describes it as even more shrouded in secrecy. Sophia
suspects that, like successive waves of French revolutionaries, Ormond
is implicated in schemes of "pillage and murder" that have been "engrafted on systems of all-embracing and self-oblivious benevolence,"
and that "the good of mankind is professed to be pursued with bonds
of association and covenants of secrecy." His society turned against its
own ideals, deformed by the requirements of secrecy.[90]

Far from forming an anti-Jacobin critique, this criticism of Ormond's secret society resembles Godwin's arguments against political
associations in *Political Justice,* a recognition that unsettles the mistaken
assumption that Ormond represents Godwin. This faulty conflation

depends on Sophia's use of Godwinian keywords in her description of Ormond's principles: "sincerity," "necessity," his "enthusiast[ic]" "disbelief" in religion, as well as his antimatrimonialism.[91] On a close reading, however, none of these apparent signs of Ormond's presumed Godwinianism holds up; though he professes that his chief "boast was his sincerity," Ormond proves duplicitous at every turn, assuming disguises and, like Carwin, "imitating the voices and gestures of others." Sophia herself makes plain the contrast between his profession of sincerity and his actual tendency toward concealment when she contrasts his appearances with his "actions."[92] Likewise, in contrast to Godwin's emphasis on virtue as universal benevolence, Ormond consistently promotes his own self-interest over the happiness of others, and where Godwin is essentially optimistic (his doctrine of necessity, after all, provides the foundation for a theory of inevitable human progress), Ormond's brand of necessitarianism leads only to nihilism. In contrast to the villains in most anti-Jacobin novels, in which "[e]ach chapter . . . provide[d] a crucible in which the . . . new philosophy could be . . . found not merely wanting, but productive of the most conspicuous evils,"[93] Ormond claims in some places to hold certain Godwinian beliefs but clearly counters these claims with his own actions. Even his arguments against marriage are less principled than they are instrumental in his effort to seduce Constantia.

The topic of antimatrimonialism, in fact, suggests the clearest divergence between Ormond's opinions and Godwin's. In *Political Justice*, in an appendix to his discussion of property, Godwin infamously laid out his arguments against marriage on four specific points: he argued that there was no guarantee that two people's "inclinations and wishes" would coincide over time (an idea related to Godwin's principal critique of promises more generally); he saw the notion that one must have a life companion as itself the result of "cowardice, and not of fortitude" or self-determination; he believed that marriages were often contracted before the parties were mature enough to make such a binding decision; and, finally, he viewed marriage as "the most odious of all monopolies," whereby men dominate women by removing them from the social, sexual, and even conversational markets. (In fact, it is conversation and not sexual intercourse that seems to be Godwin's chief attraction to women "of accomplishment"; in his ideal state, if several men are attracted to one powerful woman, "[w]e may all enjoy her conversation; and we shall be wise enough to consider the sensual intercourse as a very trivial object,"[94] a litmus test almost all of Brown's characters, male and female, seem to fail.)

Although Godwin's revised treatment of marriage attracted the attention of Smith and his colleagues, this aspect of his work was not a point on which they recorded major disagreement, and while Godwin softened his opposition to marriage over time, the gist of his critique remained in later editions. One of Godwin's chief additions in later editions concerns friendship's role in marriage, in terms that recall Mrs. Carter's conclusion to *Alcuin,* which was composed after Brown had access to the second edition. "Friendship," Godwin wrote there, "if by friendship we understand that affection for an individual which is measured singly by what we know of his worth, is one of the most exquisite gratifications, perhaps one of the most improving exercises of a rational mind. Friendship therefore may be expected to come to the aid of the sexual intercourse to refine its grossness and increase its delight."[95]

There can be little doubt that Brown had *Political Justice* on hand when he sketched Ormond's character; as many have pointed out, some phrases are so close as to suggest an "exogenous context."[96] And yet Ormond's "matrimonial tenets" (which Sophia describes as "harsh and repulsive") are not Godwin's at all. "Marriage is absurd," Ormond believes, because of "the general and incurable imperfection of the female character." Though he does base some of his opposition on the Godwinian objection to promises, Ormond uses this approach only to justify his abandonment of Helena. Constantia does not cure Ormond's misogyny; he simply declares a changed opinion to further his seduction efforts. Sophia seems ambiguous on this point: "He was suddenly changed," she says, "from being one of the calumniators of the female sex, to one of its warmest eulogists."[97] But she emphasizes verbal expressions here rather than actual beliefs; in any case she has already warned that Ormond's words are worthless.

Constantia's own views on marriage are more consistently Godwinian, though with crucial amendment. Early in the novel, before Ormond's introduction, Constantia recognizes the implications of the permanence of marriage "vows of irrevocable affection and obedience." She elaborates on this reasoning later in the novel, again using the language of Godwin's critique of promises; vowing to remain faithful in marriage would be to "abdicate the use of her own understanding" in determining when "obedience" was unreasonable or when and where "conjugal privileges" were to be admitted. She objects as well to the laws of coverture, which will deprive her of "the product of her own labor" as well as her "personal freedom": "So far from possessing property, she herself would become the property of another." Although her father's views on marriage are even more "flexible" than Constantia's (to him, "the marriage vows were . . . formal and unmeaning"), she does not abandon the institution altogether but resolves to wait for seven years before she will seriously entertain suitors.[98]

When Ormond, after abandoning Helena, steps up his efforts to seduce Constantia, he does so by appealing to her rational disposition and her intellectual habits. Specifically, he engages her in conversation: "The conversation of Ormond was an inexhaustible fund" that offered "a more plenteous influx of knowledge was produced than could have resulted from any other source." His conversation is so engaging, apparently, that Constantia forgets his behavior toward Helena. Constantia does not know, however, that Ormond's conversation is anything but unrestrained, just as his boast of sincerity actually covers his tendency to deceive. Under the pretension of unfolding to her his utopian schemes, he draws her into his confidence; to her, he celebrates sincerity as a virtue, but secretly he lays a plan "suited to the character of this lady": "He challenged her to confute his principles, and promised a candid audience and profound consideration to her arguments." He designed not to entertain her views but to undermine them: "She was unaware that, if he were unable to effect a change in her creed, he was determined to adopt a system of imposture—to assume the guise of a convert to her doctrines, and appear as devout as herself in his notions of the sanctity of marriage."[99]

Such duplicity could not be more un-Godwinian, a point underscored by Brown's decision to use Constantia, not Ormond, to voice several of Godwin's arguments against marriage and promises. Constantia's respect for marriage rests, significantly, on principles other than religious ones. Sophia chastises her friend on this point and claims that her lack of religious training leaves her "unguarded" against Ormond.[100] Constantia's views on religion are largely unformed. "[H]er habits rather than her opinions were undevout," Sophia complains, which suggests that she had some form of religious belief but no orthodox behavior. When "called to meditate on this subject, . . . her perceptions were vague and obscure." She is not an atheist; she simply has not thought much about religion, which was "regarded by her, not with disbelief, but with absolute indifference." The "modes of study and reflection" prescribed for her by her father have "unfitted her" for discussion of religious matters. Neither is her father an atheist: "Mr. Dudley was an adherent to what he conceived to be true religion. No man was more passionate in his eulogy of his own form of devotion and belief, or in his invectives against atheistical dogmas." Rather, he believes that children are too young and impressionable for religious indoctrination. Her father's training reflects his attitudes toward institutional Christianity, however. Even as he "accustom[s] her to the accuracy of geometrical deduction," he wants her to recognize "those evils that have flowed, in all ages, from mistaken piety."[101] Private piety has private consequences, he believes, and should be entered into with mature deliberation and reasoning; "mistaken piety" has material and social consequences that run counter to the happiness of humankind.

One needs only to think of the elder and younger Wielands for evidence. As in *Wieland*, religion in *Ormond* more often than not wears a sinister face, though its manifestations and effects are more various here than in the earlier novel. Martinette's tutelage under Father Bartoli offers a chief example. Religious dangers appear briefly in relation to Sophia as well. Far and away the novel's most devout character, Sophia reveals that her mother had developed a religious mania following a rapid conversion from a profligate lifestyle to Methodism under the influence of a revivalist. Unable to think on her former crimes, she goes insane. Sophia, however, marches forward under religion's banner. She not only believes in "divine superintendence," but is "mindful of the claims upon my gratitude and service which pertain to my God." She elaborates on her beliefs in the language of religious testimonial: "I know that all physical and moral agents are merely instrumental to the purpose that he wills; but, though the great Author of being and felicity must not be forgotten, it is neither possible nor just to overlook the claims upon our love with which our fellow-beings are invested."[102]

Sophia outlines her faith in explicit contrast not only to Ormond's but to Constantia's principles: Sophia believes that Constantia's lack of religious indoctrination has made her "a stranger to the felicity and excellence flowing from religion." Ormond, on the other hand, was an "enthusias[t]" in his "disbelief": "The universe was to him a series of events connected by an undesigning and inscrutable necessity, and an assemblage of forms to which no beginning or end can be conceived."[103] Because Sophia's voice so fully controls the novel's narrative, the temptation exists to read her own religious confession as the novel's moral.

Such a view, however, fails to bring to *Ormond* one of *Alcuin*'s most useful lessons: that Brown's philosophical dialogues cannot be disconnected from the question of character. He follows up this implication in *Ormond* with Sophia's ironic and perhaps disingenuous observation about the novel's villain: "Ormond was imperfectly known. What knowledge [Constantia] had gained flowed chiefly from his own lips, and was therefore unattended with certainty."[104] Sophia's warning can be read as ironic if we apply it as well to her monopolistic role as narrator. Not only does she evade the fact that everything *we* know about Ormond flows from her pen, she also seems oblivious to the possible countercharge that everything we know about *her* is "unattended with certainty" for similar reasons. Like Ormond, Sophia is not always consistent with her self-characterization. Her faith, for example, may be more fragile than she makes it seem; when she reviews Constantia's story at the novel's climax, she sees more "malignity in her fate" than she does "human agency . . . merely subservient to a divine purpose," an observation that leads her "into fits of accusation and impiety."[105] Sophia loses her monopoly on moralizing if we contrast this failure of resolution with Constantia's behavior in the finale; primed by Martinette's example of female fortitude, she protects herself by killing her attacker. In the end, Constantia makes good without God; we hear no more religious didacticism from Sophia in the novel's conclusion, where didactic morals typically find their final expression. Instead the novel leaves us to view her faith as the manifestation of character, the particular seat of her motivation, rather than as the story's inexorable lesson to be learned.

From this vantage point, the "education of Constantia Dudley" takes the laurels, as Ormond rightly predicts it will. Ormond labors to convince her (this time drawing on terms largely amenable to her Wollstonecraftian feminism) that to be the victim of rape is no crime, and that his intended assault will not affect her "claims to human approbation and divine applause," nor will it diminish the "testimony of approving conscience."[106] Ormond hopes this realization will make her a willing victim; when she vows to take her own life rather than lose "a greater good," he corrects her faulty thinking again:

> "Poor Constantia!" replied Ormond, in a tone of contempt; "so thou
> preferrest thy imaginary honour to life! To escape this injury without
> a name or substance, without connection with the past or future, with-

out contamination of thy purity or thraldom of thy will, thou wilt kill thyself; put an end to thy activity in virtue's cause: rob thy friend of her solace, the world of thy beneficence, thyself of being and pleasure?"[107]

Constantia appears to accept this reasoning so far as it extends to the preference of life as a potential victim of rape over death by suicide to prevent such a fate. So she kills him in self-defense, though she afterward uses the defense that her actions were necessary to prevent "an evil worse than death."[108]

Regarding the novel within contemporary legal and moral discourse on the topic of rape, one recent critic has argued that Ormond "represents the intended rape as a final test" of Constantia's rationality: "[B]ecause rape does not involve her consent, it cannot cause her harm."[109] Ormond's reasoning on rape and reputation puts him in line not only with *Clarissa*'s Lovelace or *Anna St. Ives*'s more comedic villain, Coke Clifton, but also with Mary Wollstonecraft. Consistent with his character, however, Ormond mouths rational truths for self-serving and pernicious ends. Constantia resists not his reasoning about reputation or responsibility but his failure to recognize the difference between her "purity" and her "will." By raping her he would not violate her purity, true. He would, however, fail to recognize that she has a will of her own and that to violate her will would be criminal.[110]

The novel's climax does not place Constantia's violence on a plane with Ormond or Martinette, whose violent acts work toward more questionable ends, so much as it refutes sentimental assumptions about gender, such as those that earlier led Constantia to ask Martinette, "[H]ow can the heart of women be inured to the shedding of blood?" In doing so, Brown undermines the assumptions on which conservative moralists felt the need to protect their wives and daughters from Wollstonecraft's ideas (and her fate), to enact a patriarchal retrenchment in the name of protecting American women from becoming "concubines of the Illuminati."[111] Instead, *Ormond* shares Wollstonecraft's belief that in order for women to play a full part and to benefit from the march of intellectual progress they would have to overcome the limitations imposed by a false sense of decorum and by essentialist notions of gender, whether they posit women as incapable of violence or of intellectual improvement.

Mixed-Sex Friendship and Conversation in the Friendly Club's Larger Circle

The tension between sincerity and politeness, particularly in mixed-sex settings, was a recurring theme not only in club members' writings but also in their social circles. As they took up these issues in their *Monthly Magazine,* in Brown's novels, and in mixed-sex society, the group's response to British radicalism and feminism—for some members qualified, but for others surprisingly persistent—remained central to their thought into the first few years of the new century.

The continued attention they gave Mary Wollstonecraft offers the best example of this enduring interest. One response to Wollstonecraft in the group's *Monthly Magazine, and American Review* seems especially pertinent given the author's decision to frame his comments as a mixed-sex parlor conversation, reminiscent in some ways of *Alcuin.* In September 1800, a regular columnist who wrote as "the Speculatist"—the prose style seems very much like Brown's—provided an account of a debate among young New Yorkers on Wollstonecraft's legacy. The account, which the Speculatist attributes to a friend, illustrates the contention that "speech" is "eternally prostituted," in polite conversation, "to the purposes of falsehood." In the essay's conversational scene, a married man who is something of a "gallant" asks a young woman, Lucy, her opinion on Wollstonecraft's *Vindication.* Two other young people are present, a young gentleman and a young woman, both of strong intellectual talents. Lucy, "whose powers were by no means adequate to an accurate decision on a question of some importance," glances around the room to ascertain the group's expectations. Fearing she will falter, the intellectual young gentleman volunteers for her that though Wollstonecraft may be criticized for style, abruptness, and lack of method, surely Lucy "must be charmed with the intrepid spirit of our authoress in stepping forth the champion of her sexes' [*sic*] rights—in combating a thousand prejudices long held sacred—in opposing reason to the force and number of her antagonists, and pointing the way to the luminous regions of truth and science."[112]

Lucy parrots this opinion, the implication clear that she is nothing more than a stage actress who has had "her part assigned her." The married gallant, having set a trap, retorts that "Miss Woolstonecraft [*sic*] has not treated her subject with so much delicacy as is requisite" and that "she talks about things which you ladies are not accustomed to mention, and calls them by their names without ceremony." When he asks the more intelligent young woman, Maria, her opinion on "our female philosopher," Maria balks and in "the name of delicacy" chooses, in the narrator's view, to "debase the purity of her mind with a false-hood, rather than to incur the terrible opprobrium of indelicacy." She responds that she has not read Wollstonecraft thoroughly but has read enough to be deterred from finishing, although she ultimately "should never qualify herself to judge correctly of so coarse a performance." Of the four people involved in the conversation, the Speculatist's friend as-serts, only one told the truth: the young gentleman who assigned Lucy her part and who was clearly disappointed by Maria's timidity (his eyes had been "fixed upon her with a thrilling expression of tender solici-tude; but instantly averted with evident chagrin" at her answer).[113]

The sketch helps to frame the Friendly Club's complicated, some-times convoluted, response to the challenge of maintaining sincerity in mixed-sex society. Its moral is clearly that "delicacy" and "gallantry"—gendered sides of the same polite coin—lead to indirection and false-hood. The narrator seems less conscious of the ease with which the young gentleman, the anecdote's center of moral and intellectual grav-ity, so easily took it upon himself to tell Lucy what she "must" think, almost as if he were doing her a favor. Two things seem significant about this scenario. First, that the sketch, at such a late date, allows such a spirited defense of Wollstonecraft to stand on the record. And second, that it places its hero—a young and earnest intellectual like club members themselves—in such a pedagogical and judgmental po-sition in relation to his female peers. The sketch reveals a conflicted approach to mixed-sex conversation; on one hand, it continues to ideal-ize truth-telling without consequence and intellectual equality between men and women, while on the other it assumes that in the current state of society, educated young men will preside over women as teachers and judges rather than meet them on equal terms as peers.

As much as civic and intellectual life, for middle-class men in the late-eighteenth-century city, was dominated by fraternal association, mixed-sex social settings like the one represented in the Speculatist's sketch took up significant amounts of club members' time, energy, and theoretical consideration. On the latter score, especially as such set-tings related to understandings of friendship, several approaches seem to have coexisted for club members, some of which were highly in-fluenced by ideas about gender like the ones Brown explored in his novels. Much of the mixed-sex society these men enjoyed took place in the homes of married members, such as Kent, Dunlap, or the Woolseys, or other married friends and relatives, such as William Johnson's brothers, erstwhile club members. But before and after Smith's death, the younger, single members of the club participated in heterosocial friendship circles that encouraged consideration of the possibilities for mixed-sex intellectual association and provided opportunities to put into practice some of the radical doctrines on women's improvement they found so compelling in their reading of Wollstonecraft and other British Jacobins. The daily interactions of a mixed-sex social and intellectual world—including walks, teas, dinner parties, parlor performances, and group readings of recently published novels and poetry—constitute a complementary intellectual culture to the one represented by club meetings proper;[114] this heterosocial culture, however, as the sketch also suggests, remained one in which boundaries of politeness were sometimes tested but where conversational convention was difficult to breach without consequence.

If Brown's *Alcuin* suggested one approach to mixed-sex intellectual culture, in which "the sexual distinction" and the erotics of conversation posed an obstacle to unrestrained conversation, other models for heterosocial society coexisted among club members. Like *Alcuin*, Smith's diary entries on this topic suggest a dichotomy not so much between public and private spheres but between sensuality and delicacy. Unlike *Alcuin*, however, Smith suggests at one point that friendship between men runs the risk of greater sensuality than mixed-sex friendships. In his autobiographical sketch of his childhood to age 11, Smith follows a lamentation on the "debas[ing]" influence of a male schoolmate, who introduced him to masturbation and other "low pursuits of vice,"[115] with a rhapsody to the "[p]recious friendship!" he sustained with a young girl named Hannah Jones, "now a wife, & a mother," whose friendship, he claims, "subsists to this day." Smith's description of this friendship, which resulted from the "fortunate" "mixture of sexes," in some respects resembles his portraits of male friendships, including a comparison of their friendship to the love between David and Jonathan, though he frames Jones as one in a series of little "mistress[es]" and also refers to their friendship as "amour." Still, the absence of the "sensuality" that arises in same-sex friendships leads Smith to conclude that mixed-sex "intercourse," at least at a "tender age," is more "refined & delicate than [friendship] between two of the same sex."[116]

In one of Brown's later literary magazines, William Dunlap put forth a different view. In response to an essay on friendship written by Brown's future brother-in-law, John Blair Linn,[117] Dunlap declared mixed-sex friendship an oxymoron. "The attachment between persons of the same sex, is called friendship," Dunlap maintained, "and perhaps can, strictly speaking, be said only to exist in relation to persons of the same sex." This argument required "[f]riendship between man and woman" to be labeled "love"; following an account of several romantic schoolboy "attachments," Dunlap declares that on his marriage, "the passion of friendship was swallowed up in the passion of love."[118]

Dunlap, of course, continued long after his marriage to participate in all-male associations and to offer expressions of friendship to Brown, Smith, and others (though perhaps without the romantic effusion that characterizes some contemporary exchanges). But his autobiographical argument helps to explain Smith's fears, expressed in his 1795 accounting of the club's brief history to that point, about the impact of marriage on fraternal association. Writing to one recently married male friend, Smith speculates that the event has "rendered life precious to you, by . . . more endearing sentiments" than those among same-sex friends, but wonders nevertheless about "changes of opinion," "revolution of ideas," or other "variation of character" that may also have resulted. "Do you view things, with different eyes[?]" he wonders.

> [A]nd tho' you love your friends as much as ever, love them from different principles? How are pleasures and how science, affected by this change? The flame of Love often outblazes the rays of Ambition; Connubial Joy saddens the once-pleasant calls of Friendship; & paternal care extinguishes the lamp of benevolent Investigation.

Smith describes here the limited resources of an economy of emotion implicit in romantic friendship. Placing energies in heterosexual romance, marriage, and parenthood depreciates other "pleasures," like science, ambition, and friendship itself, thereby jeopardizing friendship's contributions to "Investigation." Though he goes on to reassure this correspondent that he assumes the opposite—that his friend's governing passions have likely been "expanded & ennobled" by his change of situation—Smith remains ambivalent as he seeks reassurance: "Shall I be disappointed? Ay—*shall* I?"[119]

Young New Yorkers of the Friendly Club's acquaintance participated in a vibrant heterosocial intellectual culture, and though such so-

ciety contrasted somewhat with the all-male public world of civic associations as well as with the private gender-exclusive enclave of Friendly
Club meetings themselves, younger club members at the turn of the
century made concerted efforts to flout convention, even if these efforts
never resulted in women's admission to the club.[120] Two overlapping
waves of female friends were particularly important to club members
from the mid-1790s until just after the turn of the century. The first
gathered in the home of Mrs. Maria Morton, the widow of a Revolutionary-era merchant, whose eligible and intelligent daughters, Susan
and Margaret, were favorite female associates of the group until Susan
moved to Boston on her marriage to Josiah Quincy. The second, which
overlapped with the coterie that had assembled earlier at Mrs. Morton's
home, included a trio of young women—Maria Nicholson, Margaret
Bayard, and Maria Templeton—almost a decade younger than Smith,
Brown, and Johnson, and gathered at Templeton's family home as well
as the home of Bayard's married brother. Though their acquaintance
with Friendly Club members began prior to Smith's death, and though
it would eventually lead, a decade later, to the marriage of William
Johnson to Maria Templeton in 1809, this second circle cohered most
fully between early 1799 and the fall of 1800, when Margaret Bayard
married the Jeffersonian editor Samuel Harrison Smith and the couple
relocated to the nation's new capital in the District of Columbia.

Among both sets of mixed-sex friends, and in letters to female
friends and family members more generally, a style of intellectual exchange prevailed in which Friendly Club members positioned themselves as interlocutors or teachers of their female associates. Eliza Susan
Morton Quincy's later recollection of the advantageous "friendship of
Mr. William Johnson and Dr. Elihu Hubbard Smith of Connecticut,"
who were "distinguished for literature and accomplishments," described
a "course in history" supervised by the former, a point that underscores
not only the intellectual nature but the pedagogical character of the
relationship these young men established in relation to female acquaintances.[121]

This pedagogical stance—similar to the relationship the British
writer Mary Hays described with a series of male intellectuals, including Godwin, who served as her "monitors"—was a self-conscious effort to compensate for deficiencies in female education. Although such
relationships were at times described as designed for mutual improvement, they also seem to have been viewed, especially by the young men,

as a means to create ideal female companions if not future wives. "If we can mutually assist each other, in the acquisition of knowledge & virtue," Smith wrote to his friend Idea Strong, "we cannot commence [a correspondence] too speedily." Yet in the same letter Smith strikes a tutelary tone that makes plain the dynamics implicit in such an exchange. "You are not one of those unthinking girls," he assures Strong:

> [Y]our mind is not of that trifling cast, to be alive only to the rumors of the day, & the flatteries of fools. . . . To some young women the seriousness of this letter, & the importance attributed to epistolary communications, would be sufficient to terrify them from attempting to write again—especially to him who could address them such a letter. With you, or I have dreadfully deceived myself—the case will be different. You will be pleased to turn your time to some account; & to derive instruction from a source whence the mass of letter-writers expect only the gratification of vain & foolish imaginations, or a curiosity equally idle, unproductive, & contemptible. . . . You will, gladly, enter on the pursuit of those inquiries which lead to the discovery of the truths most important to be rightly known & comprehended, by rational beings.[122]

In spite of the language of mutual assistance, privately Smith characterized this letter as designed "to set her on reflecting—which is as much as I can expect to do." By providing occasion for reflection, he saw himself as doing more than offering rote instruction; he was facilitating a process that would result in her independence of thought. Nevertheless, he clearly saw himself—at some points even with older women like Susan Tracy, who had literally been his teacher when he was a child—in the position of instructor. In a letter of "counsel" and "instruct[ion]" to his sister Abby on her engagement, Smith suggests that such instruction would make young women into intellectual companions for their husbands. "It is not enough that your society be tolerable to him," Smith wrote to Abby, "you must labour to induce him to seek it, in preference to all others; or if this be not possible, at least, to make it pleasant to him, when society of a more illustrious character cannot be obtained." Women should also make themselves viable consultants on the education of their children. If wives apply themselves "to the cultivation of general literature" while their husbands labor at a profession, he wrote, "[w]ith what pleasure will he throw aside, at proper seasons, the ponderous volumes of the Law, to discuss with you, if you are qualified to take a part in the discussion, the more interesting themes which morals, policy, history, poesy & criticism, unceasingly offer to the consideration of youthful, virtuous, & glowing minds!"[123]

Club members' differing approaches to mixed-sex friendship straddled old and new orders of relations between the sexes. Though Dunlap was only five years older than Brown and three years older than Johnson, his marital status placed him in a different position from his friends when it came to heterosocial affairs. By contrast, the younger, unmarried Friendly Club members appeared to have struck up friendships with unmarried young women that sometimes may have doubled as courtship rituals but at other times seem simply designed for intellectual improvement and emotional fulfillment.[124] This description characterizes the mixed-sex circle surrounding Bayard, Templeton, and Nicholson, initiated just prior to Smith's death.[125] Documented primarily in letters from Bayard to her fiancé, Samuel Harrison Smith, who was living in Philadelphia, this circle strove to violate conventions of politeness in its efforts to establish an intellectual environment that ignored sexual distinction. Bayard and her friends formed relationships with Brown, Johnson, the Millers, Mitchill, and a young lawyer named Anthony Bleecker, who according to several accounts joined the Friendly Club following Smith's death; over time the friendships with Brown, Johnson, and Bleecker solidified most. In spite of explicit aims to defy social convention, these friendships were never free from challenges posed by polite society, especially in the wake of an anti-Jacobin backlash against Wollstonecraft, Godwin, Darwin, and other favorite writers.

Politeness worked both ways in mixed-sex conversation. According to Bayard, when she initially met Elihu Smith in the summer of 1798, the conventions of polite conversation required her participation when she might otherwise have been too shy to speak; the group's "conversation," as it progressed, "became more & more pleasing & nothing but the rules of politeness induced me from time to time to address myself to the others . . . & make it general." But certain conversational styles—displaying too much "warmth," for example—were deemed unbecoming in women, and some topics were typically placed off limits for women or for men when they were in mixed company.[126] According to her characterization of the young men, Brown and Johnson in particular expressed the belief that ideal conversation among the sexes would take place in pairs or small groups rather than in "a large & promiscuous company."[127] Bayard also recognized her male friends' aim to expand female abilities and found their company to stimulate her desire to learn. "The other afternoon at Dr. Mitchel's," she records on one occasion, "I could scarcely comprehend a sentence & lost some fine strokes of wit, because I know nothing about chemistry," a situation that prompted her resolution to improve in "the acquisition of knowledge."[128]

The kind of social interactions Bayard and her friends established with Friendly Club members drew disapproving comments from some, who apparently felt that Bayard was slighting her absent fiancé by socializing too intimately with other young men. Bayard informed one "lady, who spoke to me on this subject" that her relationship with male friends was "free from . . . gallantry" and was instead "the intercourse of rational beings," but the social judgment underscored her observation that "few young persons of different sexes meet frequently to converse on serious & general topics; their intercourse [more typically] consists of an interchange of frivolous & unmeaning compliments."[129] The type of intellectual conversation this circle cultivated was, in her view, highly extraordinary, even "strange," Bayard wrote to her fiancé, "& Maria & I talk of it with surprise. Intimacy, frequent intercourse; unreserved communication of ideas, cool, disinterested friendship & the parties [consisting of] young people of different sexes—Ah my dear friend, if you were but one of this circle, how happy should I be."[130]

At least initially, Bayard resisted some principles held by her new friends, which she characterized as "theories" that were opposed both to real-life experience and to her own Christian principles.[131] On similar grounds she wrote disapprovingly of Mary Hays's *Memoirs of Emma Courtney*[132] and responded enthusiastically to Robison's *Proofs of a Conspiracy*, which she saw as rightly countering the "spirit of innovation & inquiry,"[133] reactions that were diametrically opposed to the Friendly Club's reception of the same works. Drawing on Robison's language, she categorized Brown, Johnson, Bleecker, and Mitchill as members of the "certain class of men" a book like *Proofs of a Conspiracy* sought to oppose, those who are "more about, what may be, than about what is."[134] If she regarded their visionary principles with suspicion, however, their intellectual fervor kept her engaged. "After conversation either with Mr. Brown or Jonson [*sic*]," she wrote her fiancé, "I find my ideas better arranged, my mind more active & vigorous—Indeed the pleasure[s] of conversation have become so valuable, that I do not feel sufficient interest in the usual intercourse of society."[135]

Bayard's sense of distance from social convention appears to have been heightened by her notion that her behavior was transgressive, that it ran against the grain of social fashion. The exhilaration of this feminist self-fashioning extended from intellectual realms to social behavior. Bayard self-consciously followed Mary Wollstonecraft's example, for instance, in traveling on one occasion without an escort. After taking a stage to Brunswick, unaccompanied by a male companion, Bayard exulted in the sense of liberation afforded by her defiance of convention: "New views open before me, I am no longer content to humbly tread the paths which custom has worn in the road of life; I am for trying my strength to tread new ones; there are many obstacles in my way; the most formidable to me is the censure or ridicule of my own sex, most of whom are fright'd if they do anything not authorized by custom."[136] If other women were put off by her behavior, her fiancé was titillated by this "enterprising spirit," he wrote, noting Wollstonecraft's infamy for similar breaches of decorum. Indeed, Samuel Smith's letters constantly admonish her to increase her education and her independence, specifically by maintaining her friendships with the Friendly Club circle.

Though members held different views on the nature of mixed-sex friendship and the possibilities for unrestricted conversation in mixed-sex society, and though the circle that included Bayard appears to have challenged polite conventions on some occasions, some indications exist that the print-based republic of letters, represented in part by the group's *Monthly Magazine*, offered them a more immediate and less problematic arena for women's participation in intellectual culture. When, on one occasion, Bayard read from her commonplace book to this "little circle" of men and women, whose members preferred one another's company above "any this city could afford," Brown and Johnson encouraged her to submit "several pieces" to their magazine: "If [her writing] were in print said Mr. B—Why if it were in print, interrupted Mr. J it would be admired and extolled." Though such praise "made my face glow," she told Samuel Smith, both she and Maria Templeton agreed to become contributors to the magazine.[137]

Though she had been initially put off by Brown's habits as a moral observer (and perhaps even more by the threat that what he observed might find its way into print), Bayard eventually came to feel that his probing questions and unorthodox opinions, which she had early on derided as theoretical rather than practical, were ultimately educational and entertaining; his and Johnson's "conversation," she wrote, "is various & instructive & seems to be an inexhaustible source of pleasure."[138] Moreover, it led her to cultivate an ideal of mixed-sex friendship that aspired to transcend the "sexual distinction" Brown's characters had addressed in *Alcuin;* her ideal, she wrote to Smith, would be the standard to which she would hold him in their marriage.

Defending herself against the disapprobation heaped on her for her intense friendships with these single young men, she wrote one of her most passionate letters to her future husband. "Is it not wonderful," she exulted, that some people "should suppose, that like most of my sex, I delighted in the society of men, merely because they are men, & because their attentions have been considered as flattering." Although she admits to avoiding public walks with any one of the men individually, she does not want to consider the possibility that her weekly visits from them also might have to cease. In language that recalls British Jacobin arguments, she considers the effects of "establish[ing] principles, whose tendency is the promotion of individual & general good . . . and inflexible & uniform adherence [to which] would certainly sometimes lead us to act contrary to the established customs of the world." Rejecting the importance of the world's opinion, she vaunts her lover's to the position of greatest importance, fortified by her experience of friendship with Brown, Johnson, and Bleecker but desirous that her relationship with Harrison Smith rise above the sexual distinction. "Forget that I am a woman," she implores, and even as she worries that the fantasies she describes belong more to "imagination" than to "real life," she concludes the letter, "You can make me what you please—make me then your *friend.*"[139]

Bayard's plea poignantly demonstrates the conflicted terms by which this group sought to create new models of mixed-sex friendship and to further women's education and improvement. Yet even here she assumes she will occupy a pupil's position relative to her husband's as teacher. Undoubtedly Bayard and her "four visitants" (Brown, Johnson, Bleecker, and Templeton) experienced exhilaration as they sought to apply, in a new setting unbounded by sex, the ideals of mutual inquiry and friendship by which the club had been organized. But as Bayard's letters ultimately bear witness, such experiments could result in the disapproval of polite society and still left unequal power dynamics in place; if the social form of the conversation circle occupies a key place in the professionalization of knowledge production, the experience of this mixed-sex circle suggests that women were being trained, in part, to make their future husbands' professional lives and reputations possible.

Perhaps the most interesting aspect of Bayard's account is the record she offers of a persistent sympathy for Wollstonecraft and a continued enthusiasm for Godwin, long after popular opinion had turned against these writers. Though some Friendly Club members participated in the backlash against Wollstonecraft that followed the publication of Godwin's *Memoirs,* many members of this social circle apparently remained sympathetic.[140] Bayard herself, writing in her commonplace book in February 1799, described how moved she was by the "artless manner" of Wollstonecraft's letters to Imlay, to the point that she almost forgave her violations of the laws of society, in the expectation that her own principles would prove as firm. Ultimately she finds Wollstonecraft's ideals to have failed, as signaled by her inability to maintain them against the prejudice of society; she faults Wollstonecraft for concealing her relationship with Godwin and continuing to go under the name Imlay, actions that betray a confidence in the principle of sincerity and a false fear of society's opinion. Wollstonecraft lacked "strength of judgment," Bayard concludes. "Her imagination uncontrol'd by this principle form'd theories which it adorn'd in the most seducing actions," and her subsequent actions were such that Bayard can "love & pity Mary Wollstonecraft" but she "can not respect her."[141]

If the club's extended mixed-sex circle showed some sympathy for Wollstonecraft and continued to admire her principles, if disapproving of her behavior, Brown's personal reaction to Wollstonecraft's decline appears to have been somewhat mixed. At least as he presented himself in conversation with Bayard, Brown seems to have retreated from his earlier positions on the topic of women's intellectual development, even as he encouraged her to write for his magazine and maintained his long-standing admiration of Godwin's moral philosophy. According to Bayard, she and Brown agreed that, in the present state of society, "scientific pursuits" were "useless" for women, and hence would be a waste of their time.[142] Only a month later, during a conversation on "morality," Brown told Bayard that "the Godwinian was the most perfect" system he knew. "But said he, were I to marry, I should wish for my wife to be a Christian, with this system engrafted on her. For religion would afford that sanction & authority which would enforce obedience, & those motives which encourage to perseverance." While his wife's "obedience would be to the command [of] her God," his would be "to that of my reason[;] her motives, the approbation [of] her creator, & the reward of eternal happiness, mine the approbation of men, & the pleasure arising from the discharge of duty." Such a sentiment represents a significant concession on the subjects of gender and religion at the same time he offers a surprisingly persistent endorsement of Godwin's morality.[143]

The previous summer Brown had published *Edgar Huntly*, his fourth novel, and the final one he would write in the gothic mode. In the section of the novel that includes the ghostly reminder of Huntly's failure to publish Waldegrave's heretical memoirs, Brown presented a gendered situation that prefigures these comments to Bayard. When Huntly refuses to turn over Waldegrave's letters to his dead friend's sister, he justifies the act by arguing that she is not adequately prepared to entertain the ideas the letters contain. The concern is explicitly gendered and rooted, as *Ormond* had been, in discussions of religion and education. "Thou, like others of thy sex," Huntly writes to Mary, "art unaccustomed to metaphysical refinements. Thy religion is the growth of sensibility and not of argument." Huntly refuses to make Waldegrave the "author" of his sister's fall.[144] Brown frames this exchange in such a way that the object of critique—is the problem Mary's education or Waldegrave's doctrine?—remains ill defined. By contrast, Elihu Smith, whose situation this scene echoes, had shown no similar concern for his sisters' faith; as he had with friends like Mrs. Tracy and Idea Strong, he hoped to wean them away from Christianity, though the process was gradual and he was only reluctantly open about the extent of his own departure from Christianity. But the scenario in *Edgar Huntly* recalls more than the dilemma of Elihu Smith's unpublished diary and other textual remains; it also recalls the failure of Godwin's *Memoirs*, his attempt at biographical truth-telling gone utterly wrong. Such was the ultimate fate of British Jacobinism in America. Mary Waldegrave's very name echoes Wollstonecraft's death; her character marks the grave, perhaps, of an unqualified enthusiasm for Wollstonecraftian feminism and for the possibility of radically reforming heterosocial society at the turn of the century.

Fig. 1. William Johnson, by James Sharples, Sr., 1797. Courtesy of the Cincinnati Art Museum, lent by the National Society of the Colonial Dames of America in the State of Ohio. Sharples's portrait of Johnson, like those of other Friendly Club members, demonstrates a tension between the scientific nature of physiognomical portraiture, which aimed to represent essential aspects of the sitter's character, and the performance of social status implicit in fashion decisions, such as Johnson's decision to wear his hair in a queue, powdered. (Note the excess powder on his shoulder.)

Fig. 2. Elihu Hubbard Smith, by James Sharples, Sr., 1797. Collection of the New-York Historical Society. The Society's nameplate, not visible here, memorializes Smith's friendship with the donor, David Hosack, a fellow New York City physician. Similarly, Sharples's son gave William Dunlap a "polygraphick copy" of this portrait, and descendents of Smith's relatives donated another to Yale University to memorialize his relationship to the school. These memorials deepen the emphasis on friendship and civic association implicit in the shape of the collection itself.

Fig. 3. Charles Brockden Brown, attributed to Ellen Sharples, after James Sharples, Sr., c. 1810. Courtesy of Independence National Historical Park. Brown's three-quarter face contrasts with the profiles his fellows preferred, suggesting, perhaps, a desire to complicate the portraitist's physiognomical agenda.

Fig. 4. James Kent, attributed to a member of the Sharples family (possibly Ellen), after James Sharples, Sr., c. 1798–1810. Courtesy of Independence National Historical Park. Kent had multiple sittings for Sharples portraits, one with more formal attire and powder (currently on display at the Octagon House in San Francisco, along with a separate Sharples portrait of Elizabeth Kent holding their daughter), and this one with shorter, unpowdered hair. Kent faces a different direction in each, which seem to have been intended for different exhibition contexts.

Fig. 5. Samuel Latham Mitchill, by James Sharples, Sr., 1797. Collection of the New-York Historical Society. Sharples's portrait of Mitchill, which William Dunlap considered "unlike" its subject, carries an account of personal associations in its frame and nameplate; like the Society's copy of Smith's portrait, it was donated by David Hosack. In the nineteenth century, Society collections of former and current members would come to rival most museums in the city for the extent of their portrait collections.

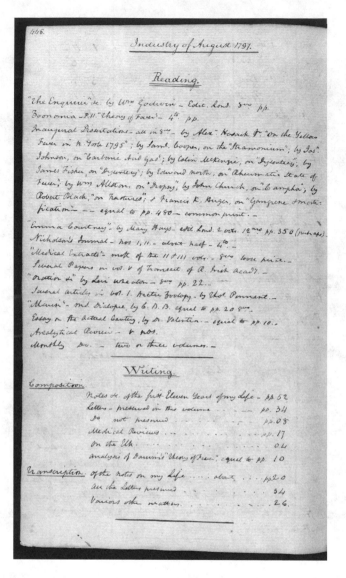

Fig. 6. E. H. Smith's "Table of Industry" for August 1797, recorded in his diary. Courtesy of the Harvey Cushing/John Hay Whitney Medical Library, Yale University. Smith's diary practice, in some ways representative of his generation, is exceptional in its meticulously detailed portrait of his circle's social and intellectual endeavors. He also used it to account for his individual productivity. His "Tables of Industry" cataloged not only what he read and wrote each month, but the number and size of the pages as well.

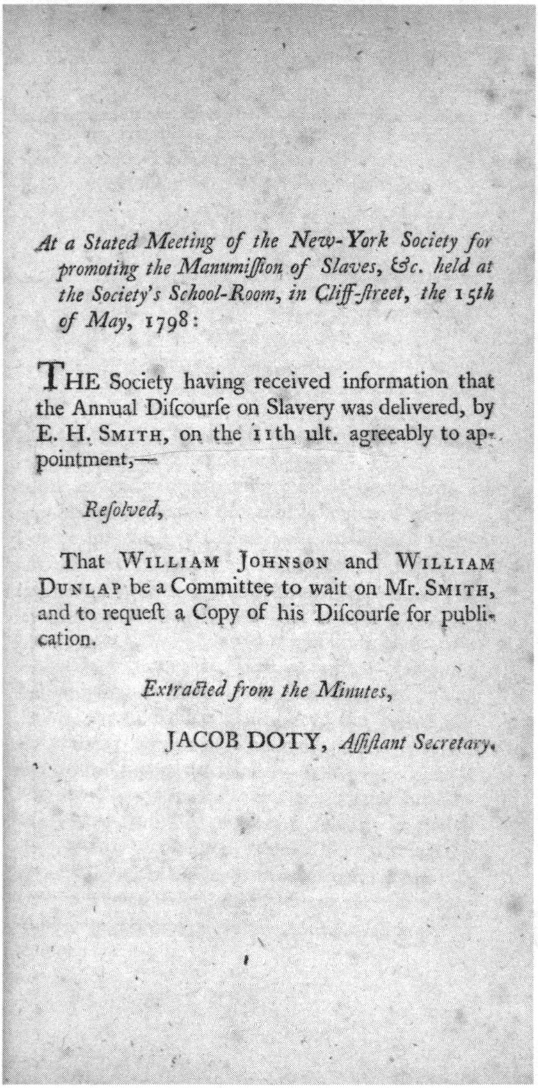

At a Stated Meeting of the New-York Society for promoting the Manumiſſion of Slaves, &c. held at the Society's School-Room, in Cliff-ſtreet, the 15th of May, 1798:

THE Society having received information that the Annual Diſcourſe on Slavery was delivered, by E. H. SMITH, on the 11th ult. agreeably to appointment,—

Reſolved,

That WILLIAM JOHNSON and WILLIAM DUNLAP be a Committee to wait on Mr. SMITH, and to requeſt a Copy of his Diſcourſe for publication.

Extracted from the Minutes,

JACOB DOTY, *Aſſiſtant Secretary.*

Fig. 7. E. H. Smith's Manumission Society Oration, delivered 11 April 1795 (inside leaf). Collection of the New-York Historical Society. Visualizing in print the formal social rituals by which such texts came into existence, published society orations functioned as public performances of friendship and voluntary association as they cultivated one's civic reputation. Here the society members designated to procure a copy of Smith's oration happen to be his Friendly Club fellows as well.

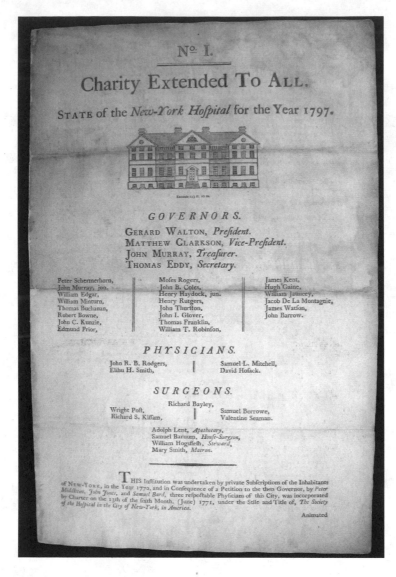

Fig. 8. *State of the New-York Hospital for the Year 1797,* title page. Courtesy of the New York Academy of Medicine Library. The first published statistical report for the hospital's activities, which appeared in the same year the *Medical Repository* was founded and was also concerned primarily with the threat of yellow fever, emphasizes the significance of civic association in the production of professional reputation. James Kent is listed among the board members, and Elihu Smith and Samuel Mitchill among the physicians. The caption at the bottom traces the institutional history of civic and professional association that resulted in the hospital's founding.

II. INDUSTRIES OF KNOWLEDGE

James Kent, Legal Knowledge, and the Politics of Print

I N William Johnson and Elihu Smith's rooms at 45 Pine Street, on Saturday evening, 30 September 1797, a rather small number of Friendly Club members—the two roommates along with Dunlap and Kent—settled into one of their liveliest discussions on record. Johnson, leading the evening's conversation, read aloud the chapter "Of Learning" from William Godwin's recently published *The Enquirer*, then turned the talk to the "utility of various kinds & modes of reading" more generally. But the ensuing discussion appears to have been dominated, uncharacteristically, by Kent, who, according to Smith's diary account of the meeting,

> recounted his late reading—criticism on the political works of Harrington, Al: Sidney, Sir T. Moore, Hobbes, Locke, Hume, Adam Smith, Sir James Stuart, Arthur Young, the Economists, Godwin—on the metaphysics of Locke, Reid, Beattie, D. Stuart, A. Smith, Hume, Godwin, Berkley, Priestley, Jonn. Edwards, R. J. Sullivan—on the improvements made in Historical Writing, not as to Style, but Manner—Historical may comprehend almost all other knowledge—Machiavel & John Adams—value of the latter's Work as a compend of political History—of the ancient writings in our City library—of Gibbon's Geo-

graphical Collections—necessity of a perfect idea of the topography of
the scene of historical relations.[1]

Caught up in this cataloging moment, Kent "tumbled over the Enquirer" (which "lay on the table," William Dunlap notes in his diary
entry for the evening)[2] "& was much pleased with it." At some point,
Dunlap read the section on priests from the essay "Of Trades and Professions," and Johnson read the section on lawyers. "Hence new discussions," Smith records, "altogether confirmatory of [Godwin's] doctrines,
as applied to in[di]viduals generally—Kent & Johnson exceptions to
the principal censure of lawyers."[3] Dunlap's diary includes the note
that Kent, at this meeting when the few religiously devout members
were not present, "remark'd that men of information were now nearly
as free from vulgar superstition or the Christian religion as they were
in the time of Cicero from the pagan superstition—all, says he, except
the literary men among the Clergy."[4]

The scene of reading—and of debates about reading's "utility"—
records a myriad of anxieties generated, for these club members and
many of their contemporaries, by transformations within the culture
of liberal professionalism, in particular by a changing relationship between reading, the social authority conveyed by professions and print,
and the concomitant movement toward prioritizing expert knowledge
and training. These anxieties throw into relief the club's relationship
to the consolidation of the early republic's institutions of knowledge
production: the publishing enterprises that grew out of club members'
professional endeavors (including literary institutions like the theater,
the novel, or the literary magazine, which Dunlap and Brown hoped
for a time could provide them with financial stability and could make
authorship itself a profession). I have labeled these institutions the early
republic's "knowledge industries," a phrase that both puns on Friendly
Club members' idealization of industry as a personal virtue and draws
attention to the ultimate goal of all their publishing projects: the dissemination of useful knowledge and professional reputation. Industries
of knowledge, as I conceptualize them, occupied sites beyond the conversational space of the club, though the scene just recounted also illustrates the relationship between the club's conversational practice and
the production of knowledge in other spaces.

James Kent's experience in New York from 1793 to 1798 offers a window onto the particular relationships this group of friends experienced

between professional consolidation and the dynamics of the rapidly expanding print culture that facilitated their participation in knowledge industries. In some ways James Kent stands apart from other club members, at least in the role the club played in furthering his career. In his case, political alliances built before he moved to the city were more immediately instrumental than the friendships he cultivated through club life. But his Friendly Club fellows offered him something other political alliances did not: a "literary life," an ideal Kent worked to make central, not marginal, to legal education in America. The club also provided him with several model attempts at joining profession with print, as well as with a set of networks already in place by which his friends attempted to distribute his printed law lectures, early attempts at a systematic approach to law that would culminate decades letter in his monumental *Commentaries on American Law*. The club also provided him with one key associate, William Johnson, who spent years as Kent's court reporter, and to whom those *Commentaries* would be dedicated.

If the Friendly Club served in part to provide a space where the specialized demands of profession did not preclude the pleasures and profits of general knowledge, Godwin again provided them with a set of ideals in this regard. As a model intellectual (what club members would have called a "philosopher"), Godwin offers the testimony of one who transcended a flawed profession (in his case the ministry) to become a professional writer, a cultural critic. Though most club members were not keen on abandoning their professions, they recognized the value of Godwin's critique. Kent, in particular, must have been charmed by Godwin's promotion of a mode of reading that so closely resembled his own. In Godwin's model, genius depended on a style of learning that placed supreme value on the interaction of one's own mind with the train of great thinkers of ages past: "Nothing . . . can be more ill founded than this imputed hostility between learning and genius." Rather, if someone wanted to "do well in any art or science," his task was first to acquaint himself with the master thinkers among his predecessors, then to take an even more "comprehensive view": "How accurately ought I to perceive the parts, or branches, as they extend themselves from the trunk, each constituting a well arranged and beautiful whole of itself, yet each dependent, for its existence and its form, upon the root by which the entire mass is sustained."[5]

Such a program resembled the one Kent had followed for several years and was the basis of his confidence that success in his profession depended on a system of accumulating general knowledge, including familiarity with several languages and the long history of Western literature. The particular branch of knowledge he and William Johnson had chosen to pursue—the study of law—depended on the "root" of broad classical learning, including familiarity with belles lettres. Kent and Johnson believed the legal profession offered the ideal arena for gathering, arranging, and exhibiting their learning, though for it to achieve this potential, they would have to guide significant efforts first to make print technologies central to the profession and then to use these technologies to secure the Americanization of the common law, the body of legal custom based on the collective wisdom of case law rather than on legislative statute.[6]

Kent and Johnson, drawing on the club's recognition of the centrality of print to the knowledge industries they hoped to shape, played a major role in this process.[7] Given the comparative success of his later career, Kent's early efforts at legal writing are brushed aside by legal historians and biographers as warm-up drills. But Kent's early career offers its own set of insights into the relationship between the literary life Kent consistently longed for and the role of print in securing the professional career that made him famous. Kent's early professional experience included participation in state politics and close association with national political leaders. On leaving Yale in 1781, he had been apprenticed by his father to Judge Egbert Benson, New York State's attorney general, and enjoyed a fleeting career upstate before suffering defeat in a congressional race in 1792. Following his congressional defeat, he relocated his young family, hoping for a more congenial intellectual, political, and social environment. Instead he found his new practice slow and the city diseased—his only child, a daughter, died from smallpox that year. Likely as a reward for Federalist loyalty, and perhaps to rescue him from financial difficulty, Columbia College's trustees (a body that included Alexander Hamilton and John Jay) named him the school's first professor of law.[8]

Kent arrived in New York City in 1793, only months before Elihu Hubbard Smith, and though he was not among the original ten members of the Friendly Club, he was invited to join early on, when some founding members began to wane in their participation. His connections to club members probably came both through networks of Yale graduates and through his participation in the city's legal circles, which included Friendly Club members William Johnson and Charles Adams, the latter of whom was admitted to the club at the same time as Kent.[9] Kent was three years older than Dunlap, eight years older than Smith and Brown, slightly more established in his career, and like Dunlap had the additional distinction of maturity that marriage conferred. These characteristics placed him in something of a senior position in the club and gave him a voice of authority. "Last evening was spent with the clubbists at K[ent]'s," writes the erstwhile law student Charles Brockden Brown on one occasion, framing Kent as prosecutor or judge: "Received from the candor of K. a severe castigation for the crimes of disputatiousness and dogmatism. Hope to profit from the lesson he taught me."[10]

If political print culture privileged anonymous publication—something Kent briefly dabbled in when he and Noah Webster collaborated under the pen name "Curtius" to defend John Jay's notorious trade treaty with the British at mid-decade—professional print culture took a very different direction. Hence Kent's publication of his introductory law lectures under his own name, which served to advance his career (gaining him his first international notice). Between his appointment to the Columbia professorship in December 1793 and the inauguration of his lectures in November 1794, Kent undertook a renewed course of reading with characteristic vigor, scouring English court reports and legal digests, and studying Bynkershoeck, Quintilian, and Cicero in original languages.[11] He then outlined nearly three dozen lectures, eleven devoted to federal law and the Constitution, and the remainder to New York's state laws. Beginning 17 November, he read two lectures a week at College Hall, at the corner of Murray Street and West Broadway, in the heart of "legal New York."[12] His audience consisted of "forty students and several other gentlemen of the city, equally distinguished for their literary accomplishments, and their zeal for the knowledge and improvement of our municipal law."[13] In Kent's mind, the study of law should not be confined to lawyers; neither should legal training separate students and practitioners from "literary accomplishment."

Kent's determination to align his career path with a transforming print culture had disappointing early results, a sign to Friendly Club members that "the literary character of our City" was not yet what they desired.[14] (The complaint anticipates club members' frustrations with other audiences, particularly in the theater.) Kent nevertheless printed the lectures, which sold for three-eighths of a dollar in New York. His friends attempted to peddle them out of state; Smith sent thirty copies to a Connecticut lawyer friend in January 1796 with instructions to "[c]onvert one or more to your own use; & dispose of the others as well as you can."[15] He also sent fifty copies to Uriah Tracy, hoping he would circulate them among fellow congressmen and others in Philadelphia.[16] Though Kent would later in life look back at these lectures as "slight and trashy productions,"[17] his friends assured him they bore the markings of genius. "I shall be grossly deceived, my brother," wrote Moss Kent shortly after receiving his copy, "if they do not introduce you to a distinguished place in the Republic of Letters & enrole your name with those of *Hume, Robertson,* & our *American Camillus* [Hamilton] as an ingenious & elegant writer."[18] Smith blamed the poor reception on New York's preoccupation with "the arts of gain" and its "neglect of elegant & useful science, of the arts of genius, taste, & society." He satirized money-grubbing senior lawyers who were too stingy to encourage their clerks to attend Kent's lectures.[19]

Still, Kent preferred the professor's rostrum and the bench, where he could read from carefully researched texts destined for print, to the more high-flying eloquence of the classical oratorical ideal, a cornerstone of legal professionalism well into the nineteenth century. Even later in his life, Kent's preference could spark derision. "I suppose Chancellor Kent could cite fifty cases to [Daniel] Webster's one on any given subject," wrote one lawyer to another, "and yet, before either court or jury, the odds in favor of Webster would be great indeed."[20] The fact aside that this comment predates the publication of Kent's famous *Commentaries,* which earned him an enormous amount of money and acclaim, this peer misses a crucial feature of Kent's exegetical strategy; in Kent's view, the temporary victories of orator over audience are less significant than the institutions of legal writing, the far-reaching potential of printed precedent.[21]

That is, Kent attempted to outweigh his audience with the sheer weight of his knowledge, printed and bound. While print has been described, in relation to early American political culture, as removing the necessity of making judges "depositaries of the law,"[22] Kent employed his strategy of extensive research, written decisions, and published reports—in short, what he called "the science of law"[23]—to make himself into just such a receptacle. His initial judicial appointments, as master of chancery in 1796 and city recorder in 1797, cemented his realization that a jurist's role was more congenial to his literary ambitions than common practice as an attorney, though the sheer pace of keeping up with both jobs (which he held in tandem) left little time for reading and writing. The jobs did "make a great deal" of money for him, he wrote his brother, but always with the goal of becoming "one of the most independent of men" in order to allow more time for reading and writing.[24]

Like Smith, Brown, and Dunlap in particular, Kent set forth his vocational self-conception in autobiographical form, writing himself into key scenes in the history of his profession. As Kent told the story of his ascension to the bench, the written "law" when he became a judge was curiously blank, a tabula rasa. Or so it appeared. "When I came to the Bench there were no reports or State precedents," he later wrote in a biographical sketch for a young lawyer who was a warm admirer.

> The opinions from the Bench were delivered *ore tenus*. We had no law of our own, and nobody knew what it was. I first introduced a thorough examination of cases and written opinions. In January, 1799, the second case reported in first Johnson's cases, of Ludlow *v.* Dale, is a sample of the earliest. The judges, when we met, all assumed that foreign sentences were only good *prima facie*. I presented and read my written opinion that they were conclusive, and they all gave up to me, and so I read it in court as it stands. This was the commencement of a new plan, and then was laid the first stone in the subsequently erected temple of our jurisprudence.[25]

In this narrative, which his contemporaries endorsed, Kent's insistence on written reports—his recognition of the importance of writing and print to the rise both of professionalism and of a native legal tradition—filled in the blank represented by "no law of our own."[26] Kent's self-history, in this paragraph, is densely packed. "Ore tenus" equals ignorance, or at least impermanence; it is extemporaneous (not based on "a thorough examination of cases") and transitory (because its "opinions" are not "written"). His rejection of this common approach, he implies, allows him to offer an authoritative legal history. Behind the printed decision, Kent reveals, lies a battle in which he came off as victor. "The judges," on one hand, whom Kent elsewhere labels "very illiterate as lawyers,"[27] harbor typical aversions to foreign precedent. Kent enters the court with researched text in hand to argue otherwise. And the sheer force of his "thorough examination," represented in his written artifact, demands their submission. Kent's victory, secured through the authority of extensive reading and printed writing, is both personal and institutional; they "gave up to *me*," an act that facilitates the erection of the "temple of our jurisprudence."[28]

Kent's most stunning exploitation of the early republic's literary culture, and the story he took most pride in telling, involved the development of written decisions and published court reporting. Kent was by no means solely responsible for these developments in the United States; as early as 1785, the same year Kent was admitted to the New York bar, the Connecticut legislature had enacted a statute requiring written opinions from judges.[29] But his storytelling matters more, his continual insistence that he brought these practices to New York's state courts, and did so in such an influential manner that his decisions as state supreme court justice and eventually as chancellor would eventually form a body of precedents on which his fellow judges and other states' courts could draw. The reputation his decisions gained allowed for both the appearance of a native legal authority and tradition, and for ensuring that common law traditions would form the heart of American jurisprudence.

Kent secured this national—even international—reputation, well before the publication of the *Commentaries*, largely through William Johnson's court reporting.[30] At thirty volumes, not including occasional digest versions, Johnson's reports, published between 1806 and 1823 (covering cases back to 1799) stand as the most extensive collaborative writing project to emerge from Friendly Club members. Johnson's role in this production involved more than simply reprinting or even reporting on Kent's decisions. "In Kent's day," one legal scholar writes, "the reporter remained a figure of great consequence—the person who selected the cases, stated the facts, summarized the views of counsel, summarized the views of those judges who gave oral opinions, and supplied annotations of his own."[31] Johnson's *Reports* secured his own professional reputation for decades. Joseph Story wrote Johnson in 1824, on the occasion of his and Kent's mutual retirement, that "your thirty volumes of Reports will form an era, not merely in the jurisprudence of New York, but of America."[32] In the public mind, Johnson was always connected to Kent; as such their friendship was the longest-lasting public remnant of Friendly Club association during club members' lifetimes.

Kent's works remained in print, read widely by law students and legal professionals, throughout the entire nineteenth century. In some ways representative of the "Federalist literary mind" of the 1790s and early 1800s, Kent's work also requires us to rethink literary-historical narratives of literary Federalism. Rather than retreating to the literary sphere represented by Joseph Dennie's *Port-Folio,* an aesthetic "counterworld to Enlightenment skepticism,"[33] Kent's career was an example of Federalist literature that did not retreat from the political public sphere or cower behind the posture of an effete "lounger."[34] Kent's writings were read long after the *Port-Folio* or the satire of the Hartford Wits had become curious artifacts for antiquarians.[35]

And yet, as Kent's early enthusiasm for Godwin would remind us, his writings tell us about much more than partisan aesthetics. In them Kent consolidated personal and professional authority and at the same time sought to extend the shelf life of the Enlightenment's definitions of literature and knowledge. Kent's simultaneous allegiance to the creation of a coherent American legal profession and commitment to a literary life broadly conceived resonates with the experience of his fellows who hoped to be philosophical members of liberal professions or, as in the case of Brown and Dunlap, who hoped to make belles lettres, the theater, novels, and print journals the site of philosophical speculation *and* vocation. In 1797 and 1798, just as political tensions within the country and between America and France began to escalate toward war, Friendly Club publishing projects moved into full swing. But the contexts for their rising professional reputations and print output—including Kent's law lectures; Dunlap's Park Theatre and early printed plays; Smith, Mitchill, and Miller's *Medical Repository;* Brown's magazine publishing and first attempts at novels—invoked contexts broader than national politics. Dunlap aimed to make the theater a tool for progressive moral education; Smith and his friends aimed to instill proper medical views and morality; and Brown aimed to do both—all in an urban setting in which civic and social authority depended, club members believed, on citizens' understandings of their political, moral, and even environmental constitutions.

⁣⁣⁣

FOUR

The Public Is in the House

William Dunlap's Park Theatre
and the Making of American Audiences

WHEN William Dunlap opened a new theater in New York in January 1798, the event represented, in a way, the culmination of five years of the Friendly Club's collaborative efforts to gain local, national, and international reputation. Dunlap had spent nearly a decade developing his craft as a playwright (he so far had ten plays to his credit) and two years as a joint manager of the Old American Company, together with the perpetually bickering rival actors, Lewis Hallam and John Hodgkinson. If the new theater's opening can be understood as a culmination of efforts, though, for club members it also signaled prospects, a singular opportunity to reach large audiences and to forward the club's moral agenda. Along with other efforts group members undertook that spring—the publication of Brown's *Alcuin;* the preparation of an American edition of Erasmus Darwin's scientific poem, *The Botanic Garden;* James Kent's appointment to the state supreme court—Dunlap's new venture embodied the group's collective ambition and its sense that members were on the cusp of the social authority they so desired. Though the new playhouse remained unfinished on opening night (the evening's original prelude piece, *All in a Bustle,* poked fun at the situation), the crowd, which one newspaper claimed was "the most overflowing house that was ever witnessed in this city," must have compensated.[1]

Decades later, the theater historian George Odell waxed romantic as he sought to capture the scene. "Something was born on the evening of January 29, 1798," he wrote, "something on which the imagination loves to dwell. I wonder how many of the actors or spectators realised that they were making history?"[2] Smith and Dunlap certainly had that sense. Smith had composed a prologue for the occasion, read on stage by the company's leading actor, John Hodgkinson, in which he aimed to inaugurate not only the new theater but an American dramatic tradition as well. He prophesied that the United States would produce performers and playwrights to rival Europe's best: "new Bettertons and Booths," "New Quins and Garricks," American versions of other celebrated actors like Pritchard, Wolfington, and Clive; he also foresaw native playwrights to rival Congreve, Jonson, Cibber, Farquhar, Steel, Cowley, Inchbald, Sheridan, Dryden, Rowe, Otway, and even "A native Holcroft, sovereign of the Stage, / To perfect morals form a future age." The only thing that would rival a homegrown Holcroft, of course, would be a "perfect Shakespere": perfect, presumably, either because he would be American, or because his philosophy would be modern.[3]

Dunlap clearly had ambitions to be, if not an American Shakespeare, then an American Holcroft, whose works he staged repeatedly throughout the 1790s. Dunlap's conception of the theater in 1798, which he shared with most of his fellow club members, was consistent with the vision of Holcroft and other Jacobin writers. Like other literary forms, he believed, drama offered "a powerful engine for the improvement of man, and . . . it only wants the directing hand of an enlightened society to make it the pure source of civilization and virtue."[4] Dunlap's circular logic—an "enlightened society" would create an enlightened stage, which would then help to generate the "civilization and virtue" that characterized an enlightened society—presages tensions that would run through his career as the new Park Theatre's manager when audiences did not always respond to the civilizing process as Dunlap and others envisioned it. Elihu Smith, outlining his poetic address for the opening night, formulated the dynamic between authors and audiences this way: "The Manager should select moral & good pieces, the Auditory should applaud & encourage them. If any thing dull, or indecent, were brought forward, it should be driven off. So all false accent, action, &c. &c. in the performance, to be discountenanced: everything proper countenanced."[5]

Charles Brockden Brown too believed that the stage offered the most "powerful mode of winning the attention, and swaying the passions of mankind," but his faith in contemporary audiences remained somewhat lower than that of his friends: "Theatres are, in themselves, capable of being converted into schools of the purest wisdom and philanthropy," he wrote in an anonymous piece in the Philadelphia *Weekly Magazine* only a few months after the Park opened in New York. "[B]ut it is too evident that, at present, popular dramas are vehicles of error and depravity, and that theatres are schools in which something very different from benevolence and justice is taught."[6] If the theater belonged in the people's hands, as Dunlap and others believed, then the people needed to be capable of shouldering that responsibility.

The relationship between authors, actors, and audiences—what Smith elsewhere called their reciprocal duties—occupied Dunlap's mind in the weeks following the theater's opening, as he composed his most ambitious play yet, a tragedy based on the story of Major John André, who was captured and executed during the American Revolution for his role in facilitating Benedict Arnold's defection to the British side. Dunlap imagined his play "impress[ing] . . . the sublime lessons of Truth and Justice upon the minds of his countrymen." He also seems to have invested the play with personal significance and selected it as his first original drama to be played in the new theater. He had conceived and even started the play years earlier but had resumed work on it in earnest the previous fall, during a visit to Boston on theater business. The recent success in Boston and New York of John Burk's drama *Bunker-Hill* (which Dunlap despised on aesthetic if not political grounds) seems to have rekindled his interest in making art from the materials of the American Revolution. While in Boston he assessed that city's efforts to produce an American literature. He purchased Royall Tyler's novel *The Algerine Captive* and Sarah Wentworth Morton's popular patriotic poems "Beacon Hill" and "Ouabi," both of which he grew to like the more he read; he also visited Bunker Hill and passed on the street "Mr. James Allen the poet, whose manuscript poem of Bunker Hill has been so often mentioned."[7] Stopping at "Attlebury" on his way home, he downed "a good dish of tea" while reviewing "Beacon Hill," when the inspiration struck him to begin composing poems to accompany John Trumbull's paintings of Revolutionary War scenes, beginning with *Death of General Warren at Bunker's Hill* (1786). He spent the rest of the trip drafting stanzas in his diary as he continued to make progress on *André*.[8]

Dunlap's personal investment in *André* shows in his decision, before the play had even been staged, to put it to press.[9] But opening night brought problems that appear to have been at least partially unforeseen. His decision to make André a tragic hero worked against him with some portions of his audience. On the play's opening night, when a fiery young American soldier, Bland, smitten with André's virtue, shows his disapproval of André's death sentence by removing his soldier's cockade from his cap and throwing it on the ground, the "veterans of the American army who were present" voiced their outrage. In response to the incident, Dunlap inserted in the preface a "sequel to the affair of the cockade," something akin to a list of errata compiled after the type has been set: General Washington forgives Bland, returns the cockade, and allows him to restore it to its rightful place in contrition. The revised sequence played in the remaining two performances, which went off without incident. But the incident leads him to offer, in his preface, which was written both after the play had debuted and after type had been set, a melodrama of American authorship, with himself as hero, and reveals a set of anxieties that seem to have countered his original confidence in the play and in his audience. "[T]he Author," he writes, referring to himself in the third person, bears responsibility for the potentially controversial decision to use "the death of Major André as the subject of a Tragedy."[10]

In the intervening years he confronted several obstacles to producing the play: "a prevailing opinion that recent events are unfit subjects for tragedy"; a fear that those who remember the actual "events expect to see them *all* recorded," and that they will fault "the poet" for "any deviation from what they remember to be fact." There were "[s]till further difficulties," he worried, to attaining "public favor." He feared that "friends of Major André (and it appears that all who knew him were his friends) will look with a jealous eye on the Poem," which takes its title character to task for "submitting to be an instrument in a transaction of treachery and deceit," though he counters by reminding them he has given André "every virtue."[11] These fears, of course, turn out to have been the wrong ones, and Dunlap seems in the preface to be left with his head spinning as he tries to grasp the composition and character of his audience.

Over the coming years, Dunlap recounted *André*'s disastrous premier in multiple versions: in the play's printed preface, in his diary, and eventually in his *History of the American Theatre* (1832). It has become, in the annals of the American stage, a legendary example of a playwright's miscalculation of an audience's response. Some accounts even frame it as a theater riot. It was also, though, an example of the very behavior Dunlap's friends seemed to sanction in their descriptions of the theater: an audience asserting its disapproval of a performance it deemed to be in error. But the situation belies the confidence Smith and Dunlap ideally placed in virtuous audiences.

Despite his willingness to revise the play and to publish a corrected scene, Dunlap sounds defensive as he pleads in the preface for his patriotic critics to allow him both an attempt at historical realism and poetic license enough to absolve him of responsibility for his characters' actions: "[S]urely," he reminds his readers, these offended "veterans . . . must remember the diversity of opinion which agitated the minds of men at that time, on the question of the propriety of putting André to death." And equally certain, if these audience members had stopped to think, they would have "mingle[d] with their disapprobation, a sentiment of pity" for the fictional but offensive Bland, since his misguided passion stems from having had his life saved, while a British prisoner, by the ill-fated André. In Bland, "the Author has drawn a generous and amiable youth," Dunlap writes, "so blinded by his love for the accomplished Briton, as to consider his country, and the great commander of her armies, as in the commission of . . . horrid injustice." But because the audience reacted angrily to the unpatriotic display Dunlap has added extra lines to smooth over the affair. After this attempt to patch up the situation, he tends to one more prefatory detail: "To the performers the Author takes the opportunity of returning his thanks for their exertions in his behalf; perfectly convinced, that on this, as on former occasions, the members of the Old American Company have anxiously striven to oblige him." This authorial performance over, "The Poem is now submitted to the ordeal of closet examination, with the Author's assurance to every reader, that as it is not his interest, so it has not been his intention to offend any; but, on the contrary, to impress, through the medium of a pleasing stage exhibition, the sublime lessons of Truth and Justice upon the minds of his countrymen."[12]

Dunlap's nod to the actors elides (or, better yet, recasts) the company's actual opening night performance. Dunlap had been annoyed most of all at the actor playing Bland, T. A. Cooper, who had only recently joined the company (after leaving a position in Philadelphia) and whom Dunlap tended to indulge because he had been mentored in London by Godwin and Holcroft. Although a talented actor (Dunlap said his Hamlet was "the best acting I ever saw"),[13] Cooper only magnified the tensions that already existed among the company's actors. He disputed with Hodgkinson over roles and, when he did not get his way, would sometimes sabotage the other actor's important scenes. He had done so, in fact, during *Zorinski,* only four nights before *André* opened, and had argued with Hodgkinson over roles in *André* as well.[14] Cooper's blundering performance during *André* 's debut angered Dunlap so much that, over thirty years later, he still had steam to let off in his theater history. "Young Bland was not the hero of the piece," Dunlap recalled, which must have irritated Cooper, since

> very little of the author's blank verse came *un-amended* from the mouth of the tragedian. In what was intended as the most pathetic scene of the play, between Cooper and Hodgkinson, the first, as Bland, after repeating, "Oh André—oh, André" . . . approached the unfortunate André, who in vain waited for *his* cue, and, falling in a burst of sorrow on his neck, cried, loud enough to be heard at the side scene, "Oh, André—damn the prompter!—Oh, André! What's next, Hodgkinson?" and sunk in unutterable sorrow on the breast of his overwhelmed friend, upon whose more practised stage cleverness he relied for support in the trying scene—*trying* to the author as well as actor and audience.[15]

Here, as in the play's preface, Dunlap defines the Author, in opposition both to the audience and his relation to the actors; but he also, in some ways, blurs these categories by writing potential and actual theater audiences and the personalities of the American Company—characters all—into the printed text of the play (and later into its history). In doing so, he makes "Author," "audience," and "actors" all players in both prefatory and retrospective dramas that represent the permeable boundaries between the new theater's various architectural spaces—gallery, pit, boxes, stage, even the side scene—themselves marked by class- and gender-based divisions.

André may have been a commercial failure, but modern critics have generally regarded it as Dunlap's best play. Moreover, historians of the period have recognized his choice of subject matter itself—the André execution—as offering, in its multiple retellings by Dunlap and others, "a sensitive barometer of the changing beliefs about the 'character' of the nation"[16] or as "figur[ing] prominently in contemporary efforts to determine the meaning of the American Revolution."[17] Other critics have focused on certain tensions within the drama—between feelings and duty, old and new definitions of "virtue," Federalist and Republican partisan ideologies (including competing visions of America's ideal relationship to Europe).[18] But Dunlap's preface also suggests the play's usefulness as a departure point for understanding how tensions between author, actor, and audience can offer insight into late-eighteenth-century Anglo-American culture more generally, including the new nation's acute preoccupation with what one critic calls "natural theatricality," or the "tension between the natural and the theatrical." As Dunlap understood such preoccupations, they related closely to anxieties about influence and authority in the relationship between an intellectual class (including artists and literary authors) and an American public.

The reaction of a portion of the audience to *André*'s production, together with Dunlap's subsequent narratives about the event, suggest a measure of public distrust generated as audiences were forced to confront "the 'real' theatricality of history."[19] In the preface to *André*, Dunlap simultaneously announces his expectation that poetic and historical writing be treated differently and betrays his fears—based in part on the events that transpired on the play's opening night—that his audiences will fail to make that distinction. And with good reason. The events of André's capture and execution in 1780 had occurred in a revolutionary context recognized by many of its participants as highly theatrical (typical of revolutionary moments);[20] furthermore, the everyday culture of politeness that had obtained for most of the century had made the concept of ritualized social performance seem routine. The disjuncture between *André*'s condemnation of such performance and the audience's failure to distinguish between poetry and fact reveals much about the constitution of audiences and society in the period. Situations like "the affair of the cockade," more importantly, though they were characteristic of audience behavior on both sides of the Atlantic in this period, set the terms by which Friendly Club members understood American audiences and reveal some fissures in their late-Enlightenment understanding of literature's relation to its publics.

The Audience Part and the Didactic Stage

Dunlap's attraction to the story of Major André—along with his earliest exposure to the theater—stemmed from his peculiar experience during the war. Like James Kent, William Dunlap, three years younger, read his way through the American Revolution, though instead of devouring Blackstone while exiled from a besieged Yale College, the New Jersey–born son of a retired British officer read "the whole of Shakespeare" while his family moved from town to town.[21] They eventually relocated to British-occupied New York City, where Samuel Dunlap's family and mercantile business would be safe from the fighting. Controlled by the British, New York offered the 13-year-old his first trip to the theater, where he saw George Farquhar's *Beaux' Stratagem* performed by British soldiers, perhaps including John André himself. Such opportunities were confined to British-controlled cities; the Continental Congress had shut down the theaters in cities they occupied. Despite an accident that had blinded him in one eye, Dunlap's main passion was painting. At age 15, the war over, he traveled alone through western New Jersey, making his way to Philadelphia, when he unexpectedly encountered Washington himself on a road near Princeton. "It was a picture," he later wrote, a *tableau vivant,* suggesting his tendency to frame events in artistic and theatrical terms.[22] Friends arranged for General and Mrs. Washington to sit for him, and he eventually gained access to them at the army's headquarters. He witnessed Washington's triumphal entry into New York on "Evacuation Day," 25 November 1783, when the British quit the city.[23]

Though Dunlap received less formal education than most of his Friendly Club compatriots, he was one of the few club members to have visited Europe. His father paid for him to study painting with the expatriate American artist Benjamin West in London. Intimidated by West's skill and criticism, Dunlap spent the better part of his three years there in coffeehouses and theaters with the painter's son, Raphael, and a group of other young friends. In the autobiographical sketches he composed later in life he framed his carefree London years as a cautionary tale against parental indulgence and youthful indolence, against lost educational opportunities in particular. "Every source of information was neglected," he later lamented.[24] In 1787 his father called him home.

If Dunlap had not gained the training as a painter his father had sent him for, he *had* acquired a deepened appreciation for the theater.

Upon returning to New York, he found that the new government had
allowed the New York stage to remain open, though some civic leaders complained that citizens should spend their money on rebuilding
the city rather than on popular entertainments. Shortly after returning, Dunlap attended a play written by an American, Royall Tyler's
The Contrast, which inspired him to try his own hand at the craft. The
result was a piece called *The Modest Soldier,* which was accepted by the
American Company but never staged. Two years later, in 1789, following his marriage to Elizabeth Woolsey, he wrote *The Father; or, American Shandyism,* influenced, as the title would indicate, by Laurence
Sterne's novel. While he continued to take part in his father's business,
he had settled on a calling as a playwright. Over the next eight years,
he saw several more plays staged. During the same years, he formed a
friendship with Elihu Smith, who had included two of Dunlap's poems
in his 1793 anthology of American verse,[25] and helped him form the
Friendly Club, whose members encouraged his efforts as a dramatist
and as a theater critic for the *New-York Magazine.* By the mid-1790s,
Dunlap had turned over his father's business to more capable merchants. Purchasing a half-interest in the American Company in 1797,
he spent the next eight years, until his bankruptcy in 1805, attempting
to make his living through the New York stage.

Friendly Club members used the opening of Dunlap's new theater
to position themselves as American literary founders. The recognition
of a new theatrical era permeates Elihu Smith's verse prologue for the
opening night. Similarly, Dunlap throughout his life, particularly in
his mammoth histories of the American theater and fine arts, portrayed himself and his friends in heroic terms as American literary pioneers. *André* opened with a prologue of its own in which the actor John
Martin reinforced Dunlap's heroism: "A Native Bard, a native scene
displays,/And claims your candor for his daring lays."[26] The lays were
daring because they were written by an American for an American audience about American scenes—a rare combination, Dunlap emphasized. As the character of American audiences was yet in construction,
Dunlap and his friends cast themselves in the role of public educators
and aimed to make the theater, like their other literary endeavors, a tool
for cultivating virtue and morality on sound philosophical principle.

By positioning themselves at the head of new literary traditions,
club members saw themselves as setting out the agenda of their choice.

For this reason, the question of the relationship between authors and audiences was front and center in Smith's prologue. It would, in fact, have been even more central to his prologue than it was in the final version, if not for a censorship of sorts by Dunlap that itself reveals much about the tension club members experienced on this issue. Consistent with club members' vision of the theater as an engine of social and philosophical reform, Smith wanted to emphasize the moral uses of the stage and to admonish audiences of their responsibilities. Dunlap, understandably, did not want to drive audiences away through excessive moralizing and was probably more wary than Smith of belligerent audience members.

Smith's outline for the prologue, preserved in his diary along with the portions Dunlap asked him to remove, allows us to see both men's programs for the theater more clearly and to speculate on the opposition Dunlap anticipated from the audience. Smith's prose outline to the poetic address served as a history of American civilization, with an emphasis on the potential for a distinctly national literature:

> The first settlers of America found it savage. From this rude begining [*sic*], they have attained to their present improved state; & our future improvement is secured by our civil & political institutions. . . .
>
> Next followed the lines [preserved in the final version] relative to the establishment of the Stage in America, & forming a counterpart to those which preceded.
>
> I came, then, to the consideration of what was necessary to such an establishment; & having noticed the difficulty of erecting an unimpeachably excellent institution, pretty much in the manner still preserved [in the final version], proceeded to remark that the duties of managers & players, & of audiences, were reciprocal.
>
> The Manager should select moral & good pieces, the Auditory should applaud & encourage them. If any thing dull, or indecent, were brought forward, it should be driven off. So all false accent, action, &c. &c. in the performance, to be discountenanced: everything proper countenanced.
>
> Taste not everywhere the same; nor even morality. Each nation requires some peculiar attention, on the part of the dramatist, who writes for it. Pernicious effects of deriving all our theatric exhibitions from other countries, as they relate to every different state of society, to follies & vices not so abundant here, & corrupt our taste & morals. . . .

Our characters [are] created or modified by surrounding circumstances. Foreign productions [are] to be received with caution; native
talents encouraged. . . .

Here followed the lines [preserved] . . . stating a great example for
patience, & perseverance. Then . . . this sentiment was [to be] exprest—
"that even feeble efforts of the american muse ought not to be absolutely
discouraged. This might repress the genius & exertions of some who
otherwise would acquire deserved eminence. That every thing is to be
hoped from patronized (by the public) competition. . . ."

Then . . . to the end [as it stands: concluding with Smith's prophecy
that American will yield native equivalents to European master players
and dramatists].[27]

For Smith, American drama is all prospect, and his prologue inau-
gurates not simply the New Theatre (as it was initially called) but the
entire American theatrical enterprise. Smith's outline makes use of a
rhetorical figure common in the early republic, a parallel between the
new nation's progress and an unfolding drama whose final scenes are
yet to be staged.[28] Compared to Smith, Dunlap is restrained on this
grand occasion. "This Prologue is not to be compared with Samuel
Johnson's" famous address, Smith wrote to Brown, a few days after
completing the requested revisions, "nor is it as good as I should have
made it, had not our Manager [Dunlap] been afraid of promising too
much, & receiving too little encouragement in doing as he ought to
do."[29] He had earlier confided to his diary that Dunlap's excisions had
left the final product with "a miserable poverty of ideas." The offensive portions of his original composition began, apparently, with his
thoughts on the "reciprocal" "duties" of managers, players, and audience, including a call for the audience to drive off "anything dull, or indecent," and continuing through his comments on the relativity of taste
and morality, in relation to a national aesthetic. The expunged lines,
which he preserves in the diary "with all their incorrectness," argue that
"Each land, each race, each social state demands / Peculiar models from
the artist's hands," and warns against the "tyrant pomp" of European
drama, which threatens to spread immorality "Through town & village,
with contagion fierce," "Infect[ing]" young and old alike, until foreign
taste rules not only the stage but all "Dress, motion, food."[30]

Smith's objections to the "contagion" of European culture do not
prevent him from idolizing British writers and using them as standards

to which American neophytes can aspire. Rather, his complaints are twofold: one, he worries that the social contexts in which these actors and writers live or lived might have required them to represent vices (even if only to combat them) that Americans simply do not have, and two, he fears that producing European plays to the exclusion of encouraging native "flowrets" will only result in blasting American writers "in their timid bloom." Dunlap allowed Smith's plea for patience with American productions to stand, and in the final version the catalog of master players and dramatists forms the entire final third of the piece. Dunlap's nervousness seems to have been for the more strident warnings against overreliance on European plays. Perhaps he worried that his audiences would not want to be lectured on their tastes, or informed of their impatience with native productions, or perhaps, as a businessman, he realized that the bulk of his company's repertoire was and would be made up of European titles, despite his own or Smith's preferences. Smith could hardly have expected Dunlap to repudiate foreign drama; Dunlap had already decided to name the theater boxes after many of the same playwrights Smith cataloged in the poem. He had also begun translating French and German pieces for the New York stage, a pattern that would dominate the next several years of his career.[31]

Despite Dunlap's insistence that Smith mute his attack on American audiences in the prologue, he had voiced a similar complaint earlier as the anonymous critic of the *New-York Magazine*'s Theatrical Register and echoed it decades later in his history of the theater. In the Register, which he conducted until he assumed a partnership in the Old American Company in 1796,[32] he took American audiences to task indirectly, by appearing to criticize himself through an anonymous review of one of his own plays. *Fontaineville Abbey*, his 1795 stage adaptation of Ann Radcliffe's *Romance of the Forest*, to the dismay of the Register had not been announced as the work of an American. "Can it be possible," the critic asked, "that the author thinks that such an avowal would operate against it?" Answering his own question years later in the *History*, Dunlap grumbled, "There can be no doubt that he did think so, and no doubt but that such an avowal at that time would have been enough to condemn the piece."[33] Whether or not this characterization was accurate, Dunlap and his friends strongly believed American audiences were set against them. "Do I not see ignorance, pride, stupidity, carelessness, & a superstitious veneration for foreign writers," Smith complained to his diary in 1795, "& a mean jealousy of an illustrious writer of our own country, go hand in hand, & as it were, conspire, against the lives of men?"[34] Smith's comments here were about medical authorship in particular, but the criticism held, he believed, for all American audiences. "[S]o precarious is every thing of the kind, in America," he wrote in anticipation of *Edwin and Angelina*'s production, "that I have no right to reckon on deriving any gain therefrom."[35]

The length of time he spent composing the prologue belies Smith's insistence to Brown that it should not be compared to Samuel Johnson's. In any case, his note to Brown also points to another "idea" Dunlap muted in the version Hodgkinson read at the opening, concerning the importance of the audience as an arbiter of morality and taste. Smith's deleted lines on respective and "reciprocal" "duties" aren't recorded in the diary, but they likely referenced and revised the climax of Johnson's prologue, which anticipated the tension between Dunlap's realism and Smith's idealism:

> Ah! let not Censure term our Fate our Choice,
> The Stage but echoes back the publick Voice.
> The Drama's Laws the Drama's Patrons give,
> For we that live to please, must please to live.[36]

Dunlap seems to have endorsed the sentiment in the last two lines, which confirm the all-importance of the audience to the enterprise's solvency. Smith seized on the idea in the second line, that the audience holds enormous power in determining what appears on or is driven off the stage. As another American stage observer from the period put it, "The public, in the final resort, govern the stage."[37] Johnson's image of the stage echoing the "publick Voice" puns on the acoustic realities of the architectural space; in England and America, eighteenth-century theatergoers were notoriously noisy, especially in the pit and galleries, to the point of drowning out the actors' lines. Recall Smith's call, in the initial draft of his prologue, for the audience to shout down "any thing dull, or indecent." Dunlap, as manager and playwright, however, was less eager to encourage such noisy dramatic censorship; given both men's characterization of theater audiences, we might doubt how willing either was to trust the crowds they observed several nights a week.

In contrast to the judicious audience participation outlined in his prologue, a description of the new theater Smith wrote for the *Commercial Advertiser* emphasized the auditory and visual rather than the oral forms of audience participation: the audience's proximity to the stage allows its members to hear better; the lack of support columns allows the audience to become integrated into the spectacle. "The audience part of the New Theater," he wrote, spending twice as much time on this section than on the stage and scenery,

> is a segment of a large circle—and of course the spectators, even in the front boxes, are brot within a very convenient distance, both for seeing and hearing. The Pit is a very convenient distance, both for seeing and hearing. The Pit is remarkably commodious. The Boxes are disposed in three semi-circular rows, from one side to the other of the stage—and the Gallery is thrown back of the upper front boxes. The total omission of pillars as supports to the boxes, avoids a common and great obstacle (in Theatres) to the view—and when the house is filled, presents an unbroken line of spectators, which forms no uninteresting part of the spectacle.[38]

The double meaning of Smith's phrase "the audience part" conveys both territorial and performative senses, the part of the theater occupied by the audience and the part it played as it contributed to productions.

Though Dunlap was not able—in Smith's mind at least—to do "as he ought" and let Smith admonish the audience regarding its moral responsibilities, Dunlap *had* endorsed a similar view of audience responsibility in his anonymous Theatrical Register. There, Dunlap had lamented the fact that more "men of respectability" did not attend the theater, where they could exercise their moral influence through their applause. A whole "class" of potential viewers absents itself, fearing the material will be "filled with obscenity and immorality": "thus is the Theatre deprived of many of those persons in whose power it would be to influence the Managers in their choice of pieces, and by their approbation or disapprobation, make this species of entertainment as pure as it is rational: for on this we may rely, no Managers will bring forward that which is displeasing to their audiences." Your children will find their way to the theaters with or without you, Dunlap warned. So, "Go to the Theatre, ye fathers; go to the Theatre, ye friends of virtue and good order; and support by your applause every chaste and moral production of the Muse."[39] The theater, in other words, was not inherently moral or immoral; it was what the audience made it, as Dunlap wrote to Thomas Holcroft in 1797: "A Theatre . . . is only good as it is a mode of communicating knowledge," in particular "that knowledge which leads to virtue, of exercising Justice or benevolence, and bestowing happiness, which *is in itself essentially good.*"[40]

Public Appeals: The Hodgkinson-Hallam Controversy

Dunlap and Smith owed at least part of their conception of American audiences to their experiences as audience members themselves. As one critic has observed of the 1790s in Britain, this was the end of an era in which "it was still possible to conceive the writer's relation to an audience in terms of a personal compact," in part because authors could "scan the audience of [their] plays" to gauge reactions and look for those they recognized from other settings.[41] Smith himself, though a regular theatergoer, wrote that he "enjoy[ed] plays very little. My taste is either very much blunted or very much refined." Despite this sentiment, during the period when he was writing his own *Edwin and Angelina,* Smith had determined that his literary productions "may as well be dramatic, as of another kind: they may, in this shape, as much advance the cause of truth, as in any other." The theater offered Smith, Dunlap, and their friends not only a vehicle for communicating moral knowledge, as Dunlap had argued to Holcroft, but an arena in which "the public" gained tangible form, an arena in which they could observe concrete audiences responding to their literary productions and those of American and foreign competitors. For the most part this experience heightened their sense that the American public was not yet ready to support literary writing as a profession, as Smith had argued in the prospectus to *Proteus.*[42]

Smith's indignation with audiences intensified when he felt his friend Dunlap or his favorite contemporary playwrights had been poorly received. When Dunlap's Gothic thriller *The Mysterious Monk* was staged in October 1796, Smith had his fair share of criticism for the play itself but harsher words—and more of them—for the audience. "The very excellencies of this Play," he told his diary, "are so many obstructions to it's popularity. Our people will not bear a simple, unbroken, & artfully natural display of passion." The actors, in this instance, deserved equal blame, being "unequal to the task" of performing it well, and being "totally incapable of forcing [the audience] to relish it," an indicator of his conception of audiences as tabula rasa waiting for powerful impressions from the stage.[43] During the play's second performance, on a double bill with an adaptation of *The Taming of the Shrew,*

Smith again studied the audience reaction and criticized the inept acting: "A thin house, for the second night of a new piece. My friend has
made some judicious curtailments in his piece since the first night, & it
was now better performed—but, still, indifferently: indifferently, as it
respects just performance, but better than usual for our performers, &
therefore very well for our audience."[44]

Smith's complaints against American audiences included jealousy
over the response given even to watered-down versions of Shakespeare:
"How much of the applause which British Plays obtain, among us,
arises from our knowing that they have been so well received at home?
And, beside the prejudice so universal against pieces of our own manu-
facture, is there not an intellectual cowardice, a fear lest others should
despise his judgement, which restrains the spectator from applauding a
cis-atlantic drama?"[45] As his own *Edwin and Angelina* was in rehearsal
he feared it would be received poorly unless "several adaptations" were
made to suit the audience. American theatergoers, he complained,
could not abide the phrases "God damn it" or "My God." So "tender
are the consciences of our people, and so careful are they of the name of
God," that even if "the character & passion of the fictitious being" on
stage required it, "this very monosyllable is not to be made free with."
He noted with some glee the ironic result: "I must exclude God from
my play."[46]

Religious austerity hardly equaled the kind of moral rigor Friendly
Club members hoped to effect through the stage. After Dunlap read
to the club his *Tell Truth and Shame the Devil,* Smith worried it might
be "too moral to succeed" in America: "Our audiences must have a
plentiful dose of fun, to make even a drop of morality palatable."[47]
Even Americans' apparent appreciation for Shakespeare, which Smith
certainly shared, didn't make him think better of the typical viewers
who probably were simply "familiar with all the principal dialogues &
characters, from their boyish days."[48] And even Shakespeare could not
compete with flashier contemporary European drama that had only
"[s]how & bustle, for interest & character & plot; & eating a pudding,
for wit & humour; [all of which] pass off better, with an audience, than
Othello & Iago, Benedick & Beatrice."[49] Occasionally Smith dealt the
audience a backhanded compliment: "Thank Heaven! our audience
was not stupid enough to relish" a particularly bad afterpiece, he wrote
on one occasion, adding, "stupid as it usually is."[50]

Such priggishness aside, club members knew the audience wielded enormous authority. Hence their concern with the stage's pedagogical potential. If audiences were to be called on as arbiters of morality and taste, they would need careful preparation for the role. Otherwise they stood vulnerable to being swayed by what Dunlap lamented as the "star system." In New York this problem played out in the relationship between the Hallams and Hodgkinson, who had feuded for years over which actor was the best beloved by audiences, and illustrates not only the significance of "the audience part" in such matters but also points to the complexity of the social and artistic situations rising from a cultural ideal of "natural theatricality." The Hodgkinson-Hallam feud came to a climax in early 1797 as Mrs. Hallam, notorious for turning up intoxicated on stage, fought off the company's attempts to oust her by appealing to her fan base.[51] Hodgkinson had finally refused to play any longer if he had to share a stage with Mrs. Hallam, who on occasion would drag the company's infighting on stage, abusing Hodgkinson verbally in the middle of a play. In March 1797, both Hallams interrupted Hodgkinson's performance in Richard Cumberland's *The Fashionable Lover* with a direct appeal to the audience that Mrs. Hallam be allowed back in the company. A group of their supporters, scattered through the theater, hissed Hodgkinson and cheered for the Hallams, though, as Smith recorded of the "riot" in his diary, the "respectable & greater part" of the audience sided against the drunken actress.[52]

The notion of a theater audience as a juridical public carried over into contemporary conceptions of print as well. Within weeks, the 30-year-old Hodgkinson published *A Narrative of His Connection with the Old American Company,* which he opened with an appropriately dramatic anecdote:

> On the 29th of March I was prevented from going on with my Character for the Evening, by a part of the audience calling for Mrs. *Hallam,* formerly an Actress in the Company. . . [who] contrary to the Regulations of the Theater . . . came through the private Door into the Theatre, where she was supported by Mr. *Hallam,* a Performer and principal Proprietor . . . who addressed the Audience, and obtained Permission for her to read . . . a Complaint of having been *driven* unjustly from the Stage . . . without any *sufficient* Cause; intimating all this had been effected by my Agency. In the Confusion which followed, I was not allowed to justify myself. After some Time, I submitted, engaging to exculpate myself by a Publication in the Papers, or elsewhere.[53]

Though the narrative (and a notary public's "Firm and Seal") speak to the text's exculpatory agenda, the opening scene also suggests a strategy by which Hodgkinson hopes not only to represent his theater audience but to convince it—and a broader reading public—that its rights have been violated as much as his. His argument concurs with Smith's assertion that the "respectable & greater part of the audience [was] favorable to [Hodgkinson], & not to [Mrs. Hallam]," even though Hodgkinson had been "so interrupted as not to be able to proceed."[54] Along with Hodgkinson's claim that he and not the Hallams deserved the audience's approbation, the scene introduces a related theme that dominates Hodgkinson's brief pamphlet: the crowd's interest in and even preference of an actor's personality over the dramatic character being portrayed on stage.

A similar scene occurred a few months later, when Mrs. Hallam eventually convinced Dunlap to let her back onstage. Some of the company supported the move, thinking that she would both "convince the public of her worthlessness" and make the other performers—the other leading actresses, in particular—more popular by contrast.[55] One night soon after Mrs. Hallam's return, Dunlap watched her closely "thro' my glass" and thought "she appeared bloated in the face, & stupid eyed & if my apprehensions do not very much wrong her, she was partly intoxicated." (Either that, he added, or "her playing is worse" than ever.) Mrs. Hallam appealed to audience members by reading a monologue prepared by one of her supporters, later printed in Philip Freneau's magazine, the *Time-Piece*. Admitting that she "may thro' inadvertency have stray'd" from a straight and narrow path, she asked the audience for mercy:

> On your indulgence still I'll rest my cause
> Will you support me with your kind applause?
> You verify the truth of Pope's fine line
> "To err is human; to forgive, divine."[56]

Dunlap called the performance her "promise of amendment," a phrase that captures the degree to which her life has become a public text, her repentance figured as revision. Here we have the real-life drama of a well-known actress reading a prepared script—in heroic couplets, no less—to a theater audience, asking for applause, not only for this performance, but to absolve her of her sins and to welcome her return to the stage. The audience welcomed her back with "three cheers."[57]

In such situations, actors appearing *as themselves* for a rapt audience (including one's supporters, performing the part of the public) demonstrate the degree to which an audience seemed ready to accept staged authenticity. An even more striking example later in the same evening involved a temporary reconciliation between Hodgkinson and Mr. Hallam: "towards the conclusion" of Richard Brinsley Sheridan's *A School for Scandal*, Dunlap writes, "in the scene prefatory to the screen scene when Charles drags Sir Peter 'into court' the characters were forgotten by the Auditors who applied every speech to Hallam and Hodgkinson instead of Sir Peter and Charles." Sheridan's scene—which enacts a reconciliation between the characters—contained several lines that "were received with shouts of applause & fixed upon the men."[58] The play had receded in the audience's consciousness, replaced by a greater interest in the relationship between the actors.

Understanding these varied attempts to organize theater and reading audiences requires careful thinking about the varied natures of the publics formed by specific cultural forms—novels, political debate and oratory, periodicals, courtrooms, parades, theater, and theater riots, for example. A better understanding of the relationship of theater audiences to other and larger publics requires consideration of what authors saw in theater audiences—a specific public in a specific public space—and the ways these encounters shaped the texts that we have come to accept as transforming the post-Revolutionary public sphere. The public organized within New York's theaters was simultaneously democratic (it both "governs the stage" and is "literary" without necessarily being literate) and class stratified; it comprised multiple audiences, or what would now be called publics and counterpublics, in its separate architectural spaces. As Dunlap himself noted, theater audiences were quite different from reading audiences, the former being more likely to uphold stricter moral standards than a private reader would.[59] But narratives such as Dunlap's and Hodgkinson's make it plain how easily the two publics, theatrical and print, could be collapsed in writers' or actors' minds, one taken as a visible manifestation of the other, and both taken as synonymous with "the public" at large.

Hodgkinson's and Dunlap's accounts contain a dense network of sometimes competing understandings of audience and its relationship to what Hodgkinson elsewhere in his narrative calls the "Public Voice." The phrase recalls Smith's instructions, in his draft prologue, for the audience to take such a law-giving role and shout down "any thing dull, or indecent." Hodgkinson's similar recognition of the audience as "umpire" in his conflicts registers more negatively in his conception of a public that robs an actor of a private life, professional dignity, and even sensibility. New York audiences, he complained, "consider Actors as Public Slaves . . . who are to have no will of their own, but are bound to be the obedient and submissive Victims of their Caprice. . . . [A]nd thus a Profession, which, to excel in, requires . . . particular *Feeling*, the Professor, on some Occasions, is not allowed to *feel at all*," a curious inversion of the theater opponents' claim that acting robbed performers of their own personalities.[60]

If audiences believed that they could access actors' real lives through these staged performances, Hodgkinson fantasized that the theater audience was a stand-in for much larger publics. In his *Narrative* he carefully attempts to organize his audience by refusing to believe the theater audience proper would have willingly refused him the chance to speak in his self-defense. Rather, the Hallams had acted "in concert" with supporters they planted there. This cabal stages its own performance in "the audience part" of the theater and exists apart from—indeed, subverts—the larger theater audience, resulting in "confusion" rather than consensus. As recourse he addresses a different public, one potentially larger but less tangible or likely to hiss him off stage, by circulating his narrative in print. The print performance enacts narrative control as it compensates for his inability to control the original scene; he offers it as a fulfillment of his "engagement with the Public," in consideration of the "Patronage" he had received from the "Citizens of New-York."[61] He seems confident that these three publics—theater, print, and citizenry—will overlap significantly enough that theatergoers (representatives of public opinion) will be won to his side of the affair.

The "public" Hodgkinson imagines hearing his appeal extends from the theater audience to the public outside the theater's walls, one governed by rational thought rather than by momentary passion or partiality, one liable to be impressed by his careful account of fact, figures, legal documents, and notary seals. It is a far cry from the crowds that drove him from the stage, or from the theatergoing public Smith sometimes describes as stupid. It bears greater similarity to Smith's description of the new theater for the *Commercial Advertiser:* contrasting Smith's idealization of "the public Voice," this other model holds that audiences are to be seen rather than heard, a sentiment that qualifies the frequently stated ideal that audiences would spontaneously police the morality of what appears on stage.

Critiquing Natural Theatricality: On Stage with André

If the audience's routine refusal to distinguish between theatrical and social performance speaks to the near-universal embrace of the *theatrum mundi* metaphor, it also helps to explain problems Dunlap faced as he staged *André* in the spring of 1798. In particular it offers insight into the difficulties club members understood themselves to face in their attempts to educate, even to govern, the same audiences that were supposed to govern public beliefs and behaviors. Appropriately, the first play produced at the Park was Shakespeare's *As You Like It*, with its famous lines describing the world as a stage and its men and women as players. With *André*, Dunlap confronted this metaphor head on. The Revolution itself had been highly theatrical—from the costumed spectacle of the Boston Tea Party to the carefully staged execution of André himself. If contemporaries framed the American Revolution as "the first act of the great drama,"[62] Dunlap's *André* curiously restaged a scene from that first act before the reverberations from the revolutionary drama had faded into silence. In launching a familiar attack on falsehood and disguise, Dunlap highlighted—perhaps inadvertently—the episode's theatricality, and so laid bare the cultural conventions by which the original events had been played out.

The original André affair had played out not quite twenty years earlier and was one of the most controversial moments in the entire war. More than any other episode in the long war, André's capture, trial, and execution played out in theatrical terms, paving the way for, but also complicating, Dunlap's later dramatization. Living in New York in 1780, as the 14-year-old son of a loyalist merchant, Dunlap had seen the saga unfold from the British side. But even those who tried Major André, found him guilty, and hanged him had seen the young British officer as a tragic figure. At the center of the real-life "tragedy" had been the issue of André's costume; when captured, he had been behind lines, dressed as a commoner. As Washington reported it to the board of officers that would try André, he had been taken in "an assumed character."[63] A gentleman, as the American officers well knew, was above the act of spying; in forsaking his army uniform André had also forsaken the performance of class distinction and took a part that was not his. To defend himself on this point was André's major concern. He wrote Washington, immediately upon his capture, in an attempt to "secure myself from an imputation of having assumed a mean character," an act that would be "incompatible with the principles that actuated me, as well as with my condition in life." Accordingly he explained in elaborate detail how and why he had "*quitted my uniform.*" He had found himself within "one of your posts . . . [a]gainst my stipulation, my intention, and without my knowledge before hand," he told Washington. He had agreed to meet Arnold but only on neutral ground. Forced by the approaching daylight to stay until the next night, he swapped his "regimentals" for other clothes and only inadvertently found himself behind enemy lines. He was on his way back to New York when three American soldiers stumbled on him and took him prisoner. Rather than a spy, he assured Washington, he had been "betrayed . . . into the vile condition of an enemy in disguise within your posts. . . . I was involuntarily an impostor."[64]

The American board of officers, however, rejected his defense and reported to Washington its finding that he should be considered a spy and, "agreeable to the law and usage of nations, it is their opinion, he ought to suffer death." André responded with another letter to Washington hoping that "[s]ympathy towards a soldier will surely induce your Excellency and a military tribunal, to adapt the mode of my death to the feelings of a man of honor." He appealed to Washington's sentimental manhood: "Let me hope, Sir, that if aught in my character impress you with esteem towards me, . . . I shall experience the operation of these feelings in your breast, by being informed that I am not to die on a gibbet."[65] Alexander Hamilton, a likely model for Dunlap's Colonel Bland, had pleaded André's cause to Washington, begging the general to let André die a gentleman's death by firing squad, as he requested, rather than condemning him to be hanged, but Washington was resolute in imposing the original sentence.

Dunlap's portrait of "the poetical character of André" as a "Hero" with "every virtue" was not far from the view of many Americans in 1780, especially the genteel corps of officers. Dunlap's final appendix to his play included an extract of a letter by Hamilton that had been published in a Pennsylvania newspaper on 25 October and reprinted widely.[66] "Never, perhaps, did a man suffer death with more justice, or deserve it less," Hamilton's account began, pinpointing the same paradox Dunlap would later highlight. Hamilton's description of André's execution illustrates the degree to which the event had been understood in theatrical terms long before Dunlap laid his hands on it:

When he was led out to the place of execution, as he went along, he bowed his head familiarly to all those with whom he had been acquainted in his confinement. A smile of complacency expressed the serene fortitude of his mind. Arriving at the fatal spot, he asked, with emotion, "Must I then die in this manner?" He was told that it had been unavoidable. "I am reconciled to my fate," said he, "but not to the mode." Soon, however, recollecting himself, he added, "It will be but a momentary pang;" and, springing upon the cart, performed the last offices to himself, with a composure that excited the admiration, and melted the hearts of the beholders. Upon being told the final moment was at hand, and asked if he had anything to say, he answered, "Nothing, but to request you will witness to the world that I die like a brave man." Among the extraordinary circumstances that attended him, in the midst of his enemies, he died universally esteemed, and universally regretted.[67]

Hamilton's narrative, which itself takes something like a theater critic's tone, foregrounds the ritual performance of the execution. André passes through an attentive audience, there to see him hung. He puts on a smile (which, artlessly, "expresse[s] . . . his mind"). He delivers appropriate lines, speaks with emotion, and "perform[s] the last offices to himself" by securing the rope around his own neck. His concern for audience reception extends beyond the immediate crowd to "the world." A similar account by an American officer also emphasizes the dramatic quality of the scene. "I never saw a man whose fate I foresaw whom I so sincerely pitied," wrote the 26-year-old Major Benjamin Tallmadge, André's guard, to one of Washington's aides-de-camp. "He is a young fellow of the greatest accomplishments [who] unbosomed his heart to me so fully, and indeed let me know almost every motive of his actions . . . that he has endeared me to him exceedingly. . . . Had he been tried by a court of ladies, he is so genteel, handsome, polite a young gentleman, that I am confident they would have acquitted him." Though masculine audience members, according to Tallmadge, were susceptible to being moved by the "unbosom[ing]" of a fraternal heart (Tallmadge himself was "obliged to leave the [execution] parade in a flood of tears"), some quality that set the male court apart from "a court of ladies" allowed them to pierce André's genteel exterior and administer justice. "But enough of André," Tallmadge closed his letter, "who, though he dies lamented, falls justly."[68]

The same set of conflicted feelings would later permeate Dunlap's drama. The play's tension between fraternal sympathy and the demands of reasoned justice have received much less critical attention, from Dunlap's time to ours, than its infamous cockade scene.[69] But Dunlap and later critics alike seem to have embellished the anecdote in part to justify their image of early American audiences as inadequately prepared for native productions. His immediate response to the play's opening night includes notice of the incident, though more muted than we would be led to expect by subsequent mythologizing. The entire passage from his diary reads, "Evening 'André & poor Soldier' in ye house 817$. The play was much applauded notwithstanding the extreme imperfectness of Cooper & some others but on Bland's throwing down his Cockade there was a few hisses."[70] Elihu Smith, also in the audience opening night, returned home and wrote, "Evening at the Theater. Saw Dunlap's 'André.' The House was full—the audience good-humored—but the piece most wretchedly played. Cooper miserably deficient."[71] Smith makes no mention of the cockade affair or any audience response to it (to the contrary, his audience is "good-humored"); in both accounts, the great weakness is Cooper's poor performance.[72]

The following day, Dunlap began to unfold a new story of the audience's response in his diary: "I find Cooper's friends [the men who had supported his move from Philadelphia, many of whom were subscribers to the building of the theater] displeas'd with André because he cut so poor a figure in it & my friends much displeased that it was done so badly. Mr Gaune, G[arrit] Kettletas & others advise me not to repeat it on monday as intended." To this point, Dunlap's focus has remained on Cooper's performance rather than the cockade in deciding whether or not to continue the run. Then: "On consulting about the Theatre I find that general satisfaction was expressed, but our warm & ignorant people, look upon Bland's action as an insult to the Country. On considering that to withdraw the play would show as an acknowledgement of its insufficiency I determine on its repetition on Monday. Make an alteration in 5th Act, by making Bland on his repentance receive the cockade again." By waiting until the final act to restore the cockade, Dunlap let the offensive scene stand as originally written and performed; angry audience members would have to wait through two more acts before Bland fully acknowledged his error. Monday morning Dunlap heard more rumors about audience displeasure: "Rain. I am told that the people are so offended at the Cockade business as to threaten to hiss off the play to night." That evening, it took in $271 despite a "[v]iolent storm of wind & rain." Contrary to warnings received earlier, "[t]he play was received with constant applause."[73]

Not until Tuesday, 3 April, when the storm that was drenching the city had intensified to the point that Dunlap shut down the theater for the evening, did the first political attack on the play appear in the public papers. At the office of his printer, the Swords brothers, to pick up the last proof sheets of the play, he "saw a bungling attack upon André" in the Republican-biased *Argus* (also known as *Greenleaf's New Daily Advertiser*).[74] By that point, he had already revised the cockade incident to make it more palatable to the entire audience, and appears to have succeeded. The paper ran two pieces on *André:* one reported on the opening, noted that "a part of the audience" had hissed the cockade scene, but said the larger part paid "more unequivocal tributes to the Author's power by their tears."[75] The other, a letter signed "Z," attacked the play on several points. First, the author complained, the play represents Washington, in refusing so many pleas for André's life, as "an unfeeling, obdurate monster!" Next, Bland, the representative American soldier, "in the presence of the general, takes off his cap, plucks therefrom the *American cockade,* dashes it to the floor, and *tramples it underfoot,* vehemently cursing his country and their cause." The letter also points out that the actor, Cooper, is British, suggests he showed anti-American zeal in trampling the cockade, and implies he will be punished upon a repeat performance. In addition to maligning Americans through these characters, the letter writer continues, the play holds up an enemy spy as "an honorable character!" and even a "martyr," rather than recognizing him for what he was, "the instrument of so black a deed" as Arnold's treason. To fill out the implication that the play is nothing more than aristocratic, Anglophilic propaganda, Z complains that the much-reverenced yeoman soldiers—"the brave and heroic veterans" who captured André—are not even included among the *dramatis personae,* and also that the play omits the court-martial, which would have placed André in a proper light as a villain.

Content, like Hodgkinson, to trust the public's judgment, Dunlap wrote and delivered a response the same day. On the fourth he followed up dinner at William Woolsey's—in company with Kent, Smith, George Woolsey, and their brother-in-law Moses Rogers—by correcting the final sheets of the drama and completing the preface. When he dropped the papers back at the printers' the following morning, the Swords brothers passed on the information that the "[a]ssailant in the Argus is one Conolly an Irishman," not the "veterans" Dunlap had assumed were the disapproving audience members and to whom, accordingly, he had addressed the preface. That day his response to Z appeared in the *Argus*, addressed, "To the crookedest and last letter in the Alphabet, Z." (Dunlap punningly signed his letter, written in the third person, with the straightest letter, "I.") The *Argus*'s correspondent, he suggests, must not have seen the play, or perhaps simply was not capable of comprehending it, since it both defended André's execution and praised Washington in no uncertain terms. After quoting several lines as example, Dunlap notes places where he had praised the common soldiers, including André's captors. He omitted the capture and court-martial scenes, he implies, because they would have, through their sheer theatricality and spectacle, detracted from the play's more philosophical patriotism. Though he had already altered the play to have Bland, repentant, resume wearing the cockade, Dunlap defended the scene as originally played. The act was private, witnessed only by Washington, who clearly disapproves of Bland's actions. Bland, Dunlap argues, demonstrates the influence of blind and uncontrolled passions; André, while made more tragic by his virtue, clearly demonstrates that evil consequences can flow from one fatal mistake. Z might have understood these points better, Dunlap concludes, if he had not "seen everything through the mist of prejudice and error."[76]

The ongoing exchange revealed the distance between Dunlap's idealized audience and this incorrigible audience member, who in Dunlap's mind could not comprehend the rules that governed the literary public sphere. Dunlap had assigned Saturday, the seventh, for the play's third performance, for which proceeds traditionally went to the playwright, if a local figure. The evening brought Dunlap $329, despite the continuation that day, in the *Argus*, of the letter exchange, with Z weighing in again.[77] Most of the letter reiterates Z's original complaints, though in harsher terms. André, for example, is now denounced as "contemplat[ing] nothing less than butchering in cold blood our brave citizen soldiers." In one of his more interesting arguments, the letter writer seizes on one of Dunlap's defenses, that the cockade scene was protected by the privacy of the exchange between Washington and Bland. These "sophisms," complained Z, could not "convince me the author acted right, by introducing a scene of so degrading a tendency; if it were performed in private as you assert, would it have remained there yet, but when brought on a stage, it becomes a transaction of public notoriety, and therefore ceases to be a private deed, or taking it literally in your own words its [*sic*] a libel on the general, by insinuating he ever talked in private, what in public would meet his severest censure."[78] Dunlap, who left the next day for Philadelphia on theater business, never responded to this attack, and the exchange ended.

This chronology deserves such a careful recital for the several questions it raises about reciprocal expectations of authors and audiences in the period. It demonstrates that the infamous protest to the original scene may have been less vehement than critics and historians typically assume; the larger problem was Cooper's poor performance, and even the *Argus,* the vehicle for the arguments made by Z, had reported on the general audience's tearful approbation for the play as a whole. Dunlap's initial decision to insert Bland's contrite resumption of the cockade later in the play, though it does perhaps demonstrate his class bias against "warm & ignorant" veterans, was made and even performed before the partisan newspaper attacks began. It also demonstrates the audience's difficulty maintaining the difference between stage performance and real life, between literary characters and the characters of those who created or portrayed them. Should an author be blamed for a character's actions? Should an actor? Is it possible for a character to act in character without an author or actor endorsing the behavior or without an audience responding indignantly? To what degree can "privacy" be represented on the stage, a "vehicle" for "public transaction"? Can a playwright represent a revered public figure, have him interact with fictional characters, without "insinuating" the original would have behaved as his character does on stage?

This final question seems to get closest to the heart of Dunlap's challenge in staging *André*: how, exactly, to have Hallam perform the part of a figure as revered as Washington. Staging Washington opened the possible reading that his character and motivations for his original judgment were being called into question. Exactly what part had Washington been playing, eighteen years earlier, and for what audiences? As described by Hamilton and others, André performed well at the execution; he fitted the noose around his own neck, blindfolded himself, and uttered a final speech that moved his audience to tears. Though he does not stage the execution, Dunlap preserves the question of its theatricality in the prolonged consideration of how André will die. As André raises the question with Bland:

O, think and as a soldier think,
How must I die—The *manner* of my death—
Like the base ruffian, or the midnight thief,
Ta'en in the act of stealing from the poor,
To be turn'd off the felon's—murderer's cart,
A mid-air spectacle to gaping clowns:—

. . . .

Let me, O! let me die a soldier's death,
While friendly clouds of smoke shroud from all eyes
My last convulsive pangs, and I'm content.[79]

André takes as his chief concern his performance on the gibbet before an American audience. He would prefer to die offstage, or, perhaps, behind a curtain of smoke. Dunlap does not allow his audience the curiosity that led trains of American spectators to pass John André's corpse for a better look at the dead man. And well he did not, wracked as the dramatic culture of the early republic was with tension between natural theatricality and stage performance, in which actors and characters were sometimes confused. In the case of Washington, Dunlap's efforts to demonstrate his humanity, despite the sentence, carried the perverse possibility that the general might come off cold and obdurate. If André already seemed, as Z had complained, too sympathetic, a melodramatic hanging scene could not have helped.

Partisans, Philosophers, and Playwrights

Did *André* play out a partisan part of its own, as Z and later critics have argued? If we take Dunlap's claims for the play seriously, that it had no partisan agenda, what other moral lessons might it seek to convey? Using the cockade incident as a departure point, much recent criticism on *André* follows Z to suggest that the play reveals a Federalist agenda on several fronts: its attention to gentlemen officers at the expense of André's yeoman captors; its generation of negative reaction from anti-Federalist publications; its author's grumbling about the play's "warm & ignorant" opponents; and especially its inclusion of the cockade scene itself, read as an anti-French statement, given that the cockade originally signified America's alliance with France during the Revolution.

Much of this speculation, however, misreads the evidence. Though the play does comment carefully on post-Revolutionary America (largely through characters' speculations about what independence will mean), its main concerns cannot be reduced to Federalist propaganda for several reasons. First, Dunlap's Federalism itself has been overstated. Though Dunlap was not outspoken on partisan matters, in private he derided partisans generally and Federalist enthusiasts like his brothers-in-law in particular. Three months after *André's* appearance, Dunlap allowed to be staged, as part of a benefit for one of the company's actresses, an afterpiece called *The Federal Oath, or Americans Strike Home.* Despite its Federalist bias, he execrated it and its author in his diary. "The benevolent intention of the benevolent [playwright] in his piece—of patch'd work," he sneered, "is to inculcate some grand and novel political truths, Such as, that, we ought to damn all Frenchmen, and that 'two yankee boys can beat four mounseers.'"[80]

Evidence within Dunlap's play also suggests problems with reducing *André* to political propaganda. Dunlap almost certainly modeled the headstrong Bland on Hamilton himself, a move that would hardly seem friendly to high Federalists, given Bland's character flaws.[81] Rather than taking overt sides in debates over America's relation to Great Britain and France, however, *André* disavows all European culture, and in spite of Dunlap's failure to include the yeoman captors as characters, Washington and the other gentlemen officers comment warmly on the valor and virtue of common soldiers.

Even granting the audience the authority to assign the cockade incident an anti-French meaning, it is not at all clear it would have been widely understood that way. A few weeks after the play opened, Americans learned of the scandalous "XYZ Affair," in which agents of the French government demanded bribes of American envoys in order to stave off war between the two countries. In the rise of anti-French sentiment that resulted, when the demands were made known to the general public in April and May of 1798, thousands of young men volunteered to enlist if the country went to war. If *André's* "failure" were simply due to a poor political climate for its initial staging, Dunlap could have revived it in the wake of the XYZ Affair to what should have been great success. Opinion on the matter was nowhere near universal, however; in Philadelphia on 8 May, fights broke out between Federalist youths wearing black cockades and Republicans wearing red.[82] Though the black cockade had symbolized fraternal fellowship with France during the Revolution, by the spring of 1798 it was being worn by those with least sympathy for France, suggesting that Bland's action in the cockade scene could have been read as an anti-Federalist gesture as easily as an anti-French one.

Dunlap, however, declared his intention in the play's spoken prologue to avoid "party-spirit" and aimed instead "to impress . . . the sublime lessons of Truth and Justice upon his countrymen."[83] Although his characters do stage debates on topics of immediate political importance—the French Revolution looms heavy in the background—Dunlap's primary concerns are philosophical, beginning with an issue fundamental to the theatrical enterprise in which he participates and the larger literary understanding he represents:

> Our Poet builds upon a fact to-night;
> Yet claims, in building, every Poet's right:
> To choose, embellish, lop, or add, or blend,
> Fiction with truth, as best may suit his end;
> Which, he avows, is pleasure to impart,
> And move the passions but to mend the heart.[84]

These prefatory passages efficiently capture the play's aims—and difficulties. "Truth and Justice," not partisan politics, are the key terms. In Dunlap's vocabulary they signal, first, the absolute refusal of duplicity or disguise, and second, the importance of subordinating individual to public good. The first issue arises in relation to André's capture, behind lines wearing civilian clothes. As such, he played the part of "the spy" and was captured, tried, and executed. For this crime André has already repented when we first meet him in the play: "[B]e cautious ever to admit/That duty can beget dissimulation," he tells Bland. The second issue arises with André's sentence, which Dunlap represents as a sacrifice that cuts against sentiment and fraternal sympathy in the name of the greatest good. Weighed in the balance, justice demands that Washington sacrifice André in order to protect the political rights of future generations. The play gets at these truths using a dialogical or conversational method similar to Brown's *Alcuin* and to his fiction more generally. In addition to these two larger topics of debate, the play stages dialogues on several grand issues of post-Revolutionary society: America's relation to Europe; the motivations for war and love of country; the tensions between head and heart; and—related to the question of "fictions" and "truths"—the difficulties caused by tensions between stage performance and the social theatricality of everyday urban life.[85]

Several of these issues come together in Dunlap's repeated atten-

tion to the theatricality of war itself. On one hand, war is real in a
way no "mimic scenes" can be, and Dunlap keeps this point in view
from the preface forward. Bland's assertion on his first entrance that
"[t]he Briton . . . plays at no mimic war" underscores both the Revolution's performative dimensions and the ways in which war's realities
cut through any artificial principles of politeness or civility. But on the
other hand, the play also makes clear that "acts" of war share much with
acting in the theater. Seward, a 30-year-old member of Washington's
staff, who harbors Romantic sentiments about the utopian energies the
American Revolution will unleash, calls attention to the international
audience for the ongoing conflict, and, anachronistically gesturing toward France's coming decades, predicts that the American example will
lead "other nations [to] break their galling fetters / And re-assum[e] the
dignity of man." Seward's partner in this dialogue, M'Donald (as his
name implies, the voice of a moderate moral philosophy that shares
much with the Scottish Common Sense school), responds that "acts"
are less important than the motives that generate them. Are those who
rise up to break "Coercion's iron yoke" in all cases motivated by virtue,
or can the same acts be carried out for a spurious "love of property"?
After all, he points out, "mercenary Europeans" have flocked to the
colonies to join the war,

> So wanting in the common sense of nature,
> As, without shame, to sell themselves for pelf . . . and yet call
> Their trade the trade of honor.

Though M'Donald acknowledges his own temptation to fight from
motivations of vengeance ("My son is—butcher'd—") he ultimately
claims to "love this country for the sake of man" and "hope[s] my every
act / Has been the offspring of deliberate judgment."[86]

Though M'Donald contrasts his own motives with those of "mercenary Europeans" he quickly turns to his own reasoned response to
André's case:

> Without inquiry [the mercenary Europeans] murder, and yet call
> Their trade the trade of honor—high-soul'd honor—
> Yet honor shall accord in act with falsehood.
> O that proud man should e'er descend to play
> The tempter's part, and lure men to their ruin!
> Deceit and honor badly pair together.

Turning the conversation in this direction, M'Donald calls into question André's motivations for deceit and does so using theater metaphors. He also calls into question the performance rituals of honor culture by associating them with base deception. In so doing, he reverses the dynamics of what theater critics refer to as "metatheatrical commentary"; rather than using the vocabulary of the theater self-referentially, to critique the theater as an institution, Dunlap has his characters use theatrical terms to critique the theatricality of the larger society. Seward argues that his reasoning "[t]astes not of charity" for one who owes his ill fate to "fickle Fortune," but M'Donald responds sharply that André's predicament resulted directly from misdeed, not misfortune. Washington moderates this debate (as he does all the others he witnesses) by "*Sportively*" warning Seward that they had better clear the stage before M'Donald begins "to rail." Without disagreeing with M'Donald, he adds:

> Worthy M'Donald, though it suits full well
> The virtuous man to frown on all misdeeds;
> Yet ever keep in mind that man is frail;
> His tide of passions struggling still with Reason's
> Fair and favorable gale[.]

Washington leaves to sleep, and M'Donald is left alone to sing his praises in terms that reveal his recognition that Washington's moderation is ideal: "By nature, or by early habit," the General is "grac'd"

> With that blest quality which gives due force
> To every faculty, and keeps the mind
> In healthful equipoise, ready for action;
> Invaluable temperance—by all
> To be acquired, yet scarcely known to any.[87]

Here is the order, the discipline, and the reason Dunlap's play endorses.

A good portion of Dunlap's project in *André* rests on Washington's moderation. Indeed, these early dialogues function as much to develop Washington's character—good humored, reasoned, sympathetic—as they do to lay out specific debates about liberty and order, or about motives for war. Though not all audience members understood Dunlap's Washington the way he hoped they would, these early dialogues set the stage for the difficult decision to lay aside fraternal sympathy in the name of reason and impartial justice. Dunlap is bound, of course, by the historical fact that Washington did not pardon André, that he did not even change the mode of execution from hanging to death by firing squad, as Hamilton and others begged him to.[88] At the time, Hamilton had feared that "[w]hen André's tale comes to be told, and present resentment is over, the refusing him the privilege of choosing the manner of death will be branded with too much obduracy."[89] Dunlap's Washington, justifying his decision, acknowledges the multiple audiences that submit him to their scrutiny. "I know the virtues of this man, and love them," Washington assures Bland,

> But the destiny of millions, millions
> Yet unborn, depends upon the rigour
> Of this moment. The haughty Briton laughs
> To scorn our armies and our councils. Mercy,
> Humanity, call loudly, that we make
> Our now despised power be felt, vindictive.
> Millions demand the death of this young man.[90]

Not only does Washington perform for a world stage (including "haughty Briton[s]," who rudely scoff like a disapproving theater audience), but for millions of unborn Americans, recalling the trope of the new nation unfolding like a drama: in Washington's lines, the most significant audience is yet unborn.

What seems jarring here is the degree to which Washington's sentiments, in the context of the drama, cannot compete with others Dunlap introduces: first, Bland's emotional appeals to the bond of friendship; second, Dunlap's plot twist that suggests Bland's father, currently a British prisoner, will be executed in revenge if André dies, a dramatic maneuver amplified both by André's generous efforts to forestall British revenge and by Dunlap's introduction of Mother Bland and her two younger children, who wonder innocently when their father will be home; third, Dunlap's creation of a character named Honora, who, as confirmed by documents published after André's death, had been his youthful love but had been forbidden by her father to marry André. In the historical record she marries someone else, and André, distraught, joins the king's army on the eve of the American war; in *André*, she arrives in the American camp, just as he prepares to go to the gallows, with the story that her marriage was a ruse invented by her father to get rid of André. The scene between Honora and Washington, wherein she pleads for André's life, moves Washington to turn away and, as the stage directions indicate, hide his eyes with his hand. "[M]y heart is torn in twain," he tells his officers. When he learns that the British have just executed an American soldier, he stops wavering ("Why, why, my country, did I hesitate!") and calls for André's execution.

Writing these scenes, Dunlap finds himself in a double bind. He has introduced this escalating parade of distraught figures—bosom friend, American mother, star-crossed lover—in part to let Washington demonstrate his humanity, by showing sympathy for each of them, but moreover to demonstrate the heavy weight of justice, for André's life must act as a sacrifice to the greater good of millions yet unborn. Ideally, a sympathetic and sentimental Washington would have softened the blow that inevitably falls with André's death. But Dunlap also forced the audience to watch Washington reject such sentimental pleading time and again, to demonstrate both his fortitude and his republican elevation of the national above the personal. Though Dunlap clearly aims for Washington to demonstrate "healthful equipoise,"[91] the conventions of sentimental drama work against him, and Washington comes off as cold and unfeeling.

By pitting a sentimental Washington against the later advocate of justice, Dunlap takes up the philosophical debates that attracted him to the radicalism of Godwin and Holcroft, the same debates that fueled so many other Friendly Club conversations and literary projects. Washington's crucial invocation of "unborn millions" echoes one of the most notorious passages in *Political Justice:* the anecdote of Archbishop Fénelon and his servant, in which Godwin argued that, given a choice between saving one or the other from death, the preference should be given to Fénelon. In making such a choice, Godwin wrote, "I should have been promoting the benefit of thousands who have been cured by the perusal of [his political satire, *Telemachus*] of some error, vice, and consequent unhappiness." The benefits of this choice would extend infinitely, since each person so cured has "become a better member of society, and has contributed in his turn to the happiness, information, and improvement of others."[92] Such impartial justice should be rendered, Godwin argued, even if the servant were his parent or benefactor, even if *he* were the servant himself. But the contrast Dunlap has established between fraternal sentiment and the demands of justice also leaves him open to the charges Z brought in the *Argus*, that his portrait of Washington renders him an "unfeeling, obdurate monster."

Dunlap's Jacobin defense of one of Washington's most controversial acts left him open to objections from across the political spectrum. Just as many readers rejected Godwin's scenario as naïve, if not dangerous, some of Dunlap's audience members reacted similarly to the principles promoted by Dunlap's play. Others, like Z, could not recognize any radicalism in Dunlap's play that resembled their own. Nevertheless, *André*'s failures may help to explain the extraordinary success Dunlap achieved, beginning in the fall of 1798, with translations and adaptations of a series of plays by August von Kotzebue. Here was a Shakespeare and Holcroft combined, some thought. Dunlap, though he resented American audiences' more ready embrace of a European than American playwright, found in Kotzebue a model for combining sentimental spectacle with Jacobin philosophy; his adaptations of Kotzebue's plays went over well with New York audiences.[93]

Miscalculation or no, the "equipoise" modeled by Dunlap's Washington reflects club members' efforts to discern truth and embrace it impartially. It also allows clearer understanding of the nature—and remarkable consistency—of the united literary endeavors in which the group engaged. Dunlap's theater, financially demanding as it was, likely reached more audience members during the club's existence than all their other writing combined, and so club members idealized it as a venue for the dissemination of moral knowledge, as a medium through which they could impress on their fellow citizens principles they valued. "There are many who cannot, and still more who will not, read," Dunlap wrote in response to a friend who challenged him on the morality of the theater, "but [they] will receive the lessons of wisdom when impressed by the exertions of others."[94] Dunlap's reception model derives partly from Locke, partly from Godwin. Such "impressions" would be irresistible. The mundane operations of the theater, however, as Dunlap knew well and as his diary demonstrates brilliantly, could make that ideal seem far off. The sometimes motley crowds in the theater provided club members with a picture of "audience" that influenced their disparaging attitudes toward American readers more generally. Club members left the theater recognizing their dependence on an audience's judgment, whether or not they felt that judgment could be trusted. The tension between what they aimed to offer, and an audience's willingness to receive it, made their pursuit of truth and their efforts to disseminate it a delicate, ongoing dance.

FIVE

"Here was fresh matter for discourse"

Yellow Fever, the *Medical Repository,*
and *Arthur Mervyn*

O N a Tuesday morning near the end of October 1796, Charles Brockden Brown wrote a letter from New York, where he had been living for two months in William Dunlap's home, to his older brother James, in Philadelphia, to reassure him that the city's yellow fever season had passed—without alarm, compared to the previous year's outbreak—and that he and his friends were safe. Dismissing his brother's calls to "[c]ircumspection," Brown wrote that he could not help but "admire the exaggerations of rumour, and the multiplying and enlarging efficacy of distance," an observation that prompted an extended meditation on imagination and sensory perception, topics he would take up later in his fiction. Unlike physical objects, he wrote, which are "diminished by distance," the fever and other "imaginary spectacles . . . grow into gigantic dimensions, in proportion to their actual distance from us."[1] In 1796, to describe yellow fever as an imaginary spectacle would have struck some as odd; the threat of annual epidemics was quite real, and James Brown's concern was justified. The disease had taken 750 lives in New York's densely populated waterfront neighborhoods in the summer and fall of 1795; dozens—hundreds, and even thousands in the worst cases—had died almost every summer since 1791 in urban American seaports from Boston to Charleston. In 1793,

Brown's family had fled the worst North American epidemic yet, when between four thousand and five thousand Philadelphians—roughly a tenth of the city's population—died in a three-month period.[2]

Brown's focus on the relationship between the fever and imagination, however, suggests that he was already considering the fever's potential as a fictional device to generate interest, suspense, even sublime terror in an audience. Fear of the fever, he wrote, worked in much the same way as fear of the dark, a "disease" he had suffered from since childhood. "[W]hen in the dark," he wrote,

> if an unlucky incident calls my attention to the imperfect gleam, which may be darted from a neighbouring lamp along the ceiling, or to that more imperfect glimpse, which will be produced by the faintest starlight, when reflected from irregular and polished surfaces[,] I find myself seized by unwelcome shrinkings, and hasten to the asylum which sleep, or light or company, or abstract meditation, may afford me. I have never had recourse, in this phantastic distress, to the best expedient, but when all others fail me, that is, the endeavour to *reason down* my perturbations, and dispeople, by more energy of argument, the aerial world of "calling shapes and beckoning shadows dire."[3]

The connections Brown draws in this letter between fear and fever, darkness and a distempered imagination, seem appropriate for someone who would eventually be known as the founder of American gothic fiction; his confession that he feared the dark is intriguing for the same reason. More significantly, the letter both models and represents imaginative processes, as Brown imagines himself in "phantastic distress" brought on by an imaginary danger, then demonstrates how one should carefully and rationally dissect this fear. As he "*reason[s] down* [his] perturbations" and cures himself of "unwelcome shrinkings," he invokes a clear science of the mind, rooted in Hartleyan and Lockean vocabularies of "associations" and "impressions." Still, the reluctance with which he resorts to reason suggests that he remains caught between the pleasures and imperatives of imagination (explicitly associated with the "aerial world" of literature exemplified by the line from Milton's *Comus*) and a desire to represent himself as a rationalist.

Over the next five years, during his increasingly lengthy residencies in New York, he would establish his reputation as a novelist by writing stories that were sometimes fraught with similar tensions. Nonetheless, his fever fiction would consistently seek to subordinate literary genres to the purposes of moral observation and rational inquiry. Brown's novels not only participated in medical debates but also held up characters who modeled behaviors appropriate and inappropriate to a fever season. In so doing he aimed to use the novel form to intervene in social affairs and to generate authority for literary authorship in the new American republic and the republic of intellect.

Readers of Brown's fiction may be tempted to regard as perverse his selection of the gothic novel, with its typical traffic in terror, as the vehicle by which he would "reason down" fear of the fever and set such public examples. Yet in diagnosing the disease of "fear," Brown implies that various factors—age, experience, reflection, habit—may themselves provide sufficient "cure[s]." He might have added that literary narrative itself could serve as a prophylactic, particularly if it conjures up terror in order to habituate or perhaps even to inoculate a reader to fear's unhealthy side effects. Years later he would encourage Margaret Bayard to read his novel *Edgar Huntly* precisely so she could "immur[e]" her mind to "such scenes & images."[4] Brown's medical language is telling. In the fall of 1796, while he contemplated the fictional possibilities yellow fever afforded, Elihu Smith was hard at work—sometimes in the same room—on his own fever gothic, a medical history of "The Plague of Athens," intended for publication in the first issue of the *Medical Repository,* which would appear that fall, edited by Smith along with future club members Samuel Latham Mitchill and Edward Miller.[5]

If Brown used yellow fever to create some of his most compelling fictional settings, Smith aimed to fix his professional reputation by writing about it as well. He began his medical publishing career in 1796 by treating New York's 1795 epidemic in a collection of essays edited by Noah Webster. His next two years would be spent promoting particular medical understandings of the fever, through his correspondence and in the *Repository.* Like Brown he hoped his literary strategies would accommodate a broad audience: "I hope to attract common, as well as medical, readers—& they must be amused," Smith wrote in his diary of his essay on the Athenian plague. "The taste of our professional men is not yet sufficiently correct to relish the beauties of a simple style."[6] These literary concerns—which go beyond preoccupations with mere amusement or taste—were means to more significant ends than reputation; they were matters of life and death. Smith had written with utopian hopefulness in his contribution to Webster's collection that "[w]ere it possible to impress the truth vividly on the minds of the great body of citizens; to rouze men into action; to excite a generous disregard for temporary advantages, and a lively interest for the future welfare of themselves and their posterity; a few weeks might enable us to bid defiance to death, in many of the forms in which he now assails us."[7]

Brown's *Arthur Mervyn*, even more than his earlier fever writing in magazine serials and in *Ormond*, similarly aimed to "impress . . . truth[s]" about the fever on his reading audience. In early 1798, having completed his philosophical dialogue, *Alcuin, Sky-Walk, or Man Unknown to Himself*, and a good portion of *Wieland*, he began *Mervyn*'s serialization in the Philadelphia *Weekly Magazine*, where he had started and aborted several other serial novels that winter and spring.[8] *Arthur Mervyn* seemed poised to be Brown's greatest success; it opened dramatically with a benevolent doctor who discovers a fever victim near death on his doorstep and takes him in as a patient. Although he chose to set the novel in Philadelphia's major outbreak of 1793, Brown had just survived Philadelphia's 1797 epidemic and had at least contemplated a plan of his own to tend fever victims that year, in an epidemic that killed close to 1,250 people. (As Philadelphia's 1797 fever raged, Smith wrote a terse, one-lined letter to Brown, who had not kept his New York friends updated on his condition or whereabouts: "Charles, are you dead?") Fever was on everyone's mind as spring turned into summer in 1798. With the opening chapters of *Mervyn* safely on deposit with the *Weekly Magazine*'s editor and the manuscript for his first completed novel, *Sky-Walk*, also at press, Brown returned to New York, where he would spend the remainder of the summer living with Smith and Johnson. Arriving in the city on Independence Day, with his career as a fiction writer just gaining momentum, he had little idea that his Philadelphia publishers would be dead by summer's end, cutting *Mervyn*'s serialization short and consigning *Sky-Walk* to oblivion. (The manuscript was never recovered.) Nor did he imagine that in New York he would confront yellow fever more directly than he ever had, surviving an epidemic season that left him infected and Smith dead.

If the fever, in taking Elihu Smith's life, bore at least part of the responsibility for the Friendly Club's eventual disintegration, it had also, from 1795 to the turn of the century, called out the group's collective social and intellectual energies as nothing else had and provided its members with a particularly dramatic context for fashioning identities and reputations as "men of observation." The yellow fever debates epitomized the burgeoning late-eighteenth-century world of information. The recurring epidemics, writes one media historian, generated an "incredible rush of communication": newspaper essays, articles, notices, open letters, personal correspondence, diary accounts, drawing room discussions, broadsides, poetry, political satire, and every other "channel of communication" imaginable, "from word-of-mouth rumor to learned medical treatise," was a conduit for information and misinformation about the fever. The omnipresence of death created an industry for knowledge about the source, treatment, prevention, and social effects of the fever, including journalistic accounts and especially necrologies. Well into the nineteenth century, American presses turned out pamphlets, columns, and health codes, one medical student's inaugural dissertation after another, all arguing the fine points of the fever's origins, transmission, and treatment. As a concrete body of early American writing, this work is so large that it should perhaps be considered a second set of constitutional debates, this one concerned not with the previous decade's U.S. Constitution but with comprehending the constitutions of America's soils and climates, as well as the impact of the fever on its manners and populations.

The "rush of communication" precipitated by yellow fever was itself the subject of extensive commentary.[9] Rumors about the fever seemed self-regenerative, as Brown had complained to his brother. Smith expressed similar concerns about the proliferation of fever stories; in their constant retellings, such accounts "acquire[d] redoubled horror" until cities found themselves in "a violent state of alarm."[10] The virtual subindustry of print that emerged on the subject, along with unregulated rivers of rumor, gave rise to a "situation of the public mind," in Smith's words, in which the diversification and protraction of the debates made it increasingly difficult for "the medical world," let alone the general population, to accept the simple "truth" of the explanations he and his colleagues offered.[11] "It is time that something was done to relieve the minds of the ignorant from this overwhelming, this destructive Terror," Smith resolved in his diary at the height of New York's first major outbreak: "[T]his malady of the mind . . . [is] a thousand times more dreadful & pernicious than all corporal evils."[12]

Because unmanaged information yielded the worst possible audience responses, the appearance of yellow fever in so many American cities generated acute anxiety for men like the Friendly Club's members, who conceptualized their social standing as rooted in being better informed than their fellow citizens. Smith mined the city's libraries in order to benefit from historical sources on epidemic diseases. Desperate for authentic intelligence from neighborhoods and cities other than their own, he and other club members sought, even prior to New York's 1795 epidemic, to establish correspondences with physicians and acquaintances in other cities, particularly in Philadelphia.[13] Noah Webster's collection on the subject convinced Smith that a more regular publication was needed to collect and distribute accurate information as widely as possible.[14] He began to outline a proposal for a medical journal in July 1796 and published it, in partnership with Mitchill and Miller, that November. Addressed, "To the Physicians of the United States," the circular called out to a broad set of potential contributors. "[T]he variety of subjects comprehended in this undertaking," they anticipated, "will put it in the power of almost every other class of citizens, as well as of physicians, usefully to aid in its execution."[15] Smith extended similar calls through his own correspondence: "If there is any sensible, well-informed Physician settled near you," he wrote to a friend in Georgia, "I will thank you to let me know; & also to send me his name & address." Such correspondences would not only bring information back to him from remote parts but also open a channel by which his publication could find distribution.[16]

Such urgency stemmed from the conviction that words and imagination—the very stuff of fiction—had moral and even physical effects. The stories one hears or the scenes one imagines can influence what one actually sees, can affect literal and metaphoric *views*, an idea that runs consistently through the group's fever writing. In the *Monthly Magazine* for August 1799, for example, we find anonymous letters, purportedly from "a Gentleman in Philadelphia to his Friend in England," which lament that "[n]umerous and stubborn facts" about the fever, "drawn from various parts of the United States," are being blocked from public view by "invented" "[t]ales, most absurd." "[S]o blinded by prejudice or interest are some minds," the gentleman writes, "that having once shut their eyes, they obstinately determine not to re-admit the light, lest their fortunes might suffer, or the reputation of a favorite city be impaired."[17]

Smith's "The Plague of Athens" literalizes the notion that stories can supplant sight. Published in the *Repository*'s inaugural issue, Smith's essay climaxes in the assertion that the ancient plague of Athens (which struck during the Peloponnesian War) and contemporary yellow fever epidemics were essentially the same disease. As part of his catalog of symptoms, gleaned from sources as varied as Hesiod, Thucydides, and modern historians like Gibbon and De Pauw, Smith suggests "that the *vision* was impaired" in plague victims and that some suffered "a total loss of the substance of the eyes." As happened in modern epidemics, Smith continued, rumors and superstition also shut out accurate views. "Thucydides enlarges, with consummate eloquence," he writes, "on the terrible influence which this calamity exercised over the minds of his countrymen." Friends, fearing contagion, refused assistance to friends. Victims were denied lodging. Famine reigned. Worst of all, a "superstitious horror seized on every heart, and weighed down every spirit, when they remembered the interdictions of the Oracle . . . and imagined . . . the effects of the vengeance of the offended Gods." No ritual or observance, however, could stop the plague's spread, and the results were devastating: "For it inflicted the most dreadful pains on all who experienced it; spared neither age, nor sex; destroyed near 5000 of the flower of the Athenian armies, with an immense multitude of the poor; and did not disappear until after it had . . . reduced the powerful republic of Athens to the very verge of ruin and despair."[18] The major warning is obvious: modern republics will suffer the same way if appropriate measures are not taken or if the wrong authorities are granted the public's trust.

Smith's self-conception as a medical observer foregrounds the importance of clear sight. Hiking, during the high point of New York's 1795 epidemic, to the top of a prominent hill, he sought to "survey the town, in all it's parts, advantageously & at my leisure." He filed his findings—a description of the ups and downs of street elevation and building density—in his diary under the heading "FACTS, RELATIVE TO THE FEVER," clearly confident in his powers of observation.[19] Similarly, Smith's description of the "situation of the public mind" created by yellow fever invokes a metaphor of standpoint or perspective, whose shadowy side Brown explores in the letter to his brother already quoted. "Plague operates by invisible agents," Brown writes. "We know not in what quarter it is about to attack us."[20] If this situation leaves most people flailing in and fearing the dark, someone must exist, by contrast, open-eyed and observing. Like Smith, Brown crafted a professional identity as an observer—a "moral observer," as he describes himself in the preface to *Arthur Mervyn*. As such he will note the material effects of storytelling and aim to legitimate writing—even the writing of novels—as a useful professional endeavor and as a contribution to moral and scientific knowledge. Consider the language of observation, fact-gathering, and exhibition in the prefaces to Brown's other novels: "[I]t is the business of moral painters to exhibit their subject in its most instructive and memorable forms. If history furnishes one parallel fact, it is a sufficient vindication of the Writer" (*Wieland*); "America has opened new views to the naturalist and politician, but has seldome furnished themes to the moral painter. . . . It is the purpose of this work to profit by some of these sources; to exhibit a series of adventures, growing out of the condition of our country" (*Edgar Huntly*).[21] In these descriptions Brown not only articulates a desire to "exhibit" useful information but also hopes to construct a position of authority for "the Writer" as an arbiter of knowledge about the new nation and its citizens.[22]

The *Medical Repository*'s founding can be understood as part of a broader consolidation of the medical profession in America, as medical associations strengthened ties to political institutions and other established forms of social authority, and as broad-ranging medical reform emphasized the creation of information networks among practitioners. Such consolidation and reform came only gradually, as various sources of information struggled, at this moment, for dominance of an expanding public sphere.[23] Along with Brown's fever writing, the medical journal emerged within this moment of simultaneous anxiety and self-confidence. In addition to sharing a field of knowledge production on the fever, evident in their common commitment to particular medical doctrines, they shared a conviction that literary forms could serve as useful avenues for disseminating medical information to a broad readership. If words and imagination could further the disease, language also had the potential for more salutary effects. More specifically, the group's concern for storytelling in epidemic contexts stemmed not only from its competition with other sources of knowledge on the fever but also from its members' particular understanding of the relationship between storytelling and the body, evident in the minute attention they paid in medical practice and in their writing to the decomposing bodies of fever victims. Such local concerns had broader implications as they epitomized debates on the politics of information, the professionalization of print, and the distribution of useful knowledge: the specific concerns of their idealized republic of intellect.

Fever Writing and Cultural Authority in and around an Epidemic

Recognizing the similarities among club members' various professional and authorial self-understandings requires readers to take seriously Brown's statement, in the preface to *Arthur Mervyn*, that his novel constitutes a "venture" into "medical and political discussions [of yellow fever] . . . afloat in the community."[24] The prefatory remark provides another reminder that Brown's novel constitutes only a small part of the printed and spoken responses to early American yellow fever epidemics. The hyperproduction of fever stories resulted in part from the bitterly entrenched divisions among physicians that emerged in Philadelphia in 1793 and only deepened over the following decades. The primary contentions concerned transmission and treatment; was yellow fever an imported contagion, or the domestic product of environmental causes like soil, diet, sanitation, and atmosphere? Was it best treated by mild means—quinine ("the bark") and wine—or by more dramatic measures, like the bloodletter's lancet or mercury purges? Importantly, each side of these debates relied on skillful storytelling to visualize the invisible workings of the disease. "Importationist" or "contagionist" narratives pictured a communicable (or "catching") fever shipped from the West Indies in sailors' and immigrants' bodies and material goods. On the opposing side, "climatists," "sanitationists," or "non-importationists" argued that the fever was not communicable person to person but generated, rather, in the polluted atmosphere that arose from common city filth, or in the stagnant air of poorly ventilated housing. No one knew at the time (and no one would guess for another century) that the disease *did* come by ship, though not carried by infected sailors or their material goods but by female *Aedes aegypti* mosquitoes, packed under the lids of water casks like so many illicit stowaways.[25]

The *Repository*'s editors designed the journal, from the start, not only to participate in these increasingly national and international debates but to win them. Smith's former teacher, Benjamin Rush, had convinced him that Philadelphia's 1793 epidemic originated locally. His experience in New York in 1795 cemented that belief, and he remained a fierce partisan for local-origin theories until he died. Edward Miller, a decade older than Smith, had known Rush since the early 1780s, when both had served as physicians to the Revolutionary Army. Miller completed his formal training under Rush at the University of

Pennsylvania, taking a bachelor of medicine in 1785 and a doctor of medicine in 1789. From Dover, Delaware, he had taken a keen interest in Philadelphia's situation in 1793 and became one of Rush's regular medical correspondents.[26] He moved to New York following its 1795 epidemic at his brother Samuel's insistence that the city required his skills after losing a number of physicians to the fever that fall. His arrival was highly anticipated by Smith and Mitchill, who both joined the staff of the New-York Hospital as physicians that June. (See Fig. 8.) Mitchill's appointment in particular was designed to ally the hospital with the college's medical school.[27] Six years older than Smith, he had received his medical training in Edinburgh, where he graduated in 1786, and had been a professor of chemistry, natural history, and agriculture at Columbia College since 1792. With both the hospital and college dominated by climatist-sanitationists, New York's local debates in the 1790s had a preponderance of physicians on one side and cautious politicians, a merchant-dominated Health Committee, and some portions of the general public on the other. Though debates in New York never reached the level of vitriol that characterized Philadelphia's response, New York's physicians and citizen-observers like Noah Webster participated fully in the contentious interstate and international exchanges on the topic.

Whether living in New York or Philadelphia, Brown too was surrounded by these debates day in and day out.[28] Most recent criticism of his fever novels, however, pays far less attention to the fever as an actual medical crisis than to the seductive potential of "contagion" as a metaphor. Certainly contagion held metaphoric currency in the eighteenth century; Brown himself, in *Arthur Mervyn,* draws analogies between fever and seduction, friendship, debt, romantic infatuation, panic, sympathy, dirty jokes, prostitution, debauchery, sadness, and a lover's anxieties.[29] Rather than forming a consistent pattern, however, these various references to figurative infections, contractions, and contagions suggest that "contagion" and disease are too easy as metaphors.[30] Brown's novel and the story of Elihu Smith's death inadvertently offer stark warnings that the impulse to make disease a metaphor diminishes the experience of actual victims and those who care for them.[31]

Brown's fever stories are better understood if they are situated within the broader range of information called into existence by epidemics. New Yorkers first encountered a surge in writing about yellow fever in response to Philadelphia's situation in 1793, which pointed dramatically to the fever's disruption of an accurate information flow between cities. As James Kent wrote to his brother upstate, "communication with Philadelphia" by October, when the fever was at its peak, had become "completely prevented," along with the bonds of fellowship with the distraught Philadelphians. "[A] Committee sits every Evening at the Coffee-House, & the citizens Patrole the Wharves & Shores every night to prevent any Philadelphian from arriving," Kent wrote. This ad hoc group, which would later become the city's official Health Committee, aimed "to break all communications with Philadelphia."[32] They even published a broadside warning against the consumption of Philadelphia goods. The strategy would benefit New York "if the disease was easily communicated," Kent commented, but some of the city's physicians already blamed "the Atmosphere of Philadelphia" instead. Nor were medical explanations the only ones being offered. The Reverend Dr. John Mason preached that the epidemic, like Indian hostilities on the Western frontiers, signaled God's judgment on Americans for forgetting him so quickly after delivering them through the Revolution. (Mason was particularly indignant that the Christian God had been neglected in the newly ratified Constitution.) New Yorkers shouldn't take comfort in escaping Philadelphia's fate, Mason warned, for "[a] sovereign God has made them an example of his righteous vengeance," and their city could be next.[33]

Such statements make it clear that the politics of information, in an epidemic setting, was intimately bound with problems of social authority rooted in competition among the professions. In New York's 1795 epidemic, primed by watching Philadelphia's experience from afar, government officials as well as physicians and general citizens scrambled to find appropriate responses. Battles ensued over the regulation of public knowledge, even as the means of conveying information continued to multiply. In the spring of 1795, prior even to New York's first major outbreak, the Health Committee, newly made official by Governor George Clinton, issued broadsides about a fever currently raging in the West Indies and warned ships they would face quarantine and inspection before they could enter the city's port. More broadsides followed in the fall, as the city's epidemic got seriously underway. One such publication in early August reassured citizens that the fever was contained and alarm unwarranted, though it also warned of the need for public vigilance and sanitary precautions.

The Health Committee represented politicians' efforts to stem the disease; its membership was dominated by merchants but included some members of the Medical Society of the State of New York (a weekly discussion circle of gentleman physicians since the 1740s, made the official state society in 1794), the College of Physicians, the staff of the New-York Hospital, and other physicians in private practice.[34] In spite of their shared memberships, these groups clashed at the turn of the century over public health policy. Much confusion stemmed from various meanings of the word "communication," always loaded in epidemic contexts. During the first weeks of the 1795 epidemic, the Health Committee called on the Medical Society "to communicate their sentiments and exchange ideas on the subject of the present epidemic in the upper part of the city." The society responded with a resolution to "meet every Tuesday evening during the continuance of the present epidemic, and that the members communicate to the Society a statement of their practice respecting fevers in general, the numbers of their patients, their residence, occupation, and events, with such remarks and observations on particular cases as they think proper."[35]

Such a cooperative spirit did not last long. The Health Committee soon accused the College of Physicians of withholding information on patients.[36] Angry doctors complained that the committee was only partially informed regarding the fever.[37] While the committee claimed to be anticontagionist in doctrine (in line with Rush and Smith), it took measures that seemed motivated by fear of contagion, such as demanding that doctors send their patients to the newly opened Bell Vue hospital, located well out of town to the northeast, or quarantining incoming ships with any sign of sickness on board. Physicians considered these measures an encroachment on their authority to determine the best treatment of victims. The debate over the fever's origins presented further problems. Though the Medical Society had officially declined to weigh in on the controversial question of "whether the late epidemic was imported or generated among us," its report on the 1795 epidemic, which included recommendations to the city government, was essentially a sanitationist document: "The accumulation of filth in the streets; this being composed chiefly of dead animal and vegetable substances, is, when exposed to a hot sun, a source of noxious effluvia, which has a tendency to produce the most fatal effects."[38]

Over the coming years the society repeatedly expressed frustration that its sanitary recommendations were never fully acted upon by the corporation of the city.[39] For their part, the official statements of the

Health Committee were designed to stem panic in the moment and, when collected and published after the fact, to demonstrate how active and industrious the committee had been. A volume of *Letters from the Health Office* that followed the 1798 epidemic seems especially calculated in this regard, as it depicts the health commissioners busily trotting about the city sniffing out what they believed were the sources of contagion, such as a load of spoiled beef in a merchant's basement.[40]

In response to confused and conflicting governmental responses, only some of which made their way into the public prints, texts began to emerge from several other quarters, all offering competing explanations and recommendations: popular or journalistic accounts, sermons, scientific treatises, and medical writing, including the *Medical Repository*, whose editors also published their ideas about the fever elsewhere. The first popular journalistic accounts of the fever had emerged in Philadelphia in the midst of the 1793 epidemic. Mathew Carey initially dominated the market with his famous *Short Account of the Malignant Fever*, which appeared in multiple editions before the epidemic had even subsided.[41] In New York, following the 1795 epidemic, a young man named Matthew Livingston Davis, who would later go on to be one of Aaron Burr's chief lieutenants, followed Carey's example and attempted the same sort of instant history. Of all the New York accounts, this one would seem to uphold the alliance between sanitationist doctrine and democratic politics; Davis blames the large number of Irish immigrant deaths in 1795—perhaps up to two-thirds of the 750 people who died—on escalating rents that resulted from European political unrest, rapid urban growth (the number of families in the city had doubled between 1790 and 1795), and "luxury and pride" among landholding New Yorkers. Davis praises the Health Committee but has little good to say about physicians in general, whom he sees as overinvested in their own reputations.[42]

Clergymen also competed to offer explanations and advice. Some told their congregations, as the Reverend Mason had in 1793, that the fever was a form of divine retribution. The Dutch Reformed minister William Linn, Brown's future father-in-law, numbered among the offenders on this front. In a published sermon he declared, "If we have suffered public judgments, there must be public sins which have occasioned them; for God *doth not afflict willingly, nor grieve the children of men.*"[43] Smith, Brown, and the majority of their friends had no patience for such views. Smith complained in his diary that ideas like these would only hamper efforts to find the sources of disease and remove them. "All the churches, on the Continent, are, I suppose, now opened to besiege the Almighty, as he is called, with petitions," Smith wrote from his apartment during the 1795 epidemic. "At this moment, a Methodist, who dwells in the house opposite, is beseeching the Deity, with nasal twang; & praying him to remove *his judgements,* from New York. . . . [A]nd our Corporation or Magistracy have tho't fit at this time, to renew the laws for the religious observance of Sunday; & for restraining the Goats from going in the Streets. But there is no end to the absurdities on this subject."[44]

Smith and friends placed greater faith in a diverse body of sanitationist writing. Benjamin Rush received Smith's unending loyalty. As early as the spring of 1794, Smith wrote to Rush that he eagerly awaited his account of "the late Fever in Philadelphia," which he hoped would transcend "contentions of opinion" among physicians and prepare an "opening . . . for the ready reception of truth."[45] Smith, Mitchill, and Rush also encouraged the participation in these debates of learned laymen like Webster.[46] At least initially, proponents of local origin theories considered Webster's intervention a boon to their cause.[47] He demonstrated that debates should not discredit the profession generally and that citizens could aid physicians in their broader contest for solutions. These alliances reflected ways in which an older model of the republic of letters was still in place: both protodisciplinary and yet concerned with consolidation of a class-based professional authority.

As representatives of very different approaches to publishing anticontagionist doctrine, the *Repository*'s editors illustrate various kinds of cultural work this writing performed. They also illustrate a primary reason the sanitationist cause was so compelling: its ability to generate images for what seemed to be the invisible sources of infection. Mitchill blamed the fever on "the gaseous oxyd of azote," which he also called "pestilential fluids" or "septon."[48] (The latter term eventually became his favorite.) This was the invisible substance some observers referred to as "contagion," though Mitchill and his sanitationist colleagues believed it to be an atmospheric condition rather than something generated in victims' bodies or spread by personal contact.[49]

Mitchill aimed to publicize his "Doctrine of Septon" not simply for academic purposes but to effect immediate social intervention. He held that oxygen and septon existed on a principle of balance. Following Priestley and Lavoisier, Mitchill viewed oxygen as the foundation of life; "septon" (a name Mitchill derives, like *septic,* from the Greek word for "putrescent") was the "principle of dissolution." When the two combine in disproportionate volumes, he argued, they release "pestilential fluids" into the atmosphere. In order to counter the progress of pestilence, Mitchill took various measures, from inventing a machine called the Oeleopile to remove foul air from courtrooms, to prescribing the use of alkalis—lime and potash in particular—to neutralize septon. For this reason, he encouraged urban residents to whitewash the interiors of their homes with lime; some even ingested it as a self-protective measure. Otherwise, a "redundant acidity . . . would prevail and destroy the balance of powers in the natural world." Fever would result, and decomposition, beginning even before a fever victim has died, would threaten atmospheric pollution and perpetuate an epidemic.[50] Septic air, Mitchill and most other sanitationists believed, resulted from a mixture of rotten animal and vegetable matter: street droppings, privy pits, spoiled goods, and the made land on which the city was expanding year by year, some of which was filled with dead animals, oyster shells, and other refuse. In addition to countering such effluvia with alkalis Mitchill recommended eliminating meat from one's diet, since rotten meat could generate contagion in the alimentary canal just as easily as if it were left outside to poison the atmosphere with tiny particles of decomposing matter.

Mitchill approached the fever from his perspective as a professor of chemistry. Initially his publications on the topic were highly technical and relied primarily on his creative synthesis of established scientific authorities and his own reasoning, especially on chemical subjects. His theories gained international attention—including translation into German—though they received high-profile criticism as well. Later he realized that imaginative prose, familiar correspondence, and even poetry may offer more effective vehicles for delivering his arguments to general readers; in addition to publishing scientific pamphlets and articles in the *Repository,* Mitchill wrote magazine essays addressed to housewives and exchanged public correspondence with figures like Webster on the question of what should be done with street manure, one possible source of noxious effluvia.[51]

Mitchill wrote gripping prose, images as vivid as the smells he described were pungent. Yellow fever was not a "catching disease," he wrote, communicable from one person to another like "the *small pocks.*"[52] To counter such assumptions, he described the effects of septic fluids on the body's internal processes in a gothic mode, likely leaving readers feeling as if the very air they were breathing might be working corrosion through their systems. In a 1796 letter to a New York congressman, for example, published in the *New-York Magazine* and reprinted in one of his medical students' inaugural dissertations, Mitchill argued that "[p]estilential fluids, thus exhaling from the surface of the earth, may completely surround the human body, and be applied to the whole cuticular and pulmonary surface, as well as to the entire mouth and nostrils: and the like productions, generated in the alimentary canal from corrupted food, may be spread all along the intestinal tube, so that the internal surface from the gullet to the anus, may at times be partially or entirely disordered by them."[53]

Mitchill's gothic body metonymically invoked a larger social body, also vulnerable to disease. To some observers, especially in 1795, the preponderance of Irish immigrants among the dead implied that the epidemic itself had purged the social body of disorder or waste.[54] Neither Smith nor Mitchill held such views. Smith discusses New York's Irish population in his early fever essays, and although he imagines their particular susceptibility to intemperance and a meat-heavy diet, he acknowledges the difficulty of only recently having escaped from English oppression, and he does not blame them for generating or carrying the disorder.[55] Mitchill is even more sympathetic to the immigrants' plight. He, like Matthew Davis, implies "the poor" (never ethnically distinguished) are the victims of commercial interests; but rather than dwell, as Davis had, on the sources of poverty, he lays most of the blame with municipal leaders who have allowed the city's expansion into the rivers and harbor on newly made ground. "[A] vast proportion of Water and Front-Streets," Mitchill wrote as part of a Medical Society report in 1799, "have been made out of the most exceptionable materials," including "bones, oyster-shells, wood-shavings, street-scrapings, offals, and in short every thing else, save good earth, gravel or sand." The city was being built, in other words, on diseased foundations. And not only the new waterfront lots; Mitchill's version of the social body metaphor became increasingly literal in other accounts he wrote: "If my information is correct, the exhalations from privies and sinks in many parts of this city [and] [t]he vapours issuing from barrels of putrefying beef have poisoned a number of our citizens. Many stores, yards and cellars abound with substances equally detrimental to health; and in addition to this, it deserves to be mentioned that human carcases, buried and accumulated for a long series of years, have poisoned the air in many parts of christendom, and that by the concurrence of both municipal and spiritual authority."[56]

Even so, dead animal and human bodies did not pose the only danger. Mitchill finally telescoped the seat of the social body's disorder into the bodies of representative citizens and not just the poor. In one pamphlet he argues in great detail that animals, including humans, carry a significant amount of "manure" within their bodies, which results in stomach problems, often a symptom of yellow fever. "A source of poisonous effluvia," he wrote, "thus seems to exist in our own bodies, sufficient to disturb the animal machine excessively, and even to effect its destruction. [The] great quantities of butcher's meat, poultry and fish which we consume, are the materials which chiefly afford the gaseous oxyd. . . . [A]s long as we gorge ourselves with animal food, and dwell among its putrefactive recrements, the poisonous gaseous oxyd of azote proceeding therefrom, must be expected to disturb both our respiratory and digestive functions, and be followed by distress and woe."[57]

As a member of a New York health committee following the epidemic of 1798, Mitchill called for tighter regulation of all forms of decomposing matter, including "temples of Cloaecina," or privy pits, which spilled over into neighboring cellars that sometimes served as crowded housing for immigrant families. Mitchill's point is plain: to overlook the recommendations of his committee was to ensure that inhabitants would "continue to *eat*, and *drink*, and *respire* a part of their OWN EXCRETIONS."[58] They will, in other words, become like the disease itself, which gorges on human flesh, eliminating the distinction between body and waste. Believing that his "inquiry has brought contagion home to our doors, and traced it to its seat within our bodies," Mitchill declared, "Henceforth much of the labour employed in tracing the origin of fevers in foreign places, and their introduction in ships to our own ports, may be considered superfluous."[59]

Such descriptions allow for two key observations. The first regards what might be called their imaginative dimension. Clearly these theories owe as much to the physician's imagination as they do to any empirical science. But Mitchill's accounts significantly differ from importationist claims (equally imagined rather than empirically demonstrated) that West Indian trade imported the fever. Rather, Mitchill identifies as the culprit something even plainer to anyone who approached the waterfront district on a hot late summer afternoon: the overwhelming stench of the city—something you can smell, taste, almost feel as it folds around you, fills your nostrils, and turns your stomach. His accounts translate olfactory observations into verbal and visual images, a method for locating the fever's sources he believed was more empirical than attempts to trace the coincidence of incoming ships with outbreaks of the disorder.[60] Second, and perhaps more importantly, Mitchill's descriptions place significant emphasis on social authority. He aims to trump both religious and municipal leaders the same way he has trumped his medical opponents, by convincing the general public to follow his advice. Not surprisingly, Mitchill's multiple career paths included stints in the U.S. House and Senate, where he sought to enact legislation based on his scientific speculations: a utopian collapse of literary, medical, and state authority, with poet-physicians holding the reins of government.

Medical Eloquence and Sympathetic Stomachs

The *Medical Repository* shared with *Arthur Mervyn* an assumption that great nations are built on exemplary writing that explores in minute detail unmapped terrains—cultural, geographical, geological, atmospheric. The concern for the poetics of medical discussion perhaps came naturally to Smith and Mitchill, both of whom composed poetry on medical and nonmedical subjects, but Smith's diary entries frame his notion of "medical eloquence" as a deliberate strategy for creating a general, educated audience. (So concerned was Smith with the journal's "literary character" that he asked for Brown's writerly opinion, particularly regarding his "Plague of Athens.")[61]

When the *Repository* debuted in the fall of 1797, it positioned itself as responding directly to the eruption of fever stories that followed Philadelphia's 1793 and New York's 1795 epidemics. Smith, who clearly conceived of the magazine as a vehicle for his own writing and reputation, took an approach that was slightly different from Mitchill's; he emphasized the visual not so much by creating harrowing images for what cannot be seen, but by foregrounding medical observation—not only through the rise of anatomical knowledge through dissection, which was also happening at this moment, but also by observing the environment. Smith's hike to the hilltop, for example, allowed him to survey the city, looking for places where the land was not level and buildings too densely packed. As a sanitationist, he believed the sources of the fever would be visible, even if effluvia were not. One medical historian describes Smith's fever writing as providing a "verbal map" of the fevered city. The same mindset drove one of the editors' medical allies, Valentine Seaman, to publish in the *Repository* what some historians consider the first spot maps used to trace the progress of an epidemic.[62]

The *Medical Repository* shares with Brown's fever writing an emphasis on the difficulties of controlling information and its effects in the midst of an epidemic. A distempered public mind meant that individual imaginations, if unbalanced, could leave citizens more susceptible to the fever than they might otherwise be. The ability of the fever to dominate conversation and thought was only part of the problem. Writing in his diary during New York's 1795 outbreak, Smith dramatizes the dilemmas faced by citizens and social bodies:

> Wherever you go, the Fever is the invariable & unceasing topic of conversation. . . . People collect in groups to talk it over, & to frighten each other into fever, or flight. I saw, in Maiden-Lane, this morning, a Carman, at a Cabinet-maker's, taking in a load of Coffins. A number of persons, of various colors, ages & sexes, were staring, half-dismayed, at this unwelcome sight. Here was fresh matter for discourse. In one shape, or other, the fever is constantly brought into view; & the soul sickens with the ghastly and abhorred repetition.[63]

Like death, fear, in Smith's description, nullifies distinction. The scene distresses Smith not only because any "number of persons" can "frighten each other into fever" (a literal threat, according to his medical understanding), but also because the "discourse" that replaces an "unwelcome sight" (when fever clouds one's views) is more exaggerated than it is informed. Brown dramatizes these dangers of imagination in a similar scene he used in both a Philadelphia magazine serial ("The Man at Home") and in *Ormond:* a nervous Philadelphian observes the nighttime burial of an assumed fever victim, then retreats, fearing contagion, to his home, where he dies, "an example," the narrator intones, "of the force of imagination." Smith's street scene is even more sinister; the dead bodies in his narrative are not even present but simply suggested to the imagining onlookers by the load of newly finished coffins. The idea of corpses—imagined or real—as "fresh matter" is both oxymoronic and chilling, and suggests that partial or erroneous information diseases, even as it generates, discussion.

The *Repository*'s editors clearly intended their journal as an antidote. Fancying themselves as exerting top-down control over the dissemination of medical information, the editors hoped to enlist a broad audience in stemming local panic and promoting the climatist cause.[64] They aimed as well to confer professional legitimacy on all who published there. In the context of fever debates this meant validating a community of physicians and informed gentlemen who endorsed the climatists' medical agenda. The *Repository,* Smith wrote in his diary, would separate sheep from goats among physicians; as the observers put themselves on display and subjected themselves to public scrutiny, the spurious would be "exposed," and "men of real talents" would assume "a more elevated rank in the eyes of their fellow-citizens."[65]

The fiction of a unified American medical community depended on a projection of a unified public sphere. In this way the *Repository* resembled those who claimed to represent the "popular voice" while dismissing opponents as dangerous or ignoring them altogether.[66] Debate was limited to the nuances of the climatist position; contagionist doctrines appeared only as the subject of merciless review essays.[67] In the editors' minds, such silencing of opponents' voices was not sinister; it was necessary to convince American decision-makers of the need for precautions that would, they believed, prevent more deaths. In order to construct a national medical audience, the *Repository* assumed the form of popular literary miscellanies, including a broad variety in content and genre. Like literary journals (which also commonly named themselves "repositories," "cabinets," or "museums") the *Repository's* structure mimicked other cultural forms that were distinctly visual in their self-presentation. With an emphasis on collection and exhibition, popular miscellanies, imitating mineral cabinets, sought to organize knowledge and transfix the gaze, creating meaning in the association of differing objects. Accordingly, each issue was broken up into small selections of periodical essays, specialized observations, reviews, foreign and domestic "medical news," and correspondence. The final category included letters to the journal's editors as well as public correspondence between prominent medical figures, or letters from public health officials to municipal leaders. On occasion these exchanges were "representations of correspondence" rather than letters that had their origins in private circulation. These public exchanges were framed as familiar letters to offer an audience the sense that it overheard privileged information from trustworthy sources.[68] All these forms were popular eighteenth-century genres, occupying an ill-defined border between belles lettres and moral or scientific instruction.

Two examples from the *Repository*'s store of medical writing—Samuel Mitchill's poetic rendering of his "Doctrine of Septon" and Edward Miller's essays on the stomachs of yellow fever victims—illustrate beliefs these writers shared with Smith and Brown about specific relationships between storytelling, fever, and the body. The deteriorating flesh of fever victims provided a compelling text for the competing interpretations of medical observers and others; nuanced narrations of symptoms, climaxing in the "decomposition" of the stomach as signaled by the black vomit, featured regularly in the volumes, pamphlets, clinical anecdotes, and periodical essays that circulated during and after epidemics. These diseased bodies, dead or alive, come to figure, in medical writing and fiction alike, as a trope of deteriorating discourse, both polluted and polluting. But the analogy between a fever-producing atmosphere and a degenerating public sphere took on literal as well as allegorical meanings in epidemic contexts. These writings shared with Brown's a medical belief that the gut reactions produced by fevers and by fever rumors demonstrated the stomach's unique susceptibility both to disease and to terror, a belief that underscores the precarious state of these writers' potential readers.

Published in the *Repository*'s first volume, Mitchill's poem contains both the basic principles of his medical system and his response to the reception issues at stake for his readers. The poem follows Erasmus Darwin's *Botanic Garden* by beginning with an apostrophe to Popean "Gnomes!" who observe the decomposition of "Organic relics": "Subdued by Death, whose fury nothing spares," they "[t]urn back to Earth, or change again to Airs." Mitchill's gnomes redeem Pope's; their association with the earth is positive rather than negative, for they are masters of mineralogy. These sympathetic spectators (who look on "with pity and with pain") have witnessed gestation and birth as well as death. They have seen living forms "excit[ed]" "Till, aged grown, the exhausted fabric drops, / Each function fails, and every motion stops." They understand that oxygen is the vital principle, and that "Grim Septon, arm'd with power to intervene" aims to "disconnect the animal machine." Then, as Mitchill explains in the marginal gloss, we see the "[e]ffects of Septon and its compounds on the mind and body, in producing disease":

Within the great Disorganizer lurks,
And plans, unseen, his undermining works;

. . . .

Next, bolder grown, the Tyrant, with a frown,
Bids Scurvy break the blood and vessels down;
Lepra and Serpigo attacks begin,
And sores and blotches desolate the skin;
Shews greedy cancer how he best may thrive,
And gorge and feast on human flesh alive;
Tells Fever, as in ambuscade he lies,
An hundred ways to take us by surprise;
To Intermittent, Plague, and Hectic joins
And Causos, Typhus, Synocha combines;
Possessing each, and all, as war they wage,
Sporadic force, or epidemic rage.[69]

Heeding the almost universal impulse among fever observers to personify the disease, Mitchill characterizes Septon as a literary villain, whose attempts at subversion and seduction aim not to violate female chastity but to "undermin[e]" the universal principle of balance. If every body contains within it the seeds of Septon, only those whose equilibrium is unsettled—by atmosphere, climate, diet, or fear—will fall prey to disease as Septon gains the upper hand. The unsettled balance allows Septon to speed up the natural course of degeneration through aging and allow death and decomposition early entry onto the scene. Once disease has ravaged its human hosts, "foul mephitic vapours" begin to "rise" from corpses as Septon "seduces" "[u]nwary oxygen" to his side. Finally, though, the gnomes "impede the Demon's deadly course" by marshalling "bands" of "celestial" alkalis, who provide "neutral chains" to bind Septon. The "[o]peration of calcareous earths," the gloss explains, including "alkaline salts, oily substances, clay, etc." triumph over Septon by "attracting" and neutralizing "pestilential airs."[70]

Mitchill litters his poem with literary allusions to familiarize his characters by association. The verses rewrite popular and classic literature—the Bible, Greek mythology and epic poetry, seduction motifs in contemporary novels—in order to secure a broader audience for his doctrines of local origins and noncontagion. The poem attempts to convey in poetic form what Mitchill and his friends had long argued: that the unregulated decomposition of organic matter—both vegetable and animal—generates disease. Mitchill, like Smith, links such decomposing matter with a figure of corrupted communication. In the middle of the poem we find an extended analogy between Septon's generation of disease and Satan's deception of Eve in the Garden of Eden:

—Thus, when of old, as pious men believe,
The serpent whisper'd in the ear of Eve.
The subtle fiend a fit occasion sought,
With hellish guile, to poison human thought;
With winning guile seduced her easy faith,
And gave the fruit of knowledge, but of death:—

. . . .

Hence Pain, hence Sin, their wasteful course began;
Thro' all her offspring vile corruption ran;
And Man, depraved, to vice and error hurl'd
Still proves the Septon of the moral world.[71]

The degeneration of physical matter has corollaries in morals and language. Original sin becomes the "poison[ing of] human thought," indicating Mitchill's inability to separate moral from medical lessons. Both are intertwined, too, like the serpent encircling the tree of knowledge, with issues of communication. Those with "easy faith" will be vulnerable both to misinformation and to vice; in either case, the body's balance of excitement is unsettled, rendering it vulnerable to disease.

Mitchill's poem is likely the most fanciful description to emerge from the fever literature. A more typical example, though just as dramatic, comes from the inaugural dissertation of a Columbia medical student, written in 1803:

[The fever] is ushered in by a general degree of langour, listlessness, want of recollection, and disinclination to all kinds of active exertion; to which soon succeeds the febrile shivering, which again having continued an infinite period of time, is followed by an intense degree of heat— quickened and laborious respiration—pulse, for the most part, frequent, full, hard and throbbing—skin dry—tongue whitish and moist, having an appearance peculiar to diseases of membranous inflammation—bowels generally costive, great oppression at the precordia, attended also with acute pains of the head, back, and loins, with a suffusion of the whole countenance, but particularly of the eyes. . . . [T]he patient is restless, sleeps little, and awakes without being refreshed; the thirst also

... being excessive. These symptoms, if not relieved, only prove to be the precursors of another set of symptoms infinitely more dangerous, and to which the assistance of the physicians can afford very little relief. The pulses sink; they become weak, very frequent, and often intermittent. The state of the tongue is infinitely more alarming, having changed from a whitish color to one almost approaching black. The redness of the countenance generally, and eyes in particular, is now followed by a yellow color. The whole body often takes on the same appearance. The vomiting ... now becomes incessant, and the matter ejected ... appears now to be the effect of a morbid change having taken place in [the stomach]. Hemorrhages from the nose and mouth are not unfrequent. The patient is by turns sensible and delirious. Subsultus tendinum, and coldness of the extremities now succeed, when the patient may be said to be struggling with death, which unfortunately soon follows.[72]

The sprawling sentences, punctuated by sharp graphic phrases, manage to capture both the alarming intensity of the patient's experience (the dashes suggest a gasping for fresh air) and the clinical resistance to it (enclosing the physician's masterful scrutiny of physical effects). The fevered body makes radical changes in appearance as it approaches death, with shifts in color corresponding to levels of deterioration. According to one medical historian the four colors most often associated with the fever's progression—red, bluish-white, yellow, and black—were still linked, in the late eighteenth century, with theories of medicine in which "the body's four humors were associated with one of the known elements: blood with fire, phlegm with water, black bile with earth, and yellow bile with air." The color-coded humoral theory fit a seasonal schematic and "a [set of] specific psychological effect[s] (blood with spring and the sanguine temperament; phlegm with the winter and the phlegmatic temperament; black bile with autumn and melancholy; and yellow bile with summer and the bilious or choleric temperament)."[73] White to black, red to yellow, cold to flushed to clammy, the transitions read like the seasonal life cycle in fast forward, until the yellow and black of the late-summer, early-autumn "bilious" fever season manifest themselves through the body, which, jaundiced and ejecting black vomit, begins to decompose even before burial.

As in this account, many medical narratives described the fever as disabling body and mind. Most accounts called special attention to the stomach and the brain and dictated the terms by which club members processed their own experiences. "I do not understand my own case," Brown wrote to Dunlap following Smith's death, "but see enough to discover the combination of bodily and mental causes have made deep inroads on the vital energies of brain and stomach."[74] His perception returns in *Arthur Mervyn*'s infection scene, when Arthur "senses" he has inhaled a "vapour, infectious and deadly": "I seemed not so much to smell as to taste the element that now encompassed me. I felt as if I had inhaled a poisonous and subtle fluid, whose power instantly bereft my stomach of all vigour. Some fatal influence appeared to seize upon my vitals; and the work of corrosion and decomposition to be busily begun."[75] Brown's belief that physical and mental exhaustion facilitate infection remains continuous from fact to fiction. The most feared symptom, evidence of a vitiating of the stomach's "vital energies," the black vomit also signaled death's immanent approach. The brain's vital energies, when sapped by the fever, yielded to a loss of reason or a derangement of the imagination, thereby increasing susceptibility.

The relationship between brain and stomach, and between those organs and fear, found its most careful expositor in Edward Miller, with whom Brown lived during the final stages of Elihu Smith's disease. In the yellow fever patient, Miller explains, "miasmata," embedded in swallowed saliva, first invade the stomach, which then draws "into morbid sympathy various parts of the head, limbs, back &c. then the heart and arteries, and, successively, many other parts of the body."[76] The stomach is the organ in greatest sympathy with the brain ("as is often observed in the sudden loss of appetite . . . by the arrival of joyful or afflicting intelligence"). This sympathetic nature renders it particularly vulnerable to "terror." The connection between storytelling, fear, and the body is explicit. A person who has ingested pestilential miasma, Miller argues, might still stave off infection if the body's "equilibrium of excitement" can be preserved by avoiding "frightful" spectacles or "alarming" stories that would unsettle a delicate balance.[77] Some authors conveyed specific advice on how to treat irritated brains and stomachs; one graduating medical student recommends yeast for stomach problems, "followed with nourishing antiseptic drinks, such as milk-punch, lemonade, porter diluted with water, &c.," and for troubled brains suggests "sinapsims, composed of rye-meal, vinegar, and mustard, applied to the soles of the feet, blisters to the ankles, to the inside of the thighs, and to the head."[78] Rush and his followers, including Smith and Miller, recommended bloodletting to relieve these and other symptoms. But Miller's contributions also emphasize clearly the importance of regulating language about the fever. With the likelihood that fevers would continue to haunt the American landscape, and in the context of an overabundance of fever discourse, the need was clear for a carefully cultivated audience, one trained to separate fever rumors from "medical eloquence."

Arthur Mervyn's Omnivorous Gaze

When Brown completed *Arthur Mervyn,* following Smith's death, he described the novel's epidemic as generating both a surfeit of diseased bodies and a corrosion of social discourse. The novel unfolds through a proliferation of competing narrative voices, including contradictory characterizations of Mervyn himself, crucial information knowingly withheld, misinformation unwittingly passed on, language barriers that prevent communication, misreadings of appearances, conversations overheard illicitly though often fortuitously, letters lost and found, and forgeries. One might argue that the central preoccupation of the novel's twentieth-century critics—the question of Mervyn's reliability as a narrator—testifies to Brown's success in generating narrative suspense through these strategies. But the guessing game equally crucial to the novel's plot (Where did this fever come from? How are we to respond?) centers on ways in which the epidemic pretext for Brown's American gothic threatened to undermine the body politic by fragmenting scientific observers and the public mind more generally.

Arthur Mervyn, like all of Brown's work, shares with his friends' medical writing a fundamental concern with sensory evidence, visual evidence in particular. Eyes abound in the novel, from Arthur's need to see things with his "own eyes," which "sparkle with pleasure" when he has original information to convey, to the restless eyes of Watson's corpse, to Stevens's confidence in physiognomy, as he trains his eyes on Arthur, to Achsa's Jewish eyes, which against her will communicate the secret of her heredity.[79] Certain characters—Welbeck in particular—shrink from being the objects of observation, but "new light" continues to be thrown on them nonetheless.[80] From these optical allusions emerges an understanding of the relationship between how one sees and how one behaves, between one's "views" and one's actions.[81] Mervyn's central educational experience, for this reason, involves a lesson in epidemiology by the virtuous physician Medlicote, modeled in part on Smith, who teaches him how to "view" the fever by training his gaze on the apparently invisible: "He combatted an opinion which I had casually formed, respecting the origin of this epidemic, and imputed it, not to infected substances imported from the east or west, but to a morbid constitution of the atmosphere, owing wholly, or in part to filthy streets, airless habitations and squalid persons." Mervyn's "casually formed" opinions on the fever (and his behavioral responses to it) are as cloudy as the contaminated atmosphere of the city until he learns to see clearly the fever's origins.[82]

Sight, in *Arthur Mervyn,* is not a tragic or fallen sense; Brown's notorious suspicion of "appearances" reinforces rather than undermines this claim. Appearance implies uncertainty; observation requires rigor. Even in the novel's preface Brown visualizes language as a pestilential vapor; fever "discussions," like putrid miasmata, are "afloat," hovering over the "community." Positioning himself as a "moral observer" of this polluted environment, Brown explains what a writer does in such a setting by emphasizing the visual aspects of the fever and its effects above all else. Even human "passions and motives" are offered as "displays," classified like artifacts in a cabinet, framed for public viewing.[83]

Such language recalls the *Medical Repository*'s mission to unite and inform "men of observation"; the continuity between Brown's concerns and those of his medical-writing friends is illustrated well by contrasting the novel's two major introductions to the fever. The first occurs in the opening paragraphs, narrated by Dr. Stevens, who saves a fever-stricken Mervyn and functions for much of the novel as an amanuensis of the young man's bizarre adventures:

> Returning one evening, somewhat later than usual, to my own house, my attention was attracted, just as I entered the porch, by the figure of a man, reclining against the wall a few paces distant. My sight was imperfectly assisted by a far-off lamp; but the posture in which he sat, the hour, and the place immediately suggested the idea of one disabled by sickness. It was obvious to conclude that his disease was pestilential. This did not deter me from approaching and examining him more closely.
>
> . . . His throbbing temples and burning skin indicated a fever, and his form, already emaciated, seemed to prove that it had not been of short duration.
>
> There was only one circumstance that hindered me from forming an immediate determination in what manner this person should be treated.

My family consisted of my wife and a young child. . . . We ourselves enjoyed good health, and were hopeful of escaping with our lives. Our measures for this end . . . did not consist of avoiding the receptacles of infection, for my office requires me to go daily into the midst of them; not in filling the house with the exhalations of gun-powder, vinegar, or tar. They consisted in cleanliness, reasonable exercise, and wholesome diet. . . . To take this person into my house, and bestow upon him the requisite attendance was the scheme that first occurred to me.[84]

Stevens's opening paragraphs deserve to be quoted at length because they make so plain the nature of Brown's participation in "medical discussions" of the disease; the narrator-physician informs his audience immediately where he stands on debates over the fever's etiology. Remaining safe, Stevens explains, doesn't require fleeing the city, avoiding infectious sites, or filling the air with substances popularly believed to counter the poison of pestilence. Rather, simple sanitary measures at home, along with careful attention to personal fitness, will allow him to conduct business even in the "receptacles of infection" without putting himself or his family at risk. Stevens, contemporary readers would have recognized, promotes the sanitationist cause.

The medical implications of these opening scenes—in which the diseased body figures as a text to be read and interpreted—become even more persistent when we contrast the physician's discovery of a yellow fever victim (quite literally on his doorstep) with Arthur Mervyn's own narration, thirteen chapters later, of his initial encounter with rumors of the epidemic. According to the account he gives Stevens, Mervyn first hears of the fever while boarding in the country with a Quaker farmer named Hadwin, whose 15-year-old daughter kindles in him a "passion" that resembles a "disease" in its potential to destroy "either . . . [his] integrity or [his] existence."[85] Ethical dilemmas proliferate until one situation trumps all domestic concerns; following him from Philadelphia, news of the yellow fever epidemic had arrived in the form of

a rumour, which had gradually swelled to formidable dimensions; and which, at length, reached us in our quiet retreats. The city, we were told, was involved in confusion and panick, for a pestilential disease had begun its destructive progress. Magistrates and citizens were flying to the country. The numbers of the sick multiplied beyond all example; even in the pest affected cities of the Levant. The malady was malignant, and unsparing.

The usual occupations and amusements of life were at an end. Terror had exterminated all the sentiments of nature. Wives were deserted by husbands, and children by parents. Some had shut themselves in their houses, and debarred themselves from all communication with the rest of mankind. The consternation of others had destroyed their understanding, and their misguided steps hurried them into the midst of the danger which they had previously laboured to shun. Men were seized with this disease in the streets; passengers fled from them; entrance into their own dwellings was denied to them; they perished in the public ways.

The chambers of disease were deserted, and the sick left to die of negligence. None could be found to remove the lifeless bodies. Their remains, suffered to decay by piecemeal, filled the air with deadly exhalations, and added tenfold to the devastation.

Such was the tale, distorted and diversified a thousand ways, by the credulity and exaggeration of the tellers. At first I listened to the story with indifference or mirth. Methought it was confuted by its own extravagance. The enormity and variety of such an evil made it unworthy to be believed. I expected that every new day would detect the absurdity and fallacy of such representations. Every new day, however, added to the number of witnesses, and the consistency of the tale, till, at length, it was not possible to withhold my faith.[86]

Beneath the second passage's images of devastation, which will only intensify as the narrative, like the disease, progresses, lurk tensions fundamental to Brown's fiction: between appearances and truth, representation and reality, imagination and observation. The "tale, distorted and diversified in a thousand ways" suggests a narrative that expands as it decomposes, much like the fever's paradoxical "destructive progress," or like the corpse that "decay[s] by piece-meal," simultaneously extending its bodily boundaries as it "fill[s] the air with deadly exhalations." The mass response, as described here, inverts Stevens's discovery of Mervyn on his doorstep; common "credulity" starkly contrasts with Stevens's detached observation of the fever itself. Mervyn, narrating this sequence, reminds his audience repeatedly that these images were not yet based on his own observations. Rather, he represents the "distorted and diversified" news from the city as a rumor with a weighty life of its own, a rumor that "swelled" until it filled the farmhouse like an unwanted guest.[87]

In contrast to these responses, Stevens's reaction to the fever-stricken Mervyn establishes a clear behavioral code for fever seasons, wedding the sympathetic identification idealized in eighteenth-century moral philosophy to the cool scientific gaze of the physician. Visibly moved by Mervyn's "manlike beauty" and rustic appearance, Stevens had "scarcely ever beheld an object," he explains, "which laid so powerful and sudden a claim to my affection and succour."[88] According to contemporary medical ethicists, such sympathy was essential to physicians' success, but it also rendered them particularly vulnerable. It was, Benjamin Rush argued in an 1801 medical lecture, "sometimes so powerful, as to predominate over the fear of death; hence we observe [physicians] to expose, and frequently sacrifice their lives, in contending with mortal epidemics," and thus the "graveyards of Philadelphia alone, hold the precious relics of three and twenty members of our profession, who have died martyrs to this affectionate and heroic sympathy, since the year 1793."[89] But Stevens's response says as much about clear-sighted observation as it does about sympathy. He diagnoses Mervyn, even in the partial light of a "far-off lamp," *before* sympathy stakes its claim, emphasizing his empirical skill over his sensibility.

In contrast to Stevens's actions, the fever appears in Mervyn's account not through a physician's observation but as verbal representation. Between rumor and observation, Mervyn repeatedly demonstrates, resides the danger of imagination, the principal threat to accurate information about the fever. People either circulate fantastic fever stories, or, in fear, they shut themselves off "from all communications," as if simple conversation—the very naming of the fever, or the breath expelled and inhaled while speaking—could facilitate infection. Their "understanding" precluded, they leave "chambers of disease" deserted, refuse aid to those who could be cured (leaving the sick to die of "negligence," not pestilence), and abandon corpses in the street, acts that will result only in further pollution and a "tenfold" increase of "the devastation." Fear deprives the powerless of their usual protections; men desert women and children. As the city turns topsy-turvy, public officials, living in the national capital by virtue of their public office, retreat to country manors and estates. Back in the city, that which is most private—the deathbed—is turned out of doors, as victims fall "in the public ways." Rather than removing themselves from danger, such blind steps have "hurried" Philadelphians "into the midst" of it.

Represented as a rumor, this account has more to say about fever stories than about the fever itself. The "tales of sorrow" continue to interfere with accurate information as Mervyn makes his way into the city and the "fugitives" who clog roadways "detain every passenger with inquiries after news." Mervyn's own progress is delayed as he is "suffered to listen" to these "dialogues"; the stories excite his "panick" and cause him to fear that "the floating pestilence had already lighted on [his] frame" until "by vigorous efforts of [his] reason" he regains "some degree of composure."[90] The question posed to moral observers is this: how can one resist the "sublimity" that flows from stories of "enormous dangers" and come to more certain knowledge about the fever's origins and prevention?[91] Can one behave virtuously in the midst of an epidemic without accurate information? In a context in which terror can precipitate the disease itself, the communication breakdowns occasioned by the epidemic pose an enormous threat, as much in need of diagnosis and treatment as are fever victims themselves.

The care with which Brown differentiates between fever rumors and the fever itself recalls the medical theories put forth in the *Repository*. As Mervyn makes his way through the epidemic, the novel not only bears out Miller's descriptions of brain and stomach but also recalls Mitchill's attention to the politics and poetics of decomposing bodies. In Brown, the decomposing figures of fever victims function as a litmus test for characters, a means of determining their observational or interpretive prowess. Furthermore, decomposition serves as a natural punishment for those who fail the test. Contagionists, in other words, become sources of contagion. The merchant Thetford, *Arthur Mervyn*'s most chilling example of the misguided contagionist, receives, for his inhumane behavior, an "adequate" "retribution": "the death of his wife and child," then "the close of his own existence." Thetford's malignancy is rivaled in Brown's fiction only by *Ormond*'s Whiston, who abandons his dying sister and spreads terror by circulating fever rumors. Fleeing to the countryside, he falls sick and is left to die by other fearful contagionists. His body rots aboveground, "suffered to decay by piecemeal," furthering disease.[92]

In selecting "decomposition" as a principal trope, Brown plays vividly on the term itself: in their "theatre[s] of disaster," his fever novels stage decomposition as the body's unwriting, a gothic play on the notion of body language.[93] In *Ormond*, the black vomit "testifie[s]" to Mary Whiston's "corroded and gangrenous stomach."[94] The "lineaments" written on Wallace's face in *Arthur Mervyn* become "shadowy and death-like." Bodies lose "composure" until signs of life have been fully replaced by signs of sickness. All that remains of Thetford, Mervyn notes while exploring the dead man's home, are the "vestiges" of a body—the yellow and black marks on the bedding, ghostly script, the remains of an unwritten identity.[95] The antidote to the decomposing effects of rumor and fear, the novel suggests, is *composure* or even *composition,* the practice of countering pestilential stories with restorative ideas or information.[96] "No timidity, no ill-timed despair, of mine, shall palsy my powers," Smith wrote during the 1795 epidemic. "I grow more composed as I write." A body that retains its "composure" (its "equilibrium of excitement"), as Edward Miller suggested, can perhaps "sustain" the virus "without injury."[97] For Arthur, writing "circumscribes" the "wanderings" of the imagination and fortifies the frame. "My blood," he notes, "within the few minutes thus employed, flows with less destructive rapidity."[98] Brown's characters repeatedly pull themselves out of sickness by composing their thoughts. In *Arthur Mervyn,* Medlicote's engaging conversation and accurate information about the fever carry similar power. "As I talked with this man," Mervyn narrates, "the sense of danger was obliterated. I felt confidence revive in my heart, and energy revisit my stomach."[99]

The idea of narrative control as both prophylactic and treatment for disease is most extensively illustrated by Mervyn, who cures himself by gradually becoming the sole narrative voice.[100] Viewed against the novel's overwhelming emphasis on the need for an accurate information flow, Mervyn's progression toward narrative control signals sincerity rather than deception. Even Mervyn's apparent lies (regarding his own infection, for example) are part of a broader understanding of truth-telling, since he understands that the general populace, operating on contagionist assumptions, will not deal justly with him if they were to suspect him as a carrier of the disease.[101] The readings of the novel that most aggressively argue for Mervyn's duplicity and unreliability fail to account for the intricacy with which Brown treats the subject of informational accuracy, particularly where the fever is concerned.[102] Similarly, the critics who read the novel's second part as a repudiation of the first, as manifesting a shift in Brown's political and moral attitudes, are not attuned to recognize the informational context for the second volume, in which Mervyn systematically seeks to right Welbeck's wrongs by making himself a broker of previously concealed truths. Scientific and moral accuracy are intricately linked. Mervyn's newfound self-consciousness as a storytelling moralist—whose most urgent project is the need to narrate himself out of other people's misreadings of his actions—emerges hand in hand with his decision to apprentice himself to Stevens and to become a physician, a vocation that offers both republican rewards (opportunities "of lightening the distresses of our neighbors") and philosophical pleasure ("the means of intellectual gratification" by exploring "the whole system of nature").[103]

In one of the novel's oddest episodes, Arthur boards a morning stage for Baltimore, where he will seek to pay restitution to a handful of Welbeck's victims. Instead he offers a telling portrait of the ways in which scientific authority could seek to preserve social hierarchy. With him on the stage are "a sallow Frenchman from Saint Domingo, his fiddle-case, an ape, and two female blacks." The Frenchman plays his violin, the monkey "mounche[s] an apple," and the women "gaze with stupid wonder" out the coach's window, "chatter[ing]" with one another "in a sort of open-mouthed, half-articulated, monotonous, and singsong jargon." Mervyn takes all this in for a moment:

> I sometimes gazed at the faces of my *four* companions, and endeavored to discern the differences and samenesses between them. I took an exact account of their features, proportions, looks, and gestures of the monkey, the Congolese, and the Creole-Gaul. I compared them together, and examined them apart. I looked at them in a thousand different points of view, and pursued, untired and unsatiated, those trains of reflections which began at each change of tone, feature, attitude.[104]

Mervyn demonstrates above all, in this description, his emerging scientific aptitude, evidence of his transition from being overwhelmed by pluralistic Philadelphia to being the master of this diversity through rational observation. "If men be chiefly distinguished from each other by the modes in which their attention is employed," he notes earlier in the novel, "I may justly claim to be enrolled" in the "class" made up of "creatures of reflection."[105] The stagecoach and travel in general were chief forms, at the end of the eighteenth century, for gathering just the sort of information on which enlightened thinkers can reflect. In its democratizing function, placing people of all ranks and backgrounds into a shared intimate space, the coach provided a "stage" on which travelers performed for one another, allowing fellow riders glimpses into other social worlds.[106] For Mervyn, his companions and the passing scenery serve as a natural history diorama. He catalogs and categorizes these

others without ever throwing himself into the mix, creating for himself
a sense of critical detachment. His observations, with their unques-
tioned validity, are minute, "exact," a careful "account" of physiological,
physiognomical, and linguistic sameness and difference. He marks his
fellow passengers as different not only by the visible variation in skin
color ("sallow," "black," "noir") and the audible difference in language
but in the very way they pass their time in the coach—the Frenchman
"look[ing] seldom either on this side or that," absorbed in his own
"*tweedle-deedle*" and his monkey's antics; the monkey itself absorbed in
the physical gratification of munching an apple; the black women who,
like Mervyn, observe what they pass but in his mind are unable to comprehend or articulate what they see. Vitalized by this exercise in natural
history, Mervyn turns his classifying gaze upon his surroundings, taking "endless enjoyment" in "the shape and substance of the fence[s],
the barn[s], and the cottage[s]," and in the very "aspect of earth and of
heaven."[107]

With this brief travelogue, which foregrounds his whiteness as well
as his self-conception as an observer, Mervyn joins the fellowship of
the novel's other scientific authorities.[108] Mervyn's acts of classification
resist the stage's democratizing space and position him at the top of the
moving microcosm's social hierarchy.[109] "I was destined to be *something*
in this scene of existence," he says on his return to Philadelphia, "and
might sometime lay claim to the gratitude and homage of my fellow-
men."[110] Mervyn's conception of his relation to audience recalls both
the *Repository*'s ideal of "medical eloquence" and Brown's description of
his own historical-fictional practice as requiring "a certain license of in-
vention" in order to make facts stick. The writer of such fiction, Brown
argued in a 1799 *Monthly Magazine* essay, shares with other professionals an "enhance[d] . . . power over the liberty, property, and health of
mankind" and an obligation to "obviate, by intellectual exertions, many
of the evils that infest the world." So conceived, professional "power" is
unapologetic; it is a "common good."[111]

This connection between observation and authority is critical to
Mervyn's ability to disseminate information, to tell stories about what
he knows. Like Brown, the "story-telling moralist" behind the scenes,
Mervyn finds "the United States a new and untrodden field" in which
he can "examine objects with his own eyes" and become "entitled at least
to the praise of originality."[112] Brown's definition of professional authorship joins with Mervyn's natural history narrative in pointing to the

concerns of the republic of intellect: association, observation (and its attendant acts of organization and exhibition), and anxiety over the receptiveness of American audiences (for whom American literature is, like the new nation itself, understood to be an "untrodden field"). As Brown described these authorial and audience concerns, "The world is governed, not by the simpleton, but by the man of soaring passions and intellectual energy. By the display of such only can we hope to enchain the attention and ravish the souls of those who study and reflect." The ultimate goal of this "display" is to exhibit a "contexture of facts capable of suspending the faculties of every soul in curiosity, . . . joined with depth of views into human nature and all the subtleties of reasoning."[113]

By the novel's end, clearheaded observation and the science of storytelling (an art that counteracts the fever in his own body) have offered Arthur social authority via admission to professional fraternity. In some ways, his narrative complements the sentimental novel's marriage plot; Arthur's marriage to Achsa at the novel's close cements his drive for social authority and is the capstone, perhaps, of his professional development. Mervyn's medical bildungsroman parallels the development of his relationship with Achsa Fielding (to be consummated once he stops writing the book). They prefigure their marital union, significantly, by an exchange of their life stories and their ability to provide knowledge the other lacks. Achsa's "discourse," Mervyn tells us, is better than "cold, jejune, vexatious" books. "So versatile; so bending to the changes in occasion; so obsequious to my curiosity, and so abundant in that very knowledge in which I was most deficient, and on which I set most value, the knowledge of the human heart"—Achsa's conversational abilities help convince him that the young Quakeress, Eliza Hadwin, who "prattle[s] forever," would make a better daughter or sister than a wife. Arthur values Achsa's experience (based on her age, her previous marriage, her sexual knowledge, her firsthand observation of European affairs) because it offers him intellectual gratification. Her information quotient, in other words, outstrips Eliza's. The value he places on Achsa's conversation ultimately sustains his hierarchical position; though an oedipal reading is possible, of course, she will also play "*mamma*" to his papa. Arthur establishes his hierarchical relationship to her by reading in her eyes some information she has not readily offered (her Jewish genealogy); while she completes his education, then, she remains "obsequious to [his] curiosity," the characteristic that defines him and by which he has achieved social authority.[114]

September 1798: "New York this time has got a plague indeed"

In the spring of 1799, Brown wrote the following in *Arthur Mervyn*'s preface:

> The evils of pestilence by which this city has lately been afflicted will probably form an aera in its history. The schemes of reformation and improvement to which they will give birth, or, if no efforts of human wisdom can avail to avert the periodical visitations of this calamity, the change in manners and population which they will produce, will be, in the highest degree, memorable.[115]

The novel was set in Philadelphia's 1793 epidemic, of course, but "this city" could easily have applied to New York the previous fall, whose scenes of devastation were deeply personal and certainly fresher in his mind. When he and Johnson left the city in late September, after Smith's death, the toll was nearing four hundred. By November, over fifteen hundred more had died.[116] Brown gestures, as he presents his novel to the public, to a future citizenry affected intimately by the fever, a population whose numbers and social institutions have been permanently marked and which will respond with "schemes of reformation" not yet imagined. Brown highlights as well a variety of organizational and interpretive practices that mirror the Friendly Club's own diverse modes of synthesis and creation. The fever supplies "copious material" for medical, political, and moral observers to classify and "methodize." In keeping with his fellow club members' exhibitionary impulses, Brown's novel is itself a "display" case of "passions" and "motives." The interpreters agree that the fever has ushered in new ways of life. Manners may change, but the possibility remains that the disease will stay the same. Its "periodical" recurrence has made it familiar, its "visitations" become part of everyday life.

So much more need, then, to control it—and its effects—through careful narrative as well as through medical and political reform. Positioning himself as a "moral observer," Brown places his novelistic enterprise on a plane with the observational practices carried out by his scientific friends. In *Arthur Mervyn*, Brown's title character mimics Brown's and his friends' self-descriptions. Not only does Mervyn undergo class- and race-conscious training in observing his environment but the novel's very narrative structure depends on techniques, common to Brown's culture, of gathering, arranging, and displaying information. At the beginning of the novel's second volume, Stevens, the sometime narrator-physician, recognizes that "this season of pestilence" has provided him with "numerous" "opportunities of observation . . . and I had not suffered them to pass unimproved." So the observers among the Friendly Club regarded their own experience. The crucial terms here—"observation," "novelty," "display," "truth" (both scientific and moral)—not only imply Stevens's conviction of Mervyn's sincerity but also point toward the early national literary context in which Brown himself, as a novelist, acts as an "observer," an arranger and exhibitor of a "contexture of facts." When Brown writes, as he consistently does of his fiction, that "[f]acts have supplied the foundation of the whole," he isn't simply catering to a Puritanical audience for whom "fiction" is morally suspect; he positions his work among other literary projects—the *Repository*, for example—that seek to observe, arrange, and display facts about the nation's moral, political, and physical landscapes.

The narrative control Mervyn models at the end of the novel may also suggest an attempt to comprehend or contain the emotional devastation an epidemic wrought. Though the club's various narrative responses share generic forms as well as moral, political, and philosophical suppositions, they differ, perhaps, in their attitudes toward death itself. Medical narratives claim a logical comprehension of death's processes; *Arthur Mervyn*, by contrast, despite its urgent climatist agenda, acknowledges the epistemological limits death has posed. Brown's "methodiz[ing]" stands as an attempt to comprehend, and even to effect, social change by shaping his audience's response when the fever returns next summer, but he embraces in the preface the likelihood that "human wisdom" might not be up to the task of arriving at final answers. No aspect of Brown's experience in the 1790s brought that point home more clearly than the death of his closest friend.

Elihu Hubbard Smith spent the afternoon of 4 September 1798, his 27th birthday, in bed. For two days he had remained at home, failing to make his usual series of medical and social visits. On the twenty-sixth of August he had lain restless until after twelve, kept up by the "heat & the mosquitoes," and after a brief "imperfect slumber" was "obliged to rise, mount a horse, ride to Corlear's Hook, & thence cross to Long-Island [Brooklyn] a mile above." Such emergency calls to see patients, combined with daily rounds under a scorching sun and an eager perusal of Benjamin Rush's newly published volume of *Medical Inquiries and Observations*, left him exhausted. "[S]till feeble, but hop[ing] to get abroad tomorrow," he tried to make his bedridden days industrious by reading Brown's most recent additions to his in-progress novels, *Carwin* and the "new begun 'Stephen Calvert,'" which would follow *Sky-Walk* and *Wieland,* then at press in Philadelphia and New York, respectively. He wrote letters to his friends. The following morning he attempted a medical visit but returned home to face the inevitable: he was "scorched with fever."[117]

The afternoon of Smith's birthday, he, Johnson, and Brown wrote a group letter to Dunlap, who had taken his family to Perth Amboy. Brown wrote first, noting that Dunlap's recent letter to them had "cheared *us* poor solitary beings with this plaguey fever at our doors, in our cupboards & in our beds. Johnson & I are pretty well," he continued. "But EHS, by midnight sallyings forth, sudden changes of temperature, fatigue & exposure to a noon day sun, is made sick. perhaps it would not have been so if this Demon had not lurked in the air. Tomorrow it is hoped he will be able to answer your questions as to the prevalence & comparative malignity of this disease himself." Johnson wrote next, assuring Dunlap that "nothing interesting to an 'infidel philosopher'" had happened in his absence. He and Brown both chided Dunlap for letting religious allusions slip into his prose. He also urged Dunlap to return to New York. "The Town is the only place for rational beings," he wrote. "Under the shield of Philosophy what have we to fear? As to fever, it is a being of such unaccountable origin, such amazing attributes, and such inexplicable operations, that I deliver it over to the Doctor, to be treated *secundum artem.* That is to say, according to *his trade.*" Accordingly Smith took the pen. "These gay friends of mine," he wrote,

> have so covered the paper with their gambols that nothing but coldness and conclusion, dullness & death-heads are left for me.
>
> Had you seen me extended on my bed yesterday, rejecting (alas the while!) half a dozen supplications from the sick & confined to pills & potions, you would have trembled for the safety of your poor philosopher. To-day, however, I have sitten up 'till this hour; &, if the day be fair, tomorrow shall resume my customary functions.

Smith wrongly predicted that the fever would decline; instead, it would rage through September and October. Despite his physical condition, he tried to keep up Brown's and Johnson's playful tone, signing off the letter in the language of copyright: "By order of the Con[gress]."[118]

On Friday, 7 September, Smith attempted a medical visit. The friends learned that an older brother of Samuel and Edward Miller was dead of fever in Delaware and that Brown's Philadelphia publisher, James Watters, had died during the reigning epidemic there. With "[p]erpetual tears, & perpetual drizzling from the nose to-day, [but] in other respects better," he returned home to convalesce. For a few days his health seemed to improve. He made several medical calls and stopped by a printing office to "read a mass of papers." He made social visits in the evening, with Brown and Johnson "at Mrs. Templeton's," where they passed time with new friends, Maria Templeton and Margaret Bayard. He walked on the Battery with friends. On the tenth he noted, "Our fever increases."[119]

The next day the friends learned that the young Italian physician Joseph Scandella had arrived in New York from Philadelphia and was fever stricken. "Went to him, & removed him to my house," Smith wrote.[120] Mitchill, writing to Noah Webster, who had removed from New York to New Haven, recounted Smith's "Visit of friendship" to save Scandella, who had been on the verge of eviction from the Tontine Coffee House; by the time Mitchill wrote the letter, Scandella had died. "New York this time has got a plague indeed," he wrote. "The Scourge is applied severely and cuts deep. I am satisfied more if possible than ever of its local origin. Nobody now talks of importation."[121] In a letter on the state of New York's epidemic, Smith had assured Benjamin Rush a few days earlier that "our friend Dr. Scandella," would receive every possible assistance from "the faculty of N. York."[122] By the fifteenth, Smith confided to his diary that "poor Scandella has excited all my apprehension & sympathies. I fear that he cannot recover."[123]

It was Smith's last journal entry; the next day Scandella was dead. Smith's friends removed him from the "theatre of death and grief" to Horace Johnson's—William's brother—"whose house is spacious, healthfully situated, and plentifully accommodated."[124] Brown accompanied him briefly, then went to stay with the Millers. Horace Johnson recorded that Smith's "symptoms were particularly malignant. . . . His attack was [characterized by] vomiting and a slight pain in the back; and the same continued to death. No act or remedy could compose his stomach."[125] In Edward Miller's estimation, Brown wrote to his brother, "the disease in no case was ever more dreadfully and infernally malignant" than in Smith's.[126]

Despite the years of arguing about the disease and promoting their beliefs about its origin and treatment, the friends still found themselves left to make sense of Smith's death. In contrast to the cool generic conventions of the autopsy, more intimate forms allowed the friends to reveal that their grief threatened to reorder their entire views of the world. Echoing Brown's lamentation on "the folly of prediction and the vanity of systems," Johnson, who only days earlier had vaunted "the shield of Philosophy," wrote to Dunlap, "How fallacious is hope! How vain is theory!"[127] The gloom did not go away soon. In Perth Amboy, Brown took three days before he described for Dunlap the events leading to Smith's death. Returning to New York later in the fall the friends were haunted by Smith's absence. Johnson complained in November to a friend in Albany that "[o]ur City," in the wake of the epidemic, already "exhibits its wonted aspect of bustle, noises and gaiety.—How much are the common herd of men, superior to brutes in feeling and forethought?" The urban "bustle" contrasted the emptiness he felt: "The incidents of the few last months of my life have deeply affected me. I know not when the impressions will be effaced.—That I have escaped death, is at this time a matter of some surprize.—I estimate the tenure of my existence at a low rate.—and am able to look with indifference on its termination."[128] Edward Miller echoed the sentiment in a letter to Benjamin Rush on the last day of the year. "The loss of our friend Smith is of vast and incalculable extent," he wrote. "If his morning was so luminous, what would have been his noontide splendour?"[129]

For Brown's part, his feelings were strangely divided. His career as a writer, so encouraged by Smith earlier in the year, continued to push ahead and for the first time promised to bring financial stability. "My social hours and *schemes,* are in their customary state," he wrote to his brother the following February. "Up till eleven, and abed till eight, plying the quill or the book, and conversing with male or female friends, constitutes the customary series of my amusements and employments. I add somewhat, though not so much as I might if I were so inclined, to the number of my friends. I find to be the writer of Wieland and Ormond is a greater recommendation than ever I imagined it would be."[130] But by July, his thoughts had turned back to the fever, as the first cases of the season began to be reported. "My sensations, in this state of things are so different from my sensations last summer, that I look back with astonishment," he wrote to his brother James.

> I do not wonder that I then remained in the city, but that my mind retained its tranquility in the midst of perils the most imminent; that I

could muse and write cheerfully in spite of the groans of the dying and the rumbling of hearses, and in spite of a thousand tokens of indisposition in my own frame, is now almost incredible. I perceive that this tranquility and courage is utterly beyond my reach at present. I rejoice that there will be no domestic or social ties making me desert the city with reluctance. Those friends who then were as hard as myself are already alarmed, and all those whose safety is particularly dear to me, will vanish from this scene as well as myself.[131]

By this point, the first volume of *Arthur Mervyn* had come off the press. *Edgar Huntly* was in production. Brown and William Johnson had traveled to Connecticut that summer, where they likely visited Smith's relatives. Over the next several months Brown would struggle to throw off the "gloominess" that characterized the "out-of-nature incidents" in *Edgar Huntly*, he told his brother. Henceforth, to please his audience and perhaps to please himself, he would be "dropping the doleful tone and assuming a cheerful one, or, at least substituting moral causes and daily incidents in place of the prodigious or the singular."[132] *Arthur Mervyn*'s second volume only partly keeps that promise, but *Clara Howard* and *Jane Talbot*, his final two novels, would substitute domestic scenes for doleful tones, even if they did not mark an end to his engagement with "moral causes" and other ethical dilemmas.

Brown's critics often assume that the gloom pervading his first four novels stemmed from his recognition of the limits of Enlightenment knowledge.[133] But the disavowal of knowledge is too easy an explanation, even in the face of the fever that took Smith's life. In one signal moment in *Arthur Mervyn*, Brown offers, along with a fear that Enlightenment modes of communication and knowledge will fail, a glimmer of hope and a determination to move forward:

> I chuse the obvious path, and pursue it with headlong expedition. Good intentions, unaided by knowledge, will, perhaps prove more injury than benefit, and therefore, knowledge must be gained, but the acquisition is not momentary; is not bestowed unasked and untoil'd for: meanwhile, we must not be unactive because we are ignorant. Our good purposes must hurry to performance, whether our knowledge be greater or less.[134]

The convoluted sentences suggest vacillation and uncertainty as well as determination and fortitude. In the wake of Smith's death Brown gives what he has: his conviction that certain modes of behavior will still save lives during fever seasons—though perhaps not every life. He also demonstrates a conviction he shared with Smith, that the "national health" depended on regulating and disseminating such information, even though ignorance might not be a fully curable flaw in the human condition.

The mode of authorship upon which such dissemination depended has an analog in the generic form of the miscellany or review—the "literary museum," a form to which Brown devoted most of his career after Smith's death. Critics have called this mode of authorship an "editorial function" and see Brown's *Clara Howard* and *Jane Talbot* as working in this mode. In these novels Brown "collects" and "arranges" the correspondence of his characters in such a way that the "editor" rather than romantic author is "idealized." By seriously attending to Brown's late novels and editorial career, we can see that the trajectory from republican to "bourgeois moralist," a staple of Brown biographies, might be better understood as "a celebration of a new model of natural aristocracy, in which it is the *true* editor alone who can serve as the proper governor for the nation."[135]

Above all, Brown's novels shared with the medical writings of other Friendly Club members such attempts at bodily, narrative, and audience control. The ideas "afloat" in the community, which Brown noted in his preface, were as dangerous as the floating miasmata that generated the pest. "I cannot but admire the exaggerations of rumor," Brown had declared in the fall 1796 letter to his brother James. Because contemporaries complained so much of the dangers of rumor, Brown's choice of the word "admire" is striking. But rumor's ability to seize the imagination, to monopolize the body's "vital energies," to generate an ever-expanding audience is what the novelist and his medical writing friends most hoped to mimic.

The End of the American Enlightenment

Samuel Miller's *A Brief Retrospect of the Eighteenth Century*

NARRATIVES, like the knowledge they convey, carry with them multiple histories, characterized by contingency. Accidents accumulate in the production of texts—people meet by chance, find a weatherworn pamphlet on the street, overhear a conversation in a stagecoach, receive an invitation to a club. People organize themselves on one principle but convey information about another. The first day of January 1801, by sheer coincidence, witnessed the production of two very different texts from members of the Friendly Club, if indeed the club still met in some configuration at that date. That New Year's Day, Samuel Miller preached a sermon, probably at the Wall Street Presbyterian Church. He took as his topic a beginning: the commencement of a new century. Charles Brockden Brown, probably sitting at a desk at the Pine Street apartment he continued to share with William Johnson, wrote about an ending, in the preface to the bound edition of the third and final volume of the *Monthly Magazine, and American Review*. Regarding the sermon, "Some who heard it were pleased to express a wish that it might be published," Miller later wrote. So he set to work adding notes and soliciting subscribers.

By the time he was finished with the "amplification," however, three years had passed and the sermon had turned into two volumes totaling over a thousand pages. Published as the misleadingly named *A Brief Retrospect of the Eighteenth Century*, it would remain the work by which Miller would be best remembered, even after another half-century of continuously publishing sermons and theological debates. Brown, on the other hand, wrote in a mildly despairing tone about the difficulties of periodical publishing in America. For the next two years, under the title *American Review, and Literary Journal*, the monthly magazine the Friendly Club started would reduce to a quarterly. "[T]he commencement of another year, and a new century," Brown wrote, "render this a fit time for such a change."[1]

Much had changed, in fact, since 1793, when Samuel Miller and Elihu Smith made their separate ways to New York. (Brown had stopped through that fall on his way back to fever-decimated Philadelphia from a trip to Connecticut to meet Smith's friends.) The city's population had nearly doubled. Fever had secured a place on the annual calendar. In 1793, until news of the Terror arrived that fall, many Americans still were optimistic about the promise of the French Revolution. By 1801 political partisanship had escalated to extraordinary proportions; the previous year's presidential election—which Jefferson won on New York's Republican vote—had exacerbated the culture wars launched by countersubversives in the late 1790s. The Illuminati scare refused to go away. Though Brown and Johnson and some of their friends still privately defended Wollstonecraft's and Godwin's ideas (if not their sexual liberalism), Congregationalist conservatives had clearly put anti-Jacobinism in cultural ascendancy, President Jefferson or no.

The ongoing controversies drew lines that were sometimes unexpected. In 1801, Miller, the sole clergyman in the club's history, became embroiled in one of the late flurries in the Illuminati affair when, as he claimed, he sought to rescue Jedidiah Morse's honor from accusations that he persisted in his alarmist paranoia even though he had received credible reports from Europe that the scare was illusory. In his letter to the New York–based, Jeffersonian newspaper the *American Citizen*, edited by James Cheetham, Miller declared that Morse was a man of integrity; nevertheless, "it has always appeared to me, that as he has given undue credit to the assertions of *Robison* and *Barruel* . . . with an indiscreet and excessive zeal; yet, as he is evidently innocent of the charge so confidently brought against him in this instance, his veracity ought to be so vindicated."[2] Morse's friends chafed at the backhanded defense; the Reverend William Linn, whose daughter, Elizabeth, Brown would soon court, wrote to Morse that he had tried to dissuade Miller from publishing his letter but found "it is in vain to remonstrate with a *Democrat*."[3]

The partisanship that dominated American newspapers also threatened friendships. Not quite a decade earlier Linn had written Morse an introductory letter of recommendation for a 24-year-old Miller, on his way to Boston during a tour of New England.[4] Miller occasioned another political controversy when a letter he had written to a minister in New Haven, affirming that he "had much rather have [the deist] Mr. Jefferson President of the United States, than an aristocratic Christian," was published in a newspaper without his knowledge.[5] Although the club and its *Monthly Magazine* tried to remain above politics, and though the club's mixed-sex circle was clearly made up of both Jeffersonian and Federalist young people, years later Dunlap would suggest that partisanship played the decisive role in the group's "lingering death."[6] It seems fair to suggest that partisanship—mapped onto international culture wars between "modern philosophers" and anti-Jacobins—also brought an end to the late-Enlightenment republic of intellect.

Among Friendly Club members, Samuel Miller stands out as singular, in part for his combination of Jeffersonian politics and orthodox Christianity, and yet his two-volume *Brief Retrospect* not only offers significant insight into the dynamics of intellectual association the club represents but also offers additional explanations about the club's collapse and a glimpse into the future at the world that would replace it. Embedded in its encyclopedic investigation of European and American arts and sciences of the century that had just closed, Miller leaves an implicit record of the contests the century had witnessed between competing forms of cultural and professional authority. Miller's text also implicitly offers possible ways to understand the forces that called the club into existence and those that brought it to an end. Published only a decade after he arrived in New York City, Miller's *Brief Retrospect* is an appropriate final testament to the group's collaborative efforts to place American writing within a broader republic of intellect.

Miller came to New York in January of 1793 to accept a collegiate pastorate in the city's three Presbyterian churches. He was 25 years old, two years older than Smith and Brown. He was examined, prior to taking his position as a licentiate, in Latin, Greek, geography, logic, rhetoric, natural philosophy, astronomy, moral philosophy, divinity, ecclesiastical history, and church government. (Such a broad knowledge base suggests, perhaps, why he was particularly suited to write a work like the *Brief Retrospect.*) His ordination took place that summer. Before long, Miller had gained notice for the "air of literary refinement" that set him apart from the city's other—most of them older—preachers. Miller's son and biographer, himself a minister, later in the nineteenth century found fault with his father for having joined, during his New York years, "a literary club, which embraced some very doubtful characters, as the intimates of a clergyman," and thought the *Brief Retrospect* itself was a sign that Samuel Miller "had not yet learned to give himself whole and rigorously . . . to his bare gospel work."[7]

Yet entry into the Friendly Club's secular and mostly Federalist world did not come easy for a Jeffersonian minister of the gospel. Though he shared for years some ideas and social space with his future club members—Smith, Miller, and George M. Woolsey all became Manumission Society members at the same meeting in November 1793—he did not begin intimate association with the group until well after his brother Edward had moved to the city and assisted in founding the *Medical Repository.* (While Edward Miller and Samuel Mitchill had become regular visitors to the club around the founding of the medical journal, and Edward a regular member in April 1798, Samuel Miller was never even a visitor to the club until 5 May 1798, the first meeting after his brother became a full member.)[8] By the end of that year, however, perhaps bound more tightly to the group by Smith's death, Miller was enthusiastically at work promoting the projected *Monthly Magazine.* "[T]his is not an ordinary, nor a catch-penny, plan," he assured Jedidiah Morse, seeking his assistance in gathering Massachusetts subscribers. The magazine's editor, Miller wrote without naming Brown, was "a gentleman of undoubted learning and taste," and would receive the support of "an association, which includes some of the first literary characters in the city."[9]

Like the *Monthly Magazine,* Miller's *Brief Retrospect* acted out the principles of the republic of intellect in its inception and organization. Miller sent scores of letters across America and Europe—particularly to Scotland and Germany but also to English, Dutch, Swiss, and Swedish correspondents—soliciting information for the volume. He plied his friends' brains on their pet subjects and for their professional knowledge. Edward Miller, in fact, wrote the bulk of the chapters on medical and scientific subjects but insisted that he not be listed as a coauthor. (In a largely flattering review of the book for his *Literary*

Magazine, Brown notes that the "departments of physics and mathematics, evince a more careful and intelligent hand than the sections which belong to mere taste and fancy," an almost clear signal that he was privy to the matter of joint authorship and perhaps a sign that he preferred Edward's secularism to Samuel's moralizing.)[10]

The first two volumes constituted only the first part of Miller's projected work. As "Part First," they covered the century's "Revolutions and Improvements in Science, Arts, and Literature." The two volumes included overviews and commentaries on eighteenth-century publications in the following categories: mechanical philosophy, chemical philosophy, natural history, medicine, geography, mathematics, navigation, agriculture, mechanic arts, fine arts, physiognomy, philosophy of the human mind, classic literature, Oriental literature, modern languages, philosophy of language, history, biography, romances and novels, poetry, literary journals, political journals, literary and scientific associations, encyclopedias, education, and "Nations Lately Become Literary" (including the United States). Each of these sections has several subsections. In addition to this overview of science, arts, and literature, Miller outlined but never completed three more parts to the *Brief Retrospect:* one each for theology, moral philosophy, and politics. The two volumes he did publish constitute a work of divided mindsets and moods, by turns optimistic about the scientific progress made during the eighteenth century and pessimistic about what Miller perceived as a decline in Christian belief. Though this element may stem from the book's status as a jointly authored product, it also indicates Miller's own conflicted attractions to Enlightenment thought and science on one hand and Calvinist theology on the other.

A collaborative effort, the *Brief Retrospect* involved former Friendly Club members in various ways. In addition to Edward Miller's significant contributions, Miller consulted Charles Brockden Brown on several subjects and likely received feedback from others. He circulated proof sheets among a wide circle of friends and acquaintances and incorporated major changes or corrections as "Additional Notes." Productions by club members also receive special notice in the text.

Miller did not simply catalog, he canonized. Of the *Medical Repository* he commented that its founding, "from the peculiar circumstances of our country, may be considered as an important event in noting the successive steps of medical improvement in the United States." In addition to providing "a most useful vehicle for conveying to the public a knowledge of every improvement in the science of medicine," the *Repository* "furnishes at once very reputable specimens of the learning, talents and zeal of many American physicians," a near conflation of natural knowledge with the reputation of those who assemble it.[11] Mitchill receives special praise for his "inquiries concerning the nature and constitution of *pestilential fluids*."[12] And in the midst of a section on novels and romances that would become infamous as an antifiction screed ("Never was the literary world so deluged with the frivolous effusions of ignorance and vanity" as in the century just closed), Miller praises Charles Brockden Brown as producing the first American fiction "deserving respectful notice." Miller sees, in Brown's "several productions, a vigorous imagination, a creative fancy, strong powers of description, and great command, and, in general, great felicity of language." Although Miller's discussion of drama evinces a surprising familiarity with a range of dramatic writing, the chapter's antitheatrical prejudice almost certainly precludes the possibility of Dunlap's input. (As Miller reassures pious readers in a footnote, "[T]he author takes for granted that no reader will consider him as expressing an opinion favourable to theatrical amusements.")[13]

Such reactionary moments aside, Miller's *Retrospect* wears its Enlightenment origins on its sleeve. As Brown wrote in his review of the final product, the book itself stands unmistakably as a product of the era it takes as its subject: "One of the most remarkable improvements of the last century is the practice of reducing the whole body of human knowledge into a comprehensive and systematic order." In doing so, Miller was surprisingly catholic. Though he does not hesitate in several places to pronounce disapprobation on the thinkers under discussion (he deals particularly harshly with Mary Wollstonecraft), he also makes a point, from the beginning, that "[a] man who is a bad Christian may be a very excellent mathematician, astronomer, or chemist; and one who denies and blasphemes the Saviour may write profoundly and instructively on some branches of science highly interesting to mankind."[14] The very subtitle of the work, in highlighting "Revolutions and Improvements," takes up two terms most conservative Christians and anti-Jacobins had come to regard as anathema, and the volumes' overall celebration of science runs sharply counter to the assault of several Federalist orators and ministers on science as a handmaiden of Jeffersonian infidelity.

If Miller's *Brief Retrospect* reflects the Enlightenment orientation the club sought to preserve, it also marks that culture's eclipse. In his dedication to his political hero, John Dickinson of Delaware, Miller makes it plain that he "contemplate[s] every department of human affairs through the medium of Christian principles," and so he attempts less to let the ideas he collects compete with one another for preeminence than he aims to refract the previous century's thinking through his particularly Presbyterian lens. In doing so he counters the dominant movement among club members during the 1790s to combat clerical authority with a morality founded on reason and scientific principle. Miller, by contrast, feels that science, in spite of the progress made in the previous century, "must ever fall short of those extravagant expectations which, founded in the ignorance of human nature, and discarding the dictates of experience, cannot avoid proceeding in error, and ending in disappointment." As one intellectual historian notes, Miller's book offers a rejoinder to the progressive arguments for perfectibility that ran through Condorcet's *Outlines of an Historical View of the Progress of the Human Mind* (1794), which had so energized Smith and other club members in the year after it was published. "One cannot equate [scientific] progress with moral progress," Miller argues over and over.[15]

In so doing, Miller both counters the optimism that marks his brother's sections on science and foreshadows some important cultural developments of the nineteenth century. If the social authority of the elite clergy began its decline in the late eighteenth century, a more democratized religious authority—not the authority of philosophers or scientists—would prevail in the nineteenth. The "Second Great Awakening," already rumbling in parts of the country, would occupy much of the country through the 1830s.[16] The Revolutionary generation would prove the last to be able to put candidates forward whose religious skepticism was unabashed. Far from Elihu Smith's dream for exposing the "amazing & disgustful collection of absurdity" that makes up "all religions," Miller's book presages the subordination of science to Christianity that would characterize much of the coming century.

The *Brief Retrospect* may have taken as a departure point the beginning of a new century, but Miller also filled the book with a variety of endings. The book's "Recapitulation" in particular reveals an effort to contain the intellectual speculation the previous century had unleashed by enumerating several defining characteristics. The eighteenth century, Miller concludes, was "pre-eminently an age" of many things: the age of free inquiry, physical science, economical science, experiment, revolutions in science, printing, books, the unprecedented diffusion of knowledge, superficial learning, taste and refinement, infidel philosophy, Christian science, translations, literary honors, and finally, it was the age of literary and scientific intercourse, facilitated, he wrote, by a "republic of letters" both transnational and commercial. As in the rest of the book, Miller here waxes utopian and dystopian all at once. The members of this republic are a "highly favored generation" that has seen "improvements in science, which their fathers, a century ago, would have anticipated with astonishment, or pronounced altogether impossible," but they have also witnessed—and in some cases contributed to—"some degrading retrocessions in human knowledge" and been subjected to "the noisy pretensions of false philosophy." In summarizing the achievements and dangerous tendencies of the previous century as characteristics of an era now closed, Miller leaves himself free to set out a new agenda for his readers: "Philosophers of the Nineteenth Century!" he thunders. "[Y]our predecessors of the past age have bequeathed to you an immeasurable mass of both good and evil." Their job is to discern one from the other and thereby contribute to "that substantial advancement in knowledge which the enlightened and benevolent mind anticipates with a glow of delight."[17]

The peculiar blend of voices in Miller's book bears witness to the notion that texts have histories marked by accident. This conceptualization itself bears some similarity to the eighteenth-century preoccupation with "association," in both principal meanings of the term: the voluntary association of individuals in civil society and the association of ideas, the foundational notion of much eighteenth-century philosophy of mind. At the end of the century, though, association psychology led most Friendly Club members not to contemplations of contingency but to notions of necessity. Ideas combine, they believed, not as the result of accidental encounters but along a predestined course; for these necessitarians, the knowledge that results from this combination is as progressive as it is inevitable. By the 1820s, association, in both senses, took on nationalist dimensions that were only apparent in very nascent forms in Miller's book. The nation-state replaced friendly circles and informational networks as the milieu from which important associations were supposed to derive. And so, although the conversation circle endured as an important site of literary production, the transnational Enlightenment republic of letters met an end of sorts and nationalist literary traditions emerged full force on both sides of the Atlantic.[18]

By contrast, Brown's despair at the difficulties in editing the *Monthly Magazine* reveals the limitations of any nationalist intentions the group may have had. True, they had aimed to shape American audiences and ask for their support as subscribers. But they had also aimed to represent the new nation in larger intellectual arenas. The task had proved difficult for two main reasons, Brown believed: first, all "patronage" was "voluntary and unsolicited"; and second, the population of a single city was insufficient to generate the subscribers needed to defray the printing costs and subsidize the editorial work. Although the magazine survived for a few years reduced to a quarterly, the group probably did not survive the partisan warfare that peaked in 1800. (The account in Margaret Bayard's letters ends in the fall of 1800, when she moves with her new husband to the new capital in the District of Columbia. Sources are sparse after that.)

Its decline notwithstanding, the club clearly had learned the lesson that print culture and professional reputation were useful allies in their efforts to disseminate knowledge. Print would continue to play decisive roles in each member's life: Brown, after returning to Philadelphia in 1801, would edit two more periodicals and author political pamphlets until his death in 1810. Dunlap would issue, during the first and second decades of the new century, a collected edition of his plays and translations. He wrote biographies—including the first one of Brown—briefly edited a magazine, and later in the century authored a series of histories in which he highlighted his own and other club members' roles in the founding of American literature. Edward Miller and Samuel Mitchill continued to edit the *Medical Repository,* which gained the distinction of being the longest-running American periodical of the late eighteenth and early nineteenth centuries. After Edward Miller's death in 1812, Samuel collected and published a volume of his brother's medical works. Samuel Miller himself became one of the most prolific of former club members. Abandoning the subsequent volumes of the *Retrospect,* he took up pastoral writing as well as denominational polemics, including several contributions to fierce pamphlet wars in the first decade of the century on the comparative legitimacy of Presbyterian and Episcopalian ordination. He left New York to help found the Princeton Theological Seminary in 1813, and by the time of his death in 1850 he had over three hundred titles to his name. William Johnson and James Kent, through the first decades of the new century, were an indefatigable team in turning out volumes of printed legal decisions. "Johnson's Reports" numbered thirty volumes. Kent, who secured his influence and fame by publishing his *Commentaries* in the 1820s and '30s, dedicated his monumental work to Johnson in honor of their long-standing intellectual partnership.

Though this proliferation of texts must have been due in some measure to the youthful, utopian energy generated by the Friendly Club, the publications these men issued in later years—some of them all the way to the middle of the nineteenth century—belong to different intellectual cultures than the one they had shared in the 1790s. These new ways of thinking, however, were outgrowths, rather than rejections, of the group's Enlightenment ideals. By the 1830s, literary and scientific cultures had largely separated from one another. Moreover, within the newly separate literary and scientific circles alike, fissures began to emerge between amateurs and professionals. Younger men who had been professionally trained as physicians or scientists scorned older models of intellectual culture in which science was a leisure pursuit.[19] "Amateur" authorship (a phrase that does not quite capture the club's character or intentions) gradually gave way, in a technologically advancing, market-driven print culture, to the new culture of professionalism. But the bibliography of works by former Friendly Club members indicates that professional pursuits had dominated their publishing endeavors from the last decade of the eighteenth century on. Rather than putting their literary energies to the service of philosophical and scientific principles that transcended disciplinary and professional frameworks, their nineteenth-century endeavors were more closely aligned with the emergence of disciplinary and professional thinking. The lawyers wrote about law, ministers about religion, scientists and physicians about science and medicine. The only member who had persisted in plying his trade as an author or artist, William Dunlap, wrote long histories of the arts and the theater. Samuel Mitchill continued his existence as a literary and scientific Renaissance man, but he was clearly the remnant of an older order.

Even New York's civic culture began to segregate along professional lines. Early in the nineteenth century, former Friendly Club members were instrumental in founding civic organizations that drew men of a variety of professions to public association: the New-York Historical Society (1804) and the Literary and Philosophical Society (1814), for example. Smaller, private literary associations comparable to the Friendly Club existed through the nineteenth century, of course. William Dunlap and James Kent both belonged to the Bread and Cheese Club, one such group organized by James Fenimore Cooper in the 1820s.[20] But with rare exceptions, nineteenth-century clubs were designed more for leisure and fellowship than for the aggressive pursuit of collaborative publishing projects.

And yet something of the old order remained. In the first years of the 1800s, when Samuel Miller divided human knowledge into discrete categories, it made perfect sense for him to group "Science, Arts, and Literature" in one category. If, as the century progressed, literature and science became increasingly separate pursuits, some aspects of the Friendly Club's world demonstrated an extraordinary persistence: their confidence that imaginative fiction can convey moral truths ("the truths of the human heart," in Hawthorne's famous phrase), or the ambition for encyclopedic collection (lovingly upheld and parodied all at once in a work like Melville's *Moby-Dick*). Even Emerson's *Nature* was prompted not by a walk in the woods but a trip to the Jardin de Plantes in Paris, with its carefully classified collections.[21] Even transcendental insight, it seems, begins with associations in a materialist world. Friendly Club members shared with following generations the confidence that narrative forms can serve to make sense of—and to shape—the world of associations we inhabit.

Friendly Club Membership
and Nineteenth-Century
New York City Historiography

For historians and critics who have written about the Friendly Club, the membership roster has always played a crucial role, in part because membership has so often been taken as an index of one's political or philosophical beliefs or intellectual or social positions. William Dunlap published the earliest known account of the Friendly Club to list its members by name, in an 1813 memorial to Dr. Edward Miller in Dunlap's short-lived journal, the *Monthly Recorder*. Dunlap's sketch (cited in the introduction for its description of the club's "unshackled intellectual intercourse") seeks to use members' individual reputations as a stamp of approval for Miller's early life in New York. This version of the roster, written over a decade after the club's collapse, lists Dunlap, Kent, William Johnson, Brown, Smith, the Woolseys, Mitchill, and the Millers, as well as Anthony Bleecker and John Wells.[1]

Mitchill and the Millers began attending meetings only in the months leading up to Smith's death in 1798, and some historians have assumed they were not regular members. Samuel Miller and Samuel Mitchill, when they appear in Smith's entries, are listed explicitly as visitors. (Smith always separated visitors from members in his diary accounts of club meetings and had a habit of alphabetizing the regular members in attendance by surname.) Bleecker and Wells, mentioned in passing by Smith on only a few occasions, and never in connection with the club, apparently became active only following Smith's death.[2] Fredrika J. Teute's research on Margaret Bayard's mixed-sex circle at the turn of the century yielded new sources that link Bleecker to other club members in intimate social settings.[3] Samuel Miller endorses Dunlap's account by reproducing it verbatim in the biographical sketch that prefaces his brother's posthumous *Medical Works;*[4] we have no reason, therefore, to doubt Dunlap and Samuel Miller on the point of Wells's and Bleecker's later participation, though we have no contemporary accounts of their contributions to club activity.

Dunlap published two other versions of the club roster in the decades that followed. In his 1815 biography of Brown, whose journals (since lost) he quotes regarding some club meetings, Dunlap provides essentially the same list he had included in the *Recorder* two years earlier, with the omission of Mitchill and the addition of Charles Adams, an odd choice for inclusion, since his short-lived participation overlapped with only about half of the others listed.[5] Nearly two decades later, in his *History of the American Theatre* (1832), Dunlap uses discussions of the club and its members as a way to idealize the formative environment for his own early career. Brown, Johnson, and Smith, he says, were his closest friends among the "band of pioneers" of New York's literary culture. In this account of the club, much more removed from the scene than his previous ones, Dunlap provides some contradictions in his list, omitting the Woolseys, Wells, Bleecker, and Adams, but this time adding Richard Alsop and Noah Webster (the latter of whom, though he socialized regularly with club members, and had been a member with Dunlap and Mitchill of the earlier Philological Society, is not listed in Smith's diary as attending a single meeting).[6]

Later in the nineteenth century, other members or their biographers also used club lists to illustrate an individual's participation in pioneering groups of American writers. James Kent, in his old age, provides a partial list of "a little social literary *club*" from his early New York days—Smith, Brown, Johnson, W. W. Woolsey, and Edward Miller—though he dates the club from 1799, after Smith's death.[7] Samuel Miller's son cites the list from the *Recorder* in his 1869 biography of his father but only as a backhanded compliment to his father's literary shoulder-rubbing, which he considered slightly scandalous (and spiritually dangerous).[8] Unfortunately, after citing only a few entries from his father's early New York diaries, he apparently destroyed the originals. John

Wells's descendents, in their *Memorial of the Life and Character of John Wells* (1874), offered an amalgam of Dunlap's lists and a local historian's (see Francis, below) with no other evidence of Wells's contributions, largely for the purpose of demonstrating that their progenitor had associated with leading young intellectuals and artists of his day.[9] Richard Alsop's biography similarly notes—but is more hesitant than the Wells memorial to embrace without corroboration—a tradition that includes him as club member.[10] His name is conspicuously absent from lists published before Dunlap's theater history. Yet Smith's diary, when read closely, shows that Smith, at least, had promoted Alsop from regular visitor (as he was listed beginning in December 1795) to regular member in March 1796, when his name becomes alphabetized along with the others.[11] By this means I have determined that a similar process took place for Edward Miller during Smith's lifetime, in April 1798,[12] and that Smith also included Brown among the list of members, rather than among the visitors, as scholars sometimes describe him.[13]

In addition to making cameo appearances in latter-day biographies of individual members, the club became a regular feature in the memoirs and multivolume memorial histories of the city that began to appear in the late nineteenth century. In these contexts, the club began to take on legendary dimensions and was used largely to boost claims to the city's early intellectual prominence. John W. Francis, in his *Old New York; or, Reminiscences of the Last Sixty Years,* an 1865 revision of an 1857 discourse before the New-York Historical Society, misidentifies the club in one section as "the Drone Club" (a cognomen for some members of the Calliopean Society, a more formal group) listing as members Bleecker, Kent, Johnson, Dunlap, the Millers, and Brown; in another place he mentions "The *Friendly Club*" as existing in the early 1790s "under the presidency of General Laight," then follows up with another account of the Drones, this time listing Samuel Jones, Mitchill, Samuel Miller, John Blair Linn, William Dunlop [*sic*], Josiah Ogden Hoffman, Brown, and Wells. (Of his list, Laight, Jones, Linn, and Hoffman have no claim to membership; only Jones had even been a visitor.) Francis mentioned the club not only to bring together prominent men in a common intellectual society but to demonstrate Old New York's ability to cultivate "literary confederac[ies]" and "convivial club[s] of professional gentlemen,"[14] the latter phrase a dramatic underestimation of the club's ambitions.

In chapters on the city "at the close of the century" and "Institu-

tions and Inventions" of the early nineteenth century, Martha ("Mrs.")
Lamb's *History of the City of New York* (1877, 1880, 1896) mentions the
club, after correctly listing several of its members as founders of the
New-York Historical Society. Apparently following Francis, though,
she connects these members to both the Drone Club and the Friendly
Club. Under the Drones, which Lamb says was established in 1792, she
lists Bleecker, Kent, Dunlap, Johnson, Brown, the Millers, Mitchill,
and Josiah Ogden Hoffman. For the Friendly Club she features Gilbert Aspinwall (a new addition to the ever-expanding roster), then
includes Kent, Brown, Bleecker, Edward Miller, the Woolseys, Dunlap, Mitchill, and one more newcomer to the lineups, John McVickar
(who, like Hoffman and Aspinwall, shows up nowhere in contemporary sources for the club). Loosely following Dunlap's early account,
she writes that the Friendly Club "flourished for many years before and
a few years after the death of Washington—until annihilated by political differences. . . . [I]t met at the houses of its members in rotation
every Tuesday evening, and it was the duty of the host to direct conversation through the reading of a passage from some favorite author. At
the close of the discussion light refreshments—wine, cake, etc.—were
served without ceremony."[15] Like Francis, Lamb aims in these entries
to show that late-eighteenth-century New York was intellectually vibrant.

The *Memorial History of the City of New York* (1893), edited by
James Grant Wilson, outdoes Mrs. Lamb in the prestige of the club's
visitors:

> Nothing worthy of the name of a club appeared till, just before the war
> of the American Revolution, the Friendly Club was formed with James
> Kent, William Dunlap, Charles Brockden Brown, and Anthony Bleecker
> as the leading spirits. Several of its members conducted the first medi-
> cal journal in America, and its weekly receptions were attended by the
> intellect and wit of the city, George Washington often being a visitor.
> But the club finally went to pieces in the clash between the Federalist
> and Anti-Federalist members, some of them founding the Drone Club
> in 1792 as a successor of the Moot Club of ante-Revolutionary days, for
> the debate of purely technical questions, chiefly in the law.[16]

Washington, of course, never visited the club; its dates do not overlap
with New York's years as national capital. And though most of the club

members had encountered the president, none of them knew him intimately, though the claim has been repeated in attempts to elevate the
club's and its members' importance. Other frequently alleged visitors
have included Theodore and Timothy Dwight. Though these men, of
course, knew club members well, neither of them shows up in Smith's
or Dunlap's accounts of club meetings. In fact, it suggests something
about the club that though the Dwights were often in town on Saturday evenings when the club *did* meet, they are never included in such
gatherings, whether by their own choice, or by the members' decision
to exclude them.[17] Given the religious tension Smith and Dunlap felt
with the Dwights, their presence might have served to affect negatively
the desired atmosphere of unrestricted communication.

The following people *are* listed as visitors by Smith: Richard Alsop,
from December 1795 to mid-March 1796, when he is first alphabetized
as a regular member and then attends through the end of that year.
Henry Gahn, a Swedish immigrant, chemist, and owner of a count-
inghouse, attends as a visitor, never alphabetized, once in 1795, once
in 1796, three times in the spring of 1797, once in December 1797, once
in January 1798. Samuel M. Hopkins, a Connecticut friend, attends
regularly as a visitor in the spring of 1796 before leaving for a European
tour. (Margaret Bayard later counted him as one of the proprietors of
the *Monthly Magazine*.) Several others are listed as having visited only
once or twice: J. Mulligan, James Watson, Dr. Wheaton, Mr. Mason,
Mr. Davenport of Connecticut (the last came twice, April 1797 and
January 1798); and Samuel Jones, Sr. Edward Miller begins as a visitor shortly after he arrives in New York in 1796 and is listed as a steady
visitor from October 1797 to 28 April 1798, when he is alphabetized
for the first time; Samuel Mitchill visits four times between October
1797 and May 1798; Moses Rogers (brother-in-law to the Woolseys and
Dunlap's wife); James Sharples, twice; Mr. Boyd; Mr. Radclift, twice;
Mr. Howland (George M. Woolsey's brother-in-law); Dr. Mease; and
Samuel Miller, once (May 1798). Based on the frequency of their status
as visitors in 1798 and the diligence with which they participated in
promoting the *Monthly Magazine* after Smith's death, I have chosen to
follow Miller's and Dunlap's lead and treat Samuel Miller and Samuel
Latham Mitchill as regular members at the turn of the century, when
no contemporary record of club activity survives.

Not until James Cronin's Yale Ph.D. dissertation, a biography of

Elihu Smith, did historians of early American club culture have access to the single most important record of Friendly Club activity: Smith's diaries. And until Cronin's 1973 edition of the diaries, scholars would still have very limited access. For almost half a century the only accurate account of the Friendly Club and its membership remained Cronin's eight-page long article in the *Publications of the Modern Language Association*.[18]

BREC	Samuel Miller, *A Brief Retrospect of the Eighteenth Century. Part First, in Two Volumes: Containing a Sketch of the Revolutions and Improvements in Science, Arts, and Literature during that Period* (New York: T. & J. Swords, 1803)
CA	Charles Adams
CBB	Charles Brockden Brown
CBB, *Alcuin*	Charles Brockden Brown, *Alcuin, a Dialogue; Memoirs of Stephen Calvert. The Novels and Related Works of Charles Brockden Brown*, vol. 6 (Kent, Ohio: Kent State University Press, 1987)
CBB, *AM*	Charles Brockden Brown, *Arthur Mervyn, or, Memoirs of the Year 1793; First and Second Parts. The Novels and Related Works of Charles Brockden Brown*, vol. 3 (Kent, Ohio: Kent State University Press, 1980)
CBB, *EH*	Charles Brockden Brown, *Edgar Huntly, or, Memoirs of a Sleep-walker. The Novels and Related Works of Charles Brockden Brown*, vol. 4 (Kent, Ohio: Kent State University Press, 1984)
CBB, *Ormond*	Charles Brockden Brown, *Ormond, or, the Secret Witness. The Novels and Related Works of Charles Brockden Brown*, vol. 2 (Kent, Ohio: Kent State University Press, 1982)
CBB, *WMC*	Charles Brockden Brown, *Wieland, or, the Transformation, an American Tale; Memoirs of Carwin the Biloquist. The Novels and Related Works of Charles Brockden Brown*, vol. 1 (Kent, Ohio: Kent State University Press, 1977)
DEHS	Elihu Hubbard Smith, *The Diary of Elihu Hubbard Smith, 1771–1798*, ed. James E. Cronin (Philadelphia: American Philosophical Society, 1973)
DHAT	William Dunlap, *History of the American Theatre and Anecdotes of the Principal Actors* (New York: Burt Franklin, 1963 [1832])
DHRPAD	William Dunlap, *History of the Rise and Progress of the Arts of Design in the United States*, 2 vols. (New York: George P. Scott, 1834)
DWD	William Dunlap, *The Diary of William Dunlap (1766–1839), The Memoirs of a Dramatist, Theatrical Manager, Painter, Critic, Novelist, and Historian*, ed. Dorothy C. Barck (1930; reprint, New York: Benjamin Blom, 1969)
EAL	*Early American Literature*
EHS	Elihu Hubbard Smith
EM	Edward Miller
FC	Friendly Club

GMW	George Muirson Woolsey
H&C	J. R. Holmes and M. M. Cavnar, "A Revised Checklist of the Letters of Charles Brockden Brown," typescript, prepared for forthcoming Kent State edition of Brown's letters
HSP	Historical Society of Pennsylvania
JER	*Journal of the Early Republic*
JK	James Kent
JM	Jedidiah Morse
KP	James Kent Papers, Library of Congress
LCBB	William Dunlap, *Life of Charles Brockden Brown: Together with Selections from the Rarest of His Printed Works, from his Original Letters, and from His Manuscripts Before Unpublished,* 2 vols. (Philadelphia: James P. Parke, 1815)
LSM	Samuel Miller, Jr., *The Life of Samuel Miller, D.D., LL.D.* (Philadelphia: Claxton, Remsen, and Haffelfinger, 1869)
MB	Margaret Bayard
MBSP	Margaret Bayard Smith Papers, Library of Congress
MCK	William Kent, *Memoirs and Letters of James Kent, LL.D., Late Chancellor of the State of New York* (Boston: Little and Brown, 1898)
MMAR	*Monthly Magazine, and American Review* (New York, 1799–1800)
MR	*Medical Repository*
MWEM	Edward Miller, *Medical Works of Edward Miller, M.D., Late Professor of the Practice of Physic in the University of New-York, and Resident Physician for the City of New-York, Collected and Accompanied with a Biographical Sketch of the Author* (New York: Collins and Co., 1814)
NYAM	New York Academy of Medicine
N-YHS	New-York Historical Society
PUL	Princeton University Libraries
RL	Benjamin Rush Letterbooks, Library Company of Philadelphia / Historical Society of Pennsylvania
SBT	Susan Bull Tracy
SHS	Samuel Harrison Smith
SLM	Samuel Latham Mitchill
SM	Samuel Miller
SMP	Samuel Miller Papers, Princeton University Libraries
TD	Timothy Dwight
ThD	Theodore Dwight
WD	William Dunlap
WD, *André*	William Dunlap, *André; a Tragedy, in Five Acts: as Performed by the Old American Company, New-York, March 30, 1798, to which are added, authentic documents respecting Major André* (New York: T. & J. Swords, 1798)
WJ	William Johnson
WMQ	*The William and Mary Quarterly,* 3rd series
WWW	William Walton Woolsey

❊ NOTES ❊

Introduction

1. *Monthly Recorder* 1 (Apr. 1813): 8.

2. Henry May, *The Enlightenment in America* (New York: Oxford University Press, 1976), 233.

3. *LCBB*, 2:8; *DEHS*, 463 (6 Sept. 1798). On Scandella, see esp. 420 (23 Jan. 1798) and 463–64 (1–15 Sept. 1798); "Medical Obituary," *MR* 2:2 (1798): 226; EHS to Benjamin Rush, 10 Sept. 1798, RL. On the scope of Scandella's associations in the United States, see Antonio Pace, "Giambattista Scandella and His American Friends," *Italica* 42:2 (June 1965): 269–84.

4. CBB to James Brown, 25 Sept. 1798 (H&C #108), in *LCBB*, 2:10–11.

5. SM, "A Biographical Sketch of Edward Miller, M.D.," in *MWEM*, lx.

6. CBB to James Brown, 18 [20?] Sept. 1798 (H&C #106), in *LCBB*, 2:9–10; CBB to [?], 24 Sept. 1798 (H&C #107), in *LCBB*, 2:10.

7. CBB to James Brown, Sept. 1798 (H&C #101), excerpted in *LCBB*, 2:5. For the medical rationale for this dietary behavior, see EHS, "Letters on the Fever of 1795," in Noah Webster, ed., *A Collection of Papers on the Subject of Bilious Fever, Prevalent in the United States for a Few Years Past* (New York: Hopkins, Webb, and Co., 1796), esp. 82–86; SLM, *Remarks on the Gaseous Oxyd of Azote* (New York: T. & J. Swords, 1795), 36; and William Bay, *Inaugural Dissertation on the Operation of Pestilential Fluids upon the Large Intestines, Termed by Nosologists Dysentery* (New York: T. & J. Swords, 1797), 40–43, an inaugural dissertation SLM supervised.

8. I use the term "late Enlightenment," following Roy Porter's periodization, to indicate the late-eighteenth-century "enlightened critique of Enlightenment." See Porter, *The Creation of the Modern World: The Untold Story of the British Enlightenment* (New York: W. W. Norton, 2000), xvii.

9. EHS uses this phrase in his diary as he comments on a young New York lawyer named John Wells; notwithstanding his "superior" mind, Wells had an apparent "disrelish to mental exertion" that was the result of having paid no "systematic attention to investigation," although "[t]his defect does not appear, either constitutional, or irremediable; & he may, yet, possibly, assume that rank, in the republic of intellect, which would belong to industry and talents" (*DEHS*, 55: 12 Sept. 1795). By some accounts, Wells became a Friendly Club member after EHS's death. See Appendix. On the Enlightenment "republic of letters," see Anne Goldgar, *Impolite Learning: Conduct and Community in the Republic of Letters, 1680–1750* (New Haven: Yale University Press, 1995); Dena Goodman, *The Republic of Letters: A Cultural History of the French Enlightenment* (Ithaca: Cornell University Press, 1994); Jon Klancher, "The Vocation of Criticism and the

Crisis of the Republic of Letters," in Marshall Brown, ed., *The Cambridge History of Literary Criticism* (Cambridge: Cambridge University Press), 5:296–320; Elizabeth Heckendorn Cook, *Epistolary Bodies: Gender and Genre in the Eighteenth-Century Republic of Letters* (Stanford: Stanford University Press, 1996); and Paul Keen, *The Crisis of Literature in the 1790s: Print Culture and the Public Sphere* (New York: Cambridge University Press, 1999).

10. The phrase comes from the circular address for the *Medical Repository.* See [SLM, EM, and EHS], "An Address, &c." (New York: n.p., 1796), 7.

11. CBB to James Brown, 17 Sept. 1798 (H&C #103), in *LCBB*, 2:7–8.

12. "Medical Obituary," *MR* 2:2 (1798): 227–28, printed alongside Scandella's obituary; *Connecticut Courant*, 24 Sept. 1798; KP, Reel 2 (1794–1798), concludes with JK's record of the Scandella-Smith story. See also SLM to Noah Webster, 17 Sept. 1798, in Emily Ford Skeel, ed., *Notes on the Life of Noah Webster*, 2 vols. (New York: privately printed, 1912), 1:467–68; MB to SHS, 23 Sept. 1798 and 22 Oct. 1798, MBSP. Joseph Dennie reprinted the *MR* obituary as "American Biography. Dr. Elihu Hubbard Smith," *Farmer's Museum*, 29 Apr. 1799. For other accounts mentioned in this paragraph, see James Hardie, *An Account of the Malignant Fever, Lately Prevalent in the City of New-York* (New York: Hurtin and McFarlane, 1799), 46–47; Richard Alsop, ThD, and Lemuel Hopkins, *The Political Green-House, for the Year 1798* (Hartford: Hudson and Goodwin, 1799), first published in the *Connecticut Courant*, 11 Feb. 1799, and rpt. in *The Echo, with Other Poems* (New York: Porcupine Press, 1807), in Benjamin Franklin V, ed., *The Poetry of the Minor Connecticut Wits* (Gainesville, Fla.: Scholars' Facsimiles and Reprints, 1970), 243–45, 355; CBB, *AM,*150–54; [David Hosack?], "Sketch of the Life and Character of the Late Dr. Elihu Hubbard Smith, of New-York," *American Medical and Philosophical Register* 4 (Jan. 1814): 391–99; *LCBB*, 2:5–11; James Thatcher, *American Medical Biography* (New York: Da Capo Press, 1967 [1828]), 2:88–95; *DHAT*, 2:77–80; Evert Duyckinck, *Cyclopaedia of American Literature* (New York, 1855). Franklin B. Dexter, *Biographical Sketches of the Graduates of Yale College* (New York: Henry Holt, 1907), 4:509, describes Smith as dying while "actively employed in his professional duties," without specific reference to Scandella.

13. Milton Ellis, "Smith, Elihu Hubbard," *Dictionary of American Biography*, 17:259–60.

14. Joanne Freeman, *Affairs of Honor: National Politics in the New Republic* (New Haven: Yale University Press, 2001). In the 1790s, Federalists in particular grew anxious about anonymous public expression. See David Waldstreicher, *In the Midst of Perpetual Fetes: The Making of American Nationalism, 1776–1820* (Chapel Hill: University of North Carolina Press, 1997), 63; Christopher Grasso, *A Speaking Aristocracy: Transforming Public Discourse in Eighteenth-Century Connecticut* (Chapel Hill: University of North Carolina Press, 1999), 443; and Leon Jackson, "Jedidiah Morse and the Transformation of Print Culture in New England, 1784–1826," *EAL* 34 (1999): 2–31. Anonymity was never a predominant characteristic of publishing associated with the liberal professions (as compared to political writing, for instance), even when vocational identity was conceived in the terms of republicanism or civic humanism.

15. Frank Shuffelton, "Juries of the Common Reader: Crime and Judgment in the Novels of Charles Brockden Brown," in Philip Barnard, Mark L. Kamrath, and Stephen Shapiro, eds., *Revising Charles Brockden Brown: Culture, Politics, and Sexuality in the Early Republic* (Knoxville: University of Tennessee Press, 2004), 88–114.

16. See especially John L. Brooke, "Ancient Lodges and Self-Created Societies: Voluntary Association and the Public Sphere in the Early Republic," in Ronald Hoffman and Peter J. Albert, eds., *Launching the "Extended Republic": The Federalist Era* (Charlottesville: University Press of Virginia, 1996), 273–377; Albrecht Koschnik, "The Democratic Societies of Philadelphia and the Limits of the American Public Sphere, circa 1793–1795," *WMQ* 58:3 (July 2001); and Waldstreicher, *In the Midst of Perpetual Fetes.*

17. *DEHS,* 77 (22 Oct. 1795).

18. A. Hunter Dupree, "The National Pattern of American Learned Societies, 1769–1863," in Alexandra Oleson and Sanborn C. Brown, eds., *The Pursuit of Knowledge in the Early American Republic: American Scientific and Learned Societies from Colonial Times to the Civil War* (Baltimore: Johns Hopkins University Press, 1976), 21–32.

19. American newspapers during the 1790s increased from 96 to 234; along with "the ratio of free population per newspaper," writes John Brooke, "and the ratio of copies printed per free population," these numbers represent "the *greatest rate of growth* in the volume of the American press" in the century before the Civil War. John L. Brooke, "To Be 'Read by the Whole People': Press, Party, and Public Sphere in the United States, 1789–1840," *Proceedings of the American Antiquarian Society* 110:1 (2002): 41–118, quote on 67. From the 1790s on, newspapers served as the principal engines of partisan political cultures. See Jeffrey L. Pasley, *"The Tyranny of Printers": Newspaper Politics in the Early American Republic* (Charlottesville: University of Virginia Press, 2001).

20. Richard D. Brown, *Knowledge Is Power: The Diffusion of Information in Early America, 1700–1865* (New York: Oxford University Press, 1989), 4.

21. Ibid. The touchstone accounts of the public sphere's emergence remain Jürgen Habermas, *The Structural Transformation of the Public Sphere: An Inquiry into a Category of Bourgeois Society*, trans. Thomas McCarthy (Cambridge: MIT Press, 1989), and Michael Warner, *The Letters of the Republic: Publication and the Public Sphere in Eighteenth-Century America* (Cambridge: Harvard University Press, 1990). For an alternate take to political and literary histories of the public sphere, see Jan Golinsky, *Science as Public Culture: Chemistry and Enlightenment in Britain, 1760–1820* (Cambridge: Cambridge University Press, 1992). In my use of the term "public sphere," I attempt to abide by Charles Taylor's useful distinction between "topical common space" (defined as "common space arising from assembly in some locale") and the "public sphere," whose definition he refines as "a plurality of spaces [knit together] into one larger space of nonassembly," which is "metatopical" in nature. Charles Taylor, "Modern Social Imaginaries," *Public Culture* 14:1 (2002): 91–124, quote on 113–14.

22. Peter Dobkin Hall, *The Organization of American Culture, 1700–1900: Private Institutions, Elites, and the Origins of American Nationality* (New York:

New York University Press, 1982), esp. chaps. 5–7; Warner, *The Letters of the Republic*, esp. 43, 108; John Barrell, *The Birth of Pandora and the Division of Knowledge* (Philadelphia: University of Pennsylvania Press, 1992), xiv–xv.

23. The most important recent treatment is Robert Ferguson, *The American Enlightenment, 1750–1820* (Cambridge: Harvard University Press, 1997), originally published in *The Cambridge History of American Literature*, 8 vols., ed. Sacvan Bercovitch (New York: Cambridge University Press, 1994), vol. 1.

24. Webster offered this definition as late as the 1820s; the quote comes from his *An American Dictionary of the English Language* (New Haven: Hezekiah Howe, 1828); Warner, *The Letters of the Republic*, 122. See also Trevor Ross, "The Emergence of 'Literature': Making and Reading the English Canon in the Eighteenth Century," *ELH* 63:2 (summer 1996): 397–422. Unless stated otherwise, all italics are in the original.

25. The club's projected journal included the following "divisions": the arts, fine arts, medicine, natural history, physics, antiquities, commerce, agriculture, economics, morals, politics, religion, laws, criticism, polity, statistics, biography, literature, anecdote, poetry, manners, and miscellany, with several subheadings under each title. See *DEHS*, 79 (22 Oct. 1795). On the expansive definition of late-eighteenth-century "literature," see also Keen, *The Crisis of Literature in the 1790s*, and Clifford Siskin, *The Work of Writing: Literature and Social Change in Britain, 1700–1830* (Baltimore: Johns Hopkins University Press, 1998).

26. Ferguson, *The American Enlightenment*, 42; *DEHS*, 48 (7 Sept. 1795); EHS to ThD, 22 Nov. 1796, in *DEHS*, 265. Henry May used the FC to illustrate his category of the "moderate Enlightenment" in *The Enlightenment in America*, 232–35.

27. Michael Gilmore, for example, sees early U.S. writing as "often a matter of collaboration rather than individual authorship" and offers standard explanations for the "native novel's" "devotion to factuality": "the Puritan-Protestant dislike of fanciful embellishment, the suspicion of fictionality Americans acquired from their reading of Scottish Common Sense philosophy, and the luster of history writing among a people who learned much of their politics from Whiggish chronicles of ancient Greece and Rome." Gilmore, "The Literature of the Revolutionary and Early National Periods," in *The Cambridge History of American Literature*, 8 vols., ed. Sacvan Bercovitch (New York: Cambridge University Press, 1994), 1:550.

28. John Bender, "Enlightenment Fiction and the Scientific Hypothesis," *Representations* 61 (1998): 6–28.

29. EHS to John Aiken, 14 Apr. 1798, in *DEHS*, 438. For the published version of this letter, see *Monthly Magazine, and British Register*, July 1798.

30. Dennie reprinted the sketches in the *Farmer's Museum*, beginning 2 Sept. 1799, adding that "the late Dr. E. H. Smith, of Newyork, whose attachment to his country was never disputed, transmitted to British Editors the lives of 'certain of our own poets,' because for such modes of writing THERE WAS NO CURIOSITY IN AMERICA."

31. EHS to John Aiken, 14 Apr. 1798, in *DEHS*, 438.

32. EHS, "Proem," in *DEHS*, 360 (Sept. 1797).

33. *DEHS*, 100 (11 Dec. 1795).

Prelude. Pictures at an Exhibition

1. *DEHS,* 363 (15 Sept. 1797).

2. Christopher Lukasik, "The Face of the Public," *EAL* 39:3 (2004): 413–64; Valentijn Byvanck, "Representative Heads: Politics and Portraiture in Antebellum America," Ph.D. diss., New York University, 1998, 110–21. FC members would have been familiar with a 1789 English translation of Lavater by the British Jacobin Thomas Holcroft, one of their favorite playwrights and novelists.

3. *DEHS,* 360 ("Proem," Sept. 1797).

4. On FC members sitting for Sharples, see *DEHS,* 368 (26 Sept. 1797), 373 (2 Oct. 1797), 394–95 (25 Nov. 1797); also see *DWD,* 156 (2 Oct. 1797), 201 (4 Jan. 1798), 815 (16 Aug. 1834).

5. *Daily Advertiser* (6 July 1798); see also George Gates Raddin, Jr., *The New York of Hocquet Caritat and his Associates* (Dover, N.J.: The Dover Advance Press, 1953), 30. EHS visited the exhibition but left no critical commentary. See *DEHS,* 457 (24 July 1798).

6. Katherine McCook Knox, *The Sharples: Their Portraits of George Washington and His Contemporaries* (New York: Kennedy Graphics, Inc. and Da Capo Press, 1972 [1930]).

7. Sharples also took portraits of women, including WJ's sister, Fanny, and JK's wife, Elizabeth, pictured with their daughter, but the collection included many more men than women, perhaps suggesting a division in Sharples's practice between the collection of public characters and the business of private commissions. No advertisements for Sharples's public exhibitions mention women. In Philadelphia, Charles Willson Peale had since 1784 been assembling his own collection of "distinguished Personages," which he displayed at his Philadelphia museum. See Ellen G. Miles, "'Memorials of great & good men who were my friends': Portraits in the Life of Oliver Wolcott, Jr.," *Proceedings of the American Antiquarian Society* (1998): 123.

8. See the Appendix for details and for my rationale for including these specific individuals as members. Sharples's portrait collection also included former FC members Lynde Catlin and Richard Alsop, both merchants, the latter a poet. EHS's father, Reuben Smith, also sat for Sharples. Anthony Bleecker, who almost certainly became a member of the FC after EHS's death, sat for a portrait as late as 1810, according to Ellen Sharples's diary. See Knox, *The Sharples,* 120. The only regular members not represented in the extant or recorded collection are WWW and GMW, who were the least public of FC members and the only ones not to pursue literary publication of some sort. Portraits of the Woolseys by WD preserve more traditional familial associations.

9. Karie Diethorn, Museum Curator for Independence National Historical Park, attributes its portrait of CBB to Ellen Sharples and the one at Worcester Art Museum in Worcester, Massachusetts, to James. While CBB did visit Sharples in the summer of 1798, diary accounts do not mention his portrait being taken. Unlike the rest of the FC portraits, CBB's (like Noah Webster's and Joseph Priestley's) is a three-quarter face rather than a profile, which may suggest that he was not participating in the same round of sittings as his friends. Still,

ties of friendship likely led CBB at whatever date to select a portraitist who had been patronized by his friends; his portrait, like theirs, can be read as motivated by the prospect of joining an established and meaningful collection.

10. On the traditional significance of family contexts to eighteenth-century American portraiture, see Margaretta M. Lovell, *Art in a Season of Revolution: Painters, Artisans, and Patrons in Early America* (Philadelphia: University of Pennsylvania Press, 2005), esp. ch. 5.

11. Jack Larkin, *The Shaping of Everyday Life, 1790–1840* (New York: Harper and Row, 1988), 183; Edward Warwick, Henry C. Pitz, and Alexander Wyckoff, *Early American Dress: The Colonial and Revolutionary Periods* (New York: Benjamin Blom, 1965), 216–17; Marcia Pointon, *Hanging the Head: Portraiture and Social Formation in Eighteenth-Century England* (New Haven: Yale University Press, 1993), ch. 4.

12. Christopher Grasso, *A Speaking Aristocracy: Transforming Public Discourse in Eighteenth-Century Connecticut* (Chapel Hill: University of North Carolina Press, 1999), 387, 394. FC members were younger than the Revolution's leaders but slightly older than the group (born between 1776 and 1800) that Joyce Appleby designates "the first generation of Americans." Joyce Appleby, *Inheriting the Revolution: The First Generation of Americans* (Cambridge: Harvard University Press, 2000).

13. *DEHS*, 58 (17 Sept. 1795), 176 (10 June 1796).

14. This penchant for a bodily politics of self-expression led the friends to lap up detailed descriptions of Godwin's physical appearance from Thomas A. Cooper, an actor in WD's Old American Company who had been mentored in England by Godwin and Thomas Holcroft: "Mr Godwin is a small man delicately formed, about 40 years of age," they learned, whose "dress at present is plain with short unpowdered hair & so is Holcrofts." See *DWD*, 212 (23 Jan. 1798), 229 (4 Mar. 1798).

15. David Waldstreicher, "Why Thomas Jefferson and African Americans Wore Their Politics on Their Sleeves: Dress and Mobilization between American Revolutions," in Jeffrey L. Pasley, Andrew W. Robertson, and David Waldstreicher, eds., *Beyond the Founders: New Approaches to the Political History of the Early American Republic* (Chapel Hill: University of North Carolina Press, 2004), 79–103.

16. Vernon Parrington, *Main Currents in American Thought, Volume Two: The Romantic Revolution in America, 1800–1860* (New York: Harcourt, Brace, and World, 1927), 267–87.

17. Lukasik, "The Face of the Public," 414; Byvanck, "Representative Heads," 19.

18. T. H. Breen, "The Meaning of 'Likeness': Portrait-Painting in an Eighteenth-Century Consumer Society," in Ellen G. Miles, ed., *The Portrait in Eighteenth-Century America* (Newark, Del.: University of Delaware Press, 1993), 47; Margaretta M. Lovell, "Painters and Their Customers: Aspects of Art and Money in Eighteenth-Century America," in Cary Carson, Ronald Hoffman, and Peter J. Albert, eds., *Of Consuming Interests: The Style of Life in the Eighteenth Century* (Charlottesville: University of Virginia Press for United States Capitol Historical Society, 1994), 286–87; Miles, "'Memorials'"; Deborah Dependahl

Waters, "'All Arts Shall Flourish in Columbia's Land': The Fine and Decorative Arts of Federal New York," in *Federal New York: A Symposium,* ed. Robert I. Goler (New York: Fraunces Tavern Museum, 1990), 29; *Commercial Advertiser,* 27 Dec. 1799, qtd. in Raddin, *The New York of Hocquet Caritat,* 30. Smith's posthumous inclusion in this advertisement signals not only his local cultural capital but also a shift in the meaning of his portrait, which now served as a memorial. This is also the meaning WD assigned to the copy of Smith's portrait, which Sharples's sons gave him before the family left the city for England, in token of Dunlap's friendship with Smith. (This gift also helps explain why EHS's portrait is not among the collection at Independence Hall.) *DHRPAD,* 2:70–72; Byvanck, "Representative Heads," 26.

19. Qtd. in Wendy Bellion, "Heads of State: Profiles and Politics in Jeffersonian America," in *New Media, 1740–1915,* eds. Lisa Gitelman and Geoffrey B. Pingree (Cambridge: MIT Press, 2003), 32. These methods expanded on one of portraiture's most appealing features: its ability to reveal to sitters precisely what remained invisible to them—their own faces. Susan Stewart, *On Longing: Narratives of the Miniature, the Gigantic, the Souvenir, the Collection* (Baltimore: Johns Hopkins University Press, 1984), 125.

20. William Smith, Jr., *History of the Province of New York,* 2 vols. (1757; Cambridge: Harvard University Press, 1972), 1:226. Thanks to Jill Lepore for this reference.

One. "The Town is the only place for rational beings"

1. Sidney Pomerantz, *New York, An American City, 1783–1803: A Study of Urban Life* (New York: Columbia University Press, 1938); Paul Gilje and William Pencak, eds., *New York in the Age of the Constitution, 1775–1800* (Rutherford, N.J.: Fairleigh Dickinson University Press, 1992); Edwin G. Burrows and Mike Wallace, *Gotham: A History of New York City to 1898* (New York: Oxford University Press, 1999), chs. 19–25.

2. Robert Greenhalgh Albion, *The Rise of New York Port, 1815–1860* (New York: Charles Scribner's Sons, 1939), 5–8.

3. *The Diary,* 11 July 1793, qtd. in Pomerantz, *New York,* 287.

4. James E. Cronin, "Introduction," in *DEHS,* 1–16; Marcia Bailey, *A Lesser Hartford Wit, Dr. Elihu Hubbard Smith, 1771–1798* (Orono: University of Maine Press, 1928); James E. Cronin, "The Life of Elihu Hubbard Smith," Ph.D. diss., Yale University, 1946.

5. Eliza Newton Woolsey Howland, *Family Records: Being Some Account of the Ancestry of my Father and Mother Charles William Woolsey and Jane Eliza Woolsey* (privately printed, 1900).

6. Benjamin Franklin V, "Introduction," *The Poetry of the Minor Connecticut Wits* (Gainesville, Fla.: Scholars' Facsimiles and Reprints, 1970), xii–xiv.

7. Oral Sumner Coad, *William Dunlap: A Study of His Life and Works and of His Place in Contemporary Culture* (New York: The Dunlap Society, 1917); Robert Canary, *William Dunlap* (New York: Twayne Publishers, 1970); Oral Sumner Coad, "Dunlap, William," *Dictionary of American Biography,* 5:516–18. For autobiographical statements see *DHAT,* 2:38–69, and *DHRPAD,* 1:242–315.

8. SLM, *The Present State of Medical Learning in the City of New-York* (New York: T. & J. Swords, 1797).

9. John C. Greene, "Science, Learning, and Utility: Patterns of Organization in the Early American Republic," in Alexandra Oleson and Sanborn C. Brown, eds., *The Pursuit of Knowledge in the Early American Republic: American Scientific and Learned Societies from Colonial Times to the Civil War* (Baltimore: Johns Hopkins University Press, 1976), 1–20, quote on 16.

10. EHS to John Allen, 24 Jan. 1796, in *DEHS*, 126. Smith complains in this letter of the city's failure to establish "some permanent Institution, friendly to literature & useful knowledge."

11. JK to Moss Kent, 18 May 1796, KP.

12. *DWD*, 1:336–37 (5 Sept. 1798).

13. Peter Clark, *British Clubs and Societies, 1580–1800: The Origins of an Associational World* (Oxford: Oxford University Press, 2000). On the "deliberative public sphere," see John L. Brooke, "To Be 'Read by the Whole People': Press, Party, and Public Sphere in the United States, 1789–1840," *Proceedings of the American Antiquarian Society* 110:1 (2002): 41–118. The male civic space I describe was interdependent with but distinct from print publics, which in some ways granted easier access to women and members of lower classes. The mixed-sex social world that spilled from parlors into public promenades like the Battery, Broadway, and the Bowling Green, and even the elite social settings that gave some women access to political discussion and influence, stood apart from the all-male associations I describe. On African-American association in the same period, see Craig Wilder, *In the Company of Black Men: The African Influence on African American Culture in New York City* (New York: New York University Press, 2005); Joanna Brooks, *American Lazarus: Religion and the Rise of African-American and Native American Literatures* (New York: Oxford University Press, 2003), esp. ch. 4.

14. Paul Allen, *The Life of Charles Brockden Brown* (Delmar, N.Y.: Scholars' Facsimiles and Reprints, 1975), 20–31. See also Caleb Crain, *American Sympathy: Men, Friendship, and Literature in the New Nation* (New Haven: Yale University Press, 2001), ch. 2.

15. Allen, *The Life of Charles Brockden Brown*, 17, 22.

16. Though Brown's group had produced literary compositions for one another to critique, the Hartford group met not only for conversation and internal literary performance but also for joint literary production intended for publication. The Hartford group included friends with whom Smith corresponded regularly after leaving Connecticut: Theodore Dwight, whose older brother Timothy had been one of the original Wits; Mason Fitch Cogswell, like Smith a poet and physician; Richard Alsop, who lived in New York from late 1795 to early 1797 and was a Friendly Club member during most of that time. See Cronin, "Introduction," in *DEHS*, 9–12. On the "minor" Wits see especially Franklin, "Introduction," *The Poetry of the Minor Connecticut Wits*, xi–xxvi. For Smith's inclusion of Alsop with the regular club members, see *DEHS*, 141 (19 Mar. 1796), where he is alphabetized among the list of members for the first time. Francis Parsons, without documentation, refers to the Wits as a "friendly club." See Francis Par-

sons, *The Friendly Club and Other Portraits* (Hartford: Edwin Valentine Mitchell, 1922), ch. 1. David Shields indicates that the term "friendly club" might have been used generically for earlier groups. See "British-American Belles Lettres," in *The Cambridge History of American Literature,* ed. Sacvan Bercovitch, 8 vols. (New York: Cambridge University Press, 1994), 1:321. The term "Friendly Society," by contrast, typically referred to mutual insurance associations for working men.

17. Founded in 1768 as a debating society by future Connecticut Wit David Humphreys, the Brothers in Unity over time broadened to include literary discussion more generally. Christopher Grasso, *A Speaking Aristocracy: Transforming Public Discourse in Eighteenth-Century Connecticut* (Chapel Hill: University of North Carolina Press, 1999), 398n15, 399. On JK as a member of the Linonian Society, see Cronin, "Introduction," in *DEHS,* 3. On young men's groups, see also Glenn Wallach, *Obedient Sons: The Discourse of Youth and Generations in American Culture, 1630–1860* (Amherst: University of Massachusetts Press, 1997), esp. ch. 3; Albrecht Koschnik, "Fashioning a Federalist Self: Young Men and Voluntary Association in Early Nineteenth-Century Philadelphia," *Explorations in Early American Culture* 4 (2000): 220–57.

18. The most thoroughly documented survey of these groups between 1786 and 1806 remains Eleanor Bryce Scott, "Early Literary Clubs in New York City," *American Literature* 5 (Mar. 1933): 3–16. Scott acknowledges but opts not to untangle the contradictory accounts of FC membership; see also Thomas Bender, *New York Intellect: A History of Intellectual Life in New York City, from 1750 to the Beginnings of Our Own Time* (Baltimore: Johns Hopkins University Press, 1987), 28; and David S. Shields, "Dining Clubs and Literary Culture in Federal New York," in *Federal New York: A Symposium,* ed. Robert I. Goler (New York: Fraunces Tavern Museum, 1990), 35–40. Several historians from the nineteenth century to the present, including Bender, follow the nineteenth-century antiquarian John W. Francis's mistake to collapse the FC with the Calliopean Society. See Calliopean Society Papers, N-YHS. In "The Science of Lying," in Edward Watts and Malini Schueller, eds., *Messy Beginnings: Postcoloniality and Early American Literature* (New Brunswick: Rutgers University Press, 2003), David Shields reads the Calliopean Society as anti-Enlightenment (celebrating "lying" and indolence, denigrating science), which suggests another significant difference between the Calliopeans and the science-minded FC. However, Shields may be mistaken to identify the group as Federalist in politics; its members included such leading Republicans as Tunis Wortman, and its records indicate a Republican bias throughout the 1790s; members for a time, in the wake of the Revolution in France, addressed one another as "citizen."

On the remaining groups: The N-YHS holds minutes for the Sub Rosa dining club and Manumission Society, several volumes of which are in Elihu Smith's handwriting. For the Mineralogical Society's formation and founding membership, see *DEHS,* 456–62, passim (16 July–23 Aug. 1798). On the Emigrants, see "Original Poetry" ("The Citizens of New-York establishing a Society for the Relief of EMIGRANTS, gave rise to the following lines"), *New-York Magazine* (Nov. 1794): 703–4. On the Anacreontic Society, see *Laws and Regulations of the Columbian Anacreontic Society, as Revised, Amended, and Agreed to the 6th*

Day of March 1800 (New York: G. F. Hopkins, 1800). The Uranian Society minutes are at the New York Public Library. On the Medical Society, see Daniel C. Calhoun, *Professional Lives in America: Structure and Aspiration, 1750–1850* (Cambridge: Harvard University Press, 1965), 28–36. On Mechanics, see Anthony Gronowicz, "Political 'Radicalism' in New York City's Revolutionary and Constitutional Eras," in Gilje and Pencak, eds., *New York in the Age of the Constitution*, 105. On the Marines, see *Marine Society of the City of New-York, in the Province of New-York, in America* (New York: John Harriman, 1800), one of several successive reprints of a Revolutionary-era charter to organize granted by King George III. On New York's Masonic lodges, see John L. Brooke, "Freemasonry and the Public Sphere in New York State, 1784–1830," unpublished paper, Organization of American Historians meeting, Louisville, Ky., 11 Apr. 1991, cited by permission. On the Missionary Society, see *LSM*, 104–6. On the Black Friars, see SLM's oration to that group. On the Democratic-Republicans and Tammany, see Alfred Young, *The Democratic Republicans of New York; The Origins, 1763–1797* (Chapel Hill: University of North Carolina Press, 1967), esp. ch. 18.

On the Horanian Literary Society, see Scott, "Early Literary Clubs," 10, and John Anderson, ms. diary, N-YHS; John's brother, Alexander Anderson, who studied medicine at Columbia under SLM, also mentions the Horanians and several other groups in his own diary, located at Columbia University. Alexander Anderson describes the formation of a smaller more private "Conversation club" similar in format to the FC: see entries for 4 Aug. 1797, 6 Sept. 1797, and 12 Sept. 1797; on a "Philanthropic Society" he had long planned to organize, see 31 Dec. 1797. He was also invited to join several groups, including the Calliopeans, but apparently declined. On 2 Feb. 1796, he mentions having had, at a friend's, "the pleasure of Dr. Mitchill's company & conversation," during which Mitchill "mentioned the plan for a Literary Coffee House." See 2 Feb. 1796, though I have found no other evidence for this plan. The demands of civic association required the strict management of one's time. Approached by a group of young men forming a new literary society, Smith assessed their prospects, determined that the initial meeting was unproductive, and resolved "not to do anything further" with them in spite of the "politeness" of their invitation (*DEHS*, 440: 24 Apr. 1798); a few days later he and several other club members attended the "Society for free Debate—where we were entertained by the ridiculousness of some, & the good sense others" (440: 26 Apr. 1798). Earlier he had been invited to help form a "Humane Society" and after several lackluster organizational meetings of its trustees determined to have no more "Evening[s] wasted" on this group, which apparently formed to promote the revival of drowning victims (169: 23 May 1796).

19. *DEHS*, 440 (26 Apr. 1798).

20. Allen Walker Read, "The Philological Society of New York, 1788," *American Speech* 9 (Apr. 1934): 131–36; Jill Lepore, *A Is for American: Language in the New Nation* (New York: Alfred A. Knopf, 2001), 15–18. On the relationship between the Philological Society and FC, see my Appendix.

21. *New York Journal and Daily Patriotic Register*, 23 July 1788; Sarah H. J. Simpson, "The Federal Procession in the City of New York," *N-YHS Quarterly*

Bulletin 9:2 (July 1925): 39–56; Lepore, *A Is for American,* 15–17; Laura Rigal, *The American Manufactory: Art, Labor, and the World of Things in the Early Republic* (Princeton: Princeton University Press, 1998), ch. 1, emphasizes the importance of the nation's "builders" in the Philadelphia Grand Federal Procession; David Waldstreicher, *In the Midst of Perpetual Fetes: The Making of American Nationalism, 1776–1820* (Chapel Hill: University of North Carolina Press, 1997), 103–7; Paul Gilje, "The Common People and the Constitution: Popular Culture in New York City in the Late Eighteenth Century," in Gilje and Pencak, eds., *New York in the Age of the Constitution,* 48–73; Simon P. Newman, *Parades and the Politics of the Street: Festive Culture in the Early American Republic* (Philadelphia: University of Pennsylvania Press, 1997), 70–71.

22. On the occasion of Washington's funeral procession in 1799, FC members could have been found in several different "companies." Mitchill could have marched with Columbia faculty, the Tammany Society, or New York state politicians. SM could have marched with the Masons or with his ministerial colleagues. WD, like SM, could have proceeded with the Masons but seems to have been less attached to that group in 1799 than to the Anacreontic Society, which sponsored a special musical performance at St. Paul's chapel, following the procession.

23. Gilje, "The Common People and the Constitution."

24. Writing about the Grand Federal Processions of 1788, which divided marchers into groups of artisans and craftsmen, merchants, and liberal professionals, David Waldstreicher uses the term "federal feeling" to describe the ideological work such spectacles performed. Contemporaries used the term as they sought to maintain the appearance of political unanimity and fraternal inclusiveness while still upholding elite social hierarchies. The Federal Processions proliferated in so many states, according to Waldstreicher, because they could bring so many into the "stylized order [of] the new public sphere of the nation whose coin of admission was the display of patriotic sentiments." See Waldstreicher, *In the Midst of Perpetual Fetes,* 90–92, 103–7, quote on 105.

25. See, for example, the serial "The Club," printed in the *New-York Magazine* in 1790–91, which was succeeded by the Calliopeans' serial "The Drone." The authors of both serials make themselves and their fellows into literary characters, though they protect their real names. Several cartoons, too, are related to this genre of the "peep" into an exclusive or allegedly seditious club. Clark, *British Clubs and Societies,* reproduces several cartoons and lithographs that work in this genre.

26. Margaret Jacob, *Living the Enlightenment: Freemasonry and Politics in Eighteenth-Century Europe* (New York: Oxford University Press, 1991).

27. In the early 1790s, civic associations still petitioned state assemblies for charters; New York's "General Society of Mechanics and Tradesmen" had existed since 1785 but was denied a charter in 1786 and 1791. Its defenders pointed to the class biases behind the denials and argued that mechanics had as much right to be incorporated as did banks: "Those who assume the airs of 'the well born' should be made to know that the *mechanics* of the city have *equal rights* to the merchants, and that they are as important a set of men as any in the community."

After the mechanics ran a slate of their own candidates in 1791, they finally won a charter the following year. In the minds of their supporters, a mechanics association operated as a check on larger, wealthier organizations. "A Friend to Equal Rights," *New-York Journal,* 30 Mar. 1791, in Young, *The Democratic Republicans,* 201.

The debate over the rights of free association came to a head in 1794 following a rural insurrection in western Pennsylvania (the "Whiskey Rebellion"), which Federalists sought to attach to the rise of Democratic-Republican political societies in several states. George Washington, speaking to the third Congress, famously referred to these opposition societies as "self-created," by which he meant that they existed outside the aegis of state charters. When defenders argued that such "Patriotic Societies" existed for the laudable purpose of "free public discussion" and information about "the actions and proceedings of government," Federalists questioned the accuracy of the information such groups disseminated and the character of the societies' leaders. Fisher Ames, a Massachusetts member of the House of Representatives, denounced the groups precisely because they were not public enough; they operated in darkness, he argued, removed from public view. "Combinations" of men could promote reputation and civic pride, particularly if they were sanctioned by the government, but they could also foment sedition. Through the remainder of the decade, many Federalists would advocate for tighter government control of association and the press and take measures, in the Alien and Sedition Acts of 1798, to stem opposition sentiments. See "Proceedings in the House of Representatives on the President's Speech," 24–27 Nov. 1796, in Lance Banning, ed., *Liberty and Order: The First American Party Struggle* (Indianapolis: The Liberty Fund, 2004), 182–83.

28. In spite of these Federalist sympathies, Smith recorded his frustration with Federalist actions on several occasions. See, for examples, *DEHS* 269 (4 Dec. 1796), where he praises John Quincy and Thomas Boylston Adams for being "neither Frenchmen, nor Britons" but "Americans," and EHS to Sally Pierce, 25 Dec. 1796, in *DEHS,* 277, where he writes, "A Federalist, & a Democrat, in the party-acceptation of those terms, are equally detestable." On 442 (30 Apr. 1798) he hopes for Noah Webster's return to "moderantism" after a period of extreme Federalist rhetoric.

29. WWW to Oliver Wolcott, Jr., 6 Mar. 1794, qtd. in Young, *The Democratic Republicans,* 395.

30. EHS to Joseph Dennie, 5 Mar. 1797, in *DEHS,* 299. Linda Kerber, *Federalists in Dissent: Imagery and Ideology in Jeffersonian America* (Ithaca: Cornell University Press, 1970), ch. 1.

31. *DWD,* 323 (6 Aug. 1798): "Kent had just been reading Mad[ame] Roland and is highly delighted with her, my brother[-in-law, William Woolsey] attacked her. The Millers were brought up & condemn'd as democrats." Edward Miller is alphabetized as a regular member for the first time in *DEHS,* 440 (28 Apr. 1798). He and Mitchill had been regular visitors since the previous fall.

32. SM to JM, 3 Apr. 1799, SMP, copy in Samuel Miller, Jr.'s handwriting and inaccurately filed as a "Letter to the American Monthly Magazine."

33. See *Monthly Recorder* 1 (Apr. 1813): 8.

34. Bender, *New York Intellect*, ch. 2–3.

35. Allan Silver, "Friendship in Commercial Society: Eighteenth-Century Social Theory and Modern Sociology," *American Journal of Sociology* 95 (1990): 1474–1504; Anne Lombard, *Making Manhood: Growing Up Male in Colonial New England* (Cambridge: Harvard University Press, 2003), 79. Benjamin Franklin's account of his Philadelphia Junto earlier in the century demonstrates that the new friendship made the progress of knowledge complementary to commercial enterprise and empire as well as to civic projects like the creation of the Library Company of Philadelphia. See Benjamin Franklin, *The Life of Dr. Franklin, Written by Himself* (New York: T. & J. Swords, 1794), 110, 112.

Friendship underwent other transformations in meaning over the course of the eighteenth century as colonial connotations of "patronage" gave way to new egalitarian models and patriarchal metaphors gave way to fraternal ideals. See Gordon Wood, *The Radicalism of the American Revolution* (New York: Alfred Knopf, 1992); Jay Fliegelman, *Prodigals and Pilgrims: The American Revolution against Patriarchal Authority, 1750–1800* (Cambridge: Cambridge University Press, 1982); Mark Kann, *A Republic of Men: The American Founders, Gendered Language, and Patriarchal Politics* (New York: New York University Press, 1998), ch. 5. In the early nineteenth century, leaders of both political parties, drawn largely from the landed gentry, positioned themselves as "friends" rather than "fathers" of "the people" in an attempt to garner broad electoral support; such attempts, however, can at times smack of insincere ploys to curry favor with constituents more than they were signs of elites' willingness to cede authority to democratic masses. See Alan Taylor, "From Fathers to Friends of the People: Political Personas in the Early Republic," *Journal of the Early Republic* 11 (Winter 1991): 465–91. For other treatments of eighteenth-century friendship, see Julie Ellison, *Cato's Tears and the Making of Anglo-American Emotion* (Chicago: University of Chicago Press, 1999); Andy Trees, *The Founding Fathers and the Politics of Character* (Princeton: Princeton University Press, 2004); Fred Dallmayr, "Derrida and Friendship," in Eduardo Velasquez, ed., *Love and Friendship: Rethinking Politics and Affection in Modern Times* (Lanham, Md.: Lexington Books, 2003), 550; and Crain, *American Sympathy*.

In the account that follows I am indebted to Elizabeth Maddock Dillon's argument that late-eighteenth-century voluntary associations were "productive of private identity rather than responsive to preexisting forms of subjectivity," as private forms of friendship provided the emotional energy upon which the most durable public associations and expressions depended. Dillon, *The Gender of Freedom: Fictions of Liberalism in the Literary Public Sphere* (Stanford: Stanford University Press, 2004), 186, 185. Dillon's account resembles Silver's of friendship in Scottish Enlightenment thought: "a model of universal sociability in which anti-instrumental personal relations do not play a retreatist role, but pervade society as a source of moral order." Allan Silver, "'Two Different Sorts of Commerce'—Friendship and Strangership in Civil Society," in Jeff Weintraub and Krishan Kumar, eds., *Public and Private in Thought and Practice* (Chicago: University of Chicago Press, 1998), 50, 66.

36. Historians of gender emphasize romantic friendship's realms of emotion

and eroticism, including kissing, hugging, holding hands, brushing the tear of sensibility from one another's cheek, sharing beds, and, though explicit references are rare, even some genital contact. The corporeal dimensions of romantic friendship signaled the degree to which such affection was supposed to transcend words: "Have we not often held each other's hand, & looked one at the other, hours in silence?" EHS once wrote to a male cousin, who had apparently asked for a reaffirmation of his love. As this example demonstrates, physical affection also provided the basis for later literary expressions of devotion in the diaries and familiar correspondence that facilitated both romantic friendship and Enlightenment intellectual association. See esp. Anthony Rotundo, *American Manhood* (New York: Basic Books, 1993).

37. Crain, *American Sympathy*, 67. Drawing on CBB's letters to young male friends, Crain argues that young men in the new nation "could express emotions to each other with a fervor and openness that could not have been detached from religious enthusiasm a generation earlier and would have to be consigned to sexual perversion a few generations later" (35). Letters between romantic friends took classical and biblical models, such as in EHS's invocation of the friendship between Jonathan and David in a letter to his married friend ThD. On a recent visit, Smith had "discovered . . . in your eye, your voice, your manner, that tenderness which I felt in my own bosom, & which once mutually constituted so large a portion of our happiness." EHS's confession to ThD that "I feel for you all that Jonathan felt for David" is accompanied by a muted apology for using "the expressions of a lover" to convey his feelings. EHS to ThD, 30 Aug. 1796, in *DEHS*, 209. The language of courtship and marriage repeatedly features in EHS's diary, where he casts his friendship with WJ, for example, in marital terms; while WJ was visiting family in Connecticut, EHS described himself as "a forsaken lover, a widowed turtle." EHS to Mr. & Mrs. Lovegrove, 19 June 1796, in *DEHS*, 179. The subsequent reunion was "like the meeting of husband & wife" (203: 13 Aug. 1796).

38. Robert Fothergill, *Private Chronicles: A Study of English Diaries* (London: Oxford University Press, 1974); Stuart Sherman, *Telling Time: Clocks, Diaries, and English Diurnal Form, 1660–1785* (Chicago: University of Chicago Press, 1996); Susan Clair Imbarrato, *Declarations of Independency in Eighteenth-Century American Autobiography* (Knoxville, Tenn.: University of Tennessee Press, 1998). Though it deals with nineteenth-century diaries of young men in a different social condition and professional situation than Smith's, Thomas Augst's *The Clerk's Tale: Young Men and Moral Life in Nineteenth-Century America* (Chicago: University of Chicago Press, 2003), ch. 1, contains an excellent discussion of young male New Yorkers' participation in a long humanist tradition of diary keeping.

39. EHS to Fanny Smith, 24 Dec. 1796, in *DEHS*, 275.

40. *DEHS*, 44 (4 Sept. 1795).

41. *DEHS*, 45–46 (6 Sept. 1795). CA, John and Abigail's son, did not last long as a member. Prone to bad business deals and heavy drinking, he died shortly before his father lost the presidency to Thomas Jefferson in 1800. See Peter Kafer, *Charles Brockden Brown's Revolution and the Birth of American Gothic* (Philadel-

phia: University of Pennsylvania Press), 84–85; David McCullough, *John Adams* (New York: Simon and Schuster, 2001), esp. 567–70. EHS's friendship with CA once gave him the opportunity for an hour-long conversation with John Adams on the challenges historians would face in trying to recount the American Revolution. See *DEHS*, 268 (30 Nov. 1796).

42. "Connubial Joy saddens the once-pleasant calls of Friendship," EHS wrote to one bachelor friend. EHS to Joseph Strong, 14 Feb. 1797, in *DEHS*, 291. Marriage did not necessarily prevent fraternal association, of course. JK was married before he joined, and remained one of the most faithful attendees until he moved from the city in 1798. WWW and WD, also married before the club formed, were among the group of regulars as well. GMW married in 1797 and remained nearly as active as he had been. EHS mentions marital status only for those who fall away from activity.

43. On one occasion, for example, Smith made a positive evaluation of a Welsh clergyman's character by assessing his conversation along with his physiognomy and a letter of recommendation from a friend in Connecticut (*DEHS*, 48: 7 Sept. 1795). A week later, a "*queer* man, Dr. Williamson of N. Carolina" made a much less favorable impression by "possess[ing] of himself the whole conversation," telling "long stories" accompanied by "fantastic gesticulations, & strange contortions" (56: 14 September 1795). When former club member (and Smith's brother-in-law) Thomas Mumford returned to town for a visit, Smith found it difficult to "keep conversation alive" because of Mumford's verbal inertia: "[H]is words come forth slowly, & lingeringly; he chiefly confines himself to answering questions . . . [and so] my inquiries have only drawn from him a few imperfect pieces of information." (44: 5 Sept. 1795). Conversation was also crucial to mixed-sex company, of course, and Smith also evaluated the utility of exchanges in such settings; on one occasion at the home of married friends, for example, "We discoursed on the nature of the First Cause: On freedom of inquiry, & opinion; on Rousseau, & Petrarco; on [Thomas Holcroft's novel] 'Anna St. Ives'; on the means of extinguishing false sensibility; & finally, in an imperfect manner, on my own passion [a recent unrequited infatuation], experience, cure" (44: 4 Sept. 1795).

44. *DEHS*, 275 (24 Dec. 1796); 269 (3 Dec. 1796); 158 (23 Apr. 1796); 44 (4 Sept. 1795). Other frequent classifications include "egotistical," "bland," "wholesome," "interesting," "medical and friendly," and "multifarious."

45. *Monthly Recorder* 1 (Apr. 1813): 8. The ideal of "unregulated conversation" contrasts with the format of the highly institutionalized literary and debating clubs that met in the 1790s. The Calliopean Society, for example, whose 700-page minute book is among the collections of the New-York Historical Society, was founded in the late 1780s for "the express purpose of improving education" in New York. It was divided into classes for disputation, composition, oratory, and "questions," a group that would apparently select the topics for disputation. These questions ranged from "Whether polygamy is useful to society?" to "Whether the Theatre ought to be tolerated in this place?" (Both topics were decided in the negative.) The group also debated scientific questions, such as the cause of earthquakes, whirlwinds, wind, or the usefulness of mountains. Unlike

the FC, the Calliopeans imposed strict penalties—monetary fines, group censure, and even expulsion—for violating bylaws, which included a vow of secrecy and the requirement that members rise to address the president.

46. "On Conversation," *MMAR* (July 1800): 87.

47. David Shields, *Civil Tongues and Polite Letters in British America* (Chapel Hill: University of North Carolina Press, 1997), esp. chs. 2 and 6, quote on 175.

48. *DEHS*, 107 (19 Dec. 1795).

49. *DEHS*, 152 (3 Apr. 1796); 142 (22 Mar. 1796).

50. *DEHS*, 143 (24 Mar. 1796); 44 (5 Sept. 1795).

51. *DEHS*, 163 (7 May 1796).

52. *DEHS*, 269 (3 Dec. 1796); 160 (30 Apr. 1796).

53. *DEHS*, 99–100 (11 Dec. 1795), composed originally in July 1794.

54. See, for examples, *DEHS*, 88 (12 Nov. 1795), where he reads to SBT; 118 (1 and 2 Jan. 1796), at CBB's house in Philadelphia, where Smith and Brown read to one another from their journals; and 197 (5 Aug. 1796), where they steal away from company to read together in EHS's journal.

55. *DEHS*, 359 (11 Sept. 1797).

56. For example, Rhys Isaac finds in the eighteenth-century proliferation of diaries, autobiographies, and "first-person novels" a sense of self as "distinctive," "unique," and "more or less sustained by an introspective story of that self." See Isaac, "Stories and Construction of Identity: Folk Tellings and Diary Inscriptions in Revolutionary Virginia," in Ronald Hoffman, Mechal Sobel, and Fredrika Teute, eds., *Through a Glass Darkly: Reflections on Personal Identity in Early America* (Chapel Hill: University of North Carolina Press, 1997), 206–37, quote on 216.

57. *DEHS*, 144 (22 Mar. 1796).

58. *DEHS*, 94 (2 Dec. 1795); 144 (22 Mar. 1796).

59. EHS to Idea Strong, 29 Mar. 1796, in *DEHS*, 147–48.

60. EHS to John Williams, 25 Dec. 1795, in *DEHS*, 114–15.

61. EHS to ThD, 5 June 1796, in *DEHS*, 174–75.

62. Jon Klancher, "The Vocation of Criticism and the Crisis of the Republic of Letters," in Marshall Brown, ed., *The Cambridge History of Literary Criticism*, vol. 5 (Cambridge: Cambridge University Press), 296–320; Dena Goodman, *The Republic of Letters: A Cultural History of the French Enlightenment* (Ithaca: Cornell University Press, 1994), 96.

63. Smith's image of mutual penetrations recalls Jeffrey Masten's examinations of the erotics of collaborative male friendship in the Renaissance, though Smith uses this language with male and female correspondents alike. Masten, *Textual Intercourse: Collaboration, Authorship, and Sexualities in Renaissance Drama* (New York: Cambridge University Press, 1997).

64. Smith, "November 1796. General Preface to the Month," in *DEHS*, 242.

65. *DEHS*, 399 (2 Dec. 1797).

66. William Hartley, *Observations on Man, His Frame, His Duty, and His Expectations* (London: Joseph Johnson, 1791). Communal reading was also a central part of late-eighteenth-century social life in mixed-sex company, where novels and poetry seemed to have prevailed. See, for example, *DEHS*, 176 (7 June 1796).

67. *BREC,* 2:17–19; G. J. Barker-Benfield, *The Culture of Sensibility: Sex and Society in Eighteenth-Century Britain* (Chicago: University of Chicago Press, 1992).

68. *DEHS,* 160 (30 Apr. 1796).

69. *DEHS,* 50 (10 Sept. 1795).

70. See Spectator No. 2, in Erin Mackie, ed., *The Commerce of Everyday Life: Selections from* The Tatler *and* The Spectator (New York: Bedford St. Martin's, 1998), 83–88.

71. The merchant presence in the club, which sets this and similar late-eighteenth-century circles apart from similar groups in the nineteenth century, would decline over the course of the decade until only the Woolseys remained. See Bender, *New York Intellect,* 28. On the significance of club life to merchants, see Richard D. Brown, *Knowledge Is Power: The Diffusion of Information in Early America, 1700–1865* (New York: Oxford University Press, 1989), 112–17.

72. FC members and their close associates are listed as being elected Manumission Society members on the following dates: WWW (19 Nov. 1789), WD (15 May 1792), WJ (proposed 19 Feb. 1793; balloting not recorded, though he was an active member afterward), EHS, GMW, and, though not yet a Friendly Club member, SM (19 Nov. 1793); CA (17 Feb. 1795); JK (19 May 1795); also not yet FC members, SLM is mentioned in the minutes for 17 Nov. 1795 and EM (15 Nov. 1796). EHS kept the society's minute books from 17 Feb. 1795 until 17 July 1798, the last entry before his death that fall. The club's extensive involvement in the Manumission Society is best illustrated by the elections of 17 Jan. 1797: WWW was elected as first vice president and chair of the standing committee; WJ as second vice president and secretary of the trustees of the African Free School; EHS reelected as secretary; GMW as registrar; WD as secretary of the standing committee. After 1801 only WWW remained an active member. See New York Society for the Manumission of Slaves, Minutes, esp. vols. 6 and 9, N-YHS. For one historian's take on the society, see Shane White, *Somewhat More Independent: The End of Slavery in New York City, 1770–1810* (Athens: University of Georgia Press, 1991). JK and SM, at least, owned a slave or slaves without apparent concern that they were violating the principles on which the society was established. See *MCK,* 99; *LSM,* 90.

73. Goodman, *The Republic of Letters.*

74. Kent and Mitchill addressed the state's Agricultural Society; Johnson the Phi Beta Kappa Society at Yale; Mitchill the Tammany Society and the Black Friars; Samuel Miller the Freemasons; Miller and Smith the Manumission Society.

75. Tammany had sponsored the American Museum, which was open for its members to "have free access thereto" for viewing contents or reading books. See *New-York Magazine* (May 1791): 248–49 for regulations.

76. Theodore Albert Zunder, *The Early Days of Joel Barlow, A Connecticut Wit* (New Haven: Yale University Press, 1934), 190–91.

77. One bound series of the *Gazette of the United States* in the collections of the Library Company of Philadelphia is missing several of the Ella-Birtha-Henry poems, which have been carefully removed using a razor or knife, thereby emphasizing the portable nature of such poetry.

78. See *DEHS*, 273 (19 Dec. 1796), for example, as well as later articles by CBB, "A Student's Diary," and "Distinction between Poetry and Prose," in his *Literary Magazine, and American Register* (Dec. 1803): 165–66 and (Nov. 1804): 583–86.

79. Charles Bennett, "A Poetical Correspondence among Elihu Hubbard Smith, Joseph Bringhurst, Jr., and Charles Brockden Brown in *The Gazette of the United States*," *EAL* 12 (1977–78): 277–85.

80. *Gazette of the United States*, 20 Apr. 1791.

81. An earlier, more melancholic poem, which featured unrequited love and a suicide, had been rejected by Fenno as "not exactly calculated for this paper"; Ella seems to have responded by conceding the editor's taste for patriotic rather than romantic verse, his poem calculated to create federal feeling. Once the correspondence grew in popularity, however, Fenno relented and printed Ella's initial offering. See Bennett, "A Poetical Correspondence," 278.

82. "Sonnet II. Sent to Mrs. —— ——, with a Song," *Gazette of the United States*, 19 Mar. 1791.

83. "To Ella," *Gazette of the United States*, 23 Mar. 1791.

84. "Ode. To Birtha," *Gazette of the United States*, 2 Apr. 1791.

85. "To Ella," *Gazette of the United States*, 16 Apr. 1791.

86. "Sonnet Written after hearing a Song sung by three Sisters," *General Advertiser*, 25 Apr. 1791. One of the sisters "P*yn*" was Dolley Payne, later Dolley Madison, to whom CBB had written poems as early as 1789.

87. "Sonnet," *Gazette of the United States*, 27 Apr. 1791. For the entire correspondence, removed from its original newspaper context, see Franklin, ed., *The Poetry of the Minor Connecticut Wits*, 889–927.

88. Jerome McGann, *The Poetics of Sensibility* (Oxford: Oxford University Press, 1998).

89. The original Della Cruscan poetic exchange was published in British papers in the late 1780s, conducted principally between Robert Merry and a mixed-sex group of poetical correspondents. Many of these poems were included in Philadelphia publisher Mathew Carey's volume of selected British and American verse in 1791; their popularity with American readers may also be confirmed by the fact that CBB's father, Elijah, meticulously transcribed dozens of them into a commonplace book he devoted to poetry. Della Cruscan poetry appeared in the *New-York Magazine* (June 1790): 366 and in similar publications throughout the 1790s. In his own anthology, Smith included a poem by "Philenia" (Sarah Wentworth Morton) called "Lines, Addressed to the inimitable Author of the Poems under the signature of Della Crusca." EHS, ed., *American Poems, Selected and Original* (Litchfield, Conn.: Collier, 1793), 184–85. In the same month that Henry entered the Ella-Birtha exchange, the *General Advertiser* printed a poem under the signature "Dela Crusca" (7 Apr. 1791). EHS makes positive references to a longer poem by Merry, *The Pains of Memory*, in his diary, and chided Joseph Dennie for dealing harshly with the British poet. EHS to Joseph Dennie, 18 June 1797, in *DEHS*, 326–27. In this letter Smith also suggests that Dennie undertake an effort to reprint selections from great modern poetry in English,

which would add value to his *Farmer's Museum*, as it "would supersede the necessity of a large library of poetry."

90. EHS acknowledged the role such poetic collaboration could play in solidifying friendship in a letter to his erstwhile collaborator ThD. "[H]aving, in some sort, taken our leave of the Muses, we had bidden adieu to each other," Smith wrote of what he feared was their waning friendship. "[R]elinquishing the bond of union which was created by the combined & consentaneous cultivation of one department of literature, there is left between us no common center of attraction, no medium of connection." EHS to ThD, 26 Aug. 1797, in *DEHS*, 349.

91. EHS, "Epistle to the Author of the Botanic Garden," in Erasmus Darwin, *The Botanic Garden* (New York: T. & J. Swords, 1798).

92. *DEHS*, 79 (22 Oct. 1795). The prospectus for the imagined journal doubles as the preface to the second surviving volume of EHS's diary. His diagnosis of the American newspaper scene was fairly accurate. See Jeffrey L. Pasley, *"The Tyranny of Printers": Newspaper Politics in the Early American Republic* (Charlottesville: University Press of Virginia, 2001).

93. *DEHS*, 77 (22 Oct. 1795).

94. Ibid.

95. *DEHS*, 78 (22 Oct. 1795.)

96. *DEHS*, 78–79 (22 Oct. 1795.)

97. SM to JM, 3 Apr. 1799, SMP.

98. CBB to Armit Brown, Dec. 1798 (H&C 111), in *LCBB*, 2:11.

99. *DEHS*, 74 (17 Oct. 1795).

100. *DHAT*, 143–44, 156.

Two. Dangerous Associations

1. *DEHS*, 283 (24 Jan. 1797). Smith drafted the letter twice in the diary. See *DEHS*, 247–52 (following the entry for 19 Nov. 1796), and EHS to ThD, 22 Nov. 1796, in *DEHS*, 256–66. On ThD's discussion of the letter with SBT, see 283 (24 Jan. 1797); for his further circulation of the letter see 298 (2 Mar. 1797).

2. *DEHS*, 283 (24 Jan. 1797). Smith himself shared both sides of the exchange with other friends, including GMW. See *DEHS*, 296 (22 Feb. 1797).

3. While he realized that his parents would have to confront his opinions "at some time," he still wanted to "put them off . . . to a period, for which they may be gradually prepared. But this I could not hope for, living with them." See *DEHS*, 45 (5 Sept. 1795).

4. See, for example, CBB to Joseph Bringhurst, 30 October 1795 (H&C #60); see also Bernard Rosenthal, "The Voices of *Wieland*," in Rosenthal, ed., *Critical Essays on Charles Brockden Brown* (Boston: G. K. Hall, 1981), 104–25.

5. *DEHS*, 48 (7 Sept. 1795). These thoughts respond to his reading of Condorcet's *Outlines of an Historical View of the Progress of the Human Mind*, a philosophical defense of human perfectibility, which had been published posthumously in Paris earlier that year. Condorcet, part of the Girondist phase of the French Revolution (with which Smith and many other Americans sympathized) had been put to death by the Jacobins in 1793. Smith began work on an English

translation—never completed—in the fall of 1795. As Leonard W. Levy demonstrates in *Blasphemy: Verbal Offense against the Sacred from Moses to Salman Rushdie* (New York: Alfred A. Knopf, 1993), chap. 12, blasphemy prosecutions were virtually nonexistent at the end of the eighteenth century, although antiblasphemy statutes remained a prominent part of most states' laws. EHS may have feared that in the increasingly volatile religious and political climate, including debates in Connecticut over religious establishment, such laws could become more rigorously upheld.

6. [EHS], letter to editor, *Monthly Magazine, and British Register* (July 1798): 1–3. See also *DEHS*, 438, for the original draft.

7. Cronin, "Introduction," in *DEHS*, 12n41. See 49 (8 Sept. 1795) for an uncomfortable conversation with Woolsey on "perfectibility," and 183 (1 July 1796) for the comments on Woolsey's religious opinions, which left Smith "somewhat melancholly."

8. Richard Hofstadter, *The Paranoid Style in American Politics and Other Essays* (New York, 1965); David Brion Davis, ed., *The Fear of Conspiracy: Images of Un-American Subversion from the Revolution to the Present* (Ithaca: Cornell University Press, 1971); Gordon S. Wood, "Conspiracy and the Paranoid Style: Causality and Deceit in the Eighteenth Century," *WMQ* 39 (1982): 401–41. Ed White, "The Value of Conspiracy Theory," *American Literary History* 14:1 (2002): 1–31, offers a compelling defense of conspiracy theory.

9. *DWD*, 343 (28 Sept. 1798).

10. Stanley Elkins and Eric McKitrick, *The Age of Federalism* (New York: Oxford University Press, 1993); Daniel Boorstin, *The Lost World of Thomas Jefferson* (New York: H. Holt, 1948); David Waldstreicher, *In the Midst of Perpetual Fetes: The Making of American Nationalism, 1776–1820* (Chapel Hill: University of North Carolina Press, 1997); Saul Cornell, *The Other Founders: Anti-Federalism and the Dissenting Tradition in America, 1788–1828* (Chapel Hill: University of North Carolina, 1999). On partisanship and literary culture: Lewis Simpson, "Federalism and the Crisis of Literary Order," *American Literature* 32 (1960/61): 253–66; William Charvat, *The Origins of American Critical Thought, 1810–1835* (Philadelphia: University of Pennsylvania Press, 1936); Laura Rigal, *The American Manufactory: Art, Labor, and the World of Things in the Early Republic* (Princeton: Princeton University Press, 1998); William Dowling, *Literary Federalism in the Age of Jefferson* (Columbia: University of South Carolina Press, 1999). On partisanship and the public sphere more generally: John L. Brooke, "Ancient Lodges and Self-Created Societies: Voluntary Association and the Public Sphere in the Early Republic," in Ronald Hoffman and Peter J. Albert, eds., *Launching the "Extended Republic": The Federalist Era* (Charlottesville: University Press of Virginia, 1996), 273–377; Leon Jackson, "Jedidiah Morse and the Transformation of Print Culture in New England, 1784–1826," *EAL* 34 (1999): 2–31; Albrecht Koschnik, "The Democratic Societies of Philadelphia and the Limits of the American Public Sphere, circa 1793–1795," *WMQ* 58: 3 (July 2001).

11. Jan Golinski, *Science as Public Culture: Chemistry and Enlightenment in Britain, 1760–1820* (Cambridge: Cambridge University Press, 1992), 184–86.

12. Seth Cotlar, "The Federalists' Transatlantic Cultural Offensive of 1798,"

in Jeffrey Pasley, Andrew Robertson, and David Waldstreicher, eds., *Beyond the Founders: New Approaches to the Political History of the Early American Republic* (Chapel Hill: University of North Carolina Press, 2004), 278–79.

13. Susan Juster argues that religion has been largely left out of discussions of the eighteenth-century public sphere because Habermas's influential conception seemed so "antithetical to religious belief." Her study of Revolutionary-era popular prophecy shows religion's significance in "some of the more recessed corners of the bourgeois public sphere—those barely visible spaces (makeshift chapels, street corners, peddlers' bags, print shops, market stalls, the back rooms of inns and taverns, prisons, insane asylums) where faith and reason met, not to vanquish one another but to jostle energetically for the soul of the believer." Juster, *Doomsayers: Anglo-American Prophecy in the Age of Revolution* (Philadelphia: University of Pennsylvania Press, 2003), 16.

14. Christopher Grasso, *A Speaking Aristocracy: Transforming Public Discourse in Eighteenth-Century Connecticut* (Chapel Hill: University of North Carolina Press, 1999), 443–48.

15. Ibid.; Colin Wells, *The Devil and Doctor Dwight: Satire and Theology in the Early American Republic* (Chapel Hill: University of North Carolina Press, 2002); Jonathan Sassi, *Republic of Righteousness: The Public Christianity of the Post-Revolutionary New England Clergy* (New York: Oxford University Press, 2001); Ruth Bloch, *Visionary Republic: Millennial Themes in American Thought, 1756–1800* (New York: Cambridge University Press, 1985).

16. Michael Warner, *The Letters of the Republic: Publication and the Public Sphere in Eighteenth-Century America* (Cambridge: Harvard University Press, 1990); Larzer Ziff, *Writing in the New Nation: Prose, Print, and Politics in the Early United States* (New Haven: Yale University Press, 1991); Christopher Looby, *Voicing America: Language, Literary Form, and the Origins of the United States* (Chicago: University of Chicago Press, 1996); Jay Fliegelman, "Introduction," *Wieland and Memoirs of Carwin the Biloquist* (New York: Penguin, 1991), in tandem with *Declaring Independence: Jefferson, Natural Language, and the Culture of Performance* (Stanford: Stanford University Press, 1993).

17. See *DEHS*, 77 (22 Oct. 1795).

18. JM, *A Sermon, Exhibiting the Present Dangers, and Consequent Duties of the Citizens of the United States of America. Delivered at Charlestown, Apr. 25, 1799. The Day of the National Fast* (Hartford: Hudson and Goodwin, 1799), 8.

19. *DEHS*, 273 (19 Dec. 1796).

20. *DEHS*, 298 (2 Mar. 1797).

21. *DEHS*, 247 (18 Nov. 1796).

22. EHS to SBT, 16 Feb. 1797, in *DEHS*, 295.

23. Fliegelman, *Declaring Independence*, 32, 2.

24. EHS to SBT, 16 Feb. 1797, in *DEHS*, 295.

25. Tim Fulford, *Romanticism and Masculinity* (New York: St. Martin's Press, 1999), 77.

26. Grasso, *A Speaking Aristocracy*, 350.

27. EHS to ThD, 22 Nov. 1796, in *DEHS*, 259.

28. See *DEHS*, 70–71 (11 Oct. 1795). The same quality Smith enjoyed al-

lowed ThD to pen some of the most sharp-edged Federalist satires of the French Revolution and Jefferson's presidency. See Benjamin Franklin V, "Introduction," *The Poetry of the Minor Connecticut Wits* (Gainesville, Fla.: Scholars' Facsimiles and Reprints, 1970), xvii–xviii.

29. *DEHS*, 245 (9 Nov. 1796).

30. Smith, "Notes from Recollections of My Life from My Birth till the Age of Eleven," in *DEHS*, 18.

31. *DEHS*, 86 (6 Nov. 1795).

32. *DEHS*, 109–10. Catherine Kaplan has suggested to me in conversation that SBT may have introduced EHS to Wollstonecraft, and not the other way around; the letter containing Tracy's defense of *Vindication* is dated 25 Jan.1794, before the extant volumes of EHS's diary open.

33. *DEHS*, 86 (6 Nov. 1795).

34. EHS to SBT, 15 Dec. 1795, in *DEHS*, 104.

35. EHS to ThD, 13 May 1796, in *DEHS*, 166.

36. EHS to SBT, 31 Aug., 1796, in *DEHS*, 210.

37. EHS to SBT, 18 Jan. 1796, in *DEHS*, 122.

38. Ibid.

39. EHS to ThD, 5 June 1796, in *DEHS*, 174–75. EHS's answers, however, likely confirmed some of ThD's fears: "I do not consider the titles, in use in the United States, as of much consequence," he writes, "yet I acknowledge that I would rather they were intirely disused" except when they convey information about a person's chosen "occupation." In writing to ThD, then, he had used the title "Counsellor at Law" but neglected an additional "Esquire" because "no information is conveyed" by it. If his previous letter had been "short, & inelegant," he added, ThD might be consoled to know that the originals in the diary suggested all his letters from that period were of similar length and style.

40. *DEHS*, 180 (22 June 1796), 181 (25 June 1796).

41. *DEHS*, 184 (2 July 1796).

42. EHS to ThD, 30 Aug. 1796, in *DEHS*, 209.

43. Ibid.

44. EHS to ThD, draft letter, Nov. 1796, in *DEHS*, 248–49.

45. Ibid., 249.

46. EHS to ThD, 22 Nov. 1796, in *DEHS*, 259, 261.

47. *Gazette of the United States*, 1 June 1791, 38, rpt. in Franklin, ed., *The Poetry of the Minor Connecticut Wits*, 910.

48. Qtd. in Steven Watts, *The Romance of Real Life: Charles Brockden Brown and the Origins of American Culture* (Baltimore: Johns Hopkins University Press, 1994), 31, 56.

49. EHS to ThD, undated draft, follows entry for 19 Nov. 1796, *DEHS*, 251.

50. Ibid., 251–52.

51. Ibid., 249; EHS to ThD, 22 Nov. 1796, in *DEHS*, 265.

52. Ibid., 266.

53. EHS to SBT, 16 Feb. 1797, in *DEHS*, 294.

54. Ibid., 294–95.

55. EHS to SBT, 28 Aug. 1797, in *DEHS*, 352.

56. Ibid., 353.

57. *DEHS*, 391 (10 Nov. 1797).

58. Vernon Stauffer, *New England and the Bavarian Illuminati* (New York: Columbia University Press, 1918); Gary Nash, "The American Clergy and the French Revolution," *WMQ* 22:3 (July 1965): 392–412; Henry May, *The Enlightenment in America* (New York: Oxford University Press, 1976), 252–77; Larry Tise, *The American Counterrevolution: A Retreat from Liberty, 1783–1800* (Mechanicsburg, Pa.: Stackpole Books, 1998), chs. 18–19; Michael Leinesch, "The Illusion of the Illuminati: The Counterconspiratorial Origins of Post-Revolutionary Conservatism," in W. M. Verhoeven, ed., *Revolutionary Histories: Transatlantic Cultural Nationalism, 1775–1815* (New York: Palgrave, 2002), 152–65. For another reading of *Wieland* in the context of the Illuminati crisis, see Charles Bradshaw, "The New England Illuminati: Conspiracy and Causality in Charles Brockden Brown's *Wieland*," *New England Quarterly* (Sept. 2003): 356–77.

59. The group's friend MB documented SLM's acquaintance with Robison; see MB to SHS, 22 June 1798, MBSP. She wrote that SLM had verified that Robison was "a man of strictest integrity & his motives certainly were good." She also calls SLM a "disciple" of the very type of "Philosophy" Robison so violently opposed, and so his "certain[ty] that whatever account he gave might be depended upon" should carry special weight. In a later letter, after her fiancé accuses Robison of being motivated by party spirit, she writes again that "Dr. Mitchel who from his own principles would oppose this book, yet assured me that he was a man of integrity, & that whatever he asserted might be depended on as truth, altho' his conclusion might be faulted; Dr. M. was surprised at [Robison's] undertaking such a work, as he did not think very highly of his understanding." SLM had not yet read the book. A year earlier Dr. Rodgers, another New Yorker with ties to Edinburgh, had received a letter from a Dr. Ershine of Scotland, "which spoke highly of the author [Robison] as a man, & recommended his work as calculated to stem the torrent of irreligion which overflowed the world." MB to SHS, 12 July 1798. EHS makes no similar notice of SLM's testimony on Robison's behalf.

60. For a useful overview of Robison, see Stauffer, *New England*, 199–214; on Barruel see 215–28.

61. See *DEHS*, 319, 325, 331.

62. ThD, *An oration, spoken at Hartford, in the state of Connecticut, on the anniversary of American independence, July 4th, 1798* (Hartford, Conn.: Hudson and Goodwin, 1798), 30.

63. EHS to Samuel Miles Hopkins, 7 Nov. 1797, in *DEHS*, 390.

64. *DEHS*, 412–13 (1 Jan. 1798).

65. Ibid.; *DWD*, 241 (11 Apr. 1798).

66. *DEHS*, 458 (29 July 1798).

67. *DWD*, 339 (14 Sept. 1798).

68. "Miscellany. For the Farmer's Museum," *Farmer's Museum* (5 Aug. 1799): 1–2. Catherine Kaplan discusses Dennie's repudiation of Morse's theories briefly in "'He Summons Genius . . . to His Aid': Letters, Partisanship, and the Making of the *Farmer's Weekly Museum*, 1795–1800," *Journal of the Early Republic* 23:4

(winter 2003): 545–71, esp. 559–60, as an example of the diversity of Federalist thought on such issues as commerce and religion. Dennie suggested Morse return to his ministry and his practice of geography and leave international politics alone. He suggests too that Morse is motivated by a desire for fame.

69. *DWD,* 323 (6 Aug. 1798).

70. *DWD,* 324 (10 Aug. 1798).

71. For the installments, see *DWD,* 152–59, 163–65, 168, 172, 322, 345 (1 October 1797–14 October 1798).

72. EHS to ThD, 22 Nov. 1796, in *DEHS,* 265. The passage is from Smith's long letter to ThD. CBB's most recent biographer underestimates the sincerity of his religious crisis in the 1790s. See Peter Kafer, *Charles Brockden Brown's Revolution and the Birth of American Gothic* (Philadelphia: University of Pennsylvania Press, 2004), ch. 3.

73. As early as 1795, CBB had contemplated an anti-Christian novel, scraps of which survive in what Steven Watts called the "Ellendale" fragments. See Watts, *Romance of Real Life,* 57–58.

74. TD, *Travels in New England and New York* (New Haven: Timothy Dwight, 1821), 1:515. This portion of TD's work was composed sometime between 1796 and 1805.

75. EHS, CBB, and WJ to WD, transcribed in *DWD,* 336 (5 Sept. 1798); *DEHS,* 156 (13 Apr. 1796); EHS to SBT, 18 Jan. 1796, in *DEHS,* 122.

76. *Memoirs of Carwin the Biloquist* appeared in serial form in CBB's *Literary Magazine, and American Register* between Nov. 1803 and Mar. 1805, although a substantial portion was completed, apparently, in the fall of 1798. On these dates, see Michael Cody, *Charles Brockden Brown and the* Literary Magazine: *Cultural Journalism in the Early American Republic* (Jefferson, N.C.: McFarland, 2004), 184n13. In *Wieland,* after the disastrous effects of Carwin's agency are all too clear, a character named Ludloe shows up in Philadelphia hunting for Carwin, who is "engaged in schemes, reasonably suspected to be, in the highest degree, criminal, but such as no human intelligence is able to unravel" (149). In *Memoirs,* the action of which takes place prior to the events narrated in *Wieland,* Carwin counters by disclosing that Ludloe is an agent for a secret society whose membership requires "inviolable secrecy" under pain of death (322). If Carwin submits himself to Ludloe's reeducation, he may earn a "post, in which you will be invested with divine attributes, and prescribe the condition of a large portion of mankind" (320). The sequel ends before we learn if Carwin ever became an initiate.

77. Robert Levine, for example, discussing the relationship between the Illuminati scare and *Ormond* (1799), views CBB "in the late 1790s, particularly in his association with the conservative members of New York's Friendly Society, as a Federalist in the making." Robert Levine, *Conspiracy and Romance: Studies in Brockden Brown, Cooper, Hawthorne, and Melville* (New York: Cambridge University Press, 1989), 25. Jane Tompkins, though she mentions neither the FC nor the Illuminati, maintains that CBB's novel was Federalist propaganda. Tompkins, *Sensational Designs: The Cultural Work of American Fiction, 1790–1860* (New York: Oxford University Press, 1985), ch. 2. Shirley Samuels reads *Wieland* as antideist as well as anti-Jeffersonian in "Infidelity and Contagion: The Rheto-

ric of Revolution," *EAL* 22 (1987): 183–91; "*Wieland:* Alien and Infidel," *EAL* 25:1 (1990): 46–66; and *Romances of the Republic: Women, the Family, and Violence in the Early American Nation* (New York: Oxford University Press, 1996), ch. 2.

78. For example: "The fact that the strongest members of the Friendly Club were staunch Federalists accounts, in part at least, for Brown's gradual conversion to more conservative principles." David Lee Clark, *Charles Brockden Brown: Pioneer Voice of America* (Durham: Duke University Press, 1952), 131. Much of the most recent critical work on CBB questions the narrative of his radical-to-conservative shift. Steven Shapiro, Phillip Barnard, and Mark Kamrath, eds., *Revising Charles Brockden Brown: Culture, Politics, and Sexuality in the Early Republic* (Knoxville: University of Tennessee Press, 2004).

79. Levine, *Conspiracy and Romance,* 42.

80. John Limon, *The Place of Fiction in a Time of Science: A Disciplinary History of American Writing* (New York: Cambridge University Press, 1990), 31. Gordon Wood notes, but does not account for, CBB's difference from the anti-Illuminati conspiracy theorists in "Conspiracy and the Paranoid Style," 436–37.

81. Levine, *Conspiracy and Romance,* ch. 1. Levine is on safer ground when he resists the impulse to "reduce [CBB's] writings to a series of political statements, [which] would finally only crudely distort his literary intentions and methods" (25). My reading counters, along with arguments for CBB's Federalism, criticism that attempts to make CBB into a Calvinist or Quaker apologist, such as Michael Schnell, "'The Sacredness of Conjugal and Parental Duties': The Family, the Twentieth-Century Reader, and *Wieland*," *Christianity and Literature* 44:3–4 (1995): 259–73; and Marshall N. Surratt, "'The Awe-Creating Presence of the Deity': Some Religious Sources for Charles Brockden Brown's *Wieland*," *Papers on Language and Literature* 33:3 (1997): 310–24; Richard P. Moses, "The Quakerism of Charles Brockden Brown," *Quaker History* 75:1 (1986): 12–25; Joel Porte, "In the Hands of an Angry God: Religious Terror in Gothic Fiction," in G. R. Thompson, ed., *The Gothic Imagination: Essays in Dark Romanticism* (Pullman, Wash., 1974), 42–64; Michael Gilmore, "Calvinism and Gothicism: The Example of Brown's *Wieland*," *Studies in the Novel* 9:1 (spring 1977): 107–18.

82. CBB, *WMC,* 74.

83. Ibid., 250.

84. Franklin, ed., *The Poetry of the Minor Connecticut Wits.*

85. Jon Klancher discusses this mode of magazine publishing and its relationship to the British public sphere in the same period in *The Making of English Reading Audiences, 1790–1832* (Madison: University of Wisconsin Press, 1987).

86. Note CBB's self-referential joke: Damon's name echoes the word *dæmon*, which figures prominently in *Wieland*'s discussion of disembodied voices; the anecdote that immediately follows this one in the *Memoirs* includes a conversation on "the subject of invisible beings," another reminder of *Wieland*'s dæmonic concerns.

87. CBB, *WMC,* 259–60.

88. Warner, *The Letters of the Republic,* and his *Publics and Counterpublics* (New York: Zone Books, 2002), chap. 2; Walter Hesford, "'Do You Know the Author?': The Question of Authorship in *Wieland*," *EAL* 17 (1982–83): 239–48.

89. Nancy Ruttenburg, *Democratic Personality: Popular Voice and the Trial of American Authorship* (Stanford: Stanford University Press, 1998), 267.

90. CBB, *WMC,* 260. Ruttenburg notes and rightly disagrees with a strain of CBB criticism that reads Carwin as the "democratic threat" posed by "common people." For Ruttenburg, though, Carwin is still *Wieland*'s "common-man protagonist," and an "apt figure for conservative fears of the verbal excesses of democratic personality" (*Democratic Personality,* 185). My argument presumes that Carwin is not so much an outsider but the ultimate expert on the inner workings of publics.

91. CBB, *WMC,* 297. In his discussion of the sociology of secrets and secret societies, Georg Simmel identifies the secret as the core of modern individual consciousness. See "The Secret and the Secret Society," in Kurt H. Wolff, ed., *The Sociology of Georg Simmel* (Glencoe, Ill.: Free Press, 1950), 307–78.

92. Compare this to the scene in *Wieland* in which Carwin, who has just entered the Wieland family circle, comes close to exposing himself as the source of mysterious voices the other characters have heard by laying out his entire modus operandi; he "was disposed," he tells the friends, "to question whether the voices heard in the temple, at the foot of the hill, and in [the] closet, were not really uttered by human organs" and explains to them "the power of mimickry" and the "illusion of the fancy" (CBB, *WMC,* 75).

93. The early-eighteenth-century Camisards or "French Prophets" were driven from the same region that had centuries earlier fostered the Albigensian heresy. They resettled in London, where they set about recruiting converts. Believers in the direct intervention of the Holy Spirit and the constant presence of angels (whom they were occasionally allowed to see), they practiced a form of "trance preaching" or speaking under the influence of God's spirit. In 1707 a wealthy Camisard follower named Francois Mission published an account of the Camisard revolt accompanied by convert testimonials; it was translated into English as *A Cry from the Desart* and distributed liberally in London. The idea of the senior Wieland converting to the Camisard religion (in London, no less, not long after Camisard leaders had fled there from southern France) packs even more meaning than the evocation, through the allusion to the Albigenses, of the same sort of dualism that would preoccupy Wieland junior. In popular thinking, the Camisards were connected both to Quakers and to Shakers (or Shaking Quakers; the latter came to the American colonies in 1744). Clarke Garrett, *Spirit Possession and Popular Religion: From the Camisards to the Shakers* (Baltimore: Johns Hopkins University Press, 1987), 17–21. The Camisard preoccupation with spirit possession, similar in certain respects to the Quaker notion of the "inner voice," provides another link between the elder Wieland's faith and CBB's religious upbringing.

94. CBB, *WMC,* 19. Erasmus Darwin, *Zoonomia, or, the Laws of Organic Life: vol. I* (New York: T. & J. Swords, 1796), 439, 448, 462.

95. CBB, *WMC,* 203–4. For the Shakespearean quotation in context, see *Macbeth,* Act I, Scene 5, lines 51–52. The lines are Lady Macbeth's: "Come, thick night, / And pall thee in the dunnest smoke of hell, / That my keen knife see not

the wound it makes,/Nor heaven peep through the blanket of the dark,/To cry 'Hold, hold!'"

96. CBB, *WMC*, 215–16, 5, 3.

97. Leigh Eric Schmidt, *Hearing Things: Religion, Illusion, and the American Enlightenment* (Cambridge: Harvard University Press, 2000), esp. ch. 4.

98. Jodi Dean, *Publicity's Secret: How Technoculture Capitalizes on Democracy* (Ithaca: Cornell University Press, 2002).

99. John Cosens Ogden, *A View of the New England Illuminati: who are indefatigably engaged in Destroying the Religion of the United States; under a feigned regard for their safety—and under an impious abuse of true religion* (Philadelphia: James Carey, 1799), 3, 9. Ogden's reversal is consistent with CBB's inversion of a scenario presented in ThD's *An Oration:* "[T]he spirit of Jacobinism, differs very essentially from all other spirits. The zeal of an enthusiast in religion, though violent, and often pernicious, yet will stop short of acknowledged crime—it will shrink from cool deliberate murder. But the Jacobin is not satisfied with guilt of a common dye. He delights in murdering the wife of his bosom, in destroying the life of a smiling infant, in plunging a dagger into a parent's heart" (25). *Wieland*'s plot defiantly counters ThD's claim; Theodore Wieland, "an enthusiast in religion," willingly murders his family when he believes God requires it. It is tempting to consider the possibility that CBB named Theodore Wieland for EHS's zealous friend.

100. If CBB's fiction is less concerned with the existence of an actual order of the Illuminati than it is with popular representations of such conspiracies, such a distinction has particular bearing on the Illuminati scare as it relates to Habermasian discussions of the public sphere. Habermas's original narrative placed European Freemasonry among the cluster of social institutions that helped give birth to the public sphere; Freemasonry in particular typified his notion that "the coming together of private people into a public was . . . anticipated in secret, as a public sphere still existing behind closed doors [as long as] publicity [still] had its seat in the secret chanceries of the prince." Secrecy, for Habermas, relates to publicity as both characteristic of its earliest emergence and as an earlier social form that eventually gave way to "open associations[,] access to which . . . was relatively easy." Following this account, the transition from courtly secrecy through secret societies (or "internal" publics) to a democratic public sphere has been a staple feature of the literature on the public sphere's emergence. Habermas, *The Structural Transformation of the Public Sphere: An Inquiry into a Category of Bourgeois Society*, trans. Thomas McCarthy (Cambridge: MIT Press, 1989), 35. John Brooke has similarly argued that for "thousands of aspiring young men" in the new nation, "an introduction to—and indoctrination in—the cultural configuration of the public sphere would come in the blue light of the lodge-room, as they were inducted into the mysteries of Freemasonry." John L. Brooke, "Freemasonry and the Public Sphere in New York State, 1784–1830," unpublished paper, Organization of American Historians meeting, Louisville, Ky., 11 Apr. 1991, page 5, quoted by permission.

101. John Robison, *Proofs of a Conspiracy against All the Religions and Govern-*

ments of Europe, Carried on in the Secret Meetings of Free Masons, Illuminati, and Reading Societies. Collected from Good Authorities (New York: George Forman, 1798), 150–51.

102. Ibid., 155.

103. TD, *The Duty of Americans, at the Present Crisis: Illustrated in a Discourse, Preached on the Fourth of July, 1798* (New Haven: Thomas and Samuel Green, 1798), qtd. in Grasso, *A Speaking Aristocracy,* 352. Significantly, TD's concerns here go beyond denouncing the same "self-created" Democratic-Republican societies George Washington famously targeted in his farewell address.

104. TD had sarcastically dedicated his satirical poem *The Triumph of Infidelity* (1788) to Voltaire. See Wells, *The Devil and Dr. Dwight,* 34.

105. TD, *A Discourse on Some Events of the Last Century: Delivered in the Brick Church in New Haven, on Wednesday, January 7, 1801* (New Haven: Ezra Read, 1801), 16.

106. TD, *The Duty of Americans,* 17.

107. EHS to Sally Pierce, 9 June 1797, in *DEHS,* 324; EHS to SBT, 18 Jan. 1796, in *DEHS,* 123.

108. *DEHS,* 199 (7 Aug. 1796).

109. WJ uses these two phrases in a group letter from himself, CBB, and EHS to WD, 4 Sept. 1798, in *DWD,* 336.

110. *DEHS,* 448 (6 June 1798).

111. *DEHS,* 450 (19 June 1798).

112. EHS to ThD, 26 Aug. 1797, in *DEHS,* 350.

113. *DEHS,* 440 (26 Apr. 1798), 451 (25–27 June 1798).

114. *DWD,* 343 (28 Sept. 1798).

115. *DWD,* 345 (10 Oct. 1798).

116. CBB, *EH,* 131–33.

117. Christopher Grasso makes a similar observation as the point of departure for *A Speaking Aristocracy.*

118. *DWD,* 345 (10 Oct. 1798); Clark, *Charles Brockden Brown,* 171.

119. JK recuperated his Christian faith in the new century, though he allied himself with Episcopalianism rather than Congregationalism. In 1847, he recalled EHS, almost fifty years dead, as a "terrible free thinker." Qtd. in John Theodore Horton, *James Kent: A Study in Conservatism, 1763–1847* (1939; reprint, New York: Da Capo Press, 1969), 116n188.

Three. Unrestrained Conversation and the "Understanding of Woman"

1. *DEHS,* 243 (5 Nov. 1796).

2. *DEHS,* 244 (6 Nov. 1796), 267 (23 Nov. 1796).

3. EHS addressed "profanity" earlier in the same entry. That day he had attended rehearsals for his *Edwin and Angelina,* and worried that he would have to revise it to suit the taste of "our audience" by eliminating one "venerable monosyllable": God. *DEHS,* 243 (5 Nov. 1796).

4. *DEHS,* 246 (12 Nov. 1796), 281 (9 Jan. 1797). Though WD's piece was reviewed favorably—if briefly—in England, where it later received the distinc-

tion of being the first American play to appear on the London stage, it had no particular success at home and was quickly forgotten; it remains undiscussed in scholarship on his work.

5. WD, *Tell Truth and Shame the Devil: A Comedy, in Two Acts* (New York: T. & J. Swords, 1797), 23.

6. Both of these provocative assessments come in letters to friends who were faithful Christians. See CBB to Joseph Bringhurst, 30 October 1795 (H&C #60); EHS to ThD, 22 Nov. 1796, in *DEHS*, 262.

7. David Bonnell Green, "Letters of William Godwin and Thomas Holcroft to William Dunlap," *Notes and Commentaries* (Oct. 1956): 442–43.

8. EHS initially read parts of *Political Justice*'s first edition in 1795; his most rigorous reading, in May and June of 1797, involved the Philadelphia printing of the second edition, which FC members read against the first edition in order to assess the revisions. Unless noted otherwise, all citations to *Political Justice* will be taken from the Philadelphia edition. William Godwin, *Enquiry Concerning Political Justice, and Its Influence on Morals and Happiness* (Philadelphia: Bioren and Madan, 1796).

9. EHS to John Williams, 15 Apr. 1797, in *DEHS*, 309. Williams had attacked EHS's principles and associated Godwin with Nicolas Boulanger (a minor philosophe who wrote on religious psychology) and Thomas Paine.

10. See EHS to SBT, 16 Feb. 1797, in *DEHS*, 294. For their most sustained discussion of *Political Justice,* with Mrs. Tracy's objections implicit in EHS's responses, see EHS to SBT, 18 Jan. 1796, in *DEHS*, 123–24. In this letter EHS claims only to have read one half of one volume of *Political Justice* but says, nonetheless, that he believes the work "approaches nearer to truth, than any preceding system" (124).

11. Their daughter Mary, of course, would later marry Godwin's young admirer, Percy Bysshe Shelley. In a reciprocal circuit of transatlantic intellectual influence, Mary and Percy Shelley would both be inspired by CBB's novels, which were inspired by Mary's parents. See Eleanor Sickels, "Shelley and Charles Brockden Brown," *PMLA* 45:4 (Dec. 1930): 1116–28; Thomas Love Peacock, *Memoirs of Shelley, with Shelley's Letters to Peacock* (London: Frowde, 1909), 193–94; Pamela Clemit, *The Godwinian Novel: The Rational Fictions of Godwin, Brockden Brown, Mary Shelley* (Oxford: Oxford University Press, 1993).

12. Nicola Trott, "The Coleridge Circle and the 'Answer to Godwin,'" *RES* New Series 41:162 (1990): 212–229.

13. *DEHS*, 86 (6 Nov. 1795).

14. These writers would not have claimed the term "Jacobin," which generally referred to the most violent wave of French revolutionaries. Like FC writers they sympathized most with the more moderate Girondists. By the end of the decade the self-proclaimed "anti-Jacobins" in England had made use of the term liberally with respect to Godwin and others, and it has stuck ever since.

15. William Godwin to WD, Jan. or Feb. 1796, in Green, "Letters of William Godwin and Thomas Holcroft," 442.

16. FC members were aware of Coleridge within months of the spring 1796 publication of *Poems on Various Subjects,* his first collection, and numbered him

and Robert Southey among the Godwinians. They first heard of Coleridge in a letter sent prior to the volume's printing. *DEHS*, 199 (7 Aug. 1796); see also 229 (12 Oct. 1796), 296 (25 Feb. 1797).

17. This comment was provoked by Wollstonecraft's *A Short Residence*. *DEHS*, 208 (26 Aug. 1796).

18. John Neal, *American Writers: A Series of Papers Contributed to Blackwood's Magazine (1824–1825)*, ed. Fred Pattee (Durham: Duke University Press, 1937), 68.

19. Harry R. Warfel, *Charles Brockden Brown: American Gothic Novelist* (Gainesville: University of Florida Press, 1949), 44; *DEHS*, 171 (27 May 1796). Most critics who cite the letter—including Warfel—do not note that this draft was never sent. See *DEHS*, 184 (3 July 1796).

20. ThD, *An Oration, Delivered at New Haven on the 7th of July, A.D. 1801, before the Society of the Cincinnati* (Hartford: Hudson and Goodwin, 1801), 26–27. ThD takes particular issue in this oration with Godwin's views on marriage.

21. EHS wrote in the fall of 1795 that he had not yet read *Political Justice*, though friends had told him Godwin's principles resembled his own. See *DEHS*, 46 (6 Sept. 1795). Caleb Crain, though he assumes EHS introduced the book to CBB, cites evidence of CBB's reading *Political Justice*—and his particular attention to discussions of promises and sincerity—as early as 1793. See Crain, *American Sympathy: Men, Friendship, and Literature in the New Nation* (New Haven: Yale University Press, 2001), 85. Peter Kafer notes that CBB's father transcribed portions of *Political Justice* into his commonplace book before 1795. See Kafer, *Charles Brockden Brown's Revolution and the Birth of American Gothic* (Philadelphia: University of Pennsylvania Press, 2004), 66. Crain's and Kafer's insights together suggest that the latter is wrong to frame EHS as a Godwinian seducer who led astray the young Quaker CBB; it may even have been the case that CBB read the book first—perhaps his father's copy—and was one of the "friends," along with George Woolsey, who recommended it to EHS.

22. Godwin, *Political Justice*, 303.

23. Ibid., 83–84.

24. Cathy Davidson, *Revolution and the Word: The Rise of the Novel in America* (New York: Oxford University Press, 1986), 10.

25. An advertisement for *Political Justice* appears in the Philadelphia *Federal Gazette*, 8 May 1793. The *New-York Magazine* drew excerpts from "On the Composition of Government" 4:7 (July 1793): 404 and "On the Mode of Excluding Visitors" 1:9 (Sept. 1796): 489. The Philadelphia *American Universal Magazine* printed "Godwin on Monarchy" in May 1797, a few months after he had been cited as "the celebrated Godwin" in the Philadelphia *City Gazette* for 16 Mar. 1797.

26. W. M. Verhoeven, "Performing Rebellion: Charles Brockden Brown and the Jacobin Legacy in America," *Profils Americains* 11 (1999): 121–33.

27. *DEHS*, 146 (27 Mar. 1797). WD had received one from Holcroft in Jan. 1796.

28. *DWD*, 227 (27 Feb. 1798).

29. *DEHS*, 420 (23 Jan. 1798), 428 (27 Feb. 1798); *DWD*, 255 (11 May 1798).

30. It is difficult to determine at what point Godwin became aligned, in some Federalists' minds, with Thomas Jefferson. In March 1796, in relation to the Virginia resolutions, and around the same time most FC members began pursuing *Political Justice* in earnest, EHS's friend, the Pennsylvania Republican Dr. Michael Leib, read aloud from Godwin on democracy and secrets—from the sections on the American president and on responsibility—to the Pennsylvania House of Representatives. See *Washington Spy* (17 Mar. 1796). This politicization of Godwin would have made EHS and other FC Federalists uncomfortable. EHS continued to correspond with Leib and call on him when in Philadelphia, in spite of fears that partisanship would damage friendship. On the partisan response to Godwin by the turn of the century, see Burton R. Pollin, "Godwin's Letter to Ogilvie, Friend of Jefferson, and the Federalist Propaganda," *Journal of the History of Ideas* 28:3 (July 1967): 432–44.

The FC discussed Godwin's writings on several occasions, and EHS's fellow Federalists among the group apparently were also sympathetic to Godwin. In his second draft of his 22 Nov. 1796 letter to ThD, EHS backs *Political Justice* with the endorsement of WWW, the most religiously conservative Federalist in the FC (*DEHS*, 262). EHS also defends Godwin from what he felt was ThD's unfair characterization; if he would only read *Political Justice*, EHS argued, he could "hardly find fault with it. His metaphysics are those of Mr. [John] Locke & President [Jonathan] Edwards" (250)—the latter of whom was ThD's grandfather.

Additional evidence suggests that early objections to Godwin stemmed from religious rather than partisan motivations: JK finished reading *Political Justice* in early 1796, at a moment when, EHS records, "Both [Kent] & his wife [were] charmed with Godwin & Holcroft's Works," something that led EHS to entertain "hopes of their conversion" to rational philosophy (147: 29 Mar. 1796). Shortly after JK finished reading the book, the club discussed it at a 2 Apr. 1796 meeting, focusing in particular on the topics of sincerity and promises (152). JK's younger brother, a Federalist politician in Western New York, reported in the fall of 1796 that after reading into the book's second volume, he found Godwin "as eloquent & forcible a Writer as I ever read & that he inculcates the most amiable Morality. It is the ardent wish of my Soul," he wrote to his brother, "to be [a] Man of Taste & disinterested Benevolence, such as he most elegantly describes him in his Seats of human Happiness." Moss Kent to JK, 17 Nov. 1796, KP.

31. Godwin, *Political Justice*, 239, 238.

32. Susan Branson, *These Fiery Frenchified Dames: Women and Political Culture in Early National Philadelphia* (Philadelphia: University of Pennsylvania Press, 2001), 35–49.

33. *DEHS*, 208 (26 Aug. 1796).

34. EHS to SBT, 31 Aug. 1796, in *DEHS*, 210–11.

35. *DEHS*, 382 (21 Oct. 1797).

36. *DEHS*, 386 (5 Nov. 1797).

37. Compare this to Paul Keen's account of the British Jacobins' conception of this republic as "a network of assumptions and practices which collectively defined a professional community . . . whose essential feature was this commitment

to serving the public good through the promotion and diffusion of knowledge."
Keen, *The Crisis of Literature in the 1790s: Print Culture and the Public Sphere*
(New York: Cambridge University Press, 1999), 84.

38. Godwin's preface was withdrawn from the first edition. He first printed
it in 1831 with a comment on the political context of the novel's original publication. William Godwin, *Caleb Williams*, Standard Novels No. II (London:
Colburn and Bentley, 1831), xix.

39. M. H. [Mary Hays], "On Novel Writing," *Monthly Magazine* [London]
4 (Sept. 1797): 180–81.

40. EHS to CBB, 25 Aug. 1797, in *DEHS*, 349; EHS to CBB, 16 Sept. 1797,
in *DEHS*, 364.

41. EHS to CBB, 7 May 1796, in *DEHS*, 164.

42. EHS to Abigail Smith, Jr., 4 Apr. 1797, in *DEHS*, 307.

43. This apparent difficulty in locating these writers' politics underscores
the need articulated by the critic W. M. Verhoeven for closer attention to the
"cultural dynamics of the *evolution of the reception* of Euro-American radicalism
in the 1790s." W. M. Verhoeven, "Performing Rebellion," 123.

44. EHS to Idea Strong, 21 Oct. 1797, in *DEHS*, 382. As Henry May has
rightly noted, the FC was primarily (though not exclusively) Federalist in politics and at the same time was predominantly deist or otherwise critical of established Christianity. May, *The Enlightenment in America* (New York: Oxford
University Press, 1976), 233–34. Thomas Bender suggests that May overstates
the club's religious radicalism. Though Bender is correct, inasmuch as he calls
attention to the lack of unanimity on religious principle among group members,
I think May's categorization applies to the majority and accurately characterizes
the club's corporate identity. Of the members at the time of EHS's death, May's
description fits EHS, WJ, and JK, and possibly CBB and WD as well, although
they are more difficult to locate than the first three in terms of political partisanship. Of the group's self-identified Jeffersonians, SLM and the Millers, only
SM was an orthodox Christian in the 1790s. This leaves the Woolseys alone to
fit the stereotype of religious *and* political conservatives. While the political and
religious composition of the club is more diverse than either May or Bender allows, the union of moderate Federalism with moderate deism did predominate.
Bender, *New York Intellect: A History of Intellectual Life in New York City from 1750
to the Beginnings of Our Own Time* (Baltimore: Johns Hopkins University Press,
1987), 28–29.

45. I'm indebted on this point to Seth Cotlar, response to a session of the
Society of Early Americanists, Norfolk, Va., 2001, copy in my possession, cited
with permission. The problem of defining "radicalism" here may be even more
complex than Cotlar implies. The conflation, by some critics, of religious skepticism, Godwinianism, political "radicalism" generally, and Jeffersonianism specifically is particularly difficult to sustain. As Verhoeven also points out, defining
Godwinianism itself with any consistency is itself problematic given the con-
tinually shifting nature of Godwin's own beliefs in these years, and the distance
between Godwin's radicalism and that of Paine or of the class-driven political
radicalism of the London Corresponding Society and the other associations that

provoked the treason trials in England at mid-decade. Verhoeven, "'This blissful period of intellectual liberty': Transatlantic Radicalism and Enlightened Conservatism in Brown's Early Writings," in Philip Barnard, Mark L. Kamrath, and Stephen Shapiro, eds., *Revising Charles Brockden Brown: Culture, Politics, and Sexuality in the Early Republic* (Knoxville: University of Tennessee Press, 2004), 8–9.

46. *Ormond,* published in January 1799, offers a practical example of the kind of challenge posed here; in spite of some critics' assumptions that the novel responds to (or may even be modeled on) Godwin's *Memoirs* of Wollstonecraft, we do not know with any certainty at what point CBB, his friends, or other American readers actually read the book. Although the contents of Godwin's publication were glossed in a letter reprinted from the British *Gentleman's Magazine* in the July 1798 issue of the anti-Jacobin, Philadelphia-based *Porcupine's Gazette,* the book itself was not advertised in American newspapers until the summer of 1799, when Mathew Carey published an American edition in Philadelphia. The book's earlier circulation in America is difficult to trace. Neither EHS nor WD mentions it in his diary in 1798, although rumors about it and other texts by both Godwin and Wollstonecraft receive frequent mention. In Feb. 1799, a member of the FC's mixed-sex social circle read Wollstonecraft's "Letters to Imlay," the third volume of the *Posthumous Works* Godwin also published in early 1798, which contained much of the *Memoirs'* controversial material, but the *Posthumous Works* and *Memoirs* were not reviewed in the club's *MMAR* until August 1799, in an essay sympathetic to Wollstonecraft's principles but disapproving of her behavior. While certain aspects of *Ormond* suggest that CBB may have read or been familiar with the book while he was composing his novel at the end of 1798, we cannot be sure.

47. His effusive comments on Roland come in response to his reading of her *Appeal to Posterity. DEHS,* 117 (28 Dec. 1795).

48. EHS to CBB, 27 Mar. 1796, in *DEHS,* 146.

49. *DEHS,* 84 (1 Nov. 1795).

50. Chandos Michael Brown, "Mary Wollstonecraft; or, the Female Illuminati: The Campaign against Women and 'Modern Philosophy' in the Early Republic," *JER* 15 (fall 1995): 389–424, esp. 399.

51. TD, *The Nature, and Danger, of Infidel Philosophy, Exhibited in Two Discourses, Addressed to the Candidates for the Baccalaureate, in Yale College* (New Haven: George Bruce, 1798), 79. See also ThD, *An Oration . . . before the Society of the Cincinnati,* 27. Conflating religion and politics, ThD offers Federalism as an antidote to godless anarchy. See p. 7.

52. Godwin had been attacked as an "atheist philosopher" in a popular anti-Jacobin satire, *The Pursuits of Literature* (1794–98), by T. J. Mathias, which also recommends Barruel and Robison.

53. *Edgar Huntly* and *Jane Talbot* each contains characters who were rationalists but who have reconverted to Christianity, though the characterizations of these conversions are always mediated by interested parties and hence require greater care than critics sometimes take as they seek CBB's personal opinions or biographical content through his fiction.

54. Linda Kerber, *Women of the Republic: Intellect and Ideology in Revolutionary America* (Chapel Hill: University of North Carolina Press, 1980), 222–24.

55. Branson, *Fiery Frenchified Dames*, 22. Branson follows a speculation made earlier in the early twentieth century that CBB was the editor of one Philadelphia publication for women, the *Ladies Magazine*. There is no foundation for the claim, however, which is highly unlikely given the fact that CBB was intensely involved in legal studies at the time. See Kafer, *Charles Brockden Brown's Revolution*, 219–20n4.

56. Catherine O. Kaplan, "Elihu Hubbard Smith's 'The Institutions of the Republic of Utopia,'" *EAL* 35:3 (fall/winter 2000): 294–336.

57. Based on his reading of *Emma Courtney*, EHS wrote in a letter to CBB that Hays "appears to have studied Godwin, Holcroft, &c. with assiduity." EHS to CBB, 16 Sept. 1797, in *DEHS*, 364. Hays quotes both authors throughout, and cites *Caleb Williams* as a model in her preface, but her book also reveals Wollstonecraft's influence. EHS could not have known that Hays had inserted material from several of Godwin's letters to her into the novel and took him as the model for her heroine's rational monitor, Mr. Francis.

58. *Alcuin* was published in the spring of 1798 in New York by the Swords brothers, who also served as printers for EHS's *Medical Repository*, Dunlap's plays, and several other projects from club members. A serial version appeared in a slightly different (and conservatively edited) form as "The Rights of Women" in March and April numbers of the Philadelphia *Weekly Magazine*. This version, in keeping with James Watters's editorial policy, omitted anything politically controversial, including a full eleven pages of Mrs. Carter's most spirited arguments in favor of women's participation in political life. Robert D. Arner, "Historical Essay," in CBB, *Alcuin*, 290–98; S. W. Reid, "Textual Essay," in CBB, *Alcuin*, 329–36.

59. *DEHS*, 211 (31 Aug. 1796). Cf. EHS to Idea Strong, 9 June 1797, in *DEHS*, 323.

60. CBB, *Alcuin*, 11, 13, 19.

61. Ibid., 15.

62. Ibid., 16, 18.

63. See Arner, "Historical Essay," 286.

64. Fredrika J. Teute, "'A Republic of Intellect': Conversation and Criticism among the Sexes in 1790s New York," in *Revising Charles Brockden Brown*, 162.

65. CBB, *Alcuin*, 3–5.

66. Ibid., 3, 5.

67. Bruce Burgett, "The Problem of 'Sex' in Malthus and Brockden Brown," in *Revising Charles Brockden Brown*, 136.

68. CBB, *Alcuin*, 32.

69. Dietmar Schloss, "Intellectuals and Women: Social Rivalry in Charles Brockden Brown's *Alcuin*," in Udo J. Hebel, ed., *The Construction and Contestation of American Cultures and Identities in the Early National Period* (Heidelberg: Universitätsverlag, 1999), 356–57.

70. William Godwin, *The Enquirer. Reflections on Education, Manners, and Literature. In a Series of Essays* (Philadelphia: Robert Campbell and Co., 1797), viii.

71. EHS to CBB, 16 Sept. 1797, in *DEHS,* 364; Arner, "Historical Essay," 274.

72. CBB, *Ormond,* 252, 291.

73. See the advertisement, for example, in the New York *Commercial Advertiser,* 29 Jan. 1799.

74. Robert Levine, *Conspiracy and Romance: Studies in Brockden Brown, Cooper, Hawthorne, and Melville* (New York: Cambridge University Press, 1989); Julia Stern, *The Plight of Feeling: Sympathy and Dissent in the Early American Novel* (Chicago: University of Chicago Press, 1997).

75. Hana Layson, "Rape and Revolution: Feminism, Antijacobinism, and the Politics of Injured Innocence in Brockden Brown's *Ormond,*" *Early American Studies* 2:1 (spring 2004): 160–91.

76. The reviewer attacked the novel on aesthetic grounds as well: "We shall only add," he concluded, "that, *if* a want of perspicuity, *if* a want of elegance in style, *if* a want of imagination, *if* a want of nature in the delineation of character, *if* a want of incident, *if* a want of plot and connection, and finally, *if* a want of common sense, be excellencies in a novel, the author of Ormond, Wieland, Arthur Mervyn, &c. &c. has a fair claim to the laurel of pre-eminence in 'the temple of Minerva.'" The last phrase refers to William Lane's Minerva Press, the publisher of the 1800 London edition of *Ormond,* known for its cheap editions. Minerva published Bage's *Hermsprong* as well as some anti-Jacobin fiction but was regarded with suspicion by conservatives since its targeted public was so broad. Antijacobin Review 6 (Aug. 1800): 451.

77. CBB, *Ormond,* 29, 33.

78. CBB, *Alcuin,* 40, 46.

79. CBB, *Ormond,* 34.

80. Ibid., 28, 3.

81. Ibid., 119–20, 22.

82. Ibid., 72, 76, 77.

83. Ibid., 189–204.

84. Ibid., 28, 186, 191.

85. Ibid., 206, 205, 201–202.

86. M. O. Grenby, *The Anti-Jacobin Novel: British Conservatism and the French Revolution* (New York: Cambridge University Press, 2001); Keen, *Crisis of Literature,* 194.

87. Paul Lewis, "Attaining Masculinity: Charles Brockden Brown and Woman Warriors of the 1790s," *EAL* 40:1 (2005): 37–55.

88. Robert Hare, "Charles Brockden Brown's *Ormond:* The Influence of Rousseau, Godwin, and Mary Wollstonecraft." Ph.D. diss., University of Maryland, 1967.

89. Thanks to Evert van Leeuwen for calling this distinction to my attention.

90. CBB, *Ormond,* 252.

91. Critics who compare Ormond's "maxims" to Godwin's often are forced to admit that Ormond contradicts Godwinian principles at almost every turn. Sydney Krause, for example, argues that CBB assumed "he could depend on a certain recognition factor, at least for the tenor, if not for the literal terms of

[Godwin's] ideas" ("Historical Notes," in CBB, *Ormond,* 411), but at the same time has to concede that Ormond's tenets "may seem a less than coherent pastiche of Godwinism, suggesting either that Brown had only superficially digested the material, or that he was trying to rework his Godwin from memory" (412). In spite of acknowledging that on some points Ormond's opinions run "completely counter" to Godwin's, Krause still sees them as a transparent window onto "Brown's viewpoint," without fully considering the implications of the narrative scaffolding. CBB presents these views from the perspective of the novel's villain, as filtered through an unreliable narrator who, like Mrs. Fielder in *Jane Talbot,* would be less than friendly to Godwin in the first place (416). Robert Hare offers a similar caveat to Krause's, in regard to *Memoirs of Carwin*'s Ludloe: "Ludloe is engaged, in fact, in a Godwinian project of which Godwin himself certainly would not have approved" ("Charles Brockden Brown's *Ormond,*" 115). He notes Brown's characters' departures from Godwinian principle on several occasions but still believes that Brown uses these characters to critique Godwin.

92. CBB, *Ormond,* 114–15.

93. Grenby, *The Anti-Jacobin Novel,* 101.

94. As Mark Philp points out, Godwin added to these arguments substantively in the revisions, suggesting, for instance, that people would likely form voluntary, stable partnerships rather than be sexually promiscuous. Philp, *Godwin's Political Justice* (Ithaca: Cornell University Press, 1986), 180–81.

95. Qtd. in ibid., 183.

96. Krause, "Historical Notes," in CBB, *Ormond,* 411.

97. CBB, *Ormond,* 159.

98. Ibid., 84.

99. Ibid., 177, 179.

100. Ibid., 180, 179.

101. Ibid., 179.

102. Ibid., 227, 224.

103. Ibid., 180.

104. Ibid., 180–81.

105. Ibid., 264.

106. Ibid., 258–59.

107. Ibid., 285.

108. Ibid., 291.

109. Layson, "Rape and Revolution," 188.

110. Layson cites CBB's later magazine essay "Objections to Richardson's *Clarissa,*" in which he argues that because Clarissa has suffered an "involuntary violation" she should not be guilty or fear social stigma. Layson, "Rape and Revolution," 189.

111. TD, *The Duty of Americans, at the Present Crisis: Illustrated in a Discourse, Preached on the Fourth of July, 1798* (New Haven: Thomas and Samuel Green, 1798), 21.

112. "Original Communications: The Speculatist: No. II," *MMAR* 3:3 (Sept. 1800): 162.

113. Ibid., 163.

114. Teute, "'A Republic of Intellect.'" The paragraphs that follow would not be possible without Teute's research on MB, which has opened up significant new biographical materials on CBB's circle.

115. In an effort at sincerity that anticipates Godwin's frank recounting of Wollstonecraft's sexual history, EHS admits that "in common with many of my acquaintances, I had not the virtue, so deeply was the habit fixed, of wholly emancipating myself from this pernicious practice, till after I had entered my eighteenth year." He frames his intellectual development in part as the solution to the problem: "[L]ove & science elevated my mind above the low & exclusive gratification of the senses" (*DEHS*, 26).

116. *DEHS*, 27. Consistent with his comments here, in his unpublished utopian sketch EHS outlined a state-sponsored system of coeducation for young people, compatible with Wollstonecraft's—and Mrs. Carter's, in *Alcuin*—contention that gender-segregated education results in separate intellectual cultures for adult men and women. See Kaplan, "Elihu Hubbard Smith's 'The Institutions of the Republic of Utopia.'"

117. Linn, writing as "I.O.," had concluded a piece in which he argued for friendship's compatibility both with Christian fellowship and universal benevolence with the assertion that "[f]riendship subsisting between persons of a different sex, is of a nature still more refined than that which prevails between men," due to women's exertion of greater "gentleness," "amiableness," and "more eloquence of persuasion" than men possess. Anticipating the middle-class domesticity that was just emerging in American culture, Linn saw men as providers and protectors who will "encounter the roughness and jarring of the world from which [women] would shrink." I.O., "The Traveller, No. II," *Literary Magazine, and American Register* 1:2 (Nov. 1803): 89–90.

118. W.D. [William Dunlap], "Attachment between persons of the same sex. To the Traveller. The Traveller, no. IV," *Literary Magazine, and American Register* 1:4 (Jan. 1804): 247–48.

119. EHS to Joseph Strong, 14 February 1797, in *DEHS*, 291.

120. For a study of romantic mixed-sex friendship among Philadelphians of the same generation, see Lucia McMahon, "'While Our Souls Together Blend': Narrating a Romantic Readership in the Early Republic," in Jan E. Lewis, ed., *The Emotional History of the United States* (New York: New York University Press, 1998), 66–90.

121. Eliza Susan Morton Quincy, *Memoir of the Life of Eliza S. M. Quincy* (Boston: John Wilson and Sons, 1861), 58. Quincy's memoirs were composed for her children in 1821. She is the Morton sister referred to as "Miss Susan" in EHS's diary.

122. EHS to Idea Strong, 29 Mar. 1796, in *DEHS*, 148.

123. EHS to Abigail Smith, 18 Oct. 1796, in *DEHS*, 235.

124. Similarly, McMahon's account of mixed-sex friendship cultures in Philadelphia emerges from the context of courtship rituals and "romantic love." See "'While Our Souls Together Blend,'" esp. 67–68.

125. MB had met EHS and found him "a young man of this place of uncommon talents & information," whose conversation "delighted & entertained"

her. The friendship was facilitated through SLM. See MB to SHS, June 1798, MBSP. The dates for some of MB's letters seem to be mistaken; EHS's diary dates his initial meeting with MB as 22 June 1798, not 2 July as the placement of her letter to SHS in her correspondence would suggest.

126. MB to SHS, 20 May 1800. Political conversation in particular makes MB uncomfortable, though over time she clearly becomes more adept at it.

127. WJ's aversion to crowds was apparently due in part to shyness. After one walk, during which WJ had expressed his friendly feelings toward MB, she wrote to SHS that WJ was "not a man of words—Maria [Templeton] & I are the only ladies he visits." MB to SHS, [28?] Feb. 1800.

128. MB to SHS, 26 Feb. 1800.

129. MB to SHS, 3 May 1800.

130. MB to SHS, [28?] Feb. 1800.

131. MB to SHS, 20 Feb. 1800.

132. "If originality gives value it then has this merit, for not only the plot, but many of the sentiments are new.—But alas its originality is only that of most modern writers, who with boldness hitherto unknown, call not only the systems of politics, & religion errors, but even morality is among those causes which impede general happiness & virtue." She takes particular umbrage at the disrespect writers like Hays apparently show for "the Christian system of morality." MB to SHS 19 June 1798. Her account enlivened SHS's desire to read it: SHS to MB, 17 June 1798.

133. MB to SHS, 22 June 1798. MB was reading Robison a few weeks before EHS would take it up. SHS thought Robison was motivated by partisan politics. See MB to SHS, 12 July 1798.

134. Using language that signals her familiarity with writers like Bage and Godwin, MB believed "that were they to turn their thoughts on the present existing state of things & on man as he is, it would be more productive of utility to society, than by these speculations about future possibilities." Such theorizing, she notes, was responsible for "the premature birth of liberty in France. . . . Had those Philosophers who wished regeneration of their nations, awaited the slow but certain progression of Truth, how many calamities would have been avoided." MB to SHS, 20 Feb. 1800.

Her opposition to their philosophy did not prevent MB from maintaining her friendships with them. Regarding Anthony Bleecker's rejection of "the Christian doctrines," MB took some comfort that "his disbelief arises from no enmity to religion but from those dictates of his reason, which he says he could not resist," and in his assurance that his disbelief was not due to "fashion, or to get rid of its restraints on vice." MB to SHS, 30 Aug. 1799. MB's tolerance for their beliefs may have been heightened by the fact that her fiancé, who would soon be Jefferson's choice as editor of the partisan *National Intelligencer,* apparently shared some of their philosophical and intellectual leanings.

135. MB to SHS, 17 May 1799. For a rare expression of her own religious doubts, see MB to SHS, 18 May 1800.

136. MB to SHS, 22 May 1799. SHS's affinity with FC members is apparent in his response to MB's adventure. He was "charmed," he wrote, "with the

enterprising spirit which has electrified you." SHS to MB, 24 May 1799. Over the next year and a half he encouraged her to cultivate her friendships with the young men, convinced that their society would improve her suitability as his intellectual companion. See, for example, SHS to MB, 11 May 1800.

137. MB to SHS, 23 May 1800. The critical praise was not always reciprocal; as a reader, MB found CBB's writing distasteful, and it initially almost prevented her from pursuing his acquaintance. CBB sought out the criticism of these female friends; Maria Templeton read *Ormond*, before it was printed, on CBB's specific request that she provide her opinion of Constantia's conduct. Maria Templeton to MB, Dec. 1798. MB had read *Wieland* in the fall of 1798, before she had formed her friendship with CBB, and found it devoid of "instruction": "I began this book with prepossessions in its favour & I finish it, displeased with the author & sick from its effects," in part because of the vicarious sensations produced by "language so nervous & irresistible, that it almost metamorp[hize]s the reader into the actor, & fills him with the same terrors, infects his understanding with the same errors, the which he cannot afterwards correct." After she knew him better she still regarded his novels cautiously. She perused *Arthur Mervyn* at his request, though its descriptions of yellow fever, perhaps too close to home, replaced "the sweetness of sound slumber" with "nothing else but scenes of death." She "positively refused" to read *Edgar Huntly*, "& told him I could not consent to frighten away friend Sleep, for the sake of criticizing his writings." In response CBB "condemned the weakness of my mind, & advised me to strengthen it by immuring it to such scenes & images." MB to SHS, 11 Mar. 1800. CBB's fiction, according to one Philadelphia publication, was never very popular with female readers. See the unsigned review of John Davis's mock epic *The Philadelphia Pursuits of Literature* in the *Philadelphia Repository and Weekly Register* 5:9 (2 Mar. 1805): 71. MB writes, however, of at least one female reader in New York who relished CBB's novels as "works adapted to her taste."

138. MB to SHS, 26 Apr. 1800.

139. MB to SHS, 3 May 1800.

140. Like other Americans who initially admired Godwin, JK probably underwent a change of heart after Godwin published the *Memoirs* of his wife; it is unclear whether or not he was ever an unabashed fan of Wollstonecraft herself, but it is significant to note that even his postmortem evaluation is to some degree equivocal. In his copy of her *Vindication*, following a long biographical sketch of its author, he wrote:

> The fundamental principle on which the whole argument of this work
> is founded is that, except in affairs of love, sexual distinctions ought to
> be disregarded, and women considered in the light of rational creatures.
> The author discovers great energy of mind, vigor of fancy, and command
> of language, but several of her opinions are fanciful, and some of her
> projects romantic. Mr. Holcroft, in his "Anna St. Ives" (who in her leading features is a mere child of the imagination), has the same doctrine,
> that "mind has no sex"; that woman is not inferior to man; that, in a perfect state of society, no domestic appropriation of separate property can

subsist, but all would combine, in one universal effort of mind, to dispel error and propagate Truth. This is the genuine Godwinian philosophy.

Though the tone here is undoubtedly dismissive, JK the Federalist jurist seems to take greatest umbrage over matters of property rights. Qtd. in *MCK*, 239. SM would, in *BREC*, exult in Wollstonecraft's decline: "[I]f we may consider the life of that remarkable woman as a commentary on her doctrines it is plain that the destruction of chastity is the native fruit of her admired system" (2:288–90).

141. MB, Commonplace Book, 26 Feb. 1799, MBSP.

142. MB to SHS, 14 Apr. 1800. EHS had taken a very different view. Cf. his diary entry for 2 Aug. 1798, when he visited "Miss Templeton, for the purpose of explaining to her more fully the doctrine of Chemical Affinity—than she had comprehended it from the perusal of Lavoisier." *DEHS*, 459.

143. MB to SHS, 20 May 1800.

144. CBB, *EH*, 133.

Prelude. James Kent, Legal Knowledge, and the Politics of Print

1. *DEHS*, 371 (30 Sept. 1797).

2. *DWD*, 151 (30 Sept. 1797).

3. *DEHS*, 371 (30 Sept. 1797).

4. *DWD*, 151 (30 Sept. 1797).

5. William Godwin, "Of Learning," in *The Enquirer. Reflections on Education, Manners, and Literature. In a Series of Essays* (Philadelphia: Robert Campbell and Co., 1797), 282–95.

6. As late as 1834, Johnson sounded a defensive note about the role he and Kent had played in securing the common law's reception in the United States. It was "brought over with our ancestors," Johnson told one correspondent, "and modified and adopted by the people of the several states according to their local & political circumstances." WJ to S. Du Ponceau, 30 July 1834, HSP.

7. John Langbein, "Chancellor Kent and the History of Legal Literature," *Columbia Law Review* 93:3 (Apr. 1993): 547–94. See also James Horton, *James Kent: A Study in American Conservatism, 1763–1847* (1939; reprint, New York: Da Capo Press, 1969); Perry Miller, *The Life of the Mind in America, from the Revolution to the Civil War* (New York: Harcourt Brace Jovanovich, 1965), esp. 99–238; Lawrence Friedman, *A History of American Law* (New York: Simon and Schuster, 1973); David Raack, "'To Preserve the Best Fruits': The Legal Thought of Chancellor James Kent," *American Journal of Legal History* 33 (1989): 320–66; Carl F. Stychin, "The Commentaries of Chancellor James Kent and the Development of an American Common Law," *American Journal of Legal History* 37 (1993): 440–63.

8. Horton, *James Kent*, 71–83.

9. *DEHS*, 45 (6 Oct. 1795).

10. Qtd. in David Lee Clark, *Charles Brockden Brown: Pioneer Voice of America* (Durham: Duke University Press, 1952), 130–31.

11. *MCK*, 62.

12. Langbein, "Chancellor Kent," 559n62.

13. This was JK's description of the audience in his 1797 letter of resignation to the trustees, which they refused. In a note on the flyleaf of his personal copy of the three printed lectures, probably written much later, he recalled only "seven students and thirty-six gentlemen, chiefly lawyers and law students who did not belong to the college." See *MCK*, 77. EHS, writing in January 1796, described the audience for JK's first course as "several men, respectable for their years & situation in life," among whom "at least, thirty [were] nominal, & many real, & constant auditors" (*DEHS*, 126).

14. EHS to John Allen, 24 Jan. 1796, in *DEHS*, 127. EHS had, prior to the lectures' publication, informed Allen that he would be sending the copies, adding a recommendation of JK's character: the lectures would "be the cause of as much pleasure to his readers, as of reputation to himself. . . . I have not time to express to you the insensibility, which, almost universally, prevails here, in respect to the merit of this man; & I should feel deep regret were this effort, which he is making, with the noble design of awakening the sluggish minds of the youth of this city to a just apprehension of the importance of the profession they have chosen, not only to fail of it's effects, but involve it's disinterested author in an expense he is little able to bear." EHS to John Allen, 14 Dec. 1795, in *DEHS*, 102.

15. EHS to John Allen, 24 Jan. 1796, in *DEHS*, 127.

16. EHS to Uriah Tracy, 31 Jan. 1796, in *DEHS*, 129.

17. Qtd. in Langbein, "Chancellor Kent," 559n57.

18. Moss Kent to JK, 17 January 1796, KP, vol. 2.

19. EHS to John Allen, 24 Jan. 1796, in *DEHS*, 126–27.

20. Qtd. in Robert Ferguson, *Law and Letters in American Culture* (Cambridge: Harvard University Press, 1984), 70.

21. Kent's own praise for his friend and hero Alexander Hamilton's legal prowess emphasizes research over oratory, in terms that seem to speak to Kent's own career and strategies: "[H]e was eminently distinguished for completely exhausting every subject which he discussed, and leaving no argument or objection . . . unnoticed and unanswered. He traced doctrines to their source, or probed them to their foundations, and at the same time paid the highest deference and respect to sound authority." In his practice, "principles were stated, reasoned upon, enlarged, and explained, until those who heard" him were forced to submit to his argument. *MCK*, 305–7.

22. Qtd. in Michael Warner, *The Letters of the Republic: Publication and the Public Sphere in Eighteenth-Century America* (Cambridge: Harvard University Press, 1990), 110.

23. On JK and the "law as science" movement, see Miller, *The Life of the Mind*, 156–85; Raack, "'To Preserve the Best Fruits,'" 363–65. For the same principles described as "learned law," see Langbein, "Chancellor Kent," 566–70.

24. *MCK*, 99–100.

25. Ibid., 117.

26. See comments of John Duer in *MCK*, 112–15. Even late in life, JK described "our jurisprudence" as a "blank" when Hamilton and a small handful of

others "first began by their forensic discussions to introduce principles and to pour light and learning upon the science of law." *MCK,* 59.

27. Ibid., 58.

28. *MCK,* 117.

29. Langbein, "Chancellor Kent," 572n122.

30. Ibid., 571–84.

31. Ibid., 578.

32. Qtd. in ibid., 580n155.

33. William C. Dowling, *Literary Federalism in the Age of Jefferson: Joseph Dennie and the* Port-Folio, *1801–1811* (Columbia: University of South Carolina Press, 1999), 46.

34. Laura Rigal, *The American Manufactory: Art, Labor, and the World of Things in the Early Republic* (Princeton: Princeton University Press, 1998), ch. 4.

35. For another look at the surprising persistence and variety of literary Federalism, see Edward Cahill, "Federalist Criticism and the Fate of Genius," *American Literature* 76:4 (Dec. 2004): 687–717.

Four. The Public Is in the House

1. Heather S. Nathans, *Early American Theatre from the Revolution to Thomas Jefferson: Into the Hands of the People* (New York: Cambridge University Press, 2003), 148.

2. George Odell, *Annals of the New York Stage,* 15 vols. (New York: Columbia University Press, 1927–49), 2:7.

3. EHS, "Occasional Address, Spoken by Mr. Hodgkinson on the Opening of the New Theatre," *MMAR* 1:3 (June 1799): 239.

4. *DHAT,* 3.

5. *DEHS,* 415 (following 6 Jan. 1798).

6. "Philo" [CBB], "To the Editor of the Weekly Magazine. On Theatres," *Weekly Magazine* (14 Apr. 1798), 323–24, in CBB, *Literary Essays and Reviews,* ed. Alfred Weber and Wolfgang Schäfer, in collaboration with John R. Holmes (Frankfurt, Germany: Peter Lang, 1992), 4–8.

7. *DWD,* 177 (2 Dec. 1797): "He is a man upwards of 50, odd in his manners & appearance & very slovenly. My Landlady tells me he is an Atheist & the popular report is that he keeps his Coffin in his bed chamber & sometimes sleeps in it."

8. Like most other writing produced by the club, *André* unfolded within the context of the group's intellectual association. From late December to late February, WD also read the play to his wife (*DWD,* 199: 21 Dec. 1797), to his brother-in-law TD (214–15: 27 Jan. 1798), to a larger group of men and women at one of the Johnson brothers' homes (226: 25 Feb. 1798), and he let some of the acting company look over it to begin contemplating casting (225: 22–23 Feb. 1798). Once he had a satisfactory draft, he left the manuscript with Smith and Johnson; a few days later they were proofing the initial galley pages, which they would collect from the printer along with the opening pages of CBB's at-press dialogue, *Alcuin* (231: 12 Mar. 1798).

9. WD also "procured" from JK "a pamphlet containing the proceedings of the Court martial respecting André published by order of Congress," which he planned to append to the play's printed version (227: 28 Feb. 1798). WD obtained this pamphlet too late in the process to have used it to ensure historical accuracy, as has sometimes been claimed. More likely he hoped its inclusion would help boost sales.

10. WD, *André*, iii.

11. Ibid., iii–iv.

12. Ibid., vi.

13. *DWD*, 231 (17 Mar. 1798).

14. *DWD*, 225–28 (25 Feb.–4 Mar. 1798).

15. Qtd. in Robert H. Canary, *William Dunlap* (New York: Twayne Publishers, 1970), 95.

16. Andy Trees, "Benedict Arnold, John André, and his Three Yeoman Captors: A Sentimental Journey or Virtue Defended," *EAL* 35:3 (2000): 246–73, quote on 247.

17. Michael Meranze, "Major André's Exhumation," in *Mortal Remains: Death in Early America,* ed. Nancy Isenberg and Andrew Burstein (Philadelphia: University of Pennsylvania Press, 2003), 123–35, quote on 124.

18. Joseph J. Ellis, *After the Revolution: Profiles of Early American Culture* (New York: W. W. Norton, 1979), ch. 5; Norman Philbrick, "The Spy as Hero: An Examination of *André* by William Dunlap," *Studies in Theatre and Drama,* ed. Oscar G. Brockett (The Hague: Mouton, 1972), 97–119; Canary, *William Dunlap,* ch. 4; S. E. Wilmer, "Partisan Theatre in the Early Years of the United States," *Theatre Survey* 40:2 (November 1999): 1–26.

19. Jay Fliegelman, *Declaring Independence: Jefferson, Natural Language, and the Culture of Performance* (Stanford: Stanford University Press, 1993), 79, 91.

20. Ibid., 89–94; Jeffrey H. Richards, *Theater Enough: American Culture and the Metaphor of the World Stage, 1607–1789* (Durham: Duke University Press, 1991), chs. 11–13.

21. Qtd. in Ellis, *After the Revolution,* 121. The fullest WD biography remains Oral Sumner Coad, *William Dunlap: A Study of His Life and Works and of His Place in Contemporary Culture* (New York: The Dunlap Society, 1917). Autobiographical sketches appear in *DHAT,* 2:38–69, and *DHRPAD,* 1:242–315.

22. *DHRPAD,* 252.

23. Ibid., 254.

24. Ibid., 258.

25. EHS, ed., *American Poems, Selected and Original* (Litchfield, Conn.: Collier, 1793).

26. WD, *André*, vii.

27. *DEHS,* 414–16 (6 Jan. 1798).

28. Richards, *Theater Enough,* ch. 13.

29. EHS to CBB, 9 Jan. 1798, in *DEHS,* 417.

30. *DEHS,* 215 (6 Jan. 1798).

31. The naming of boxes itself generated some tension between author and actors and demonstrates WD's desire to prioritize the former; a few weeks be-

fore the New Theatre opened, Hodgkinson "suggested an Idea of naming the boxes from the principal dramatic Authors & Actors of Great Britain," WD wrote in his diary. "I changed it to ye dramatic Authors of Europe to the exclusion of the Actors & adopted it" (207: 14 Jan. 1798).

32. Despite a lack of indisputable evidence for WD's authorship of these columns, it has been commonplace, ever since Mary Bowman made the argument in 1927, to assume WD was the unnamed critic. Whether or not WD wrote these essays, they are consistent with his views expressed elsewhere. See Bowman, "Dunlap and the 'Theatrical Register' of the *New-York Magazine*," *Studies in Philology* 24 (1927): 413–25; Fred Moramarco, "The Early Dramatic Criticism of William Dunlap," *American Literature* 40 (1968): 9–14.

33. *DHAT*, 137, qtd. in Bowman, "Dunlap and the 'Theatrical Register,'" 418. The incident illustrates the flexible definition of "American" in the period: while later generations of American writers would consider it servile to adapt British works for an American audience, here the final product is authentically "American."

34. *DEHS*, 67 (5 Oct. 1795).

35. *DEHS*, 56 (13 Sept. 1795).

36. Samuel Johnson, "Prologue Spoken by Mr. Garrick at the Opening of the Theatre Royal, Drury Lane, 1747," in *The Norton Anthology of English Literature*, 2 vols., 5th ed., ed. M. H. Abrams et al. (New York: W. W. Norton and Co., 1986), 2310.

37. Unnamed critic, writing in 1805, qtd. in Lawrence Levine, *Highbrow/Lowbrow: The Emergence of Cultural Hierarchy in America* (Cambridge: Harvard University Press, 1988), 29.

38. EHS "Communication. The New Theater," *Commercial Advertiser* (31 Jan. 1798), qtd. in Odell, *Annals*, 2:7.

39. [WD?], "Theatrical Register," *New-York Magazine* 5:11 (Nov. 1794): 653–56.

40. WD to Thomas Holcroft, 29 July 1797, in *DWD*, 118.

41. Jon Klancher, *The Making of English Reading Audiences, 1790–1832* (Madison: University of Wisconsin Press, 1987), 14.

42. *DEHS*, 421 (31 Jan. 1798), 56 (15 Sept. 1795), 79 (22 Oct. 1795). On this topic more generally, see James E. Cronin, "Elihu Hubbard Smith and the New York Theatre (1793–1798)," *New York History* 31 (1949):136–48.

43. *DEHS*, 240 (31 Oct. 1796).

44. *DEHS*, 244 (7 Oct. 1796).

45. Ibid.

46. *DEHS*, 243 (5 Nov. 1796).

47. *DEHS*, 246 (12 Nov. 1796).

48. *DEHS*, 266 (23 Nov. 1796).

49. *DEHS*, 280 (7 Jan. 1797).

50. *DEHS*, 140 (16 Mar. 1796).

51. Billy J. Harbin, "The Role of Mrs. Hallam in the Hodgkinson-Hallam Controversy: 1794–97," *Theatre Journal* (May 1980): 213–22.

52. *DEHS*, 303 (29 Mar. 1797).

53. John Hodgkinson, *A Narrative of His Connection with the Old American*

Company, from the Fifth September, 1792, to the Thirty-First of March, 1797 (New York: J. Oram, 1797), 3.

54. *DEHS,* 303 (29 Mar. 1797).

55. *DWD,* 59 (4 June 1797).

56. *DWD,* 63 (5 June 1797).

57. *DWD,* 53 (31 May 1797).

58. *DWD,* 53–54 (31 May 1797).

59. *DHAT,* 188.

60. Hodgkinson, *Narrative,* 22.

61. Ibid., 3, 11.

62. Benjamin Rush, qtd. in Richards, *Theater Enough,* 281. See all of chs. 9–13 for transformations of the world-as-stage metaphor during and after the Revolution.

63. "Trial of Major John André," appended to WD, *André,* 87.

64. John André to George Washington, 24 Sept. 1780, in WD, *André,* 88–89.

65. John André to George Washington, 1 Oct. 1780, in WD, *André,* 104–5.

66. For the full text of the letter, see Alexander Hamilton to John Laurens, 11 Oct. 1780, in Harold C. Syrett, ed., *The Papers of Alexander Hamilton* (New York: Columbia University Press, 1961–), 2:460–70.

67. In WD, *André,* 108.

68. Benjamin Tallmadge to Colonel Wadsworth, 4 Oct. 1780, in Worthington Chauncey Ford, ed., *Correspondence and Journals of Samuel Blachley Webb,* 3 vols. (Lancaster, Pa.: Wickersham Press, 1893–94), 2:293–94. For treatments of the affair that highlight the fraternal sympathy of American officers for André, see Sarah Knott, "Sensibility and the American War for Independence," *American Historical Review* 109:1 (Feb. 2004): 19–40; Caleb Crain, *American Sympathy: Men, Friendship, and Literature in the New Nation* (New Haven: Yale University Press, 2001), 1–15.

69. Philbrick, "The Spy as Hero"; Ellis, *After the Revolution;* Wilmer, "Partisan Theatre." Wilmer makes this case most forcefully and most problematically, because he fails to examine closely several key pieces of evidence he cites. For example, he reads the title of WD's uncompleted novel, *The Anti-Jacobin,* as indicating the projected book's agenda, when in fact it satirizes ultra-Federalist conspiracy paranoia and models its title character on TD, from whose politics and religion WD dissented. Wilmer also overstates the partisan motivations for WD's dislike of Burk's *Bunker-Hill* and *Female Patriotism.* The objections reflected WD's views as a playwright that the plays were poorly written and sensationalistic, and the author, in negotiating New York runs, offensive and arrogant. Smith, a stauncher Federalist than WD himself, noted that *Female Patriotism* was "*dammed*" by its New York audience, but despite his personal dislike for Burk he was willing to admit the play was "better than his 'Bunker Hill'—& indeed was not fairly treated" (*DEHS,* 437: 13 Apr. 1798). Furthermore, Wilmer ignores or dismisses his own evidence that popular audiences seem to have "forgotten" party politics when engrossed in *Bunker-Hill*'s spectacle, as well as the fact that WD's play sides roundly against Bland and is careful to criticize André, even if it emphasizes his virtue.

In January 1798, just after he had completed *André*, WD listened politely while TD read to him from "a poem he composed for New Years verses, but did not publish. It is a bitter invective against all frenchmen innovators and infidels: I thanked him but gave no opinion" (207: 21 Jan. 1798). He did solicit TD's opinion, however, by asking him to return the favor and sit as audience for an early reading of *André*. "[H]e made some judicious remarks," WD wrote. "He approves of the sentiments attributed to André and Washington: he corrected me in several instances" (214–15: 27 Jan. 1798).

70. *DWD*, 236–37 (30 Mar. 1798).

71. *DEHS*, 434 (30 Mar. 1798).

72. The commonly cited detail that the "feeling excited by the incident was propagated out of doors" wasn't introduced by WD into the historical record until he wrote his 1832 theater history. *DHAT*, 223.

73. *DWD*, 237–38 (2 Apr. 1798).

74. *DWD*, 238 (3 Apr. 1798). This letter was reprinted the following day, 4 Apr., in the *Time-Piece*, from which Freneau had resigned only a few weeks earlier. See Wilmer, "Partisan Theatre," who mentions the *Argus* attacks and cites the *Time-Piece*, without noting that they are printing the same letter.

75. Qtd. in Philbrick, "The Spy as Hero," 114.

76. Qtd. in ibid., 114–15.

77. *DWD*, 239 (7 Apr. 1798). WD regarded the play as a failure and never again staged it in its original form. Most critics have followed his cue on this point. But only occasionally did a play run for more than three nights in a season, and the average receipts for the play—just over $472 per night—were nearly a hundred dollars over the average night that season. Perhaps WD's despair over the play, fueled by the public controversy it generated and the contention it caused among the actors, led him to regard it as more of a failure than it was; the degree to which he bemoaned its failure reveals the high expectations he had entertained for it.

78. Qtd. in Philbrick, "The Spy as Hero," 115.

79. WD, *André*, 23–24.

80. *DWD*, 304 (29 June 1798).

81. Heather Nathans notes the predominance of Federalists among the new Park Theatre's merchant subscribers, but she also points out that WD on several occasions made decisions that discount easy assumptions about partisan influence on his management. Nathans, *Early American Theatre*, 142–49, 158–61.

82. Steven J. Novak, *The Rights of Youth: American Colleges and Student Revolt, 1798–1815* (Cambridge: Harvard University Press, 1977), 40.

83. WD, *André*, iv.

84. Ibid., vii.

85. Lucy Rinehart rightly suggests that WD's use of the "discursive, deliberative, and democratic" dialogue form itself indicates an antiauthoritarianism that underlies WD's work more generally and may be a specific reaction to the Sedition Acts' attempts to curtail public political discussion. See Rinehart, "'Manly Exercises': Post-Revolutionary Performances of Authority in the Theatrical Career of William Dunlap," *EAL* 36:2 (2001): 263–93, quote on 277.

86. WD, *André*, 15–17.

87. Ibid., 17–18.

88. On Hamilton and André, see Broadus Mitchell, *Alexander Hamilton: The Revolutionary Years* (New York: Thomas Y. Crowell Co., 1970), 208–12; Crain, *American Sympathy*, 5–10.

89. Qtd. in Mitchell, *Alexander Hamilton*, 213.

90. WD, *André*, 32.

91. Ibid., 18.

92. William Godwin, *Enquiry Concerning Political Justice, and Its Influence on Morals and Happiness* (Philadelphia: Bioren and Madan, 1796), 113–14.

93. *DHAT,* 2:81–96; Sylvester Linus Kreilein, "August von Kotzebue's Critical Reception in New York City (1798–1805): A Study in Early American Theatre Criticism," Ph.D. diss., University of Wisconsin–Madison, 1989. See esp. 212–42 for contemporary debates about Kotzebue's morality and politics.

94. WD to John Murray, 1803, in *DHAT,* 188.

Five. "Here was fresh matter for discourse"

1. CBB to James Brown, 25 Oct. 1796 (H&C #77), Library Company of Philadelphia.

2. Following its dramatic 1793 epidemic, Philadelphia experienced milder episodes in 1794 and 1796, but death tolls surged again in 1797 (1,250) and 1798 (3,500). Following New York's 1798 epidemic, which killed 2,000, the worst outbreaks came in 1805 and 1822. See John Duffy, *A History of Public Health in New York City, 1625–1866* (New York: Russell Sage, 1968), esp. chs. 5–7; Susan E. Klepp, "Appendix I: 'How Many Precious Souls Are Fled?': The Magnitude of the 1793 Yellow Fever Epidemic," in *A Melancholy Scene of Devastation: The Public Response to the 1793 Philadelphia Yellow Fever Epidemic,* ed. J. Worth Estes and Billy G. Smith (Canton, Mass.: Science History Publications/USA for the College of Physicians of Philadelphia and the Library Company of Philadelphia, 1997), 178.

3. CBB to James Brown, 25 Oct. 1796 (H&C #77).

4. MB to SHS, 11 Mar. 1800, MBSP.

5. *DEHS*, 238–39 (27, 28, and 29 Oct. 1796).

6. *DEHS*, 321 (8 June 1797).

7. Noah Webster, ed., *A Collection of Papers on the Subject of Bilious Fever, Prevalent in the United States for a Few Years Past* (New York: Hopkins, Webb, and Co., 1796), 106.

8. The nine-chapter serial ran in James Watters's Philadelphia *Weekly Magazine of Original Essays, Fugitive Pieces, and Interesting Intelligence* from 16 June to 23 August 1798, until Watters's death cut the publication short. CBB had treated yellow fever in "The Man at Home" (*Weekly Magazine,* 3 Feb.–28 Apr. 1798), which ran for thirteen numbers before being succeeded abruptly by CBB's "A Series of Original Letters" (21 Apr.–2 June 1798), which in turn gave way, also unfinished, to *Arthur Mervyn*. A portion of the yellow fever episode in "The Man at Home" was used verbatim in chapter 7 of *Ormond* (in the Monrose-Baxter incident). I read "The Man at Home" and the nine serialized installments

of *Arthur Mervyn* as marked, then, by EHS's medical beliefs but not yet by his death.

9. David Paul Nord, "Readership as Citizenship in Late-Eighteenth-Century Philadelphia," in *A Melancholy Scene*, 24–25.

10. *DEHS*, 57 (16 Sept. 1795).

11. EHS made these comments in an unsigned review of John B. Davidge, *A Treatise on the Autumnal Endemic Epidemic of Tropical Climates, Vulgarly Called the Yellow Fever; Containing its Origin, History, Nature, and Cure; Together with a Few Reflections on the Proximate Causes of Diseases* (Baltimore: Pechin, 1798), in *MR* 2:1 (Aug. 1798): 82. EHS's authorship of the review is established in *DEHS*, 447–49.

12. *DEHS*, 62 (25 Sept. 1795).

13. Cf. Philadelphia following the 1793 epidemic, as described in Nord, "Readership as Citizenship," 25–26.

14. Like EHS, SLM had contributed to Webster's volume, which they believed had not received the circulation it deserved. EHS notes in his diary that the failure of Webster's predominantly climatist-sanitationist collection of essays directly resulted in the *Repository*'s founding (*DEHS*, 185: 9 July 1796). On Webster's medical writings generally, see C.-E. A. Winslow, "The Epidemiology of Noah Webster," *Transactions of the Connecticut Academy of Arts and Sciences* 32 (Jan. 1934): 21–109.

15. EHS, SLM, EM, "To the Physicians of the United States," circular pamphlet, 1796, NYAM, 7.

16. EHS to Samuel Smith, 31 July 1796, in *DEHS*, 194.

17. "Extract of a Letter from a Gentleman in Philadelphia to His Friend in England, dated July 7, 1799," *MMAR* 1 (Aug. 1799): 324–27, quote on 325. This letter unequivocally champions the theory of local origins.

18. EHS, "The Plague of Athens," *MR* 1:1 (July 1797): 3

19. *DEHS*, 75 (20 Oct. 1795).

20. CBB to James Brown, 25 Sept. 1796 (H&C #77).

21. CBB, "Advertisement," in *WMC*, 3; CBB, "To the Public," in *EH*, 3.

22. For a very different take on the relationship between "literary" and "scientific" writing in CBB's career, see John Limon, *The Place of Fiction in the Time of Science: A Disciplinary History of American Writing* (New York: Cambridge University Press, 1990).

23. Peter Dobkin Hall, *The Organization of American Culture, 1700–1900: Private Institutions, Elites, and the Origins of American Nationality* (New York: New York University Press, 1982), ch. 7; Lisbeth Haakonssen, *Medicine and Morals in the Enlightenment: John Gregory, Thomas Percival, and Benjamin Rush* (Atlanta: Rodopi, 1997), 192.

24. CBB, *AM*, 3.

25. Donald B. Cooper and Kenneth F. Kiple, "Yellow Fever," in *Cambridge World History of Human Disease*, ed. Kenneth F. Kiple (New York: Cambridge University Press, 1993), 1101. Despite their misunderstanding of the fever's origins, sanitationists like the *Repository*'s editors contributed toward prevention inasmuch as they filled in marshes and removed other standing water where

mosquitoes bred. They also contributed to efforts to import fresh drinking water. See Gerard T. Koeppel, *Water for Gotham: A History* (Princeton: Princeton University Press, 2000).

26. See EM to Benjamin Rush, 5 Nov. 1793, RL, in which Miller informs Rush that since the middle of July Dover has experienced a "Bilious Colic" epidemic of its own. In EM to Benjamin Rush, 31 Dec. 1793, RL, he congratulates Rush on his *Inquiries*, which he thinks will "demolish all candid and rational opposition." He also slights Mathew Carey's narrative, which he cannot imagine will be read by physicians "in a serious light."

27. Their appointments came five years after the hospital had taken up residency in its newly renovated buildings on the west side of Broadway, between Duane and Anthony streets. See Eric Larrabee, *The Benevolent and Necessary Institution: The New York Hospital, 1771–1971* (Garden City: Doubleday, 1971), 109–12, 160–63.

28. Critics tend to dismiss CBB's engagement with contemporary debates about the fever and then to read the fever as social allegory, a move I obviously resist. For treatments that read "contagion" in CBB's fiction as allegorizing the French Revolution, the Illuminati scare, the Alien and Sedition Acts, the rise of a market economy, patriarchal family relations, and partisanship's effects on fellow feeling, see Robert Levine, *Conspiracy and Romance: Studies in Brockden Brown, Cooper, Hawthorne, and Melville* (New York: Cambridge University Press, 1989), 15–57; Robert Levine, "Arthur Mervyn's Revolutions," *Studies in American Fiction* 12:2 (autumn 1984): 145–60; Jane Tompkins, *Sensational Designs: The Cultural Work of American Fiction* (New York: Oxford University Press, 1985); Shirley Samuels, *Romances of the Republic: Women, the Family, and Violence in the Early American Nation* (New York: Oxford University Press, 1996), 23–43; Julia Stern, *The Plight of Feeling: Sympathy and Dissent in the Early American Novel* (Chicago: University of Chicago Press, 1997), 153–238; Philip Gould, "Race, Commerce, and the Literature of Yellow Fever in Early National Philadelphia," *EAL* 2 (2000): 157–86. For other important readings of CBB's fever fiction see William L. Hedges, "Benjamin Rush, Charles Brockden Brown, and the American Plague Year," *EAL* 7:3 (winter 1973): 295–311; Robert Ferguson, "Yellow Fever and Charles Brockden Brown: The Context of the Emerging Novelist," *EAL* 14 (1980): 293–305; Robert Ferguson, *Law and Letters in American Culture* (Cambridge: Harvard University Press, 1984), esp. 142–47; Teresa Goddu, *Gothic America: Narrative, History, and Nation* (New York: Columbia University Press, 1997); and Warner, *The Letters of the Republic*, 151–76.

29. CBB, *AM*, 86, 93, 98, 125, 131, 151, 269, 324, 334, 403, 445.

30. On this point I agree with Susan Sontag, *Illness as Metaphor; and, AIDS and Its Metaphors* (New York: Doubleday, 1990).

31. Critics who read the fever as metaphor or allegory face particular historical problems. Several readings build on Martin S. Pernick's classic argument that Philadelphia physicians' medical opinions, in 1793, broke down along partisan lines: Jeffersonian-Republican physicians like Rush held agrarian ideals and believed the fever was generated by urban filth, while Federalist physicians blamed French refugees from the West Indies and so endorsed importationist

explanations. However, recurring epidemics in multiple cities left a vast archive in which political-medical alliances do not hold up so neatly. Attempts to use the fever to locate CBB politically obscure the thing CBB shares most with his medical friends: the desire to create and govern an educated audience as a way of staving off recurring epidemics. Recent scholarship suggests that debates over origins and treatment were more complex even in 1793 Philadelphia than Pernick's original interpretation suggested. See J. Worth Estes, "Introduction: The Yellow Fever Syndrome and Its Treatment in Philadelphia, 1793," in *A Melancholy Scene*, 7–9; Pernick, "Politics, Parties, and Pestilence: Epidemic Yellow Fever in Philadelphia and the Rise of the First Party System," and "Afterword," in *A Melancholy Scene*, 119–46. Joann P. Krieg's discussion of CBB and EHS in *Epidemics in the Modern World* (New York: Twayne Publishers, 1992) is unique in its recognition of CBB's participation in medical debates; her useful discussion is flawed, unfortunately, in its assumption that EHS's endorsement of the climatist position and his concern for the health of the poor indicate Jeffersonian partisanship.

32. Duffy, *A History of Public Health*, 126–27.

33. John Mitchel Mason, *A Sermon, Preached September 20th, 1793; A Day Set Apart in the City of New-York, for Public Fasting, Humiliation, and Prayer, on Account of a Malignant and Mortal Fever Prevailing in the City of Philadelphia* (New York: Samuel Loudon & Son, 1793), 15, 20.

34. "Minutes of the so-called Medical Society of the State of New York, 1794–1806," ms., NYAM. Mitchill was a member of this society from 1795 to early 1799, when his membership was revoked for his refusal to pay fines or annual dues.

35. Ibid.

36. Duffy, *A History of Public Health*, 102.

37. *DEHS*, 59 (20 Sept. 1795).

38. "Minutes of the so-called Medical Society," 11 (21 Jan. 1796).

39. In 1802 the city council decided to create a single health board, consisting of the commissioners of health and a standing committee from the city council itself: "Uniting the medical knowledge and experience of the Commissioners of Health, with the authority of this board, would inspire confidence in the minds of the Citizens." Duffy, *A History of Public Health*, 141.

40. Richard Bayley, *Letters from the Health Office Submitted to the Common Council of the City of New-York* (New York: John Furman, 1798).

41. EHS regarded Carey's work as a "successful catch-penny," a self-aggrandizing moneymaker with little scientific value. *DEHS*, 374 (8 Oct. 1797). Carey denied that he made money from the publication.

42. Matthew Livingston Davis, *A Brief Account of the Epidemical Fever which Lately Prevailed in the City of New York; with the Different Reports and Letters of Gov. Jay, Gov. Mifflin, the Health Commission of New York, &c upon the Subject, to which is added an accurate list of those who have died of the disease from July 29, to Nov. 1* (New York: Davis, 1795).

43. William Linn, *A Discourse, Delivered on the 26th of November, 1795; Being the Day Recommended by the Governor of the State of New-York to be Observed as a*

Day of Thanksgiving and Prayer, on Account of the Removal of an Epidemic Fever and for other National Blessings (New York: T. & J. Swords, 1795), 31.

44. *DEHS,* 65 (3 Oct. 1795). EHS's secular response to the fever marks a significant difference between him and Rush. For Rush's idiosyncratic blend of Enlightenment Christianity, see Nina Reid-Maroney, *Philadelphia's Enlightenment, 1740–1800: Kingdom of Christ, Empire of Reason* (Westport, Conn.: Greenwood Press, 2001), chs. 5 and 6.

45. EHS to Benjamin Rush, 9 Apr. 1794, RL. EHS offered to serve as a conduit for information from New York and Connecticut and encouraged Rush to send copies to the latter: "The rivalship of Cities and Schools has not yet reached there; both the name & the writings of Dr. Rush are respected & valued; and the most noted Bookseller, in the state of Connecticut, informed me, but a few days since, that no Medical Works met with so ready a Sale as the first & second Volumes of the Inquiries & Observations."

46. Webster, ed., *A Collection of Papers.*

47. The *Repository's* editors initially praised Webster's medical magnum opus, *A Brief History of Epidemic and Pestilential Diseases* (Hartford: Hudson and Goodwin, 1799), but they quickly soured over his idiosyncratic approach to electrical and chemical matters in relation to meteorology and the fever. See EM to Benjamin Rush, 27 Jan. 1800, and 18 Mar. 1800 (in which he criticizes Webster's "unphilosophical notions" throughout the work generally), RL. See also several letters from Noah Webster to Benjamin Rush between 14 July 1798 and 11 Sept. 1801 complaining of the book's lukewarm reception. Though he found flaw with Webster on different points, CBB (coterminous to the exchange between EM and Rush) published his own extended and withering critique of Webster's book in the *MMAR* for Jan., Feb., Mar., and Apr. 1800.

48. SLM, *The Gaseous Oxyd of Azote* (New York: T. & J. Swords, 1795). The section called "Mitchill on Contagion" in Webster's 1795 volume redacts this pamphlet.

49. SLM's pamphlet on the gaseous oxyd was translated into German and was also included in a series of essays on nitrous oxide and other "factitious airs" published by prominent British physicians Thomas Beddoes and James Watt, *Considerations on the Medicinal Uses of Factitious Airs* (Bristol: Bulgin and Rosser, 1794–96). SLM claimed the gaseous oxyd of azote was what other scientists were beginning to call nitrous oxide, and said that an overdose (or "full respiration") of the gas would result in sudden death, which accounts for "many persons falling down dead suddenly, when struck with the contagion of the plague." His argument was refuted by Humphry Davy, who would become one of Britain's most celebrated scientists. Experiments by Beddoes, Davy, and others using nitrous oxide were seized on by conservatives as evidence of a Jacobinical enthusiasm for science. See Jan Golinski, *Science as Public Culture: Chemistry and Enlightenment in Britain, 1760–1820* (Cambridge: Cambridge University Press, 1999), chs. 6 and 7, SLM qtd. on 166. N. A. Bergman, "Samuel Latham Mitchill (1764–1831), A Neglected American Pioneer of Anesthesia," *Journal of the American Medical Association* (1 Feb. 1985): 675–78, argues that SLM, for prompting Davy's later research, should be more widely recognized as a medical pioneer. On the trans-

lation of Mitchill's pamphlet into German, see SLM's 1798 address to the state agricultural society in *Transactions of the Society for the Promotion of Agriculture, Arts and Manufactures, Instituted in the State of New-York*, vol. 1, 2nd rev. ed. (Albany: Charles R. and George Webster, 1801): 205.

50. SLM qtd. in Courtney Robert Hall, *A Scientist in the Early Republic: Samuel Latham Mitchill, 1764–1831* (New York: Columbia University Press, 1934), 35.

51. See, for examples, *New-York Magazine* (July 1796): 351–56; (Oct. 1796): 539–45; (Dec. 1796): 625–30; (Dec. 1796): 630–31; (Jan. 1797): 9; (Feb. 1797): 60–68.

52. Qtd. in James Hardie, *An Account of the Malignant Fever Lately Prevalent in the City of New-York* (New York: Hurtin and McFarlane, 1799), 9–10.

53. Rpt. in William Bay, *Inaugural Dissertation on the Operation of Pestilential Fluids upon the Large Intestines, Termed by Nosologists Dysentery* (New York: T. & J. Swords, 1797), 91.

54. In *MCK,* 105.

55. A rich body of cultural criticism addresses writing about cholera in Victorian England, pertinent to earlier contexts because the terms of the cholera debates derived directly from the yellow fever debates that preceded them. The social body metaphor, according to these critics, is so significant because it reveals how a literary construct can determine social policy. In the case of cholera: "Empirical observations of specific instances of working-class distress"—the working-classes were hardest hit by cholera, just as New York's 1795 epidemics hit Irish immigrants disproportionately—"gathered and interpreted by a middle-class (white male) expert, constitute[d] the basis for understanding distress not primarily as an individual, physiological problem (bodily infirmity) but as a sign of social disorder that requires collective (legislative) action." Cholera allowed for notions of national identity that associated distemper most closely with Irish immigrants and prostitution and set about to remedy the social situation accordingly. Mary Poovey, *Making a Social Body: British Cultural Formation, 1830–1864* (Chicago: University of Chicago Press, 1995), 57. See also Elaine Freedgood, *Victorian Writing about Risk* (New York: Cambridge University Press, 2000), ch. 2.

56. James Tillary, John R. B. Rodgers, and SLM, *Report of the Committee, Appointed by the Medical Society, of the State of New-York, to Inquire into the Symptoms, Origin, Cause, and Prevention of the Pestilential Disease, That Prevailed in New-York During the Summer and Autumn of the Year 1798* (New York: Office of the Daily Advertiser, 1799), 13, 17.

57. SLM, *Gaseous Oxyd of Azote,* 18, 20–21, 36.

58. Tillary, Rodgers, and SLM, *Report of the Committee,* 20.

59. SLM, *Gaseous Oxyd of Azote,* 18, 20–21, 36.

60. Freedgood, *Victorian Writing about Risk,* makes similar observations about sensory perception as represented by medical writers in mid-nineteenth-century Britain.

61. EHS to CBB, 9 Jan. 1798, in *DEHS,* 417.

62. See Lloyd G. Stevenson, "Putting Disease on the Map: The Early Use of Spot Maps in the Study of Yellow Fever," *Journal of the History of Medicine* (July 1965): 226–61. For the quote about EHS's descriptions, see page 240.

63. *DEHS,* 60 (20 Sept. 1795).

64. On the *MR*'s subscribers, see Richard J. Kahn and Patricia G. Kahn, "The *Medical Repository*—The First U.S. Medical Journal (1797–1824)," *New England Journal of Medicine* 337 (25 Dec. 1997): 1928. Thanks to Toby Appel at Yale University's Cushing/Whitney Medical Library for bringing this article to my attention. During its first year, the *MR* had 266 subscribers, concentrated mostly in New York, New England, and Delaware but also scattered throughout the rest of the states. The overrepresentation in the editors' home states suggests that subscription networks were largely personal. But this points to the type of information community the editors envisioned: in order to reach the people they desired as potential converts, the journal would have to bolster interest beyond a specialized audience—among influential citizens. In this the editors were to some degree successful; of the initial subscription base, more than a quarter represented professions other than medicine. In New York, as EHS informed his father in late 1797, the journal had more "subscribers . . . [who were] not physicians, than who are: more than two to one, I believe. I wish that the example of these gentlemen may be followed. For our work is not meant to be confined to mere medicine, but to include natural history & agriculture, chemistry & the arts." EHS to Reuben Smith, 10 Dec. 1797, in *DEHS*, 402.

65. EHS, "(Circular) To the Physicians, of the United States," in *DEHS*, 205 (following 17 Aug. 1796).

66. On such strategies, see David Waldstreicher, *In the Midst of Perpetual Fetes: The Making of American Nationalism, 1776–1820* (Chapel Hill: University of North Carolina Press, 1997), 108–9.

67. In a letter dated 14 Aug. 1810, fourteen years into the *Repository*'s print run, the New York physician David Hosack, an importationist-contagionist and contributor to a rival medical journal, wrote Mitchill both to invite him to contribute and to explain the need for a competitor to Mitchill's journal: "The Editors of the Repository upon this subject have conducted with so much partiality as to admit nothing into their pages that militates [?] against their favorite doctrine of the domestic origin of yellow fever." Hosack to SLM, in "Copies of Letters and Documents," ms., NYAM, 74.

68. David Shields, *Civil Tongues and Polite Letters in British America* (Chapel Hill: University of North Carolina Press, 1996), 319.

69. SLM, "The Doctrine of Septon," 189–90. The poem was included in a 15 Sept. 1797 letter to Dr. Thomas Beddoes and was published as "The Doctrine of Septon. *Attempted after the Manner of Dr. Darwin*," *MR* 1:2 (1797): 189–92. EHS wrote in his diary on 22 September that SLM had dropped off the letter and poem for him to read, "& the verses to correct. I have read—& must at least suggest corrections—for some of the verses are bad" (366). On 28 September he notes that SLM accepted his corrections (369).

70. SLM, "The Doctrine of Septon," 191–92.

71. Hall, *A Scientist*, 133–34.

72. James R. Manley, *An Inaugural Dissertation on the Yellow Fever, Submitted to the Public Examination of the Faculty of Physic under the authority of the trustees of Columbia College, in the State of New-York* (New York: T. & J. Swords, 1803), 15–17.

73. Estes, "Introduction," in *A Melancholy Scene*, 8.

74. CBB to WD, 21 Sept. 1798 (H&C #106), in *DWD*, 1:341.

75. CBB, *AM*, 144.

76. EM, "Cursory Observations on That Form of Pestilence Called Yellow Fever," in *MWEM*, 50, 67, 72.

77. EM, "Some Remarks on the Importance of the Stomach as a Centre of Association, a Seat of Morbid Derangement, and a Medium of the Operations of Remedies in Malignant Diseases," in *MWEM*, 172–74. In the inaugural dissertation cited above, James Manley suggests that any "exercise of the mind" may prove "directly stimulant to the system" and thereby predispose the body to infection. Manley, *An Inaugural Dissertation*, 28.

78. Alexander Hosack, *History of the Yellow Fever, As It Appeared in the City of New York, in 1795* (Philadelphia: Thomas Dobson, 1797), 32–33.

79. CBB, *AM*, 392, 394, 110, 229, 415.

80. Ibid., 199, 220, 247. The list could continue at length; at least two dozen other instances occur in the novel.

81. Ibid., 91, 137, 221.

82. Ibid., 161.

83. Ibid., 3.

84. Ibid., 5–6.

85. Ibid., 125.

86. Ibid., 128–29.

87. David Paul Nord, "Readership as Citizenship in Late-Eighteenth-Century Philadelphia," in *A Melancholy Scene*, 24–25, 19–44.

88. CBB, *AM*, 6.

89. Qtd. in Haakonssen, *Medicine and Morals*, 218. Caleb Crain suggests that it was common, in the eighteenth century, "to compare the spread of sympathy to the spread of disease," a comparison that underlines sympathy's dangerous side. In making this point, Crain quotes Benjamin Rush's admission that, during the 1793 epidemic, he had to struggle against his own sympathetic impulses as a way to protect himself from the fever. Certainly CBB was wary of sympathy's potential elision into seduction, but Crain misses the medical argument implicit in Stevens's decision to shelter Mervyn. See Crain, *American Sympathy: Men, Friendship, and Literature in the New Nation* (New Haven: Yale University Press, 2001), 120–22.

90. CBB, *AM*, 138–40.

91. Ibid., 130.

92. Ibid., 159–60; CBB, *Ormond*, 48.

93. CBB, *AM*, 138.

94. CBB, *Ormond*, 52.

95. CBB, *AM*, 165–66.

96. Ferguson also notes this use of "composure" in *Arthur Mervyn*. See his "Yellow Fever and Charles Brockden Brown," 304–5n29.

97. *DEHS*, 59 (20 Sept. 1795); EM, "Some Remarks on the Importance of the Stomach," 173.

98. CBB, *AM*, 413–14. Fliegelman notes the similarities between CBB's

views on writing and Rush's theories on bloodletting (which the *Repository's* editor endorsed). See Fliegelman, "Introduction," in *Wieland and Memoirs of Carwin the Biloquist* (New York: Penguin, 1991), xxiii.

99. CBB, *AM*, 141, 161. The curative powers "of conversation," EHS writes in his diary, "when interesting, removing, or superseding, the sensation of pain, . . . is so common as to be known by every one." Such an assertion was "no mean argument in their favor, who maintain the superiority of mind over matter—or, to speak more properly, of the intellectual, over the physical, man. If we have power to banish, subdue, or destroy, pain, or disease, in one instance, why not in a second, in a third, & so on forever?" (*DEHS*, 74: 17 Oct. 1795).

100. Norman Grabo, *The Coincidental Art of Charles Brockden Brown* (Chapel Hill: University of North Carolina Press, 1981), 103; for another reading of "the relationship between tale-telling and well-being," see Goddu, *Gothic America*, 31–51, quote on 32.

101. Dorothy Hale accurately recognizes the importance of Godwin's discussion of promises and promise keeping to understanding Arthur's behavior. Certainly Arthur keeps for too long his promise to Welbeck to conceal his own identity, with near-disastrous results. Arthur's decision to break the promise—a decision that allows him to narrate early portions of the novel—should be read, then, not as a sign of his duplicity but of his eventual function as a sincere information broker. See Dorothy Hale, "The Profits of Altruism: *Caleb Williams* and *Arthur Mervyn*," *Eighteenth-Century Studies* 22:1 (fall 1988): 47–69.

102. Arthur's most biting modern critic, James Russo, who imagines that Arthur is actually an impostor *posing* as the real Arthur Mervyn, ignores the epidemic setting altogether. See Russo, "The Chameleon of Convenient Vice: A Study of the Narrative of *Arthur Mervyn*," *Studies in the Novel* 11:4 (winter 1979): 381–405.

103. CBB, *AM*, 223, 220.

104. Ibid., 370–71.

105. Ibid., 265.

106. Cf. *DEHS*, 82 (29 Nov. 1795), in which he notes the stagecoach's fame for providing "ludicrous adventure" for the "humorist." EHS himself offers the following account of a ride to New Haven just after New York's 1795 epidemic had subsided:

> We were six, beside the driver: an old, greasy, gouty, lecherous Jew; a huge Irish manufacturer of Fleecy Hosiery; a South Carolina merchant; a middle-aged, decent Frenchman; a young mercantile Hamburger who spoke French & English; & myself. The Israelite was for fun and singing; but no one sung. He & the Irishman discust politics & The Fever. The Frenchman & the German, first fell on the French Emigrants, next on the Fever—& lastly upon this country. All these topics they handled, with prodigious volubility, in French. The Carolina growled a little, & muttered something on merchandise: I was silent. . . . A rambling talk, on religion, at Supper, gave opportunity to all the guests to discover their infidelity; & the Hebrew, in particular, disclaimed Moses & the proph-

ets; & emphatically pronounced this sentence, that—"from Genesis to Revelations, all is trumpery."

107. CBB, *AM;* 370.

108. On the relation of racial hierarchy to observational authority, recall Medlicote, who despite his "fortitude and virtue" depends on the "dexterity and submissiveness" of his black servant, Austin, "who makes my bed, prepares my coffee, and bakes my loaf," thereby leaving the good doctor free to "moralize upon the scene" (CBB, *AM,* 161).

109. Mervyn's actions anticipate the role of "scientific discourse" as described in Dana Nelson, *National Manhood: Capitalist Citizenship and the Imagined Fraternity of White Men* (Durham: Duke University Press, 1998), esp. 51–52.

110. CBB, *AM,* 396.

111. CBB, "Walstein's School of History," *MMAR* (Aug.–Sept. 1799): 335–38, 407–11. Critics have long realized the connection between this essay and *Arthur Mervyn;* in it CBB discusses a hypothetical work of historical fiction that parallels part I of *Arthur Mervyn* quite closely.

112. CBB, advertisement for "Sky-Walk," *Weekly Magazine* (24 Mar. 1798): 228, rpt. in CBB, *The Rhapsodist: And Other Uncollected Writings,* ed. Harry R. Warfel (New York: Scholars' Facsimiles and Reprints, 1943), 135.

113. Ibid., 136.

114. CBB, *AM,* 401.

115. Ibid., 3.

116. Koeppel, *Water for Gotham,* 64.

117. *DEHS,* 462 (27 Aug. 1798), 463 (4 Sept. 1798–5 Sept. 1798).

118. *DWD,* 335–37.

119. *DEHS,* 464 (10 Sept. 1798).

120. *DEHS,* 464 (11 Sept. 1798).

121. SLM to Noah Webster, 17 Sept. 1798, in Emily Ellsworth Ford Skeel, ed., *Notes on the Life of Noah Webster,* 2 vols. (New York: privately printed, 1912), 1:467–68.

122. EHS to Benjamin Rush, 13 Sept. 1798, RL; "Medical Obituary," *MR* 2:2 (1798): 226; *DEHS,* 458 (30 July 1798), 463 (28 Aug.–3 Sept. 1798).

123. *DEHS,* 464 (15 Sept. 1798).

124. CBB to James Brown, 17 Sept. 1798 (H&C #103), in *LCBB,* 2:7–8.

125. Qtd. in Harry Warfel, *Charles Brockden Brown: American Gothic Novelist* (Gainesville: University of Florida Press, 1949), 122.

126. Qtd. in ibid.

127. WJ to WD, 20 Sept. 1798, in *DWD,* 340–41.

128. WJ to William Pitt Beers, 29 Nov. 1798, HSP.

129. EM to Benjamin Rush, 31 Dec. 1798, RL.

130. CBB to James Brown, 15 Feb. 1799 (H&C #113), in *LCBB,* 2:97–99.

131. CBB to James Brown, 26 July 1799 (H&C #114), in *LCBB,* 2:96–97.

132. CBB to James Brown, Apr. 1800 (H&C #116), in *LCBB* 2:99–100.

133. Hedges, "Benjamin Rush, Charles Brockden Brown."

134. CBB, *AM,* 323.

135. Jared Gardner, "The Literary Museum and the Unsettling of the Early American Novel," *ELH* 67 (2000): 743–771, quote on 762.

Coda. The End of the American Enlightenment

1. "Preface," *MMAR* 3 (July–Dec. 1800), iii.
2. "Candour" [SM], *American Citizen,* 10 Feb. 1801.
3. William Linn to JM, 25 Feb. 1801, N-YHS.
4. William Linn to JM, 21 July 1792, N-YHS.
5. In CBB to SM, 16 Mar. 1803 (H&C #165), PUL, CBB writes to SM: "I have seen a political letter with your name to it, published by Gemil [Gemmill, the New Haven minister to whom Miller wrote]. I hope you mean never to forgive that betrayer of a sacred trust. I am also informed that you have denounced the review. I am anxious to hear from you on all these topics."
6. *Monthly Recorder* 1 (Apr. 1813): 8.
7. *LSM,* 128.
8. *DEHS,* 443 (5 May 1798).
9. SM to JM, 24 Dec. 1798, in *LSM,* 120. Morse apparently replied that he feared the magazine would be too democratic, to which SM replied by naming CBB and adding, "You may, I believe, fully confide in him as a Federalist. Of his learning and taste there can be no question." Of the "club, of some ten gentlemen" who would assist CBB, "seven are decided Federalists; the other three are a little Democratic, but remarkably mild and moderate men" (in *LSM,* 120). SM, of course, was one of the three democrats. It is not clear whether he expected JM to be apprised of his political views. Of the claim for CBB's Federalism, there may be reason as well for skepticism. CBB had, that same month, sent a gift copy of *Wieland* to Thomas Jefferson, along with a letter expressing his "belief that it is capable of affording you pleasure and of entitling the writer to some portion of your good opinion." Biographers and critics have long interpreted this gesture in conflicting ways. See CBB to Thomas Jefferson, 15 Dec. 1798 (H&C #109), Library of Congress. The full text is printed in David Lee Clark, *Charles Brockden Brown: Pioneer Voice of America* (Durham: Duke University Press, 1952), 163–64.
10. "Critical Notices," *Literary Magazine, and American Register* 1:6 (Mar. 1804): 419–24, quote on 419.
11. *BREC,* 1:326.
12. *BREC,* 1:279. CBB joked with SM that SLM might be dissatisfied with the modest measure of praise he received: "You have managed the Mitchellean System very dextrously, but you have mortally offended the Dr. I doubt not, by not exalting the 'Extinguishment of Pestilence' to the rank of illustrious & infallible doctrines, shedding its brightest glories on the last age." CBB to SM, 16 Mar. 1803 (H&C #165), PUL.
13. *BREC,* 2:210.
14. *BREC,* 1:xii–xiii.
15. Thomas Bender, *New York Intellect: A History of Intellectual Life in New York City from 1750 to the Beginnings of Our Own Time* (Baltimore: Johns Hopkins University Press, 1987), 43–44.

16. Nathan Hatch, *The Democratization of American Christianity* (New Haven: Yale University Press, 1991); Jon Butler, *Awash in a Sea of Faith: Christianizing the American People* (Cambridge: Harvard University Press, 1992).

17. *BREC,* 440–42.

18. Robert E. Streeter, "Association Psychology and Literary Nationalism in the *North American Review,* 1815–1825," *American Literature* 17:3 (Nov. 1945): 243–54.

19. Bender, *New York Intellect,* 70–71.

20. Albert H. Marckwardt, "The Chronology and Personnel of the Bread and Cheese Club," *American Literature* 6:4 (Jan. 1935): 389–99.

21. Elizabeth A. Dant, "Composing the Natural World: Emerson and the Cabinet of Natural History," *Nineteenth-Century Literature* 44:1 (June 1989): 18–44.

Appendix. Friendly Club Membership

1. See *Monthly Recorder* 1 (Apr. 1813): 8.

2. On Wells, see *DEHS,* 54 (12 Sept. 1795), 220 (16 Sept. 1796); for Bleecker, see 449 (12 June 1798) and 460 (9 Aug. 1798).

3. Fredrika J. Teute, "'A Republic of Intellect': Conversation and Criticism among the Sexes in 1790s New York," in Philip Barnard, Mark L. Kamrath, and Stephen Shapiro, eds., *Revising Charles Brockden Brown: Culture, Politics, and Sexuality in the Early Republic* (Knoxville: University of Tennessee Press, 2004).

4. The account does, oddly, claim that meetings were held on Tuesday nights, which was not true at least during Smith's lifetime, and which Dunlap could have verified by checking his own diary. The *Monthly Recorder* tribute is reprinted in SM, "A Biographical Sketch of the Author," *MWEM,* xxix; Miller's commentary and Dunlap's sketch are both reproduced in *LSM,* iii.

5. *LCBB,* 45.

6. *DHAT,* 143–44, 156.

7. JK to William Kent, 5 Apr. 1847, KP.

8. *LSM,* iii.

9. *Memorial of the Life and Character of John Wells, with Reminiscences of the Judiciary and Members of the New York Bar* (New York: privately printed by John Trow & Son, 1874). The passage on the club from the Wells biography serves as an index of club members' reputations (and misrepresentations about them) three-quarters of a century after the group dissolved:

> James Kent has left an imperishable name. Charles Brockden Brown wrote many fugitive pieces of merit, and several novels that had popularity in their day, but their machinery was wild and founded in superstition, and are no longer adapted to the improved taste of the age. Mr. Johnson became the distinguished reporter of the decisions of the Supreme Court of the State of New York, and of the Court of Chancery when James Kent was Chancellor, and for valuable legal treatises which he published, and for well known literary and classical attainments and social virtues. Dr. Edward Miller was a distinguished physician of his

day. Rev. Dr. Miller was a Presbyterian minister of distinction, having charge of the old Wall-street church, that stood between Nassau street and Broadway. Dr. Sam. L. Mitchell [*sic*] is well known for his scientific attainments and wide range of information. Anthony Bleecker, Esq., was a gentleman of the old family of that name—a lawyer of good position, whose literary bias was greater than his ambition for forensic fame. Dr. Hubbard Smith, by his talents, gave promise of a useful career, but died at an early age. The same may be said of Charles Adams. William W. Woolsey, Esq., was a gentleman of education,—an intelligent, successful, and influential merchant, filling a high position in society. Mr. William Dunlop [*sic*] was a lawyer distinguished for his literary contributions to the magazines of the day, and for his Biography of Charles Brockden Brown, and a History of the Arts of Design in this country. The meetings of the Club were most agreeable to Mr. Wells, as it brought him in friendly association with tastes congenial to his own, and with those who were strengthening themselves to climb "the steep where Fame's proud temple shines afar." Chancellor Kent, in after days, expressed his pleasing recollections of the many hours he had passed in the society of so many men of talents and accomplishments. The intimacy of those days continued between Mr. Wells and himself during the life of the former. (46–47)

10. Karl P. Harrington, *Richard Alsop, "A Hartford Wit"* (1939; reprint, Middletown, Conn.: Wesleyan University Press, 1969), 46.

11. See *DEHS*, 141 (19 Mar. 1796).

12. *DEHS*, 440 (28 Apr. 1798).

13. Even James Cronin, the diary's editor, seems not to have noticed Smith's habit of alphabetizing regular members. See his "Introduction," in *DEHS*, 15, and his essay, "Elihu Hubbard Smith and the New York Friendly Club, 1795–1798," *PMLA* 64:3 (June 1949): 471–79.

14. John W. Francis, *Old New York; or, Reminiscences of the Last Sixty Years* (New York: Roe, 1865), 69, 288–90.

15. Martha J. Lamb, *History of the City of New York: Its Origin, Rise, and Progress*, 3 vols. (New York: A. S. Barnes and Co., 1877–1896), 3:468, 519–20.

16. James Grant Wilson, ed., *The Memorial History of the City of New York, from its First Settlement to the Year 1892*, 4 vols. (New York: New York History Co., 1892–93), 4:233.

17. See, for examples of ThD in town but not a visitor to the club, entries regarding meetings of 8 and 15 Apr. 1797, in *DEHS*, 307, 313; and for TD, entries regarding meetings of 13 and 20 Jan. 1798, in *DEHS*, 419–20.

18. Cronin, "Elihu Hubbard Smith and the New York Friendly Club," 471–79.

{ INDEX }

Adams, Charles, 33, 42, 148–49, 244, 264–65n41, 267n72, 308–9n9
Adams, John, 40, 145, 264–65n41
Adams, John Quincy, 262n28
Adams, Thomas Boylston, 262n28
African Free School, 42, 267n72
Alien and Sedition Acts, 53, 261–62n27
Alsop, Richard, 25, 43, 57, 244–45, 247, 255n8, 258n16
American Revolution, 9, 24, 26, 43, 121, 156, 160, 174–81, 184, 197, 264–65n41
Ames, Fisher, 261–62n27
Anacreontic Society, 36, 261n22
Anderson, Alexander, 259–60n18
André, John, 156–57, 160, 174–78
anti-Jacobinism, 96, 105–7, 117–18, 122–24, 136, 232–33, 236, 279n14, 283nn46&52
Argus (New York), 178–80, 187, 296n74
association, 7, 9, 18, 22, 28–32, 41, 52, 61, 131, 223, 237, 241, 258n13, 259–60n18, 261–62n27, 263–64nn35&36
association psychology, 41, 100, 237
audiences, 47, 54, 56, 78, 93, 156–60, 162–73, 177–79, 188, 223, 230, 239
authorship, 10, 53, 75–76, 156, 159, 168, 222, 230

Bage, Robert, *Hermsprong*, 92–95, 97, 109, 285n76, 288n134
Barlow, Joel, 43, 71
Barruel, Augustin, 72–74, 85, 107, 232
Bavarian Illuminati, 30, 52–53, 71–76, 83–85, 88, 107, 110, 117, 123, 129, 232–33, 273n59
Bayard, Margaret, 134, 136, 191, 227, 239, 243, 247, 273n59, 287n114, 288nn126&133–35, 288–89n136; on Brown, 137–39, 289n137; on Hays's *Emma Courtney*, 137; on Johnson, 137–39; on Mitchill, 137, 288n127; on mixed-sex society, 136–41; as *Monthly Magazine* contributor, 138; on Smith,

136, 287–88n125; on Wollstonecraft, 138–39
Belles Lettres Club (Philadelphia), 28
Bleecker, Anthony, 136–37, 139, 243–46, 255n8, 288n134, 308–9n9
Bringhurst, Joseph, 44–46, 65
British Jacobins, 66, 97–98, 101–10, 118, 141, 155, 188, 279–80n16, 281–82n37
Brothers in Unity, 28, 259n17
Brown, Charles Brockden, 1, 3, 4–7, 20, 43, 86, 87, 151, 166, 243, 245–46, 255n9; and *Alcuin*'s unpublished sequel, 114, 116; *Antijacobin Review* on, 118; and Bage's *Hermsprong*, 92; Bayard encouraged to publish in *Monthly Magazine* by, 138; and *Brief Retrospect of the Eighteenth Century*, 234–36; on celebrity as novelist, 228–29; conversation of described, 137, 138–39; early friends of, 28, 32, 264n37, 277n100, 307nn5&12; fear of dark, 190; and female readers, 289n137; and feminism, 98, 109–10, 117–29; and Godwin, 95, 98, 111–12, 116–18, 123–26, 140–41, 232, 280n21; as infidel philosopher, 75, 87; Kent chastises, 149; on mixed-sex conversation, 136; as *Monthly Magazine* editor, 49, 138, 153, 230, 231–32, 234, 239; as moral observer, 224–25; as New York literary pioneer, 49, 244; and Philadelphia *Ladies Magazine*, 284n55; in Philadelphia *Weekly Magazine*, 108, 156, 192; politics of, 101, 105–6, 117, 118–19, 274–75nn77,78&81, 282n44; posthumous reputation of, 308–9n9; and religion, 51, 55–56, 65–66, 140–41, 274n72; sends *Wieland* to Thomas Jefferson, 307n9; Shelleys influenced by, 279n11; Smith seeks literary opinion, 206; and social aims for fiction, 104, 190–91, 196; on theater, 156; on Webster, 301n47; and Wollstonecraft, 109–11, 116–30, 141;

Brown, Charles Brockden (*continued*)
  and yellow fever, 189–90, 192, 195, 198,
  209, 213–24, 226, 228–29, 299–300n31.
  Works: *Alcuin*, 98, 106, 107–16, 118–19,
  125, 128, 130, 132, 139, 154, 192, 284n58,
  292n8; *Arthur Mervyn*, 6, 13, 192, 195,
  197, 198, 206, 213, 214–25, 229, 289n137,
  297–98n8, 305n101, 306n108; *Clara
  Howard*, 108, 229, 230; *Edgar Huntly*,
  89–91, 108, 141, 191, 196, 229, 283n53,
  289n137; "Ella-Birtha-Henry" poetic correspondence, 44–46, 267n77,
  268n89; "Ellendale" fragments,
  274n73; *Jane Talbot*, 108, 229, 230,
  283n53, 285–86n91; "The Man at
  Home," 207, 297–98n8; *Memoirs of
  Carwin*, 76–80, 81, 117, 226, 274n76,
  275n86, 285–86n91; *Ormond*, 98,
  106, 108–9, 116–29, 141, 183, 192, 207,
  219, 228, 283n46, 285n76, 285–86n91,
  297–98n8; "A Series of Original Letters," 297–98n8; *Sky-Walk*, 108, 192,
  226; *Steven Calvert*, 226; "Walstein's
  School of History," 306n111; *Wieland*,
  55–56, 74, 76, 79, 80–83, 108, 115, 117,
  127, 192, 196, 226, 228, 274n76, 275n86,
  276nn92&93, 277n99, 289n137
Brown, James, 189, 228
Burk, John, 156, 295n69
Burke, Edmund, 53, 72
Burr, Aaron, 19, 21, 201

Calliopean Society, 27, 28, 30, 259n18,
  265n45; and "The Drone," 43, 245,
  261n25
Carey, Mathew, 201, 268n89, 283n46,
  299n26, 300n41
Catlin, Lynde, 33, 255n8
Christianity, 10, 31, 54, 74, 100, 107, 127,
  137, 140–41, 146, 169, 199, 205, 210, 235,
  236–37, 274n73, 283n51, 287n117; Brown
  parodies in *Wieland*, 83, 276n93; Godwinianism viewed as an alternative to,
  105; and Smith's conflicts with Connecticut friends, 62–68
clergy, 60, 71, 74, 106, 146, 147, 201–2. *See
  also* Christianity; professions
Cogswell, Mason Fitch, 57
Coleridge, Samuel Taylor, 97, 100–101,
  104, 279–80n16

Commercial Advertiser (New York), 166–
  67, 173
Condorcet, Marquis de (Marie Jean An-
  toine Nicolas Caritat), 9, 98, 109, 237,
  269–70n5
conversation, 9, 32, 33–38, 57, 218, 265n44;
  in Brown's fiction, 112–16; and character, 265n43; curative powers of,
  305n99; error dispersed by, 76; in
  Friendly Club, 1, 23, 26, 34; gendered,
  96, 98; and knowledge production,
  146; magazines and, 48; mixed-sex,
  12, 112–16, 120, 124, 130–41; in *Monthly
  Magazine*, 35; and scientific progress,
  53; and seduction, 118; and self-knowledge, 37; and social progress, 116. *See
  also* politeness
Cooper, T. A., 101, 159, 177–78, 256n14
correspondence, 32, 33, 57; and friendship,
  59–60; and scientific investigation,
  37–38, 69; and self-knowledge, 39;
  poetic, 44–46; public, 42, 208

Darwin, Erasmus, 41, 61, 83, 97, 109, 136;
  The Botanic Garden, 46, 154, 209; *Zoo-
  nomia*, 81
Davis, Matthew Livingston, 201, 204
Deism, 53, 66, 68, 83, 88, 91, 282n44
Della Cruscan poetry, 46, 268n89
Democratic-Republican societies, 28, 31,
  71, 261–62n27
Dennie, Joseph, 31, 74, 153, 254n30, 268–
  69n89, 273–74n68
Drone Club. *See* Calliopean Society
Dunlap, Elizabeth ("Nabby") Woolsey, 93,
  162, 292n8
Dunlap, William, 3, 7, 27, 32, 42, 56, 86,
  136, 145–46, 151, 153, 189, 236, 239–40,
  246, 256–57n18, 261n22, 267n72,
  284n58; autobiographical narrative of,
  161; Bage's *Hermsprong* read by, 92;
  and Bread and Cheese Club, 241; and
  cockade controversy, 177–81, 296n72;
  critiques Smith's address for theater,
  163–68; Dwights as brothers-in-law
  of, 25, 74–75, 95, 295n69; on Friendly
  Club, 34, 233, 243–45, 247, 308n4; as
  Friendly Club founder, 33; on friendship, 133; Godwin and Holcroft as
  correspondents of, 95, 101, 167–68;

and Hodgkinson-Hallam controversy, 170–73; and Illuminati scare,
74–75, 84; as infidel philosopher, 75,
87; in London, 26, 161; marriage of,
162, 265n42; and Old American Company, 13, 98, 154–73; and Park Theatre,
154–88, 293–94n31; and Philological
Society, 29; politics of, 105, 182, 282n44,
296nn81&85; posthumous reputation
of, 308–9n9; and religion, 51, 55–56; and
social aims for fiction, 104; on theater,
155, 162, 165, 167–68, 294n32; and yellow fever in New York, 226. Works:
André, 156–62, 174–88, 292n8, 293n9,
296n77; *The Anti-Jacobin*, 75, 295n69;
Cuttgrisingwolds, 43; diary, 106, 283n46,
308n4; *The Father; or, American Shandyism*, 162; *Fontaineville Abbey*, 165; *History of the American Theatre*, 6, 49, 158,
165, 244; *The Life of Charles Brockden
Brown*, 49, 114, 239, 244; *The Modest Soldier*, 162; *The Mysterious Monk*,
168; poems, 25, 43, 162; *Tell Truth and
Shame the Devil*, 94–95, 169, 278–79n4
Dwight, Theodore, 25, 39, 58, 95, 105, 247,
264n37; on Godwin, 99, 280n20; as
Hartford Wit, 57–58, 258n16; and Illuminati, 72–76, 83, 87, 277n99; Smith's
long letter to, 50–52, 56–57, 62–64, 66–
70, 75, 87, 89, 106, 271–72n28, 272n39,
283n51; Smith's strained friendship
with, 59–71, 86–88, 269n90
Dwight, Timothy, 25, 43, 58, 63–64, 67, 71,
86, 87, 91, 95, 247, 258n16, 295n69; and
Dunlap, 292n8, 295–96n69; and Illuminati, 72–76, 83–85, 87–88, 107; on
novels and theater, 75

Enlightenment, the, 4, 9, 10, 11, 32, 39, 53,
64, 83, 122, 153, 160, 229, 233, 236–38,
259n18

Fawcett, Joseph, 69, 105
Federalists, 7, 21, 31, 91, 106, 110, 148, 160,
181–82, 234, 252n14, 262n28, 281n30,
299–300n31; and Christianity, 54,
273–74n68, 283n51; and literature,
152–53; and Park Theatre subscribers,
296n81; and "self-created societies,"
53, 71, 261–62n27

feminism, 96–98, 102, 108; in Brown's
fiction, 107–29; and Friendly Club's
mixed-sex circle, 130–41. *See also*
Hays, Mary; Wollstonecraft, Mary
Fenno, John, 44, 268n81
Francis, John, 245–46, 259n18
Freemasons, 28, 52, 72–74, 261n22, 267n74,
277n99
French Revolution, 8, 29, 47, 50, 52, 58,
71, 87, 96, 117, 121–23, 183, 184, 232,
269–70n5
Freneau, Philip, 171, 296n74
Friendly Club, 3, 6, 7, 13, 27, 137–38; and
American audiences, 160; careers influenced by, 239–40; and Coleridge's
early poetry, 279–80n16; conversational style in, 34, 96; and Darwin's
Botanic Garden, 46, 154; and Dunlap's
André, 292n8, 293n9; founding of, 22,
25–26, 162; homosociality of, 98, 108,
116, 118; and Illuminati scare, 73–75;
industry idealized by, 146; literary
journal planned by, 9, 41, 46–48; as
literary pioneers, 162–63; and Manumission Society, 267n72; meetings
of, 34, 35, 36, 40, 145, 149; membership of, 31, 33–34, 41–42, 243–48; and
mixed-sex society, 112, 131–41, 283n46;
in New York City historiography, 1,
30, 42, 243–48; organizing principles,
4, 17, 22–23, 118–19, 139; and Park
Theatre opening, 162–68; and partisan politics, 21, 31–32, 106, 233, 275n78,
282n44, 307n9; privacy of, 31; publishing projects of, 10, 42, 46, 48–49, 152,
235; reading practices of, 40, 93, 96,
145–46; after Smith's death, 136, 192,
231, 239; Smith describes, 10; Smith's
expectations of, 33; religious tension
within, 52, 55; visitors to, 247; and
Wollstonecraft and Godwin, 96–97,
102, 109–10, 116, 118, 279n8, 281n30
friendship, 17–18, 186–87, 198, 263n35;
in Brown's fiction, 112, 120–21; and
Christian fellowship, 287n117; correspondence encourages, 59–60, 69; and
difference, 52; early associations, 62, 86;
female, 120–21; and homoeroticism, 116,
263–64n36, 266n63; limits of, 69–71, 86;
and literary collaboration, 39, 42–45,

friendship (*continued*)
   269n90; and literary history, 49; male,
   132–33, 176; and marriage, 125, 133,
   265n42; mixed-sex, 59, 98, 130–41;
   professional, 6; and reputation, 36, 49;
   romantic, 133, 263–64nn36&37; and
   scientific inquiry, 36, 39, 46, 60, 69;
   and self-knowledge, 37, 39, 86; and
   social clubs, 28, 32

Gates, Horatio, 17, 19
Gazette of the United States (Philadelphia),
   44–46, 64, 267n77
General Advertiser (Philadelphia), 45–46,
   268n89
Girondists, 106, 121, 269–70n5. *See also*
   French Revolution
Godwin, William, 41, 64, 69, 134, 153,
   232, 281n30, 284n57, 287n115, 288n134;
   American conservatives attack, 107,
   136; antimatrimonialism of, 118,
   124–25, 280n20, 286n94; and Brown's
   fiction, 111–29, 285–86n91; and Christianity, 105; on clash of minds, 98,
   101; and T. A. Cooper, 159, 256n14;
   in Dunlap's *Tell Truth*, 94; Friendly
   Club members write to, 36, 97;
   Friendly Club admires persistently,
   140; necessitarianism of, 100–101; on
   political association, 123; on promises, 124, 125–26, 305n101; on reading,
   147; on sincerity, 57, 96, 100, 112; and
   Smith's strained friendships, 66, 95;
   and Wollstonecraft, 96, 103, 279n11.
   Works: *Caleb Williams*, 92–95, 97, 99,
   101, 102, 104–5, 187–88, 282n38, 284n57;
   The Enquirer, 101–2, 111, 116, 145;
   Enquiry Concerning Political Justice,
   52, 59, 95, 99–101, 102, 105–6, 111, 125,
   280nn21&25; *Memoirs of the Author
   of a Vindication of the Rights of
   Woman*, 96, 106, 118, 123, 141, 283n46,
   289n140
Godwinians. *See* British Jacobins

Habermas, Jürgen, 54, 271n13, 277n100
Hallam, Lewis, 154, 170–73
Hallam, Mrs., 170–73
Hamilton, Alexander, 19, 21, 148, 150, 175–
   76, 180, 182, 186, 291nn21&26

Hartford Wits, 28, 43, 57–58, 78, 87, 153,
   258n16
Hartley, David, 41, 61, 119, 190
Hays, Mary, 97, 101, 134, 288n132; *Memoirs
   of Emma Courtney*, 105, 109, 110, 137,
   284n57; on novels, 104–5
Hodgkinson, John, 154, 158, 170–74, 178,
   293–94n31
Holcroft, Thomas, 51, 97, 155, 187, 188,
   255n2, 281n30, 284n57; *Anna St. Ives*,
   104, 109, 129, 265n43, 289–90n140; and
   T. A. Cooper, 159, 256n14; Friendly
   Club members write to, 36
Hopkins, Samuel M., 57, 247

imagination, 189–90, 194, 196, 207, 213
Imlay, Gilbert, 96, 123
Inchbald, Elizabeth, 51, 97, 105, 109, 155
information, 6, 8–9, 28, 161, 193–94, 198–
   99, 207–8, 219, 220, 229; and conversation, 34; and foreign writers, 97–98,
   103; and professions, 40, 196, 208; and
   travel, 221

Jacobins, 52, 85, 91, 106, 269–70n5, 277n99,
   279n14. *See also* British Jacobins;
   French Revolution
Jay, John, 21, 148, 149
Jefferson, Thomas, 21, 31, 73, 232, 233, 264–
   65n41, 281n30, 288n134, 307n9
Jeffersonians, 7, 21, 53, 160, 178, 182, 232,
   299–300n31. *See also* Democratic-
   Republican societies
Johnson, Horace, 33, 88, 227
Johnson, William, 3, 20, 27, 36, 42, 86,
   145, 148, 192, 226–27, 231, 232, 243,
   246, 264n37, 267nn72&74; and Bage's
   Hermsprong, 92–94; Bayard encouraged to publish in *Monthly Magazine*
   by, 138; Brown visits Connecticut
   with, 91; and Brown's *Wieland*, 74;
   conversation described, 137, 138–39;
   as court reporter, 147–48, 239–40,
   290n6; and Dunlap's *André*, 292n8;
   as Friendly Club founding member,
   33; Godwin read to Friendly Club by,
   146; as infidel philosopher, 75, 87; literary journal planned by, 41; marriage
   to Maria Templeton, 134; mixed-sex
   friendships of, 136, 288n127; as New

York literary pioneer, 49, 244; politics of, 282n44; posthumous reputation of, 308–9n9; Eliza S. M. Quincy on, 134; shyness of, 288n127; on Smith's death, 228; and yellow fever in New York, 224

Kent, Elizabeth, 255n7, 281n30
Kent, James, 3, 7, 8, 13, 21, 28, 145, 178, 239, 243, 246, 267nn72&74, 290n6, 291–92n26; during American Revolution, 161; autobiographical narrative of, 151; and Bread and Cheese Club, 241; on British Jacobins, 36; Brown chastised by, 149; Columbia law lectures, 42, 148–50, 291nn13&14; *Commentaries on American Law*, 147, 150, 152, 240; and Dunlap's *André*, 293n9; as early Friendly Club member, 33, 148; on Friendly Club, 244; on Godwin, 146, 281n30; on Hamilton, 291n21; on legal profession, 148; on New York, 26–27; politics of, 147, 148, 150–51, 282n44; posthumous reputation of, 308–9n9; and print culture, 148, 151–52; reading habits of, 147–48, 151; on religion, 146, 278n119; as state supreme court justice, 154; Webster collaborates with, 149; on Wollstonecraft, 289–90n140; on yellow fever, 199
Kent, Moss, 150, 281n30
Kosciusko, Thaddeus, 17–19, 22
Kotzebue, August von, 98, 188

Ladies Magazine (Philadelphia), 284n55
Lavater, Johann Kasper, 18, 22, 255n2
Linn, Elizabeth, 232
Linn, John Blair, 133, 245, 287n117
Linn, William, 201, 232–33
Linonia Society, 28

magazines, as medium, 42, 46, 93, 110. *See also individual magazines*
Manumission Society, 8, 27, 42, 267nn72&74
Medical Repository, 3, 4, 5, 13, 17, 20, 46, 48, 72, 153, 191, 206–7, 215, 222, 225, 298–99n25; audience, 194, 208, 303n64; in *Brief Retrospect of the Eighteenth Century*, 235; established, 194, 196, 206,

234, 298n14; on yellow fever, 197, 201, 206, 209, 301n47
Medical Society of the State of New York, 28, 200, 204, 300n34
Miller, Edward, 3, 21, 136, 198, 227, 243, 245–47, 267n74; and *Brief Retrospect of the Eighteenth Century*, 234–35; joins Friendly Club, 234, 262n31; as *Medical Repository* editor, 194, 197, 234, 239, 267n72, 282n44; posthumous reputation of, 308–9n9; as Rush's correspondent, 299n26, 301n47; on Smith's death, 228; on Webster's fever history, 301n47; on yellow fever, 209, 213–14, 219, 220
Miller, Samuel, 3, 4, 20, 21, 136, 198, 227, 239, 243, 244–47, 261n22, 267nn72&74, 307n12; biographical sketch of, 233–34; *Brief Retrospect of the Eighteenth Century*, 231–32, 233, 234–38; as Friendly Club member, 31, 234; politics of, 232–34, 262n31, 282n44, 307nn5&9; posthumous reputation of, 308–9n9
Mineralogical Society, 8, 27, 31
Mitchill, Samuel Latham, 3, 7, 21–22, 27, 136, 201, 206, 236, 240, 243–47, 259–60n18, 261n22, 262n31, 267nn72&74, 273n59, 287–88n125, 307n12; Bayard on, 137; as Columbia professor, 198; Darwin as poetic model for, 97, 209; "The Doctrine of Septon," 209–11, 303n69; German translation of, 203; and medical education in New York, 26; ; as *Medical Repository* editor, 194, 234, 239, 303n67; as Medical Society member, 300n34; medical training of, 198; as New-York Hospital physician, 198; on nitrous oxide, 301–302n49; and Oeleopile, 203; as Philological Society member, 29; as poet, 43, 209–11; politics of, 282n44; posthumous reputation of, 308–9n9; on Robison, 72; on septon, 202–3, 209–11; as Webster's correspondent, 203; on yellow fever, 202–6, 219, 298n14, 301n48
Monthly Magazine, and American Review (New York), 3, 31, 35, 46–47, 48, 72, 130–31, 138, 194, 222, 231, 234, 239, 247, 283n46, 301n47, 307n9

Monthly Magazine, and British Register
    (London), 10, 52, 98, 104–5, 110
Monthly Review (London), 73, 86, 93, 98
Morse, Jedidiah, 31, 55, 72–75, 83, 232–33,
    234, 273–74n68, 307n9
Morton, Sarah Wentworth, 156, 268n89
Mumford, Thomas, 33, 265n43

New Annual Register (London), 98, 99
New Philosophy, 59, 106–7, 110. *See also*
    British Jacobins
New York City, 13; and American Revo-
    lution, 161; civic life in, 7, 9, 20, 22,
    28–32, 240–41, 258n13, 259–60n18;
    commerce in, 24, 26; intellectual and
    literary culture in, 26–27, 131–34, 149,
    162; post-Revolutionary growth of,
    24, 204, 232
New-York Historical Society, 22, 32, 240,
    245, 246
New-York Hospital, 19, 198, 200,
    299n27
New-York Magazine, 43, 162, 204, 268n89
newspapers, 28, 178–81, 253n19, 269n92;
    poetry in, 43–46; dominated by poli-
    tics, 47, 71. *See also individual news-
    papers*
Nicholson, Maria, 134, 136

observation, 17–18, 192–93, 195–96, 206–7,
    214, 222–25. *See also* information
Ogden, John Cosens, 83–84, 277n99
Old American Company, 7, 26, 101, 154,
    158–59, 162, 256n14

Paine, Thomas, 75
Park Theatre. *See under* Dunlap, William
partisan politics, 7, 21, 31, 36, 50, 71, 91,
    101, 160, 181–83, 232, 259n18, 261–
    62nn27&28, 307n9; and literary cul-
    ture, 55; and new political historians,
    53, 55; and religion, 54, 58; and yellow
    fever, 299–300n31
Peale, Charles Willson, 20, 22, 255n7
perfectibility, 10, 39–40, 65–68, 100, 101,
    237, 269–70n5
Philological Society, 29, 30, 43, 244
politeness, 35, 68, 160, 184; and mixed-sex
    conversation, 98, 114–15, 129–31, 136.
    See also sincerity

portraiture, 19–23, 257n19
Priestley, Joseph, 21, 41, 53, 97, 202, 255n9
print culture, 46, 78–79, 84–85, 146, 149–50,
    239; theater and, 172; women and,
    108, 138
professions, 53–54, 60, 110–11, 147, 196,
    222, 240; and print culture, 146, 239,
    252n14; and public authority, 74, 84,
    146, 197, 199–201, 206
Proteus, 41, 46–48, 55, 168, 254n25
public sphere, 27, 52–53, 78–80, 83, 106,
    253n21, 258n13, 261n24; Habermas on,
    54, 271n13, 277n100; Illuminati crisis
    and, 74, 84–85, 277n100; literary, 55;
    and religion, 55; and theater audi-
    ences, 170–73, 180; and yellow fever
    epidemics, 208–9

radicalism, 98, 105–6, 282–83n45. *See also*
    British Jacobins; feminism
reading practices, 33, 36, 40, 42, 57, 92–94,
    97, 146; and gender, 95, 266n66
republic of intellect, 4, 31, 55, 93, 100, 104,
    196, 223, 251n9
republic of letters, 4, 31, 150, 202, 237
republicanism, 6, 79, 230, 252n14
Republicans. *See* Jeffersonians; Demo-
    cratic-Republican societies
reputation, 6, 17, 21, 28, 36, 236
Richardson, Samuel, 65, 129, 286n110
Robison, John, 72, 75, 83–85, 107, 137, 232,
    273n59, 288n133
Roland, Jean-Marie ("Madame"), 106–7,
    109, 283n47
Rush, Benjamin, 25, 197, 200, 202, 213, 218,
    225, 227, 228, 299n26, 301nn44,45&47

Scandella, Joseph, 2–6, 227
Seaman, Valentine, 207
self-examination, 22, 36–37, 39–41, 107
sensibility, 41, 46, 59, 141, 263–64n36,
    265n43
Shakespeare, William, 82–83, 155, 161,
    168–69, 174, 188, 276–77n95
Sharples, Ellen, 255nn8&9
Sharples, James, 19–23, 247, 255nn7&8,
    256–57n18
Simpson, Solomon, 31
sincerity, 57, 62, 70, 100, 112, 124, 126, 130–
    31, 225, 305n101. *See also* politeness

Smith, Abigail, 105, 135
Smith, Elihu Hubbard, 7, 21, 23, 24, 26,
  27, 41, 107, 145, 151, 178, 192, 243, 247,
  251n9, 254n30, 256–57n18, 270n7,
  288n133, 308–9n9; on American audiences, 47, 165–66, 168–69; and Bage's
  Hermsprong, 92–94; Bayard on, 136,
  287–88n125; and Brown's *Alcuin*, 114,
  116; and Brown's *Wieland*, 74; on
  Carey, 300n41; Christian faith lost
  by, 34, 51–52, 55–71, 88–90, 301n44;
  on clergy, 60, 75–76; on Condorcet,
  269–70n5; and Connecticut friends,
  50–53, 56–71, 86–88; on conversation,
  34–7; 265n43, 305n99; correspondence
  of, 37–40, 56, 98, 226; death of, 2–6,
  88–89, 192, 198, 214, 227, 237, 244, 259–
  60n18, 267n74, 269n90; and Dunlap's
  André, 292n8; and Theodore Dwight,
  51, 56–57, 62–64, 66–70, 75, 87, 89, 92,
  106, 272n39; as Timothy Dwight's
  student, 25, 51, 87–89; on Federalist partisans, 262n28; on fiction, 104;
  and Friendly Club, 33, 41, 245, 258n16,
  309n13; on friendship, 12, 52, 60–62,
  69, 132–33, 263–64nn36&37; and Godwin, 95, 98, 101, 105, 106, 279nn8&10,
  280n21, 281n30; as Hartford Wit, 28,
  57–58; and Kent's law lectures, 149–50,
  291n14; Kent recalls, 278n119; and
  London *Monthly Magazine*, 10; as
  Manumission Society secretary, 42,
  259n18, 267n72; on marriage, 265n42;
  as Massachusetts Historical Society
  member, 29; on masturbation, 132,
  287n115; on medical authorship, 191,
  206; as medical observer, 195–96;
  on *Medical Repository* subscribers,
  303n64; on Mitchill's poetry, 303n69;
  as New-York Hospital physician, 198;
  as New York literary pioneer, 49, 244;
  and Park Theatre opening, 155–68;
  plans literary journal, 41; politics of,
  282n44, 299–300n31; on prayer, 66,
  76; Eliza S. M. Quincy on, 134; as
  Rush's medical ally, 202; as Rush's
  student, 25, 28, 58; stagecoach adventure of, 305n106; on theater, 163–68,
  170, 177; utopian society sketched by,
  109, 287n116; on Wollstonecraft, 96,

103, 109, 110; on women's education,
  135–36, 290n142; and yellow fever,
  191–92, 193, 197, 200, 204, 206–7,
  209, 213, 225–27, 299–300n31. Works:
  *American Poems, Selected and Origi-
  nal*, 7, 25, 42, 44, 162, 268n89; diary,
  6, 13, 17–19, 32–33, 36–7, 50, 57, 87–89,
  99, 106, 207, 248; *The Echo*, 25, 58, 78;
  Edwin and Angelina, 56, 105, 166, 169,
  278n3; "Ella-Birtha-Henry" poetic
  correspondence, 44–46, 64, 267n77,
  268n89; "Occasional Address … on
  the Opening of the New Theatre,"
  155–56, 162–68; "The Plague of Athens," 191, 194–95, 206
Smith, Fanny, 33, 107
Smith, Samuel Harrison, 134, 137–39,
  288nn132&133, 288–89nn134&136
society orations, 28, 42–43, 267n74
Southey, Robert, 96, 97, 104, 279–80n16
Strong, Idea, 38, 103, 105, 106, 110, 135, 141
Swords Brothers, 179, 284n58
sympathy, 19, 32, 177, 187, 218, 304n89

Templeton, Maria, 134, 136, 139, 227,
  288n127, 289n137, 290n142
Time-Piece (New York), 171, 296n74
Tracy, Susan Bull, 50–53, 56, 58–59, 76, 95,
  105, 135, 141; and French Revolution,
  87; and Smith: —correspondence
  with wanes, 58–60, 69–71, 86–87;
  —discusses Wollstonecraft and
  Godwin with, 97, 103, 272n32, 279n10;
  on Wollstonecraft, 108–9
Tracy, Uriah, 50–53, 69–71, 87, 95, 150
Trumbull, John, 156–57
Tyler, Royall, *The Algerine Captive*, 156;
  The Contrast, 26, 162

Volney, Count de (Constantin François
  Chasseboeuf Boisgirais), 98, 122
Voltaire (François-Marie Arouet), 27, 85,
  278n104

Washington, George, 19, 21, 29–30, 40,
  44, 161, 261n22, 261–62n27; and André
  affair, 174–76; in Dunlap's *André*, 157,
  178–88; Friendly Club supposedly
  visited by, 2, 246–47
Watters, James, 108, 227, 284n58, 297–98n8

Webster, Noah, 7, 9, 29, 30, 41, 149, 191,
    194, 198, 202, 203, 227, 244, 254n24,
    255n9, 298n14, 301n47
Weekly Magazine (Philadelphia), 108, 156,
    192, 284n58, 297–98n8
Weishaupt, Adam, 71
Wells, John, 243–45, 251n9, 308–9n9
West Indies, 24, 197, 199, 205, 299–300n31
Wetmore, Prosper, 33, 35, 42
Williams, Helen Maria, 97, 109
Wollstonecraft, Mary, 96, 98, 107, 232,
    279n11, 284n57, 287n116; American
    conservatives target, 107, 123, 129, 136;
    American reception of, 97, 102–3,
    108–10; Bayard imitates, 138; in *Brief
    Retrospect of the Eighteenth Century*,
    236; and Brown's fiction, 108–29;
    death of, 97, 103, 141; on education,
    102, 120, 128; and Godwin, 96–97;
    in *Monthly Magazine, and American
    Review*, 130–31; Smith compares to
    Susan Tracy, 59; Susan Tracy defends,
    108–9, 272n32. Works: *Elements of
    Morality* (trans.), 102; *Posthumous
    Works*, 96, 283n46; *A Short Residence in
    Sweden, Norway, and Denmark*, 102–3,
    280n17; *A Vindication of the Rights of
    Woman*, 59, 102, 108, 130, 289–90n140
Woolsey, Elizabeth ("Nabby"). *See* Dun-
    lap, Elizabeth ("Nabby") Woolsey
Woolsey, Elizabeth Dwight, 25, 162
Woolsey, George Murison, 3, 32, 34, 42,
    178, 243–44, 247, 265n42, 267nn71&72,
    280n21, 282n44

Woolsey, William Walton, 3, 25–26, 31,
    42, 178, 243–44, 265n42, 267nn71&72;
    as Friendly Club founding member,
    33, 34; on Godwin's *Political Justice*,
    281n30; on Millers, 262n31; posthu-
    mous reputation of, 308–9n9; as reli-
    gious conservative, 52, 270n7, 282n44
Wordsworth, William, 101

XYZ affair, 182

Yale College, 25–26, 50, 58, 71, 85, 89, 148,
    161, 267n74
yellow fever: and Athenian plague, 194–95;
    in Brown's fiction, 108, 117, 191, 214–23,
    299n28; clergy respond to, 199, 201;
    debates on, 8, 13, 197, 198, 200, 208,
    299–300n31, 303n67; Friendly Club
    energized by, 192; governmental re-
    sponses to, 199–202, 300n39; *Medical
    Repository* founded to address, 197;
    as metaphor or allegory, 198, 209,
    299n28; in New York, 2–4, 7, 25, 55,
    189, 193–94, 195, 197, 199, 204–6, 224–
    30, 297n2, 302n55; and partisan poli-
    tics, 299–300n31; in Philadelphia, 190,
    192, 197, 198–201, 206, 218, 224, 297n2;
    preventive measures, 4, 197, 200, 298–
    99n25; publications on, 193, 197, 201,
    209–14; rumors about, 189, 193, 214,
    217, 218–19; 230; symptoms of, 211–13,
    227, 304n77; transmitted by mosquito,
    197; treatments for, 213–14